CELEBRITY SOURCES

GARLAND REFERENCE LIBRARY
OF THE HUMANITIES
(VOL. 1176)

CELEBRITY SOURCES
Guide to Biographical Information About Famous People in Showbusiness and Sports Today

Ronald Ziegler

GARLAND PUBLISHING, INC. • NEW YORK & LONDON
1990

Library of Congress Cataloging-in-Publication Data

Ziegler, Ronald.
   Celebrity sources : a guide to biographical information about
famous people in showbusiness and sports today / Ronald Ziegler.
      p.   cm. — (Garland reference library of the humanities; vol.
1176)
    Bibliography: p.
    Includes index.
    ISBN 0–8240–5946–8 (alk. paper)
    1. Celebrities—Biography—Bibliography. 2. Biography—20th
century—Bibliography. 3. Entertainers—Biography—Bibliography.
I. Title. II. Series.
Z5304.C44Z53 1990
[CT120]
016.9202—dc20   89–11762
                                   CIP

Printed on acid-free, 250-year-life paper
Manufactured in the United States of America

For Elli

CONTENTS

Contents

ACKNOWLEDGMENTS

It has been my intention in this volume to determine the nature and extent of the current information available concerning celebrity biography, and to organize it for convenient use by a diverse clientele. Any success that I have had in doing this is attributable in large measure to the understanding and cooperation of scores of publishers, organizations, and individuals with whom I have worked during the past three years.

Much of my research was done with the aid of the bibliographical resources and other facilities at Washington State University Libraries. One facility in particular, the Interlibrary Loan Unit in Holland Library, is deserving of prolonged applause and several curtain calls for the high level of professional services rendered. The indulgent and tireless efforts of Shirley Giden, Phyllis Ritter, Dave Smestad, and Kay Vyhnanek will always be appreciated and remembered—in my book they are all celebrities.

I was also privileged to spend several months at the Library of Congress making on-site use of the unique resources of that institution. My investigation at the Library of Congress was supported in part by funds provided by the Washington State University Graduate School.

Finally, my colleagues in the Humanities and Social Sciences Public Services division of Washington State University Libraries deserve thanks for amiably assuming the burden of added duties while I was absent on professional leave assembling parts of this book.

INTRODUCTION

This book is offered as a pathfinder to information concerning the lives of individuals who have gained fame and celebrity status primarily through their ability to entertain. Their talent is displayed and their popular appeal fostered by means of the mass media (most often electronic). They are the musicians, composers, actors, directors, athletes and coaches who have become "household names" in the popular culture of North America and, often, of the world.

The audience for this work may include the academic person, the librarian seeking a thoroughgoing approach to the subject, the interested lay-person, the "fan," and students at all levels. These readers will discover many hundreds of sources and services which, in combination, constitute the information structure of popular biography about contemporary celebrities. The celebrities found herein were selected from a group of several thousand listed in the latest edition (4th ed., 1986), of the *Celebrity Register*. The publisher, Celebrity Service International, is a recognized global authority and arbiter of celebrity status—hence a unique source of verification of star rank. In *CR*'s multi-occupational listing are some 900 personalities from the areas of popular entertainment and sports. I checked membership in this core group to certify the relevancy of information sources listed in this book. Entertainers and athletes found in the third edition (1973) of *CR* but who have since died are also included because it is highly likely that they would have been retained in *CR*'s current edition. Television personalities difficult to categorize such as

Dr. Ruth Westheimer, Dr. Joyce Brothers, and Jimmy the Greek are included, while television journalists are not. Former stars who gained later (and sometimes far greater) fame in non-entertainment endeavors, e.g., Grace Kelly, Shirley Temple Black, Bill Bradley, and Ronald Reagan, have been excluded. In the sports sector I included famed coaches (Paul "Bear" Bryant, Arnold "Red" Auerbach), but not famous team owners (George Steinbrenner, Ted Turner).

I have tried to be as comprehensive as possible within the scope outlined, citing printed materials published between 1977 and 1987, with a number of titles from 1988. I have not included juvenile works (pre-teenage reading or interest level).

For the very few books that I could not examine I used descriptive information taken from the Library of Congress cataloging data. These books are identified by three asterisks (***) following the citation.

Since celebrity knows no geographical boundary, I did not use place of publication as an inclusion criterion in the biographies section. However, because language of publication was a key consideration, with rare exceptions, I cited only works in the English language. Those published in North America predominate. There are considerably more foreign sources in the non-bibliographic chapters.

The latest known edition of a work is the one I cited. When a foreign edition and a United States edition were published simultaneously, I used the latter. Reprints of books published before 1977 are not cited, although a small number of paperbound editions which are actually reprints of earlier hardbound editions may have infiltrated the list. Occasionally, paperbound editions and/or reprints of post-1977 books are cited when I could not examine the original edition.

In the non-bibliographic chapters, I listed the most up-to-date contact addresses and telephone numbers I could verify.

There are four parts to this book. Part I lists general sources that are useful for accessing information about anyone—celebrity or not. Part II gives sources for information about celebrities (including directors) in motion pictures and television. Part III contains the popular music celebrities information (including that for composers), and Part IV has information on sport celebrities (including coaches).

There are nine chapters in Part I, while Parts II through IV each have eight. Chapter numbering is consecutive throughout the book, from 1 to 33. Chapters 1, 10, 18, and 26 contain entries for reference books; 2, 11, 19, 27, collective (anthologized) biographies; 3, 12, 20, 28, periodicals; 4, 13, 21, 29, computerized databases; 5, 14, 22, 30, organizations; 6, 15, 23, 31, commercial sources and services; 7, 16, 24, 30, fan clubs; and 8, 17, 25, and 33, individual biographies. Part I's ninth chapter describes general works about celebrity and fame. The works are arranged alphabetically in a letter-by-letter style. Mc, M', and Mac are alphabetized as if spelled as Mac. Compound names are considered as one name. Common abbreviations, are listed as though spelled out. Entries are consecutively numbered throughout the book.

Chapter Descriptions

Reference Books (Chapters 1, 10, 18, 26)

Organization of the four reference chapters is by type of material. Each type is grouped under a descriptive section heading: Bibliographies and Guides, Biographical Dictionaries, Encyclopedias, Yearbooks, Indexes, Directories, and Individual Celebrity Sources. Section headings vary slightly within the four reference chapters as indicated in the table of contents.

The listings give full, descriptive annotations regardless of whether they are considered standard or specialized sources. Reference books which are also continuations must be either currently in publication or have ceased publication sometime after 1978. Individual celebrity reference sources are arranged alphabetically by name and, beneath this name heading, by author.

Collective Biographies (Chapters 2, 11, 19, 27)

Biographical anthologies containing profiles on three or more celebrities, at least one of whom is a media or sports star in *Celebrity Register*, are cited and annotated in chapters 2, 11, 19, and 27.

The works may contain autobiographies, biographies, or interviews; they may be histories with significant biographical content, anecdotal accounts, unabashed gossip material, or some combination of these biographical genres.

Books with fewer than three biographies are located with the individual biographies. Usually, those having in excess of 100 sketches are placed in the appropriate reference chapter with the biographical dictionaries. Collective audio-visual materials are to be found with the printed sources.

Annotations feature the names of all the people treated in the biographies (or when the list is prohibitively long, a representative selection). The subject index includes a complete listing of the names in the annotations.

Periodicals (Chapters 3, 12, 20, 28)

The primary criteria for inclusion were that the periodical offers celebrity biographical material on a fairly regular basis and that the title is currently in publication.

Periodicals for the early to middle teenage audience are cited when their biographical material occasionally attempts to transcend the idolatric norm.

Citations give title, place of publication, publisher, beginning date of publication, and frequency. Descriptions give any variant titles with their dates of publication, a brief indication of contents, and sources where the periodical is indexed.

"Fanzines," hybrid publications aimed at a clientele of aficionados and of a quality that varies from slick and professional to semiliterate, were excluded. While the value of these publications for celebrity biography is indisputable (in particular for material on younger stars), they tend to be ephemeral, have haphazard publication schedules, and generally defy precise bibliographic control. The best method for accessing fanzines is through inquiry to fan clubs.

Computerized Databases (Chapters 4, 13, 21, 29)

The computer chapters offer a broad selection of full-text or bibliographic database sources which can be electronically accessed for retrieval of biographical information about media and sports personalities.

I have assumed that most readers will have easy access to computerized databases in today's information-sensitized environment. Computer database searches may be conducted either on-line or on-site by a trained operator acting for the user. Increasingly, as command protocols are simplified, more and more searches will be conducted by the user acting alone.

Vendors selling the search time and access to computerized information may be database owners, gateway (intermediary) operators or, most often, specialists who write and maintain software on their own large computers, handling a number of databases for their owners.

Information given in the chapters is standardized to show: name of database, place of production, producer, subject(s), contents/size, coverage, corresponding printed source (if any), address, and telephone number.

Organizations (Chapters 5, 14, 22, 30)

Special library collections, archives, museums, associations, halls of fame and other organizations listed in chapters 5, 14, 22, and 30 have rich holdings of biographical materials. These repositories range from heavily visited museums to specialized centers for scholarly research. Some facilities, most notably, public and university libraries, have few restrictions on use. In most other instances, use of collections and services by the public is controlled and normally permitted only after prior application.

While North American locations predominate, there are some twenty foreign centers listed—primarily in the area of motion pictures.

Regardless of type, the organizations are arranged alphabetically, by name. Entry information includes (when applicable), the following elements: name, address, telephone number, purpose or philosophy, collection holdings, services offered, publication(s).

Commercial Sources and Services (Chapters 6, 15, 23, 31)

Businesses engaged in the sale and/or purchase of biographical books, artifacts, and memorabilia associated with media and sports celebrities are described in chapters 6, 15, 23, and 31.

Although the cumulative number of dealers listed in the four chapters is large, it represents a small part of the multitude of such firms throughout the world. British dealers comprise the majority of the foreign entries.

Business firm names and dealer surnames are listed together alphabetically. Each entry gives name, activity (i.e., bookstore, collector source, or service), mail address, telephone number (if known), and identification of the product or service for sale.

Fan Clubs (FC) (Chapters 7, 16, 24, 32)

Star struck as they are, fan clubs offer a mine of worthwhile celebrity information.

The clubs listed are those formed for the stars identified in the *Celebrity Register*. When there are large numbers of clubs for one individual, I approximated the total number and selected two or three from the group as representative. The list of clubs that are not celebrity specific is located in chapter 7, general sources.

Club information is placed beneath entries alphabetized by celebrity. Each entry gives club name, contact person (if any), and mail address.

Individual Biographies (Chapters 8, 17, 25, 33)

Chapters 8, 17, 25, and 33 list book-length individual celebrity biographies. Consistent with the practice used throughout this sourcebook, inclusion is based upon selection by the *Celebrity Register*. Most of the books conform to the "popular" biography genre.

Because Bob Dylan, John Lennon, Elvis Presley, and The Beatles have been the subjects of such a large number of biographies, I cited for them only those books published since 1982.

Arrangement is alphabetical by celebrity name and, beneath this name heading, by author. To the right of the celebrity name is an abbreviation (Act., Dir., Ent., Mus., or Spo.) indicating occupation. Also in this location are the death dates for celebrities who have died since 1973.

Audio-visual materials are cited and summarized using descriptive data from the *National Union Catalog*. Entries are listed by title together with the printed sources.

Books about Celebrity, Fame (Chapter 9)

The works in chapter 9 may prove useful in understanding the celebrity phenomenon. It is perhaps surprising that so few monographs are available on the subject. Because of this and the worthiness of the material, I ignored the post-1977 publication date criterion and included Daniel J. Boorstin's *The Image: Or, What Happened to the American Dream*.

Indexes

Author, title and subject indexes assure comprehensive access to the several thousand discrete celebrity information sources gathered within this book. The numbers given in the indexes refer to citation numbers, not to page numbers.

Celebrity Sources

PART I
GENERAL SOURCES

Chapter 1
Reference Books

Section 1
Bibliographies and Guides

1. *America on Film and Tape: A Topical Catalog of Audiovisual Resources for the Study of United States History, Society, and Culture.* Edited by Howard B. Hitchens, and Vidge Hitchens. Bibliographies and Indexes in American History, no. 3. Westport, CT, London: Greenwood Press, 1985. 392 p. Index.

The subjects covered in this work parallel areas in a college American Studies course curriculum: the arts, folklore, history, literature, science, and sociology. In biography, of particular note are audiovisual sources in the sections on performing arts and popular culture. Entries are arranged by title within subjects, and give information on format (motion picture, filmstrip, slides, audio cassette, videorecording, or phonodisc) sound or silent, length, release year, distributor, and a description of the contents. A distributor directory is included.

2. *Biographical Books, 1876-1949.* New York: Bowker, 1983. 1768 p. Index.

See entry below for annotation.

3. *Biographical Books, 1950-1980.* New York: Bowker, 1980. 1557 p. Index.

A volume with over 40,000 entries and covering the years 1876-1949 was published in 1983. (See citation above.) Supplements are planned for the years since 1980. This volume lists 42,152 biographical and autobiographical works published or distributed in America between 1950 and 1980. The *American Book Publishing Record* database was used to generate the entries. The main arrangement is by name. Indexing is by name/subject (Library of Congress subject headings) vocation, author and title.

4. *Biography: An Interdisciplinary Quarterly.* Honolulu, HI: University Press of Hawaii for the Biographical Research Center, vol. 1-, 1978-. (Quarterly)

Biography is primarily a scholarly journal. It is placed in the reference bibliography category of this book chiefly because of its new section (beginning with Summer, 1987; vol. 10, no. 3), "Reviewed Elsewhere," in which is presented an extensive, briefly-annotated bibliography of biographies reviewed in other journals. Of paramount interest, is the subdivision, popular biography. *Biography* is indexed selectively by: *Artbibliographies Modern, Book Review Index, Index to Book Reviews in the Humanities,* and *M L A International Bibliography.*

5. Briscoe, Mary Louise; Tobias, Barbara; and Bloom, Lynn Z., eds. *American Autobiography, 1945-1980: A Bibliography.* Madison: University of Wisconsin Press, 1982. 365 p. Index.

Over 5,000 works are cited in this book, intended as a companion volume to Louis Kaplan's, *A Bibliography of American Autobiographies*, Madison: University of Wisconsin Press, 1962. (Kaplan's work cites autobiographies published before 1945.) The main arrangement in Briscoe is by author. There is a subject index.

6. Cimbala, Diane J.; Cargill, Jennifer; and Alley, Brian. *Biographical Sources: A Guide to Dictionaries and Reference Works*. Phoenix, AZ: Oryx Press, 1986. 146 p. Index.

This annotated bibliography lists 689 English-language biographical reference books published through December, 1984. Arrangement is classified by subject, usually an occupational grouping, e.g., Sports, Music and Musicians, Stage and Film. Filing within subjects is by title. Some collective biographies are included. Indices provide detailed subject and author/title access.

7. Emmens, Carol A. *Famous People on Film*. Metuchen, NJ: Scarecrow Press, 1977. 355 p. Illustrated. Index.

This is a guide to non-theatrical films (16mm) about famous people. The films are available in North America from major distributors. Arrangement is by surname. Age level of interest is given. Entries were extracted from distributor catalogs.

8. Farrell, Mary A., comp. *Who's Whos: An International Guide to Sources of Current Biographical Information*. METRO Miscellaneous Publication No. 21. New York: New York Metropolitan Reference and Research Library Agency, 1979. 102 p. Paperbound.

Farrell lists comprehensive sources of biographical information on living persons which were published between 1970-1980. She omits sources for Canada, Great Britain and the United States. Each entry contains author, title, imprint, edition, series, brief description or evaluation, and standard notes on biographical content.

9. Milner, Anita Cheek. *Newspaper Indexes: A Location and Subject Guide for Researchers.* Metuchen, NJ: Scarecrow Press, 1977-82. 3 vols.

Predominantly North American in coverage, but with international inclusions, this guide and directory to holdings shows which institutions have what newspaper index or clipping file. Information was gathered from libraries, newspapers, historical and genealogical societies, publishers, booksellers, and selected individuals. Information given includes name of newspaper index or file, subjects covered, reference service charge, photocopy charge, newspaper loan availability, and printed catalog availability. The first (of two) main sections is arranged by subject heading, the second is geographical.

10. Slocum, Robert B. *Biographical Dictionaries and Related Works: An International Bibliography of Collective Biographies, Bio-bibliographies, Collections of Epitaphs, Selected Genealogical Works, Dictionaries of Anonyms and Pseudonyms, Historical and Specialized Dictionaries, Biographical Materials in Government Manuals, Bibliographies of Biography, Biographical Indexes, and Selected Printed Catalogs.* 2d ed. Detroit, MI: Gale Research, 1986. 2 vols. Index.

This new edition "cumulates and updates entries appearing in the first edition (1967) and its two supplements (1972 and 1978)." (Preface.) With 4,000 entries added to the cumulation, the new total is above 16,000 consecutively-numbered, annotated entries. Arrangement is by place and vocation. Separate author, title and subject indexes provide further access.

11. Wynar, Bohdan S., ed. *ARBA Guide to Biographical Dictionaries.* Littleton, CO: Libraries Unlimited, 1986. 444 p. Index.

Intended as a library selection tool, *ARBA (American Reference Books Annual)* gives complete citations and critical annotations on selected biographical dictionaries, encyclopedias and directories in all fields. Books cited were published during the last 20 years, and most continue in print. Arrangement is classified by field or discipline. There are author, title and subject indexes.

Section 2
Biographical Dictionaries

12. Andersen, Christopher P. *The New Book of People: Photographs, Capsule Biographies, and Vital Statistics of Over 500 Celebrities.* New York: Putnam, Perigee, 1986. 463 p. Illustrated. Paperbound.

Using his admittedly highly subjective selection criteria, Anderson includes the powerful, rich, accomplished and notorious of the world's living celebrities. Each entry has a short biography followed by a listing of data in standard format: birth, height, weight, eye color, zodiac, education, religion, marriages, children, interests, personal habits and traits, address and income (often estimated). Since publication of the first edition in 1981, some sixty new people have been substituted for a similar number whose celebrity proved fleeting.

13. *The Bedside Book of Celebrity Gossip: 1,500 Outrageous Barbs from One Celebrity to Another.* Edited by Celebrity Research Group. New York: Crown Publishers, Prince, 1984. 119 p. Paperbound.

The subtitle describes the content, which is alphabetically arranged by the individual barbed. Unfortunately, there is no fast access, through an index or some other means, to the barber.

14. Blackwell, Earl, ed. *Celebrity Register.* 4th ed. Towson, MD: Times Publishing Group, 1986. 561 p. Illustrated. Index.

Previous editions of *Celebrity Register* appeared in 1959, 1963, and 1973. It is the "bible" of celebrity, and inclusion is an important confirmation of status. There are about 1,700 people listed in the current edition, each with portrait and a biographical sketch of several hundred words reflecting the individual's character and personality. Celebrity Service International, parent company of the publication, maintains voluminous files on thousands of personalities. The files hold information used in the sketches, and document who is currently (or who remains) a "hot property."

15. Bronaugh, Robert Brett, comp. *The Celebrity Birthday Book*. Middle Village, NY: J. David, 1981. 492 p.

The book contains the names of celebrities of all ages "who have made a significant impact on our lives today. . . ." The first main part is an alphabetical list with birthdays, and includes professional name, full middle name, maiden name, and occupation. The second part is arranged chronologically.

16. *The Canadian Who's Who*. Toronto: University of Toronto Press, vol. 1-, 1910-. (Annual)

Before 1980, this work was published triennially, with several supplementary booklets (the *Canadian Biographical Service)* issued between editions. It ". . . is the largest and most authoritative publication of its kind in Canada, offering instant access to more than nine thousand prominent Canadians in all walks of life." (Introduction.) Biographees are chosen on merit. The *Canadian Who's Who Index, 1898-1984*, provides retrospective access to the entire backlist.

17. *Concise Dictionary of American Biography*. 3d ed. New York: Scribner, 1980. 1333 p.

This book contains over 17,000 biographical descriptions of the deceased American notables listed in its parent work, *Dictionary of American Biography*. It includes all entries from the parent volumes through 1960. There are three types of entries: minimal, median and extended, with contents ranging from name, birth/death dates and places, and outstanding achievements, to those "in which the content, style and spirit of the original biographies have been preserved as fully as possible." (Preface.)

18. *Dictionary of American Biography.* Edited by Allen Johnson, et al. New York: Scribner, 1946?-58. 11 vols. Index.

A reprint of the original twenty-volume edition, with its two supplements, published 1928-58. This authoritative standard work with its seven post-1958 supplements, the most recent published in 1981, extends biographical coverage through 1965. It now contains 17,656 biographical sketches of deceased Americans "who have made memorable contributions to our national life." Each sketch is several paragraphs long, and has a short bibliography. The author's name appears at the end. The supplementary volumes have a cumulative index.

19. *The International Who's Who.* London: Europa Publications, 1st ed.-, 1935-. (Annual)

The edition examined (51st, 1987) gives in a compact paragraph biographical data on over 18,000 of ". . . our most famous and influential contemporaries. . . " from almost every country. About 1,500 of the biographies are new; the remainder revised and updated. Information includes: name, nationality, occupation, birth place/date, parentage, marriage, children, education, career facts, publications, leisure interests, and address/telephone.

20. Jones, Barry O., and Dixon, M. V. *St. Martin's Press Dictionary of Biography.* New York: St. Martin's Press, 1986. 917 p.

A revised edition of *The Macmillan Dictionary of Biography* (1981), this work contains 7,500 sketches on individuals of all times, occupations and nationalities. "The longest entries, such as Jesus, Lenin, Marx and Mozart, run between 500 and 1,000 words. The contents are accurate and the style lively, incisive and opinionated." (Introduction.) Most entries conclude with a short bibliography.

21. Levy, Felice D., comp. *Obituaries on File.* New York: Facts on File, 1979. 2 vols. 1010 p. Index.

Almost 25,000 entries comprise this compilation of obituaries which appeared in *Facts on File* from 1940 through 1978. Scope is international, encompassing deceased with one or more of these criteria: great eminence; a moment of notoriety; or, prominence within a field. The main section lists names with age, accomplishments, and date/place of death. There are chronological and subject indexes showing location by country, occupation, and company affiliation.

22. Lewytzkyj, Borys, and Stroynowski, Juliusz. *Who's Who in the Socialist Countries: A Biographical Encyclopedia of 10,000 Leading Personalities in 16 Communist Countries.* Translated and edited by Stephen Pringle and Ulla Dornberg. New York: K. G. Saur, 1978. 736 p.

"For the first time, biographies of the leading figures in all socialist countries in all spheres of life have been collected into one volume. Included are party and political officials as well as leaders in the fields of economics, science, the military, the arts, literature and religion." (Preface.) In some cases, biographies of persons recently deceased have been included. Information presented: surname, profession, birthdate/place, education, career and honors earned.

23. *Longman Dictionary of 20th Century Biography.* Edited by Alan Isaacs and Elizabeth Martin. Consultant Editor, Asa Briggs. Burnt Mill, Harlow, Essex, England: Longman, 1985. 548 p.

"[This dictionary] includes biographies of (some 1700) individuals from different countries and cultures who have contributed to thought as well as to action. The people who are included in this dictionary, however, are people about whom it is useful . . . to have easily accessible biographical information." (Foreword.) This definition encompasses sport and entertainment figures often ignored by general sources. Sketches are a paragraph or so in length, and contain birth/death dates, family background, education, events contributing to notoriety, and a summary of achievements or misdemeanours.

24. Lucaire, Edward. *The Celebrity Book of Super Lists: Fantastic Facts about the Famous.* New York: Stein and Day, 1985. 204 p. Index.

Herein are dozens of trivia lists: "Occupations of Celebrities' Mothers," "Famous Children of Dentists," and, "One-Name Celebrities," to name but three.

25. Lucaire, Edward. *Celebrity Trivia: A Collection of Little-Known Facts About Well-Known People.* New York: Warner Books, 1980. 528 p. Paperbound.

Celebrity Trivia gathers "legitimate but little-known facts and tasty tidbits" from biographies, almanacs, encyclopedias, talk shows and interviews. Individuals are included because of their fame or notoriety, and regardless of place or century of birth.

26. Mossman, Jennifer, ed. *Pseudonyms and Nicknames Dictionary.* 2d ed. Detroit, MI: Gale Research, 1982. 995 p.

"A guide to aliases, appellations, assumed names, code names, cognomens, cover names, epithets, initialisms, nicknames, noms de guerre, noms de plume, pen names, pseudonyms, sobriquets, and stage names of contemporary and historical persons, including the subjects' real names, basic biographical information, and citations for the sources from which the entries were compiled." (Subtitle.) Over 90,000 entries under original name have five elements: birth date; death date; abbreviated key code(s) to standard biographical dictionaries; nationality; and, assumed name(s) by which the individual became known. Inter-edition supplements are published.

27. *The New York Times Biographical Service.* Ann Arbor, MI: University Microfilms International, vol. 5, no. 12-, Dec. 1974-. Illustrated. Looseleaf. (Monthly)

Volumes 1-6 (Jan., 1970 Jan., 1975) have the title, *New York Times Biographical Edition,* and appeared weekly. The service supplies a yearly average of 2,000 photomechanically reproduced biographies and obituaries from all sections of the newspaper. A name index cumulates annually.

28. Vernoff, Edward, and Shore, Rima. *The International Dictionary of 20th Century Biography.* New York, Scarborough, ON: New American Library, NAL Books, 1987. 819 p. Index.

Consists of 5,650 concise biographies of world notables, living and dead. Coverage is broad, including all areas of popular culture and sports. Individuals chosen are those who have ". . . made significant contributions during the century, even if they are relatively unknown, and those whose contributions to civilization were less than monumental but whose fame is widespread." (Introduction.) Information of a critical nature is provided along with the basic biographical facts to clarify contributions to society or to help place each subject in historical context. Entries contain a bibliography of any autobiography and all significant book-length biographies. Index by occupation and nationality.

29. *Webster's Biographical Dictionary.* Springfield, MA: G. & C. Merriam, 1980. 1697 p. Table.

". . . A work of biographical reference not restricted in its selection of names by considerations of historical period, nationality, race, religion, or occupation." However numerous the entries (short sketches of some 40,000 persons), the editors have intentionally minimized the information on contemporary celebrities in sports and the media. A revised edition (not examined): *Webster's New Biographical Dictionary.*

30. *Who's Who: An Annual Biographical Dictionary.* London: A. C. Black, ed. 1-, 1849-. (Annual)

The sub-title and imprint vary. The ancestor of the great number of "who's whos" to follow, this work attempts ". . . to list those [living people] who, through their careers, affect the political, economic, scientific and artistic life of the country. . . . [and] whose lives are of particular interest, whether because they decide our destinies, spend our money, influence our taste or because they are especially prominent in their fields--

the arts, education, medicine, sport. . . ." (Preface.) Small type and abbreviated form are used to compress as many facts as possible into a paragraph. Addresses are given.

31. *Who's Who in America.* Chicago: Marquis, vol. 1-, 1899/1900-. (Biennial)

A standard work, currently in its 44th edition (1986-1987), includes life and career data on approximately 75,000 noteworthy individuals in Canada, Mexico and the United States. Selection is based on a person's position or achievements. Each edition is fully revised, and in the 44th there is a listing of individuals included in the Marquis regional or topical directories, and a "Retiree Index" of people deleted because of retirement from active work. *Who Was Who in America* can be consulted for information on those persons who died prior to mid-1985. Combined name access to the various Marquis general, regional, and topical directories is provided by *Marquis Who's Who Index to Who's Who Books* (1985-), which continues: *Marquis Who's Who Publications: Index to All Books* (1974-1984). Yet another index, *Who's Who in America, Geographic/Professional Area Index* (42d ed.-, 1982/83-), provides place and occupational access.

32. *Who's Who in Entertainment.* Wilmette, IL: Marquis, ed. 1-, 1988?- (Biennial?) ***

Scheduled publication, December, 1988. "*Who's Who in Entertainment* provides immediate access to . . . background information on more than 18,000 notables within the entertainment community." (Publisher's brochure.)

33. *Who's Who in France.* Paris: J. Lafitte, ed. 1-, 1953/4-. (Biennial?)

Title varies: *Who's Who in France, Paris 1953-54.* Other title: *Qui Est Qui en France.* The eighteenth edition (1985-86), has over 20,000 sketches of living personalities. The text is in French. Included are the famous, those with recognized excellence in their field, and those who have made outstanding contributions to France. The abbreviated style is similar to that of *Who's Who in America* (above). Addresses are given.

34. *Who's Who in Germany.* International Red Series. Munich: Who's Who Publishers, 1956-. (Irregular)

The eighth edition (1982-83), has over 17,000 biographies of living personalities from all fields in the Federal Republic of Germany (West Germany). The text is in English, with an abbreviated style similar to that of *Who's Who in America* (above). Addresses are given. An appendix gives information on political, artistic, intellectual, economic and social life, and internationally renowned enterprises.

35. *Who's Who in Italy.* Edited by J. C. Dove. International Red Series. Chicago: Marquis, 1986. 1671 p.

This work contains some 9,000 biographies (in English) of top-ranking, living personalities in the fields of business, politics, science, the arts and entertainment. It is done in the abbreviated style of *Who's Who in America* (above), concluding with information on the various branches of Italian life and a register of leading enterprises.

36. *Who's Who in Scandinavia.* Zurich, Switzerland, Who's Who, 1981. 2 vols. (Biennial)

"A biographical encyclopedia of the international red series containing some 13,000 biographies [in English] of living prominent personalities in Denmark, Finland, Iceland, Norway and Sweden." (Title page.) Arrangement is by surname, followed by title, pseudonym, profession, birthday/place, parents, marital status, names of children, address, and personal and career information.

37. *Who's Who in the East: A Biographical Dictionary of Leading Men and Women of the Eastern United States.* Chicago: Marquis, vol. 1-, 1943-. (Biennial)

Designed as a supplement to *Who's Who in America* (above), although individuals deemed particularly newsworthy are duplicated in that source. Selection criteria are the same. The current, twenty-first edition, contains approximately 23,500 names from: Connecticut, Delaware, Maine, Maryland, Massachusetts, New Hampshire, New Jersey, New York,

Pennsylvania, Rhode Island, Vermont, Washington, D.C., New Brunswick, Newfoundland, Nova Scotia, Prince Edward Island, Quebec, and eastern Ontario.

38. *Who's Who in the Midwest: A Biographical Dictionary of Noteworthy Men and Women of the Central and Midwestern States.* Chicago: Marquis, ed. 1-, 1979-. (Biennial)

Designed as a supplement to *Who's Who in America* (above), although individuals deemed particularly noteworthy are duplicated in that source. Selection criteria are the same. The current, twentieth edition, contains approximately 17,000 names from: Illinois, Indiana, Iowa, Kansas, Michigan, Minnesota, Missouri, Nebraska, North Dakota, Ohio, South Dakota, Wisconsin, Manitoba and western Ontario.

39. *Who's Who in the South and Southwest: A Biographical Dictionary of Noteworthy Men and Women of the Southern and Southwestern States.* Chicago: Marquis, ed. 1-, 1947-. (Biennial)

Designed as a supplement to *Who's Who in America* (above), although individuals deemed particularly noteworthy are duplicated in that source. Selection criteria are the same. The current, twentieth edition, contains approximately 19,000 names from: Alabama, Arkansas, Florida, Georgia, Kentucky, Louisiana, Mississippi, North Carolina, Oklahoma, South Carolina, Tennessee, Texas, Virginia, West Virginia, Puerto Rico, Virgin Islands, and Mexico.

40. *Who's Who in the West: A Biographical Dictionary of Noteworthy Men and Women of the Pacific Coastal and Western States.* Chicago: Marquis, 1949-. (Biennial)

Designed as a supplement to *Who's Who in America* (above), although individuals deemed particularly noteworthy are duplicated in that source. Selection criteria are the same. The current, twentieth edition, contains approximately 18,000 names from: Alaska, Arizona, California, Colorado, Hawaii, Idaho, Montana, Nevada, New Mexico, Oregon, Utah,

Washington, Wyoming, Alberta, British Columbia, and Saskatchewan.

41. *Who's Who in the World.* Chicago: Marquis, ed. 1-, 1971/1972-. (Biennial)

"Biographical information on important individuals from virtually every nation is presented in the eighth edition [1987-1988]. . . ." (Preface.) Individuals were chosen from the ranks of government, religion, business, scholarship, science, education, medicine, publishing, broadcasting, international associations, performing arts, and many other areas. The selection criteria for the approximately 28,300 biographees were that of occupational stature and/or achievement. Wealth or social position was not a factor in selection.

42. *Who Was Who in America: A Companion Biographical Reference Work to Who's Who in America.* Chicago: Marquis, 1942-81. 7 vols.

Contents: vol. 1 (1897-1942), vol. 2 (1943-1950), vol. 3 (1951-1960), vol. 4 (1961-1968), vol. 5 (1969-1973), vol. 6 (1974-1976), vol. 7 (1977-1981). The "Was" books contain the sketches of 105,000 deceased biographees taken from *Who's Who in America* (above). Death date and place of interment are added. Volume seven has sketches of recently deceased world notables. The index to this set, *Who Was Who in America, with World Notables: Index,* is cited below.

Section 3
Yearbooks

43. *The Americana Annual; an Encyclopedia of Current Events.* New York, Chicago: Americana Corporation, vol. 1-, 1923-. Illustrated. Index. (Annual)

Other title: *Yearbook of the Encyclopedia Americana.* In the edition seen (1985), a section entitled "Miscellaneous" contains biography and obituary chapters. Biographies are of several paragraphs, and signed (unless prepared by the staff). Included are sketches of: Erma Bombeck, Scott Hamilton, Michael Jackson, Carl Lewis, Shirley MacLaine, Walter Payton, and non-entertainers prominent in the news during 1984.

44. *Britannica Book of the Year.* Chicago: Encyclopaedia Britannica, vol. 1-, 1938-. Illustrated. Bibliography. Index. (Annual)

"The *Britannica Book of the Year* bridges the gap between editions [of the *Encyclopaedia Britannica*]." (Introduction.) In the 1987 edition examined, the section, "Year in Review," has a chapter with about 100 signed biographies several paragraphs in length. This is followed by a chapter containing obituaries.

45. *Current Biography Yearbook.* New York: H. W. Wilson, 1955-. Illustrated. (Annual)

An annual which continues *Current Biography: Who's News and Why.* (New York: H. W. Wilson, vol. 1-, 1940-), and is cumulated from monthly numbers with the title: *Current Biography.* Each of the monthly issues has from twelve to eighteen profiles of prominent persons of various nationalities and occupations. These range in length from 2,500 to 3,000 words, giving: full name; birthdate; address; profession; objective biographical account; subject's own views, attitudes, and opinions; observations of journalists, colleagues; recent photograph; and a bibliography. Biographies are periodically updated. Obituary notices appear for those persons whose biographies have been previously published. The August, 1987 issue contains fifteen profiles, among which are those of three entertainment celebrities: Paul Hogan, Dennis Hopper, and Les Paul. Cumulated index for 1940-1985.

46. *Facts on File.* New York: Facts on File, vol. 1-, 1940-. (Weekly; annual cumulation)

Subtitle: *Weekly World News Digest with Cumulative Index.* "News in the [digest] is a correct and objective summary of what is reported in more than 50 foreign and U.S. newspapers and magazines." (Introduction.) *Facts on File Yearbook* is a compilation of the 52 weekly issues of the looseleaf *Facts on File*. There is also a *Facts on File Five-Year Index*, published as a cumulative index to the yearbook. The index or digest, used together or separately, enables fast access by name to brief biographical data concerning an event, date, full name or title/occupation of an individual.

47. *Newsmakers*. Detroit, MI: Gale Research, vol. 1-, 1985-. Illustrated. (Annual)

Formerly: *Contemporary Newsmakers*. Quarterly issues cumulate into annual hardbound volumes containing biographical profiles (with portraits), on people currently in the news. Each issue has about fifty profiles which conclude with a short bibliography of additional information sources. Concise sketches of recently deceased newsmakers are grouped in a separate obituaries section.

Section 4
Indexes

48. *Access: The Supplementary Index to Periodicals*. Syracuse, NY: John Gordon Burke Publisher, vol. 1-, 1975-. (3 issues yearly)

Designed to complement general periodical indexes, *Access* includes regional and city magazines and a balanced selection of general and special-interest periodicals. About 160 periodicals are indexed, and editorial policy forbids any overlap with *Readers' Guide* (below). The third issue is a yearly cumulation. Each issue consists of two parts: (1) authors (with full citation), and (2) subjects (citation minus title). Biographical information can be located in the subject index under surname or by occupational/talent heading, i.e. music, rock.

49. *Alternative Press Index*. College Park, MD: Alternative Press Center, vol. 1-, 1969-. (Quarterly)

About 230 alternative and radical publications which fall outside the scope of the "standard" periodical indexes are covered by this source. Articles are listed by subject, including proper names. Some subject headings for use in identifying celebrity articles: autobiographies, biographies, diaries/memoirs/letters, obituaries, and actors and actresses. Publication was suspended during 1972-73.

50. *America, History and Life.* Santa Barbara, CA: ABC-Clio, vol. 1-, 1964-. (Varying frequency)

Volume 0 (zero), issued in 1972, covers periodical literature published from 1954 until the issuance of volume 1, in 1964. Approximately 700 North American periodicals and Festschriften are surveyed for material on American and Canadian history and current life. Additionally, some 1,200 foreign periodicals covered in *Historical Abstracts* are analyzed for relevant articles. Organized in four parts: Part A, article citations/abstracts (triannual); Part B, book reviews (semi-annual); Part C, American (including Canadian) history bibliography (annual); and, Part D, index (annual). Biographees are listed as subjects in the individual issue and annual indexes. In the first three quinquennial indexes (volumes 1-15, 1964-1978) there is a merged subject, biographic, and author alphabet. The *America: History and Life* database, updated quarterly, is available for computerized literature searches.

51. *Art Index.* New York: H. W. Wilson, vol. 1-, 1929-. (Quarterly)

Some 200 domestic and foreign periodicals, yearbooks, and museum bulletins are indexed in this source which includes films and television within its scope. There is coverage overlap of biographical information from English language periodicals with that found in Wilson's *Biography Index.* In the 1985-1986 volume, under "Actors and actresses," there are "see also" references to over 110 individuals. The main body of the work consists of a mixed alphabet of subject and author entries followed by a listing of citations to book reviews. *Art Index* is computer accessible online (Wilsonline), or by subscription in quarterly cumulative updates on compact disk (Wilsondisc), starting date, September, 1984.

52. *Arts & Humanities Citation Index.* Philadelphia: Institute for
    Scientific Information, vol. 1-, 1976-. (3 issues yearly)

    This comprehensive reference to material in over 7,100
journals (1,400 fully indexed/5,700 selectively) covers, among
many other topics, those of film, TV, radio and music.
Biographical articles may be found by searching under surname
in the permuterm subject index. A source index (location of the
main entry), and a citation index complete the three-volume set.
Issues cumulate yearly.

53. *Bio-Base: A Periodic Cumulative Master Index in Microfiche
    to Sketches Found in 500 Current and Historic
    Biographical Dictionaries. 1978 Base Set.* Detroit, MI: Gale
    Research, 1978. Microfiche.

    Examined were the 1978 base set, and the 1980 first
supplement. A "master cumulation" was published in 1984.
The microfiche includes a separate booklet containing an
introduction and bibliographic key to publication codes. *Bio-
Base* is the computer output microfiche (COM), generated from
a file approaching two million entries and published as the
Biography and Genealogy Master Index, and other titles in the
Gale Biographical Index Series. Since it has not been rigorously
edited, ". . . it is thus possible to make this valuable information
available to the user in fiche form months in advance. . . ."
(Introduction.) These data are also accessible on-line through
Dialog.

54. *Biography Almanac.* Edited by Annie M. Brewer, and Susan
    L. Stetler. Detroit, MI: Gale Research, vol. 1-, 1981-.
    Paperbound. (Irregular)

    Published in editions which, since 1983, are issued in
parts. Supplements are published between editions. "A
comprehensive reference guide to more than 2,500 famous and
infamous newsmakers from Biblical times to the present as
found in over 350 readily available biographical sources."
(Subtitle to the first edition, supplement.) Listed are "special
people," under the name by which the individual is most
commonly known, with cross references from any lesser-

known name(s). Vocation, birthplace and date, death date, and sources of biographical information complete the entry. The extent of duplication with listings in the comprehensive *Biography and Genealogy Master Index*, also published by Gale, is not known.

55. *Biography and Genealogy Master Index: A Consolidated Index to More Than 3,200,000 Biographical Sketches in over 350 Current and Retrospective Biographical Dictionaries.* 2d ed. Edited by Miranda C. Herbert, and Barbara McNeil. Gale Biographical Index Series, no. 1. Detroit, MI: Gale Research, 1980. 8 vols.

Continuation of the *Biographical Dictionaries Master Index*, published by Gale since 1975, and updated by annual and quinquennial supplements. This index contains over 5,700,000 citations to listings in about 600 biographical dictionaries. Arrangement is by surname followed by one or more dictionary locator "codes." Entries are extracted from a computerized file, *Bio-Base* (available in microfiche, and on-line through Dialog). Because of its exhaustive coverage, this work must be considered virtually indispensable for use in biographical reference.

56. *Biography Index.* New York: H. W. Wilson, vol. 1-, 1946-. (Quarterly)

Published quarterly, with annual and three-year cumulations. This comprehensive source "is a guide to biographical material appearing in periodicals [about 2,600] indexed in other Wilson Company indexes, selected additional periodicals, current books of individual and collective biographies [English language, about 100 yearly], and incidental biographical material in otherwise non-biographical books [English language, about 900 yearly]." (Prefatory note.) Material indexed includes: obituaries, letters, diaries, memoirs, and bibliographies. Divided into two sections: (1) access by name of biographee (giving full name, dates, nationality unless American, and occupation, followed by the citation) and, (2) an index by occupation or profession. *Biography Index* is computer accessible online through Wilsonline, or by subscription in quarterly cumulative updates on CD ROM (Wilsondisc), starting date, July, 1984.

57. *British Humanities Index.* London: The Library Association, vol. 1-, 1962-. (Quarterly)

A quarterly index covering articles published since 1962, with annual cumulations, and superseding, in part, *Subject Index to Periodicals* (coverage, 1915-1961). Over 300 periodicals (primarily British), in the humanities and several of the social sciences are indexed by subject. In one issue examined, under the subject, "Actors and Actresses," reference is given to related headings, e.g., Astaire, Fred; Bowie, David; Winger, Debra; or, "Comedians." The annual cumulations have separate subject and author indexes; both give full bibliographical information. Book reviews are included.

58. *Canadian News Index.* Toronto: Micromedia, vol. 4-, 1980-. (Monthly)

Continues: *Canadian Newspaper Index* (vols. 1-3, 1977-1979), and is issued monthly with annual cumulations. The first three volumes index the *Montreal Star, Toronto Globe and Mail, Toronto Star, Vancouver Sun* and the *Winnipeg Free Press.* Succeeding volumes cover the *Calgary Herald, Halifax Chronicle Herald, Montreal Gazette,* the *Sunday Star* (Toronto), plus some twenty additional Canadian newspapers and magazines with news content. The index is divided by subject and personal name. The former contains references to both subjects and government and corporate names. The latter refers to individuals in the news, and includes obituaries, profiles, and news references "containing significant information." Feature sports stories concerning individuals are also indexed. Biographical coverage is not restricted to Canadians. Micromedia Ltd. provides on-line searching of the *Canadian News Index* data base, begun in 1977 and increasing at the annual rate of 72,000 records.

59. *Canadian Periodical Index: An Author and Subject Index.* Ottawa: Canadian Library Association, vol. 17-, 1964-. (Monthly)

Continues: *Canadian Index to Periodicals and Documentary Films* (vols. 1-16, 1948-1963). Issued monthly with annual cumulations, this is a general index to about 130 popular and scholarly Canadian periodicals in both the English and French languages. Subject headings are in English, with French cross references. Biographical articles are entered under surname. Book and movie reviews are listed under those headings.

60. Christian Science Monitor. *Index of the Christian Science Monitor, 1960-78*. Boston: Christian Science Publishing Society, vol. 1-, 1960-. (Monthly)

Title varies: *Cumulated Index of the Christian Science Monitor, Subject Index of the Christian Science Monitor* and, *Index of the Christian Science Monitor* (coverage, 1960-1978), *Bell & Howell's Index to the Christian Science Monitor* (coverage, 1979-1983); *Bell & Howell Newspaper Index to the Christian Science Monitor* (coverage, 1984-1986); and, *The Christian Science Monitor Index* (coverage, 1987-). Monthly, with annual cumulations. The regional editions' coverage has varied over time. As of April, 1975, format for all editions became unified. The index is divided into subject (general and specific headings), and personal name sections (of individuals who appeared in the newspaper "for some significant reason"). Sports and entertainment figures are entered under the name by which they are reported in the paper. Entry statements contain a brief summation of article content or type.

61. *Essay and General Literature Index*. New York: H. W. Wilson, vol. 1-, 1934-. (Semiannual, with annual and quinquennial cumulations)

(Volume 1 is a retrospective edition covering the years 1900-1933.) As an author and subject index to collections of essays (including Festschriften) with emphasis on materials in the humanities and social sciences, this index analyzes so much material about individuals that it serves as an index of biography. Retrospective coverage to 1900 makes *EGLI* a useful source for coverage of biography published prior to 1946 (the beginning date of *Biography Index*, above). Works about a person or overall discussion of that person's work are entered by surname, under the subdivision, "About." A cumulated index, *Essay and General Literature Index: Works Indexed 1900-1969*, is cited below.

62. *Essay and General Literature Index: Works Indexed 1900-1969*. New York: H. W. Wilson, 1972. 437 p.

The first seven cumulations of *Essay and General Literature Index* are merged into one volume, creating an index listing almost 10,000 analyzed essay collections.

63. Falk, Byron A., and Falk, Valerie R. *Personal Name Index to "The New York Times Index," 1851-1974*. Succasunna, NJ: Roxbury Data Interface, 1976-84. 24 vols.

This massive listing of the countless names contained in *New York Times Index* considerably lessens the task of discovering biographical information in the newspaper backfiles. Names ordinarily buried within a multitude of subject categories are brought together in one listing. Multiple citations to one person are arranged chronologically, often by vocational title. Obituaries are included.

64. McMann, Evelyn de R. *Canadian Who's Who Index, 1898-1984: Incorporating Canadian Men and Women of the Time*. Toronto, Buffalo, NY: University of Toronto Press, 1986. 528 p.

McMann has compiled a cumulated index of 33,230 biographical sketches found in *Canadian Who's Who (1898-1984)*, and the 1898 and 1912 editions of *Canadian Men and Women of the Time*, by H. J. Morgan. Entries note full name, year born, occupations, and volume(s) in which a sketch may be found. Cross-references for name changes, stage names, pseudonyms, and the more familiar form of a name are given.

65. *Magazine Article Summaries*. Topsfield, MA: Database Communications, vol. 1-, 1984-. (Weekly)

Formerly: *Popular Magazine Review* (1984-1987). A weekly index and abstract service to about 200 general periodicals, with monthly, quarterly, and semiannual cumulative indexes. Magazines are indexed within two weeks of their cover date. Arrangement is alphabetical by Sear's subject headings; followed by an article "headline," abstract, and citation. Biographies and news events about individuals are found under the heading, "People." A separate section of the semiannual cumulative index, a "People Index," provides extensive, convenient access to biographical articles. A computerized version is available on-line through BRS Information Technologies.

66. *Magazine Index*. Menlo Park, CA: Information Access, 1977-. (Monthly)

A computer-generated 16mm microfilm index to about 400 general-interest magazines, and accessed with a motorized (ROM) viewer. The most current five years are contained on a single, cumulated reel. Previous indexing is offered on microfiche, *IAC Magazine Index*, and is retrospective to 1977. Indexing is cover-to-cover; all articles, news, product evaluations, editorials on major issues, short stories, poetry, recipes, reviews (graded A-F), and biographical pieces. Arrangement is by interfiled authors, titles, and subjects (Library of Congress subject headings augmented by "natural" language headings).

67. *Marquis Who's Who Index to Who's Who Books*. Chicago: Marquis, 1985-. (Annual)

Other title: *Index to Who's Who Books*. Continues: *Marquis Who's Who Publications Index to All Books* (Chicago: Marquis, 1974-1984. 10 vols.). The 1975 issue of this edition was examined. It is a cumulative index to 210,000 names in corresponding editions of the Marquis biographical directories. The directories indexed: *Who Was Who in America*, *Who's Who in America*, *Who's Who in the East*, *Who's Who in the Midwest*, *Who's Who in the South and Southwest*, *Who's Who in the West*, *Who's Who in Finance and Industry*, *Who's Who in the World*, *Who's Who in Government*, *Who's Who of American Women*, and *Who's Who in Religion*.

68. *National Newspaper Index.* Los Altos, CA: Information Access, 1979-. Microfilm. (Monthly)

The *Christian Science Monitor* (Western ed.), *New York Times* (late ed. and national ed.), and *Wall Street Journal* (Eastern ed. and Western ed.), have comprised this 16mm microfilm index since 1979. Two other newspapers, the *Los Angeles Times,* and *Washington Post* were added in 1982. The index is produced independently of the (printed) *Bell and Howell Newspaper Indexes* (above). Each monthly update is a full cumulation of all material except weather charts, stock market tables, crossword puzzles and horoscopes. Older indexing cumulates on microfiche, while the most current information is displayed via a motorized film reader supplied with the index subscription. Names associated with each article or editorial are indexed separately. For broad biographical access, Library of Congress subject headings augmented with contemporary words/phrases are used. Citations for this index and *Magazine Index* (above), merge daily for online searching as the *Newsearch* database. At monthly intervals, citations are transferred to the online *National Newspaper Index, Legal Resource Index,* or *Magazine Index* databases.

69. *NewsBank. Names in the News.* New Canaan, CT: Newsbank, 1978-. Microfiche. (Monthly)

This service provides current information of biographical interest as reported in newspapers from over 100 cities in the U.S. Companion services (*NewsBank. Review of the Arts. Film and Television,* and *NewsBank. Review of the Arts. Performing Arts*), are described below. Articles on newsworthy people are indexed by name and by appropriate vocational or avocational category. People of interest for other reasons are indexed appropriately, e.g., "centenarians," "crime figures," etc. A printed index, cumulated quarterly and annually, accompanies each issue. The CD-ROM product, *NewsBank Electronic Index,* provides access to the full-text microfiche.

70. *Newspaper Index.* Wooster, OH: Bell & Howell; University Microfilms International, 1972-. Paperbound. (Monthly)

Instituted in 1972 as a combined index to the *Chicago Tribune, Los Angeles Times, New Orleans Times-Picayune,* and *Washington Post* (dropped by Bell & Howell in 1982, and continued then by Research Publications as *The Official Washington Post Index*). This combined format was abandoned in 1974, with separate indexes being published thereafter. Coverage has been expanded to an additional ten American general interest newspapers: *Atlanta Journal, Atlanta Constitution* (1980-), *Boston Globe* (1983-), *Christian Science Monitor* (1979-, see separate entry, above), *Denver Post* (1976-), *Detroit News* (1976-), *Houston Post* (1976-), *St. Louis Post-Dispatch* (1975-), *San Francisco Chronicle* (1976-), *USA Today* (1982-), and *Washington Times* (1982?-). The indexes are produced in eight monthly issues, four quarterly cumulations, and a bound annual cumulation. All "significant" news is indexed. Excluded are society announcements, self-help columns, meeting announcements, horoscopes, television schedules, comic strips, and routine weather reports. Arrangement is by subject heading, including personal names. Entries (with brief abstracts) file chronologically beneath the headings. Obituaries are indexed under "Deaths," then subdivided by name of the deceased. *Newspaper Abstracts,* with 2,000,000 records dating since 1984 from the newspapers enumerated, is available through Dialog Information Services, Inc.

71. *The New York Times Index.* New York: vol. 1-, 1913-. Paperbound. (Semimonthly)

Titles of this index have varied: *New York Times Index for the Published News* (1913-1957), superseded the *New York Times Index "Prior Series"*, consisting of the original handwritten index (1851-1912). It provides subject, geographic and personal name access to the contents of the *New York Times,* and corresponds to the editions available on microfilm from University Microfilms International. Brief abstracts of significant news, editorial and feature matter allow the index to stand alone as a chronological overview of the news. Headings are arranged alphabetically. Beneath the headings, the entries (in most cases) file chronologically. Biographical material is

found by surname; names of the deceased under "Deaths."
Cumulations are quarterly. The annual cumulated volume is
issued as the fourth quarterly.

72. *The New York Times Obituaries Index.* New York: New
    York Times, 1970-80. 2 vols.

    Volume one covers the period, 1858-1968; volume two,
1969-1978. Almost 390,000 names entered under the heading
"Deaths," in issues of *The New York Times Index* are
assembled (in two separate alphabets). The supplement extends
coverage to ". . . certain well known persons whose deaths are
listed in the 'Murders,' and 'Suicides' sections. . . ." Also new
in the supplement is the inclusion of full-text reprints chosen
from the *"Times"* of the obituaries of fifty notable persons.

73. *Obituaries from the Times, 1971-1975, including an Index
    to All Obituaries and Tributes Appearing in The Times
    during the Years 1971-1975.* Compiled by Frank C.
    Roberts. Reading, England: Newspaper Archive
    Developments, 1978. 647 p. Index.

    Two decennial volumes (1951-1960, and 1961-1970),
preceed this one. All contain reprints of selected obituaries as
they appeared in *The Times* (London). The 1971-1975 volume
examined contains about 1,000 obituaries. It has an index by
sphere of activity which includes the headings: music, theatre,
broadcasting and cinema, and sport.

74. *Popular Periodical Index.* Edited by Robert M. Bottorff.
    Roslyn, PA: Popular Periodical Index, vol. 1-, 1973-.
    (Semi-annual)

    A subject-author approach to magazines not indexed in
Readers' Guide to Periodical Literature, this index does, to an
extent, overlap the coverage of other magazine indexes. For
example, more than half of the forty currently indexed titles
duplicate those found in *Access.* Article titles which do not
adequately describe the subject are given added clarification.
Appropriate celebrity subject headings used: motion picture
directors; actors and actresses; musical groups; and musicians.
Surnames are also used as subjects.

75. *Readers' Guide to Periodical Literature.* New York: H. W. Wilson, vol.1-, 1900-. (Semimonthly)

There is an annual cumulation of the semimonthly issues. *Readers' Guide* analyzes about 200 periodicals of a general nature published in the U.S. "The main body of the index consists of subject and author entries to periodical articles arranged in one alphabet. In addition there is a listing of citations to book reviews following the main body of the index." (Prefatory Note.) Biographical articles are cited under the name of the biographee as subject. *Magazine Index* (above), indexes many more popular periodicals, but does not have the retrospective coverage. Recent years' indexing by *Readers' Guide*, may be accessed on CD ROM (Wilsondisc), or on-line (Wisonline).

76. *Social Sciences Citation Index.* Philadelphia: Institute for Scientific Information, vol. 1-, 1973-. (3 issues yearly)

The triannuals are cumulated annually and quinquennially. Subtitle: "An international multidisciplinary index to the literature of the social, behavioral and related sciences." Over 4,700 journals are covered (1,400 fully, 3,300 selectively). *SSCI* has four index components: citation, source, subject and corporate. Some useful biographical articles may be found by searching under surname in the subject index. An on-line analog of *SSCI*, the *Social Scisearch* database, consisting of about one million records and updated monthly, is searchable through the Dialog service.

77. *The Times Index.* Reading, England: Research Publications, vol. 1-, 1785-. Paperbound. (Monthly)

An index to the daily and Sunday (final) editions of *The Times* (London), including the literary and educational supplements. Subject headings refer to the United Kingdom and to the subject in general, while "foreign" aspects of a subject are subtopics beneath the name of a particular country. Personal and corporate names are used as major headings, and provide the most obvious biographical search approach. The index cumulates annually. Microfilm backfiles of *The Times* are also available from Research Publications.

78. *Who's Who in America, Geographic/Professional Area Index, 1986-1987.* Wilmette, IL: Marquis, 42d ed.-, 1982/83-. (Biennial)

This specialized index offers place and occupational access to information in its parent title, *Who's Who in America.* In the first section, entries give name and occupational description. The geographic section lists by state/province, and city. The "Professional Area Index" lists by categories including, for media and sport celebrities: arts-performing; athletics; and, communications media.

79. *Who Was Who in America, with World Notables: Index, 1607-1985, Volumes I-VIII and Historical Volume.* Chicago: Marquis, 1985. 260 p.

"This index to *Who Was Who in America* lists [112,000 deceased] biographees found in the Historical Volume (1607-1896) and in volumes I through VIII (1897-1985)."

Section 5
Directories

80. Arbeiter, Jean S., and Cirino, Linda D. *Permanent Addresses: A Guide to the Resting Places of Famous Americans.* New York: M. Evans, 1983. 290 p. Illustrated. Index. Paperbound.

The intent of this book is to identify the grave sites of the celebrated throughout the United States. Descriptions are anecdotal and directions explicit. Organization is geographical and by profession.

81. *Celebrity Service International Contact Book.* Edited by Earl Blackwell, and Donnali Shore. New York: Times Publishing Group, 1988. 310 p.

The 1988 *"Contact Book"* is the 44th edition of this concise (names, addresses, and phone numbers only), yet comprehensive directory of entertainment industry organizations, services, and agents in eight cities: New York, San Francisco, Hollywood, Washington, Toronto, London, Paris, and Rome. Some sample categories from the seventy listings given: casting directors, motion picture studios, music publishers, personal managers, press agents, theater ticket agencies, and video studios. Arrangement is by city.

82. *The Fan Club Directory.* Edited by Blanche Trinajstick. Pueblo, CO: National Association of Fan Clubs, 1975(?)-. Illustrated. Paperbound. (Annual?)

There are almost 1,000 celebrity clubs listed in the 1987 up-date issue examined. A significant number of these are located outside North America. Club name, contact, address, and category (e.g., country music, sports, wrestling, etc.) are given.

83. Jones, Thomas C., et al., eds. *The Halls of Fame: Featuring Specialized Museums of Sports, Agronomy, Entertainment and the Humanities.* Chicago: J. G. Ferguson, 1977. 464 p. Illustrated.

This sports volume is the first of several intended to cover the fields mentioned in the subtitle. Each entry contains the Hall name, location, detailed description of the governing philosophy, criteria for election to membership, contents, and biographical paragraphs about some of the athletes honored. Photographs of the Halls and honorees accompany the text. There is an appendix with addresses of "Other Sports Halls of Fame in the United States and Canada."

84. Levine, Michael. *The New Address Book: How to Reach Anyone Who's Anyone.* Rev. ed. New York: Putnam, 1986. 286 p. Paperbound.

This is an address and occupation directory to over 3,500 celebrities, corporate executives, and other very important persons (and a few non-persons, e.g., Pillsbury Doughboy), and associations.

85. *The Official Museum Directory.* Washington, DC: American Association of Museums, vol. 1-, 1980-. (Annual)

"The 1987 edition features current information on more than 6,500 museums in the United States. Special appendices are provided which list museums by name and type of collection. . . ." (Preface.) Continues: *Museums Directory of the United States and Canada.*

86. Smith, Allen. *Directory of Oral History Collections.* Phoenix, AZ: Oryx Press, 1988. 141 p. Index. ***

Provides information on collections accessible to researchers. Entries give address, telephone, key staff, collection size, hours, access restrictions, finding aids, purpose, and holdings details. Arranged geographically. A detailed subject index allows access by several means. The index entry, "Motion Picture Industry" lists seven collections, "Music," has four (and nine cross references to specific types).

87. *Star Guide.* Ann Arbor, MI: Axiom Information Resources, ed. 3?-, 1987-. Paperbound. (Annual)

Continues: *Celebrity Directory* (ed. 1-, 1984?). Addresses (only) of celebrities in film, television, music, sport, politics, royalty and other fields have been assembled in this directory, now in its third edition. There are over 2,900 listings, divided by activity into five sections. Celebrities living in North America preponderate.

88. Truesdell, Bill, comp. *Directory of Unique Museums.* Phoenix, AZ: Oryx Press, 1985. 165 p. Index. Paper.

Listed in this directory are over 250 museums. Each entry is a paragraph describing the institution's main features, open hours, address and phone number. One should be no more surprised to discover a listing for a Lurleen Wallace museum as one for washing machines or outboard motors.

Chapter 2
Collective Biographies

89. Anger, Kenneth. *Hollywood Babylon II*. New York: E.P. Dutton, 1984. 331 p. Illus. Index.

The sequel to Anger's *Hollywood Babylon* (first published in Paris in 1960 as too indelicate, or libelous, for America's publishers and readers). There are sketches on "Princess Disgrace" Kelly, "Attila the Nun" (Loretta Young), "Witch Joan" Crawford, and dozens more. Illustrated with a mixture of publicity stills and candid snapshots.

90. Cronkite, Kathy. *On the Edge of the Spotlight: Celebrities' Children Speak Out About Their Lives*. Foreword by Walter Cronkite. New York: Morrow, 1981. 318 p. Illustrated. Index.

The author writes about her life with a famous father, and that of twenty-six other sons and daughters of notables, some of whom are: Susan (Paul) Newman, John (Tex) Ritter, Christopher (William F.) Buckley, Arlo (Woody) Guthrie, Jack (Gerald) Ford, Rick (Neil) Armstrong, Jennifer (Art) Buchwald, Mary Frances (Bing) Crosby, Christie (Hugh) Hefner, Mark (Kurt) Vonnegut, Nora (Ossie) Davis, Lorenzo (Fernando) Lamas, Chris (Jack) Lemmon, Linda (Ed) McMahon, Francesca Hilton (Zsa Zsa Gabor), and Amy (Irving) Wallace.

91. Ebert, Alan. *Intimacies: Stars Share Their Confidences and Feelings*. New York: Dell, 1980. 384 p. Paperbound.

The twenty-five (approximately) profiles of celebrity women in this collection first appeared individually in magazine feature pieces by Ebert. Each is the product of an interview(s) with its subject, among whom are: Katharine Hepburn, Diana Ross, Carol Burnett, Nancy Walker, Dyan Cannon, Faye Dunaway, Joanne Woodward, Aretha Franklin, Ann Margaret, Eartha Kitt, and Goldie Hawn.

92. Fox-Sheinwold, Patricia. *Too Young to Die.* Rev. ed. New York: Bell Publishing, 1982. 317 p. Illustrated.

What do James Dean, Janis Joplin and Marilyn Monroe have in common? In addition to their celebrity, an early, violent death; the premise of this book. According to the author, "charismatic entertainers" lack patience and restraint, and disproportionately often suffer early, violent death. Ranging in time from Rudolph Valentino to John Belushi, the lives and deaths of about thirty stars are presented. A list of credits accompanies each sketch.

93. Funt, Marilyn. *Are You Anybody?: Conversations with Wives of Celebrities.* New York: Dial Press, 1979. 339 p. Illustrated.

Question and answer-formatted interviews with twenty women exploring how they coped with the associated stresses of being married to famous men constitute the premise of this book. Among those interviewed are the wives of Muhammad Ali, Tony Bennett, Lloyd Bridges, Johnny Carson, Kirk Douglas, Peter Falk, Billy Graham, Michael Landon, Jerry Lewis, Carroll O'Connor, and William Shatner. Funt discusses her own relationship with husband, Alan, in the concluding chapter.

94. Griffin, Merv, and Barsocchini, Peter. *From Where I Sit: Merv Griffin's Book of People.* New York: Arbor House, 1982. 251 p. Illustrated.

Griffin has gathered several dozen interviews from an estimated 20,000 conducted on "The Merv Griffin Show." They are grouped in five categories: "My Next Guest," "Movies and Their Makers," "Very Public Service," "Newsmakers," and "Writers."

95. Hardy, Karen, and McGuire, Rick. *Boy Crazy: An Intimate Look at Today's Rising Young Stars.* New York: New American Library, Plume, 1984. 126 p. Illustrated. Paperbound.

The original photographs (some in color) are by Hardy, graduate of the Film School at New York University. The narrative is McGuire's. This collective biography, designed by Robert Luzzi, presents pictures and profiles of 19 famous young men who star in rock bands, motion pictures, television, and on Broadway.

96. Holt, Georgia; Quinn, Phyllis; and Russell, Sue. *Star Mothers: The Moms Behind the Celebrities.* New York: Simon and Schuster, 1988. 417 p. Illustrated. Bibliography. Index. ***

97. Hotchner, A. E. *Choice People: The Greats, Near-Greats, and Ingrates I Have Known.* New York: Morrow, 1984. 415 p. Illustrated.

Hotchner gives informal account of a lifetime of friendships, associations, and brief encounters with scores of the world's chosen people. Ernest Hemingway, a longtime friend, receives top billing. Other celebrities include: Clark Gable, Dorothy Parker, Ingrid Bergman, Frank Sinatra, Marlene Dietrich, Paul Newman, Gary Cooper, Barbara Hutton, Jimmy Durante, Otto Preminger, Candice Bergen, Doris Day, Sophia Loren, Burt Reynolds, Anthony Quinn, Lee Marvin, Catherine Deneuve, and Richard Rodgers.

98. Noguchi, Thomas T., and DiMona, Joseph. *Coroner.* New York: Pocket Books, 1983. 252 p. Paperbound.

Sometimes controversial former Chief Medical Examiner for Los Angeles County, Noguchi, reveals his views on the violent deaths of various celebrities which occurred within his jurisdiction: Marilyn Monroe, Robert Kennedy, Sharon Tate, Janis Joplin, Patty Hearst's SLA associates, Natalie Wood, William Holden, and John Belushi.

99. Sarlot, Raymond R., and Basten, Fred E. *Life at the Marmont.* Santa Monica, CA: Roundtable Publishing, 1987. 314 p. Illustrated. Index.

Above Hollywood's Sunset Strip stands the luxury hotel, Chateau Marmont. Sarlot and Basten tell the story of the place through anecdotes of the (mostly media) celebrities who've been accommodated there over the sixty years of its existence. A sample of the Marmont guest list: Marilyn Monroe, Howard Hughes, Marlon Brando, Greta Garbo, Errol Flynn, Hedy Lamarr, Vivien Leigh, Judy Garland, Sidney Poitier, Diahann Carroll, Bette Davis, Burt Reynolds, Roman Polanski, Jim Morrison, Barbra Streisand, Warren Beatty, Bianca Jagger, Debra Winger, Joan Collins, Robert DeNiro, and James Dean.

100. Sealy, Shirley. *The Celebrity Sex Register: 101 Luminaries Listed, Cross-indexed, Annotated, and Compiled from Biographies (Authorized or Otherwise) Autobiographies, and Tell-All Memoirs.* Introduction by Bruce Williamson. New York: Simon and Schuster, Fireside, 1982. 206 p. Illustrated. Bibliography. Index.

This biographical dictionary/collective biography hybrid lists the liaisons of celebrities from Ashley to Zanuck. It heavily favors film people, but has a sprinkling of others introduced with a paragraph or two followed by a list of spouses and/or extra-marital conquests. Among the longer lists are those of Shelley Winters and, yes, Errol Flynn.

101. Sinclair, Marianne. *Those Who Died Young: Cult Heroes of the Twentieth Century.* New York: Penguin, 1979. 192 p. Illustrated. Bibliography. Paperbound.

Classified into chapters characteristic of their public persona or reputation ("Born to Lose"—John Garfield, James Dean, Montgomery Clift, and Zbigniew Cybulski; "Oriental Superman"—Bruce Lee) twenty-seven entertainers who died in the prime of their careers are profiled in this book. Those such as Elvis Presley and Marilyn Monroe merit twelve-page profiles, while the average length is five pages. Entertainer profiles in addition to those mentioned above: Rudolph Valentino, Jean Harlow, Carol Lombard, Gérard Philipe, Buddy Holly, Eddie

Cochran, Jim Reeves, Gene Vincent, Sam Cooke, Otis Redding, Brian Jones, Jimi Hendrix, Janis Joplin, Jim Morrison, Duane Allman, Cass Elliott, Paul Kossoff, Gram Parsons, Marc Bolan, and Keith Moon.

102. Stevens, K. G. *The K. G. Stevens Slant on Celebrity Handwriting: (Find out How Y-O-U Compare).* Foreword by Robert Cummings. Covina, CA: Tambra, 1985-. Vol. 1 Illustrated. Paperbound.

Graphologist Stevens, among other material, presents eighty personality profiles in a section titled, "Celebrity Evaluations." Each notable is given a brief handwriting personality analysis. All signatures are verified. A sequel is planned.

103. Stine, Whitney. *Stars & Star Handlers: The Business of Show.* Santa Monica, CA: Roundtable Publishing, 1985. 404 p. Illustrated. Bibliography. Index.

Stine has gathered anecdotes concerning the relationship of talent agents, business managers and press agents with the performers they handle. The arrangement is chronological, and the coverage is from vaudeville until the present—embracing scores of stars in film, television, theater, records, videos, rock concerts, and sports. Several of the contemporary stars in the book are: Bob Hope, Katharine Hepburn, Willie Shoemaker, Joan Fontaine, Mickey Rooney, Frank Sinatra, Ann-Margret, Brooke Shields, and Barbra Streisand.

104. Wilson, Earl. *Hot Times: True Tales of Hollywood and Broadway.* Chicago: Contemporary Books, 1984. 260 p. Illustrated. Index.

The "Dean of Show Business Columnists," tells humorous tales about some of his encounters with the entertainment greats of the past forty years, a few of whom are: Eddie Fisher, Elizabeth Taylor, Greta Garbo, Marilyn Monroe, and Ronald Reagan.

Chapter 3
Periodicals

105. *California.* Los Angeles: California Magazines, vol. 1-, 1976-. (Biweekly)

Formerly: *New West: The Magazine of California.* The Golden State is not all celebrities, and glitz. The variety of subject matter in this sophisticated publication reflects the extreme diversity of the State. This is not to say that the film industry and its glamorous folk are ignored; there are occasional articles about celebrities, e.g., the December, 1987 issue has a photographic piece on Kim Novak, Ingrid Bergman, Joan Crawford, Rita Hayworth and a few other stars called "The Gods Must Be Glamorous." There is also a regular film reviews department. Indexed by: *Popular Periodical Index.*

106. *Celebrity Bulletin.* London, New York: Celebrity Service International, no. 1-, 1952-. (Semiweekly?)

This bulletin reports the daily activities of celebrities and their acolytes in New York, Los Angeles, London, Paris and Rome. The bible of celebrity status, *Celebrity Register,* is also published by Celebrity Service International.

107. *Celebrity Focus.* New York: Globe Communications Corp., vol. 1-, 1987-. (Monthly)

The April, 1987 issue contained features on Jane Seymour, Marlon Brando, and Woody Allen, and departments: "Couples," "Trends," "The Good Life," and "In the Stars" (star horoscopes).

108. *Confidential.* New York: Ace Media, vol. 1-, 1988-. (Bimonthly)

Bearing strong resemblance to a "scandal magazine" of approximately the same name and content popular some thirty years ago, the new *Confidential* contains celebrity stories in a department called, "The Great and the Famous."

109. *Cosmopolitan.* New York: Hearst, Corp., vol. 132-, 1952-. (Monthly)

Continues: *Hearst's International Combined with Cosmopolitan* (1886-1952). The volume numbering continues *Cosmopolitan's.* Content targets the modern woman interested in fashion, hair and skin care, exercise, health, men, the arts and entertainment. Included occasionally are articles on celebrities. Indexed (some selectively) by: *Magazine Index, Media Review Digest, Magazine Article Summaries, Readers' Guide to Periodical Literature, Access, Biography Index.*

110. *Ebony.* Chicago, Johnson Publishing, vol. 1-, 1945-. (Monthly)

Ebony, sometimes called the *Life* magazine of Black America, publishes articles on anything of interest to its primary clientele—Black history, sports, entertainment, business, fashion and celebrity items. Indexed (some selectively) by: *Biography Index, Magazine Index, Readers' Guide to Periodical Literature, Magazine Article Summaries, Film Literature Index, Media Review Digest.*

111. *Esquire.* New York: Esquire Publishing, vol. 92-, 1979-. (Monthly)

Continues: *Esquire* (Chicago, 1933-1978), and *Esquire Fortnightly* (1978-1979). An occasional celebrity feature story is to be found with other features, interviews, humor, and fashion pieces. Regular departments include book, film and record reviews. Indexed (some selectively) by: *Readers' Guide to Periodical Literature, Magazine Index, Abstracts of English Studies, Book Review Index, Film Literature Index, Magazine Article Summaries.*

112. *Family Circle.* Mount Morris, IL: Family Circle, vol. 62-, 1963-. (17 issues yearly)

Continues: *Everywoman's Family Circle* (1958-1962), and *Family Circle* (New York, 1932-1958). There are occasional articles and interviews of celebrities to be found among the wholesome women's interest and homemaking content of this magazine.

113. *Gallery.* New York: Montcalm Publishing, vol. 1-, 1972-. (Monthly)

A "men's interests" magazine seemingly seeking the male audience somewhere between middlebrow *Playboy* (below), and far more prurient fare, *Gallery* regularly publishes celebrity interviews and features, witness two examples in the March, 1988 number: "Profile: Ted Turner," and "Alive & Kickin': The New Good Ole Boys of Country Music."

114. *Genesis.* New York: Atrium Multi-Media, vol. 1-, 1973-. (Monthly)

In the mold of *Gallery* (above), *Genesis* too, sandwiches celebrity interviews and personality profiles among its omnipresent nude photo essays. A biography of singer, Stephanie Mills, and the feature, "Rising Country Stars," appear in the April, 1988 issue.

115. *Globe.* Montreal: Globe International, vol. 1-, 1954-. (Weekly)

Former titles: *Midnight Globe; Midnight.* The Canadian analog in both content and format with *National Enquirer* (below). Regularly has short articles about celebrities.

116. *GQ.* New York: Conde Nast Publications, vol. 53-, 1983-. (Monthly)

Continues: *Gentlemen's Quarterly: GQ* (1958-1983), *Esquire's Apparel Arts* (1950-1956), and *Apparel Arts* (1931-1950). Primarily interested in men's fashions, *GQ* frequently publishes articles and interviews of well-dressed celebrities;

cases in point (January, 1988 issue): "Tom Hanks, Unpeeled,"
"Class Act: Douglas Fairbanks, Jr."

117. *In Fashion.* New York: VSI Publishing, vol. 1-, 1985-.
     (Bimonthly)
     Young adult clothing and grooming features constitute the
bulk of the contents of this magazine. While hip fashion features
may predominate, biographical/interview articles such as
"Hollywood's Hottest Couple, Charlie Sheen-Charlotte Lewis"
(January/February, 1988), are published on a regular basis.

118. *Interview.* New York: Interview Enterprises, vol. 7-,
     1977-. (Monthly)
     Continues: *Andy Warhol's Interview* (1971-1977), and,
Interview (1969-1970?). This newsprint tabloid contains well-
written and illustrated interviews with personalities in the arts,
sports, and politics. Indexed by: *Access.*

119. *Jet.* Chicago: Johnson Publishing, vol. 1-, 1951-. (Weekly)
     This is a pocket-sized version of Johnson's *Ebony*,
above, directed at a younger black audience. Every issue is
replete with pieces on show business personalities. Indexed
(some selectively) by: *Magazine Index, Magazine Article
Summaries, Readers' Guide to Periodical Literature, Infobank.*

120. *Ladies' Home Journal.* Los Angeles: Family Media, vol. 6-,
     1889-. (Monthly)
     Continues: *Ladies Home Journal and Practical
Housekeeper* (1883-1889). This magazine contains a diversity
of practical and entertainment material for women. The June,
1987 issue examined had stories about Bette Midler, and Diane
Keaton. Indexed (some selectively) by: *Biography Index,
Magazine Index, Readers' Guide to Periodical Literature,
Magazine Article Summaries.*

121. *Lady's Circle.* New York: Lopez Publications, vol. 1-,
     1963-. (Monthly)

This magazine has much in common with *Family Circle* (above), and *Woman's Day* (below). That all three thrive indicates there is a large audience (or a smaller one with a large appetite) for wholesome homemaker-type publications. *Lady's Circle* contains non-fiction features and departments, and fiction. "The Honesty and Courage of Mary Tyler Moore," and "Joanne Woodward and Paul Newman," are two celebrity articles appearing in the February, 1988 number.

122. *Life*. Chicago: Time Inc., vol. 74?-, 1978-. (Monthly)

Suspended publication, 1973-1977. Preceded by: *Life*, Chicago: 1936-1972. *Life* is a monthly general interest picture magazine for people of all ages, backgrounds, and variety of interests. Columns/departments: Portrait (1,800-2,500 word essay on some person in the news). A "movie issue" was published in 1987. Indexed (some selectively) by: *Magazine Index, Readers Guide to Periodical Literature*. "Self" indexed: 1939-1952.

123. *McCall's*. Los Angeles: McCall Publishing, vol. 48-, 1921-. (Monthly)

Continues: *McCall's Magazine* (1897-1921), and *Queen of Fashion* (1873?-1897). Very interested in the lives of celebrities and the important issues of the day, *McCall's* in its June, 1987 number published articles on surrogate motherhood, Sally Struthers, Bryant Gumbel, and Pam Dawber. Indexed (some selectively) by: *Biography Index, Readers' Guide to Periodical Literature, Magazine Index, Infobank, Media Review Digest, Magazine Article Summaries*.

124. *Maclean's*. Toronto: Maclean Publishing Co., vol. 21-, 1911-. (Weekly)

Continues: *Busy Man's Magazine* (1896-1911). Columns/departments: "People" (specializing in subjects that are of primarily Canadian interest.) Indexed (some selectively) by: *Magazine Index, Reader's Guide to Periodical Literature, Magazine Article Summaries, Canadian Periodical Index*.

125. *Mademoiselle.* New York: Conde Nast Publications, vol. 1-, 1935-. (Monthly)

This magazine emphasizes fashion, but not to the exclusion of other material of interest to women: grooming, the arts, the opposite sex, popular psychology, issues in the news, and the lives of showbusiness personalities and other celebrities. Indexed (some selectively) by: *Biography Index, Magazine Index, Readers' Guide to Periodical Literature, Magazine Article Summaries, Media Review Digest.*

126. *Memories.* New York: Diamandis Communications, vol. 1-, 1988-. (Bimonthly)

Nostalgia for sale. In its premier issue, "The Magazine of Then and Now" (subtitle), focuses heavily on the "then" people, with articles about Eddie and Liz, Lana and Johnny, Jane and Ronnie, and Elvis and the Army. *Memories* segments popular individuals and events into decades: "fifty years ago," "forty years ago," etc.

127. *Ms.* New York: Ms. Foundation for Education and Communication, vol. 1-, 1972-. (Monthly)

Gloria Steinem edits this issue-oriented periodical which also has appeal to a wider apolitical audience. Articles and/or interviews of celebrated people are published intermittently. Indexed (some selectively) by: *Magazine Index, Readers' Guide to Periodical Literature, Book Review Index, Film Literature Index, Media Review Digest, Magazine Article Summaries, Women Studies Abstracts.*

128. *National Enquirer.* Lantana, FL: National Enquirer, vol. 31-, 1957-. (Weekly)

Continues: *New York Enquirer* (1926-1957). Sensationalized news stories about celebrities—primarily actors and jet-setters.

129. *National Examiner.* West Palm Beach, FL: Globe Communications, vol. 1-, 1957?-. (Weekly)

A tabloid with a passion for the shocking headline, the *Examiner* publishes news and features about celebrities as do two of its slightly less sensationalistic checkout counter competitors, the *Globe*, and *National Enquirer* (above).

130. *Newsweek.* Los Angeles: Newsweek, Inc., vol. 1-, 1933-. (Weekly)

Absorbed: *Today*, in 1937. Rivals *Time* (below) in news and feature coverage. Sports, film and television material appears in each issue. Indexed (some selectively) by: *Biography Index, Music Index, Magazine Index, Reader's Guide to Periodical Literature, Abridged Reader's Guide to Periodical Literature.*

131. *New York.* New York: New York Magazine Co., vol. 1-, 1968-. (Weekly)

The audience for this magazine is definately urban/upscale. Moreover, there is considerable readership in many cities west of its namesake. Articles with biographical content appear intermittently. Indexed (some selectively) by: *Public Affairs Information Service Bulletin, Magazine Index, Readers' Guide to Periodical Literature, Film Literature Index, Media Review Digest, Magazine Article Summaries.* "Self" indexed: 1968-1971.

132. *New Yorker.* New York: New Yorker Magazine, Inc., vol. 1-, 1925-. (Weekly)

The standard against which all other urban audience periodicals must be measured, *New Yorker* offers occasional profiles and other biographical material on popular culture celebrities. Indexed (some selectively) by: *Abridged Reader's Guide to Periodical Literature, Magazine Index, Reader's Guide to Periodical Literature, Abstracts of English Studies, Annual Bibliography of English Language and Literature, Book Review Index, Film Literature Index, Media Review Digest, Music Index, Magazine Article Summaries.*

133. *Parade.* New York: Parade Publications, Inc., vol. 1-, 19??-. (Weekly)

This Sunday supplement magazine is inserted into many North American newspapers. Interview/profile: news figures, celebrities and people of national significance.

134. *People Weekly.* Chicago: Time, Inc., vol. 1-, 1974-. (Weekly)

Articles about celebrities—performers, artists, writers, politicians, and others with broad popular recognition created through media exposure, comprise every issue. Indexed (some selectively) by: *Abridged Reader's Guide to Periodical Literature, Magazine Index, Reader's Guide to Periodical Literature, Magazine Article Summaries.*

135. *Playboy.* Chicago: Playboy, vol. 1-, 1953-. (Monthly)

Subtitle: "Entertainment for Men." Contains regular pieces on outstanding, contemporary people. (*Playboy* interviews run between 10,000 and 15,000 words.) Indexed (some selectively) by: *Magazine Index, Film Literature Index, Media Review Digest, Magazine Article Summaries.* "Self" indexed: 1953-1983.

136. *Players.* Los Angeles: Players International, vol. 1-, 1973-. (Monthly)

This men's magazine publishes articles on fashion, entertainment, and other areas (e.g., women) of interest to its clientele—including occasional biographical features.

137. *Playgirl.* Santa Monica, CA: Playgirl, vol. 1-, 1972-. (Monthly)

Subtitle: "Entertainment for Women." The similarities of this magazine with its male mirror image, *Playboy*, above, are obvious: nude centerfolds and other pictorials, non-fiction/fiction features, and celebrity interviews and articles.

138. *The Reader's Digest.* Pleasantville, NY: The Reader's Digest Association, vol. 1-, 1922-. (Monthly)

Omnipresent in English and foreign language editions around the world, the "Digest" contains original and condensed versions of previously published material from other sources. Indexed (some selectively) by: *Biography Index, Magazine Index, Readers' Guide to Periodical Literature, Magazine Article Summaries*. "Self" indexed: 1935-.

139. *Redbook*. New York: Hearst, vol. 1-, 1903-. (Monthly)

Running title: *Redbook Magazine*. Absorbed: *American Home* (1978). Previous titles: *Redbook Magazine*, and *Red Book* (1903). Subtitle: "The Magazine for Young Adults." Feature stories regularly include interviews and other biographical material about celebrities. Indexed (some selectively) by: *Magazine Index, Readers' Guide to Periodical Literature, Magazine Article Summaries*.

140. *Rolling Stone*. New York: Straight Arrow Publishers, no. 1-, 1967-. (Bi-weekly)

Contemporary (pop/rock) music and contemporary lifestyles and issues are the concern of this important tabloid. Incisive biographies on musicians—and others. Indexed (some selectively) by: *Abridged Readers' Guide to Periodical Literature, Magazine Index, Music Index, Readers' Guide to Periodical Literature, Book Review Index, Film Literature Index, Media Review Digest, Magazine Article Summaries*.

141. *Saturday Evening Post*. Indianapolis, IN: Saturday Evening Post Co., vol. 1-, 1821-. (Monthly)

Title varies: *Atkinson's Evening Post*, and *Philadelphia Saturday News* (1839). Absorbed: *Saturday Bulletin* (1833); *Saturday News* (1839). Suspended publication from February 9, 1969 to Spring, 1971. Nonfiction articles include those about celebrities, and ordinary, but interesting personalities. Indexed (some selectively) by: *Abridged Readers' Guide to Periodical Literature, Readers' Guide to Periodical Literature, Abstrax, Book Review Index, Biography Index, Magazine Article Summaries, Magazine Index*.

142. *Seventeen*. New York: Triangle Communications, vol. 1-, 1944-. (Monthly)

"Its where the girl ends and the woman begins," states the cover motto. Role model biographies/interviews appear in *Seventeen* intermittently—recently there was one about singer, Debbie Gibson. Standard fare: non-fiction (especially fashion and grooming), humor, and other departments of interest to its audience. Indexed (some selectively) by: *Magazine Index, Readers' Guide to Periodical Literature, Media Review Digest, Abridged Readers' Guide to Periodical Literature, Magazine Article Summaries.*

143. *Spy.* New York: Spy Publishing Partners, vol. 1-, 1986-. (10 issues yearly)

The sophisticated urban liberal may read and subscribe to this cocky new general magazine with features titled: "So You're Going to Prison: A *Spy* Consumer Guide for Inside Traders, . . . and Other Very Important People on the Go," "Telling it All: Celebrity Biographies at a Glance," and "Here's the Rest of Me: The *Spy* Map of Reagan's Body."

144. *Star.* Tarrytown, NY: vol. 1-, 1974-. (Weekly)

Formerly: *The National Star.* A newsprint tabloid similar to the *National Enquirer* (above), this periodical contains articles about entertainers, the glitteratti, popular films and television.

145. *Time.* Chicago: Time, Inc., vol. 1-, 1923-. (Weekly)

Absorbed: *Literary Digest* (1937). *Time,* and *Newsweek* (above) continue as the two premier general news magazines. And, as in the latter, sports, film and television material appears in each issue. Indexed (some selectively) by: *Biography Index, Abridged Reader's Guide to Periodical Literature, Magazine Index, Reader's Guide to Periodical Literature, Book Review Index, Film Literature Index, Media Review Index, Magazine Article Summaries.* "Self" indexed: 1935-1952.

146. *TV Guide.* Radnor, PA: Triangle Publications, vol. 1-, 1953-. (Weekly)

Issued in numerous regional editions. The most popular and complete general program guide for the television viewer, bracketed by news and features (including many about TV people). Indexed (some selectively) by: *Magazine Index, Readers' Guide to Periodical Literature, Magazine Article Summaries.* "Self" indexed: 1953-1982.

147. *US.* New York: Telepictures Publications, vol. 1-, 1977-. (Bi-weekly)

Closely resembles *People Weekly* (above). *U S* concentrates on celebrity features. Indexed (some selectively) by: *Access.*

148. *USA Today.* Arlington, VA: Gannett, vol. 1-, 1982-. (Daily, except Sunday)

This is a national newspaper (satellite transmitted, regionally printed, and easily purchased from one of the ubiquitous television-shaped vending machines), heavily illustrated, and containing short news and feature articles. Of particular note to celebrity-followers is the section devoted to features and departments about entertainment people and other celebrities. Other sections for sports (including occasional biographical features), and business. Indexed by: *USA Today Index.*

149. *Vanity Fair.* New York: Conde Nast Publications, vol. 1-, 1914-. (Monthly)

Continues: *Dress & Vanity Fair* (1913). Absorbed by: *Vogue,* in 1936; resumed publication in 1983, with volume 46. This slick, trendy magazine publishes features of interest to its constituency of upwardly mobile people interested in "The Binghams of Louisville," "California Girls Michelle Phillips, Her Daughter, Chynna," Ralph and Ricky Lauren, Andrew Lloyd Webber, and the scene at Gstaad (February, 1988 issue). Indexed by: *Access, Music Index.* "Self" indexed: 1913-1936.

150. *The Village Voice.* New York: Village Voice, vol. 1-, 1955-. (Weekly)

"The Voice" is an eclectic tabloid containing news, essays, features, and commentary about life, the arts, and politics in (preponderantly) New York City. Indexed (some selectively) by: *Music Index, Book Review Index, Film Literature Index, Infobank, Media Review Digest, Magazine Article Summaries.*

151. *Woman's Day.* New York: CBS Magazines, vol. 1-, 1937-. (17 issues yearly)

A perennial item on supermarket check-out counter magazine racks, *Woman's Day* offers a cross-section of articles about homemaking, grooming, human interest, and interesting people. Indexed by *Access, Magazine Index.*

152. *Woman's World.* Englewood, NJ: Heinrich Bauer North America, vol. 1-, 1980-. (Weekly)

Volume 1 begins with no. 38. Offering the normal woman's interest fare with occasional interviews or other biographical articles about media personalities.

153. *WWD.* New York: Fairchild Publications, vol. ?-, 1976-. (Daily)

Formerly: *Women's Wear Daily* (1927-1976). This newspaper format publication is the "bible" of the fashion industry. However, sandwiched among the many trade articles are the columns "Eye," and "Arts & People," which contain the latest celebrity gossip and photographs, making these pieces a mandatory read for confirmed VIP watchers.

Chapter 4
Computerized Databases

154. *America: History and Life.* Santa Barbara, CA: ABC-Clio.

Subjects: North American history and social conditions. Contents: over 120,000 citations and abstracts from some 1,900 domestic and foreign journals, and over 2,400 other sources. Coverage: 1964-. This file updates quarterly and adds 11,000 records yearly. Corresponding print source: *America: History and Life.* Address: 2040 Alameda Padre Serra, Santa Barbara, CA 93140. Telephone: (800) 422-2546.

155. *Biodoc.* Waterloo, Belgium: Database SC.

Subject: biographies of Europeans. Contents: 60,000 records of prominent personalities in politics, sports, religion, science, the arts, etc. (in French). Coverage: 1983-. This file is updated biannually adding approximately 20,000 records. Corresponding print source: *Who's Who in Europe.* Address: B. P. 111, B-1410 Waterloo, Belgium. Telephone: (32) 02-354-8249.

156. *Biography Index.* New York: H. W. Wilson.

Subject: biography. Contents: some 50,000 references to biographies from about 2,600 periodicals and hundreds of single and collective biographical books. Coverage: July, 1984-. Updates are twice weekly. Corresponding print source: *Biography Index.* Address: 950 University Ave., Bronx, NY 10452. Telephone: (800) 367-6770.

157. *Biography Master Index.* Detroit, MI: Gale Research.

Subject: universal biography. Contents: index to biographical sketches in over 350 biographical dictionaries. Coverage: over 6,000,000 records listing people from the beginning of civilization to the present. Corresponding print source: *Biography and Genealogy Master Index.* Address: Book Tower, Detroit, MI 48226. Telephone: (313) 961-2242.

158. *Canadian News Index.* Toronto: Micromedia.

Subject: newspaper articles. Contents: indexes topics including international, national and provincial news, editorials, government activities, reviews, biographies, and sports in the *Calgary Herald, Vancouver Sun, Globe & Mail, Winnipeg Free Press, Montreal Gazette, Halifax Chronicle Herald,* and *Toronto Star.* Coverage: 1977-. The file increases at an annual rate of 90,000 records. Corresponding print source: *Canadian Newspaper Index.* Address: 144 Front St. W., Toronto, ON M5J 2L7, Canada. Telephone: (800) 387-2689.

159. *Canadian Periodical Index.* Toronto: Info Globe.

Subjects: general interest; news. Contents: some 65,000 citations to articles on current events, news, fashion, food and cooking, the arts, and sports. Coverage: 1977-. Canadian and some international items, in English and French. Updated with 6,000 records monthly. Corresponding print source: *Canadian Periodical Index.* Address: The Globe and Mail, 444 Front St. West., Toronto, ON M5V 2S9, Canada. Telephone: (416) 585-5250.

160. *Essay and General Literature Index.* New York: H. W. Wilson.

Subject: the social sciences; humanities; general interest. Contents: some 11,000 citations to collections of essays. Coverage: December, 1985-. Updates biweekly. Corresponding print source: *Essay and General Literature Index.* Address: 950 University Ave., Bronx, NY 10452. Telephone: (800) 622-4002.

161. *Magazine ASAP.* Belmont, CA: Information Access.

Subject: general periodical articles. Contents: indexing and full text of articles of approximately seventy-five periodicals selected from the *Magazine Index* database. File consists of over 90,000 records from 1983 to the present and updated monthly. Address: 11 Davis Dr., Belmont, CA 94002. Telephone: (415) 591-2333.

162. *Magazine Index.* Belmont, CA: Information Access.

Subject: general periodicals. Contents: indexing to more than 400 general interest magazines published throughout North America. Coverage is from 1973 to the present. Over 2.25 million bibliographic records are updated monthly from the related full-text database *Newsearch* (below). Corresponding print source: *Magazine Index* (computer-output 16mm microfilm). Address: 11 Davis Dr., Belmont, CA 94002. Telephone: (415) 591-2333.

163. *Marquis Who's Who.* Chicago: Marquis.

Subject: biography. Contents: biographical information on 88,000 key individuals from Canada, Mexico, and the U. S., in all fields including sports and the arts. Coverage: up to mid-1986; now listing about 106,000 people. Updating of the database varies in frequency. Corresponding print source: *Who's Who in America.* Address: 200 E. Ohio St., Chicago, IL 60611. Telephone: (800) 621-9669.

164. *MCI Insight.* East Hartford, CT: MCI International/NSI Inc.
    ***

Subject: News and feature stories. Address: 333 East River Dr., East Hartford, CT 06108. Telephone: (800) 624-5916.

165. *National Newspaper Index.* Menlo Park, CA: Information Access.

Subject: the world's news. Contents: indexing of the news as reported in large U.S. metropolitan daily newspapers— the economy, politics, international news, personalities, and sports. Coverage: material has been added since 1979; to date some 500,000 records. Updating is done mid-month from information accumulated in the related, full-text database, *Newsearch* (below). Corresponding print source: *National Newspaper Index*. Address: 11 Davis Dr., Belmont, CA 94002. Telephone: (415) 591-2333.

166. *Newsearch*. Menlo Park, CA: Information Access.

Subject: the world's news. Contents: full-text of news stories, articles, and reviews from some 500 English-language magazines and newspapers. Coverage: a daily update of 1,500 pieces from newspapers and magazines cumulates for a month until mid-month when the indexing data is transferred to *Magazine Index*, and *National Newspaper Index* (above). Address: 11 Davis Dr., Belmont, CA 94002. Telephone: (415) 591-2333.

167. *Newspaper Abstracts*. Ann Arbor, MI: University Microfilms International.

Subject: the world's news. Contents: comprehensive indexing for UMI "paper" indexes, cited and annotated above in the reference chapter under the title, *Newspaper Index*. Coverage: (for most papers) since 1984; 2,000,000 records. Corresponding print source: *Newspaper Index*. Address: 300 N. Zeeb Rd., Ann Arbor, MI 48106. Telephone: (800) 521-0600.

168. *The New York Times Biographical File*. New York: New York Times.

Subject: biographies. Contents: full text of selected biographical articles from *The New York Times* newspaper, including obituaries and profiles. Coverage: June, 1980-. About fifty stories are added weekly on newsmakers from the United States with some international coverage. Corresponding print source: *The New York Times*. Address: 229 W. 43rd St., New York, NY 10036. Telephone: (800) 543-6862.

169. *Nexis*. Dayton, OH: Mead Data General.

Subject: full text processor of material supplied by wire services, newspapers, magazines, and newsletters (approximately 150 sources). Coverage: earliest information begins with 1967, but start date varies by file. Frequency of update varies: newspapers, 24 hours; wires, 48 hours; weeklies, 1 week; monthlies, 3 weeks. Corresponding print sources vary by file. Address: P.O. Box 933, Dayton, OH 48401. Telephone: (800) 277-4908.

170. *OCLC EASI Reference Database.* Dublin, OH: OCLC Online Computer Library Center.

Subjects: multidisciplinary. Contents: nearly 1,000,000 references to current materials, primarily recently published books—compiled from the OCLC catalog of 17,000,000 records. Coverage: 1985-1988-. Updates at the rate of 200,000 records quarterly. Address: 6565 Frantz Rd., Dublin, OH 43017-0702. Telephone: (614) 764-6000.

171. *Popular Magazine Review Online.* Topsfield, MA: Data Base Communications.

Subject: general interest. Contents: some 40,000 citations and abstracts to about 200 U.S. general interest magazines. Coverage: 1984-. Updates occur weekly. Corresponding print source: *Magazine Article Summaries.* Address: P.O. Box 325, Topsfield, MA 01983. Telephone: (617) 887-6667.

172. *QuantumLink.* Vienna, VA: Quantum Computer Services.

Subjects: general interest; entertainment; sports. Contents: various files of general interest (full text) information accessible with Commodore computer hardware. Information includes movie reviews, soap opera summaries, and music and entertainment industry news. Coverage: current information from the U.S. and Canada, updated daily. Address: 8620 Westwood Center Dr., Vienna, VA 22180. Telephone: (800) 392-8200.

173. *Readers' Guide to Periodical Literature.* New York: H. W. Wilson.

Subjects: news; current events; sports; general interest. Contents: citations to articles in 182 of the most popular general interest magazines in Canada and the U.S.—including biographical sketches. Coverage: June, 1986-. 212,000 records updated twice weekly. Corresponding print source: *Readers' Guide to Periodical Literature.* Address: 950 University Ave., Bronx, NY 10452. Telephone: (800) 367-6770.

174. *Social Scisearch.* Philadelphia, PA: Institute for Scientific Information.

Subjects: social sciences and the humanities. Contents: 1.7 million citations to articles in about 1,400 important social sciences journals worldwide. Coverage: 1973-. International in scope, with updating biweekly-monthly. Corresponding print source: *Social Sciences Citation Index.* Address: 3501 Market St., Philadelphia, PA 19104. Telephone: (800) 523-1857.

175. *UPI Database.* Stamford, CT: Comtex Scientific Corp. ***

Subjects: *UPI* wire service news reports. Address: P.O. Box 4838, Stamford, CT 06907. Telephone: (203) 358-0007.

176. *VU/TEXT.* Philadelphia, PA: VU/TEXT Information Services.

Subjects: full text news stories from thirty-one newspapers or news services including the *Chicago Tribune, Facts on File, World News Digest,* and the *Washington Post.* Contents and coverage: current source of news and features, updated daily. Address: 325 Chestnut ST., Suite 1300, Philadelphia, PA 19106. Telephone: (800) 323-2940.

177. *WITZ.* Ringmer near Lewes, East Sussex, England: EDICLINE Ltd.

Subjects: entertainment; politics; general interest. Contents: 1,000 full text entries of jokes, anecdotes, and other humor by public personalities. Coverage: German and English language, 1985-. Updates are quarterly. Address: 2 Broyle Gate Cottages, Ringmer near Lewes, East Sussex BN8 5NA, England. Telephone: 44 273-813238.

Chapter 5
Organizations

178. AMERICAN BROADCASTING COMPANIES, INC.
ABC News Information Center
1926 Broadway
New York, NY 10023
(212) 887-3796

Holdings: 5,000 books and 300 periodicals subscriptions to support the network news operation; clippings file. Services: interlibrary loans and on-site use, subject to restrictions.

179. BOWLING GREEN STATE UNIVERSITY
Center For the Study of Popular Culture
Bowling Green, OH 43403
(419) 372-2981

This is the most important organization involved with scholarly activities relevant to all aspects of popular culture. Holdings: large collection of books and phonograph records. Publications: newsletter, several journals, books.

180. BOWLING GREEN STATE UNIVERSITY
Popular Culture Library
Bowling Green, OH 43403-0600
(419) 372-2450

Goal: to acquire, preserve, and provide access to primary research materials on 19th- and 20th-century American popular culture. Holdings: accessible to researchers nationally through the OCLC network and online catalog (60,000 books, 25,000 periodical issues).

181. BRITISH BROADCASTING CORPORATION
      BBC Data
      The Langham, Portland Place
      London W1A 1AA
      England
      (Tel.) 01-580-4468

Purpose: A new department formed from Reference and Registry Services, BBC Data is an information service primarily for BBC staff. Holdings: special collections in drama, film, music, broadcasting, and visual arts; clippings files. Services: information to external inquirers is by subscription via BBC Data Inquiry Service.

182. CANADIAN BROADCASTING CORPORATION
      Reference Library
      365 Church St.
      Toronto, ON M5W 1E6
      Canada
      (416) 925-3311

Holdings: 13,000 books and 160 periodical subscriptions in broadcasting, current events and drama; extensive clippings files. Services: on-site public use; interlibrary loan; photocopying.

183. CBS NEWS REFERENCE LIBRARY
      524 W. 57th St.
      New York, NY 10019
      (212) 975-2877

Holdings: 25,000 books and bound periodicals; 300 periodicals subscriptions; 27,000 microforms in the fields of broadcasting, biography, and current events. Services: on-site use for research (by appointment); interlibrary loan; photocopying.

184. LOS ANGELES PUBLIC LIBRARY
      Art, Music and Recreation Dept.; Audio-Visual Dept.

630 West Fifth St.
Los Angeles, CA 90017
(213) 626-7461

Holdings: A comprehensive collection of performing arts, and sports books (200,000 volumes), films (4,000), and periodicals. Special collections of the Olympics in Los Angeles; 300 videotapes, 5,000 audio cassettes, and large clippings files. Services: all library services are open to the public.

185. MICHIGAN STATE UNIVERSITY LIBRARIES
The Russel B. Nye Popular Culture Collection
E. Lansing, MI 48824
(517) 335-3770

Holdings: The collection holds over 25,000 pieces within four categories: comic art; popular fiction (dime novels, story magazines, pulps, juvenile series books, detective mystery fiction, science fiction, western fiction, and women's fiction); popular information materials (almanacs, Blue Books, and works popularizing knowledge or offering self-help and how-to advice); and, popular performing arts. Services: on-site use of collection; reference; photocopying; interlibrary loan.

186. NATIONAL ASSOCIATION OF FAN CLUBS
2730 Baltimore Ave.
Pueblo, CO 81003
(303) 543-6708

Purpose: to bring respect, dignity and recognition to fan clubs, and the people who work in them. Publications: *Fan Club Monitor* (quarterly); *The Fan Club Directory* (annual).

187. NATIONAL BROADCASTING CO., INC.
Reference Library
30 Rockefeller Plaza
New York, NY 10020
(212) 664-5307

Purpose: provide information services to the company, with particular emphasis on the News Division. Holdings: 15,000 books, 200 periodical subscriptions, with emphasis on current events, politics, history and entertainment. Over 500 full-length biographies of prominent personalities, and extensive biographical clippings files. Services: use by application; photocopying.

188. NATIONAL MUSEUM OF HISTORY & TECHNOLOGY (SMITHSONIAN)
Constitution Ave. at 10th St. NW
Washington, DC 20560

This renowned collection of artifacts is a public treasure visited by millions yearly. Holdings: the Division of Community Life has collections related to the history of American sports, entertainment, education, labor, organizations and business enterprises. There are over thirty sub-categories within the entertainment collection alone. Services: the resources and services of the Smithsonian Institution Libraries are available for public use. Descriptive publication: Sclar, Charlotte L. *The Smithsonian: A Guide to Its National Public Facilities in Washington, D.C.*

189. NATIONAL WOMEN'S HALL OF FAME
76 Fall St.
Seneca Falls, NY 13148
(315) 568-2936

Purpose: devoted to recognizing, honoring, and highlighting the achievements of American women. Holdings: 2,000 volumes; the stories of 38 honorees are told through portraits, photographs, brief biographies, memorabilia, and A-V presentations. Publications: a catalog describing the collection is available on request.

190. NEW YORK PUBLIC LIBRARY
General Research Div.
Fifth Ave. & 42nd St.
New York, NY 10018
(212) 930-0827

Holdings: very extensive in biography (over 80,000 titles: 7,500 biographical dictionaries and other reference works, 11,000 volumes of collective biography, 64,500 volumes of individual biography); and a great amount of uncatalogued material. Services: reference; interlibrary loan; photocopying facilities, all open to the public. Publication: *Guide to the Research Collections of the New York Public Library.* Chicago: American Library Association, 1975.

191. SMITHSONIAN, See: NATIONAL MUSEUM OF HISTORY & TECHNOLOGY (SMITHSONIAN)

192. SOUTHERN METHODIST UNIVERSITY LIBRARY
Oral History Collection on the Performing Arts in America
Dallas, TX 75222
(214) 692-2253

Holdings: over 188 taped interviews of individuals in all the performing arts. Publication: *Oral History Collection on the Performing Arts in America.* Dallas, TX: Southern Methodist University, 1984.

193. 20TH CENTURY FOX FILM CORPORATION LIBRARY
Box 900
Beverly Hills, CA 90213
(805) 203-2782

Goal: to service writers, producers and production crew members with research materials for production of motion pictures and television shows. Biographical holdings: books, clippings, photographs of authors and actors; materials about celebrities outside the film industry. Services: collection restricted to on-site use; (limited) photocopying.

194. UNIVERSAL CITY STUDIOS
Research Dept. Library
100 Universal City Plaza
Universal City, CA 91608
(213) 985-4321

Holdings: over twenty thousand books and periodical volumes, pamphlets, movie stills, and 7,000 clippings files covering the popular arts, history, and biography. Services: inquire by telephone (no open public services).

Chapter 6
Commercial Sources and Services

195. ABBOTT, WARING (Collector Source)
     78 Franklin St.
     New York, NY 10013
     (212) 925-6082

   For sale: photographs of movie, TV and music personalities.

196. ALDINE BOOKS (Bookstore, Service)
     4663 Hollywood Blvd.
     Los Angeles, CA 90027
     (213) 666-2690

   For sale: performing arts books; out of print book searching.

197. ALLEN, D. C. (Bookstore)
     208 Chicago St., Box 3
     Three Oaks, MI 49128
     (616) 756-9218

   For sale: performing arts books; automobile books.

198. APPLAUSE THEATRE BOOKS (Service)
     100 W. 67th St.
     New York, NY 10023
     (212) 496-7511

   For sale: mail order performing arts books.

199. BACKSTAGE BOOKS (Bookstore)
     P.O. Box 3676
     Eugene, OR 97403-3676
     For sale: mail order performing arts books.

200. BARR, NANCY (Collector Source)
     506 Windermere Ave.
     Interlaken, NJ 07712
     For sale: 10,000 original photographs of show business
stars.

201. (WALTER   R.)   BENJAMIN,   AUTOGRAPHS,   INC.
     (Bookstore, Collector Source)
     P.O. Box 255 Scribner Hollow Rd.
     Hunter, NY 12442
     For sale: mail order autographs; music books.

202. BLUE MOON RECORDS (Bookstore, Collector Source)
     307 Cedar Ave.
     Minneapolis, MN 55454
     For sale: performing arts books; phonograph records.

203. BOOK   CITY   COLLECTABLES   (Bookstore,   Collector
     Source)
     6625 Hollywood Blvd.
     Hollywood, CA 90028
     For sale: movie, television, and rock 'n roll books;
autographs;   photographs;   movie   and   fan   magazines;
memorabilia.

204. BOOK FINDER (Service)
     80 Seneca St.
     Geneva, NY 14456
     For sale: out of print book searching service.

205. BOOK QUEST (Service)
     P.O. Box 636
     Arlington, TX 76010

(817) 265-8903

For sale: mail order out of print book searching service.

206. BOOK SEARCH (Service)
9105 Rothery Ct.
Springfield, VA 22153
(703) 451-4055

For sale: book searching (no in-house stock).

207. BOOKS 'N' THINGS (Bookstore)
34 East 7th St.
New York, NY 10003
(212) 533-2320

For sale: performing arts books; movie and television books.

208. BOOK STORE (Bookstore)
132 East Third Ave.
San Mateo, CA 94401
(415) 343-2751

For sale: performing arts books.

209. BUCKABEST BOOKS AND BINDERY (Bookstore, Service)
247 Fulton St.
Palo Alto, CA 94301
(415) 325-2965

For sale: performing arts books; bookbinding and restoration; out of print book searching.

210. CARDUNER, ART (Bookstore)
6228 Greene St.
Philadelphia, PA 19144
(215) 843-6071

For sale: performing arts books.

211. CELEBRITY LOOK-A-LIKES (Service)
7060 Hollywood Blvd.
Los Angeles, CA 90028

(213) 272-2006

Starting business a decade ago with one Jimmy Carter and one Gerald Ford, Ron Smith's company now has dozens of Ronald and Nancy Reagans, Clark Gables, Elvises, Barbras, Woodys, and Queens of England. Smith hires out look-alike contractees whose fees are based on the real celebrity's popularity.

212. CELEBRITY-LOOK-ALIKES & SOUND-ALIKES (Service)
P.O. Box 2386
Northridge, CA 91323
(818) 886-5406

Another of several such services hiring out imitation famous faces and voices.

213. CELEBRITY SERVICE INTERNATIONAL, INC. (Service)
1780 Broadway, Suite 300
New York, NY 10019
(212) 245-1460

8833 Sunset Blvd., 401
Los Angeles, CA 90069
(213) 652-9910

This is a major service maintaining biographical files on over 350,000 celebrities. The files have accumulated over the course of nearly fifty years. Access to these data is limited since the primary purpose is to document celebrity activities for publication in the daily(?) *Celebrity Bulletin*, and in editions of the *Celebrity Register*. Other services: a daily updated telephone service to gain instant information on major personalities; an international calendar of social events for party-goers, charities, social planners and jet setters; and, a business services division geared to handling activities relating to openings and new products including the appearance of celebrities. The head of the service is Earl Blackwell, nicknamed by the media, "Mr. Celebrity." *Celebrity Bulletin* (yearly subscription price 480 pounds) is published in the United Kingdom by Celebrity Service Ltd., 10 New Bond St., London W1Y 9PF.

214. CINEMA BOOKS (Bookstore)
4753 Roosevelt Way NE
Seattle, WA 98105
(206) 547-7667

For sale: movie and television books; performing arts; out of print book searching.

215. CIVIC CENTER BOOKS (Bookstore)
360 Golden Gate Ave.
San Francisco, CA 94102
(415) 885-5072

For sale: performing arts books.

216. COMMON READER (Bookstore, Service)
P.O. Box 32
New Salem, MA 01355
(617) 544-3002

For sale: mail order performing arts books; biography; out of print book searching.

217. CONSOLIDATED POSTER SERVICE (Collector Source)
341 West 44th St.
New York, NY 10036
(212) 581-3105

For sale: mail order from a large library of movie stills.

218. COSMOPOLITAN BOOKS (Bookstore)
7007 Melrose Ave.
Los Angeles, CA 90038
(213) 938-7119

For sale: show business books; phonograph records.

219. COX, A. E. (Service)
21 Cecil Rd., Itchen
Southampton, Hampshire SO2 7HX
England
(Tel) 0703 447989

For sale: movie books; entertainment.

220. DEFOREST RESEARCH SERVICE (Service)
     780 North Gower St.
     Los Angeles, CA 90038

     For sale: DeForest conducts fee-based searches for biographical and other information.

221. DRAMA BOOKS (Bookstore, Collector Source, Service)
     511 Geary z
     San Francisco, CA 94102
     (415) 441-5343

     For sale: performing arts books; cinema and mass media; magazines; memorabilia; out of print book searching.

222. GALELLA, RON (Collector Source)
     17 Glover Ave.
     Yonkers, NY 10704
     (914) 237-2988

     For sale: candid photographs of entertainment and sports celebrities.

223. GALEWITZ, H. (Bookstore)
     143 Northern Pkwy.
     Plainview, NY 11803
     (516) 938-4167

     For sale: performing arts books.

224. GATTO, JOHN TAYLOR (Bookstore)
     235 West 76th St.
     New York, NY 10023

     For sale: popular culture books; television.

225. GREENBLATT USED BOOKS (Bookstore)
     7771 Santa Monica Blvd.
     Los Angeles, CA 90046

     For sale: drama books; biography.

226. GRIFFIN BOOKS (Bookstore)
     3 Lois Ln.

Poughkeepsie, NY 12603
(914) 454-6765

For sale: biography books; performing arts.

227. GUNAWAN, SUSIANA (Collector Source)
Cempaka Putih Tengah #33
Jakarta 10510
Indonesia

For sale: celebrity photographs.

228. HALL'S NOSTALGIA (Bookstore, Collector Source)
21-25 Mystic St.
Arlington, MA 02174

For sale: baseball books; ice hockey; rock 'n roll.

229. HARRIS SEARCH AND RESEARCH (Bookstore, Service)
145 East 37th St.
New York, NY 10016

For sale: performing arts books; out of print book searching.

230. INTERNATIONAL BOOKS (Bookstore, Service)
P.O. Box 6970
Washington, DC 20032

For sale: mail order performing arts books; out of print book searching.

231. (HERM) LEWIS AND ASSOCIATES (Collector Source)
P.O. Box 580
Yucca Valley, CA 92284
(714) 364-3195

For sale: mail order photographs of television, movie, and rock stars.

232. LIBRA BOOKS (Bookstore, Service)
18563 Sherman Way
Reseda, CA 91335
(213) 344-5400

For sale: biography books; performing arts; out of print book searching.

233. LIDO, SERGE (Collector Source)
     4 Rue Chernoviz
     75016 Paris
     France
     (Tel) 1 527 6598
     For sale: photographs of French film stars and musicians.

234. LUBRANO, J. & J. (Bookstore, Collector Source)
     P.O. Box 47, Main St.
     South Lee, MA 01260
     (413) 243-2218
     For sale: mail order music books; autographs; performing arts.

235. MCCOOK, THOMAS L., JR. (Bookstore, Collector Source)
     2464 Gravey Dr. NE
     Atlanta, GA 30345
     For sale: performing arts books; music; autographs.

236. MARK TWAIN BOOK & GIFT SHOP (Bookstore)
     213 Hill St.
     Hannibal, MO 63401
     (314) 221-2140
     For sale: biography books.

237. MEYERBOOKS (Bookstore)
     P.O. Box 427
     Glenwood, IL 60425
     (312) 757-4950
     For sale: mail order show business books.

238. MONITOR INTERNATIONAL (Collector Source)
     17-27 Old St.
     London EC1V 9HI

England
(Tel) 01 253 6281

For sale: photographs of international movie and sports superstars.

239. NBC-TV (Collector Source)
30 Rockefeller Plaza
New York, NY 10020
(212) 664-4444

For sale: photographs of stars of NBC television shows.

240. OAK LAWN BOOKS (Service)
P.O. Box 2663
Providence, RI 02907
(401) 941-6840

For sale: mail order movie books; jazz books.

241. OKMAN'S HAPPY ENDINGS (Bookstore)
20418 Califa St.
Woodland Hills, CA 91367
(213) 346-8934

For sale: movie and television books; biography.

242. OTHER BOOKS (Bookstore)
483 Bloor St., West
Toronto, ON M5S 1Y2
Canada
(416) 961-5227

For sale: performing arts books.

243. PENGUIN PHOTO COLLECTION (Collector Source)
633 Fifth Ave.
New York, NY 10022
(212) 758-7328

For sale: photographs of entertainment superstars.

244. PERFORMING ARTS BOOKS (Bookstore, Collector
    Source, Service)
    90 East 10th St.
    New York, NY 10003
    (212) 982-9440

    For sale: movie and television books; memorabilia;
appraisal service; out of print book searching.

245. REMEMBER WHEN (Bookstore, Collector Source, Service)
    2431 Valwood Pkwy
    Dallas, TX 75234
    (214) 243-3439

    For sale: memorabilia; search service.

246. RETNA LTD. (Collector Source)
    414 Park Avenue South
    New York, NY 10016
    (212) 683-6560

    For sale: photographs of pop musicians, celebrities, TV
and movie stars.

247. (GEORGE) SAND BOOKS (Bookstore)
    9011 Melrose Ave.
    Los Angeles, CA 90069
    (213) 858-1648

    For sale: biography books; cinema and mass media.

248. SAVRAN'S BOOKS (Bookstore, Service)
    301 Cedar Ave.
    Minneapolis, MN 55454
    (612) 333-3872

    For sale: performing arts books; out of print book
searching.

249. SECOND DEBUT BOOKS (Bookstore, Service)
    2827 1/2 De La Vina
    Santa Barbara, CA 93105
    (805) 687-2781

For sale: biography books; performing arts; out of print book searching.

250. SHEPARD, WILLIAM P. (Bookstore)
     2035 North Brower
     Simi Valley, CA 93065
     (805) 526-3285

     For sale: pulps; movie and fan magazines; first editions.

251. STAR DATA RESEARCH (Service)
     c/o Brenda Scott Royce
     263A W. 19th St. No. 915
     New York, NY 10011

     For sale: research service (any performer or show, information on stars, reviews, etc.).

252. STARKIVES, INC. (Service)
     320 E. 65th St.
     New York, NY 10021
     (212) 517-2984

     For sale: access to a computerized database of celebrity information containing the names and backgrounds of 5,000 personalities from TV, movies, sports, music and other fields. A TV monitor attachment enables clients to view current color photographs of the celebrities.

253. STORY PRESS (Collector Source)
     Postfach 4226
     1000 Berlin 30
     East Germany
     (Tel) 030 85 45 202

     For sale: photographs of television, movie and music personalities.

254. THEATREBOOKS, INC. (Bookstore, Service)
     1576 Broadway No. 312
     New York, NY 10036
     (212) 757-2834

For sale: performing arts books; drama; out of print book searching.

255. THEATRICANA, INC. (Service)
P.O. Box 4244, Campus Sta.
Athens, GA 30605
(404) 548-2514
For sale: mail order performing arts books.

256. THREE L'S NOSTALGIA & COLLECTORS' SHOP (Collector Source)
Rt. 30
P.O. Box 35
Reading, PA 17577
(717) 687-6165
For sale: mail order memorabilia.

257. TOPIX-FOTO (Collector Source)
320 East 42nd St.
New York, NY 10017
(212) 599-0610
For sale: photographs of show business personalities, and other celebrities.

258. VINTAGE MAGAZINE SHOP LIMITED (Bookstore)
Vintage House, Great Windmill St.
London WC2
England
(Tel.) 01 439-8525
For sale: magazines only, thousands of movie magazines; sports; pop music; rock music.

259. WASHINGTON SPEAKERS BUREAU, INC. (Service)
123 N. Henry St.
Alexandria, VA 22314
(202) 684-0555

For sale: speeches given by the likes of: Jim Valvano, Lou Holtz, Fran Tarkenton, Joe Theismann, Red Auerbach, Diane Sawyer, Henry Kissinger, Leslie Stahl and Bill Cosby.

260. WORDS WORTH (Bookstore)
    30 Brattle St.
    Cambridge, MA 02138
    (617) 354-5201

    For sale: performing arts books.

261. WURLITZER-BRUCK MUSIC (Bookstore, Collector Source, Service)
    60 Riverside Dr.
    New York, NY 10024
    (212) 787-6431

    For sale: performing arts books; autographs; photographs; out of print book searching.

Chapter 7
Fan Clubs

262. ALIBI FAN CLUB (COUNTRY & WESTERN MUSIC)
    Rt. 1, Box 15
    Ochelata, OK 74051

263. AMERICAN BANDSTAND MEMORY CLUB (POP MUSIC)
    P.O. Box 131
    Adamstown, PA 19501

264. COUNTRY MUSIC ASSOCIATION FAN CLUB
    c/o Amy J. Allen
    4129 Pinar Dr.
    Bradenton, FL 33507

265. COUNTRY MUSIC FAN CLUB
    c/o Bob Dalton
    1 Citadel Dr.
    Toronto, Ont. M1K 4S1
    Canada

266. FRIENDS OF VETERAN SOAP ACTORS
    c/o Denise Clifton
    P.O. Box 6039
    Bluefield, WV 24701

267. HOLLYWOOD STUDIO COLLECTORS CLUB (Same as STUDIO COLLECTOR'S CLUB)
     3969 Laurel Canyon Blvd., Suite 450
     Studio City, CA 91604

268. INTERNATIONAL FAN CLUB ORGANIZATION
     P.O. Box 177
     Wild Horse, CO 80862-0177

269. INTERNATIONAL RODEO FANS
     c/o Ellen Boyle
     121 Shonnard Pl.
     Yonkers, NY 10703

270. NATIONAL ASSOCIATION OF FAN CLUBS
     2730 Baltimore Ave.
     Pueblo, CO 81003

271. NATIONAL BASEBALL FAN ASSN.
     P.O. Box 4192
     Mt. Laurel, NJ 08054

272. THE SILVER SCREEN EXCHANGE
     R.R. 1, Box 33
     Kingston, NY 12401

273. SOAP OPERA FANS' EXCHANGE
     c/o Colleen Acosta
     2830 La Pine Ave.
     Central Point, OR 97502

274. VIEWERS FOR QUALITY TELEVISION
     Donna Dean, Co-President
     2700 Knollwood Ct.
     Plano, TX 75075

Chapter 8
Individual Biographies
(Multi-talent Entertainers)

ANN-MARGRET. Ent.

275. Peters, Neal, and Smith, David. *Ann-Margret: A Photo-Extravaganza and Memoir.* Introduction by Ann-Margret. New York: Delilah Books, 1981. 250 p. Illustrated. Paperbound.

ASTAIRE, FRED. Ent. 6/22/87

276. Adler, Bill. *Fred Astaire, a Wonderful Life: A Biography.* New York: Carroll & Graf, 1987. 191 p. Illustrated. Playography. Filmography. Videography. Song Listing. Discography. Bibliography.

277. Astaire, Fred. *Steps in Time.* New Foreword by Ginger Rogers. New York: Da Capo Press, 1981. 327 p. Illustrated. Paperbound.

278. Carrick, Peter. *A Tribute to Fred Astaire.* London: R. Hale, 1984. 188 p. Illustrated. Filmography. Discography. Videography. Index.

279. *Fabulous Fred Astaire [Videorecording].* Video Yesteryear Recording, 684. Reel Images, 198?. 1 videocassette, 71 min., sd., b&w, 1/2 in., VHS.

Summary: Includes a segment of a "Person to Person" Astaire interview with Edward R. Murrow, plus the variety television special, "An Evening with Fred Astaire," originally broadcast Nov. 17, 1958.

280. Freedland, Michael. *Fred Astaire.* New York: Grosset & Dunlap, 1977. 183 p. Illustrated. Index. ***

281. Green, Benny. *Fred Astaire.* London, New York: Hamlyn, 1979. 176 p. Illustrated. Filmography. Discography. Bibliography. Index.

282. Pickard, Roy. *Fred Astaire.* New York: Crescent Books, 1985. 192 p. Illustrated. Filmography. Bibliography. Index.

283. Thomas, Bob. *Astaire, the Man, the Dancer.* New York: St. Martin's Press, 1984. 340 p. Illustrated. Bibliography. Index.

BARYSHNIKOV, MIKHAIL. Ent.

284. Alovert, Nina. *Baryshnikov in Russia.* Text and photographs by Nina Alovert. Translated from the Russian by Irene Huntoon. New York: Holt, Rinehart and Winston, 1984. 212 p. Illustrated. Index.

285. *American Ballet Theatre: Dancing for Love [Motion Picture].* Washington, DC: WDVM-TV, 1978. 1 reel, 28 min., sd., col., 16mm.

Summary: This is a backstage look at the life of a ballet dancer, profiling Baryshnikov and the ABT during the premiere of his production of *Don Quixote* at the Kennedy Center.

286. Baryshnikov, Mikhail. *Baryshnikov in Color.* Edited by Charles Engell France. Photographs by Martha Swope and others. New York: Abrams, 1980. 64 p. Illustrated. Paperbound.

287. *Baryshnikov, the Dancer and the Dance [Videorecording].* Script by Marilyn Nissenson. Produced and directed by Tony Cash. Long Branch, NJ: Kultur International Films, 1983. 1 videocassette, 82 min., sd., col., 1/2 in.
    Summary: This video profiles Baryshnikov, including his performance of *Configurations* choreographed by Choo San Goh. The presenter is Shirley MacLaine.

288. LeMond, Alan. *Bravo, Baryshnikov!* Photographs by Lois Greenfield and others. New York: Grosset & Dunlap, 1978. 96 p. Illustrated. Index. Paperbound.

289. Smakov, Gennady. *Baryshnikov: From Russia to the West.* New York: Farrar Straus Giroux, 1981. 244 p. Illustrated. Index.

BENNY, JACK. Ent. 12/26/74

290. Benny, Mary Livingstone; Marks, Hilliard; and Borie, Marcia. *Jack Benny.* Garden City, NY: Doubleday, 1978. 322 p. Illustrated. Index.

291. Josefsberg, Milt. *The Jack Benny Show.* New Rochelle, NY: Arlington House, 1977. 496 p. Illustrated. Index.

BERLE, MILTON. Ent.

292. Berle, Milton. *B. S., I Love You: Sixty Funny Years with the Famous and the Infamous.* New York: McGraw-Hill, 1987. 286 p. Illustrated. Index.

BOMBECK, ERMA. Ent.

293. King, Norman. *Here's Erma!: The Bombecking of America.* Aurora, IL: Caroline House, 1982. 166 p.

BURNETT, CAROL. Ent.

294. Burnett, Carol. *One More Time.* New York: Random House, 1986. 359 p. Illustrated

295. Latham, Caroline. *Carol Burnett, Funny Is Beautiful: An Unauthorized Biography.* New York: New American Library, Signet, 1986. 192 p. Illustrated. Paperbound.

BURNS, GEORGE. Ent.

296. Blythe, Cheryl, and Sackett, Susan. *Say Good Night, Gracie: The Story of Burns & Allen.* New York: E. P. Dutton, 1986. 304 p. Illustrated. Index.

297. Burns, George. *Gracie: A Love Story.* New York: Putnam, 1988. ***

298. Burns, George. *The Third Time Around.* New York: Putnam, 1980. 219 p. Illustrated.

CAESAR, SID. Ent.

299. Caesar, Sid, and Davidson, Bill. *Where Have I Been?: An Autobiography.* New York: Crown Publishers, 1982. 280 p. Illustrated.

CARSON, JOHNNY. Ent.

300. Corkery, Paul. *Carson: The Unauthorized Biography.* Ketchum, ID: Randt, 1987. 239 p. Index.

301. Smith, Ronald L. *Johnny Carson: An Unauthorized Biography.* New York: St. Martin's Press, 1987. 245 p. Illustrated. Index.

302. Tennis, Craig. *Johnny Tonight!* New York: Pocket Books, 1980. 224 p. Paperbound.

CAVETT, DICK. Ent.

303. Cavett, Dick, and Porterfield, Christopher. *Eye on Cavett.* New York: Arbor House, 1983. 250 p. Illustrated.

CHER. Ent.

304. Bego, Mark. *Cher!* New York: Pocket Books, 1986. 219 p. Illustrated. Discography. Filmography. Paperbound.

305. Taraborrelli, J. Randy. *Cher, a Biography.* New York: St. Martin's Press, 1986. 322 p. Illustrated.

COSBY, BILL. Ent.

306. Adler, Bill. *The Cosby Wit: His Life and Humor.* New York: Carroll & Graf, 1986. 125 p. Illustrated. Bibliography.

307. Johnson, Robert E. *Bill Cosby: In Words and Pictures.* Ebony/Jet Special Issue. Chicago: Johnson Publishing, 1986. 192 p. Illustrated. Paperbound.

308. Latham, Caroline. *Bill Cosby, for Real.* New York: Tom Doherty Associates, A TOR Book, 1985. 148 p. Illustrated. Bibliography. Paperbound.

309. Smith, Ronald L. *Cosby.* New York: St. Martin's Press, 1986. 218 p. Illustrated. Discography. Filmography. Videography. Index.

DAVIS, SAMMY, JR. Ent.

310. Davis, Sammy, Jr. *Hollywood in a Suitcase.* New York: Morrow, 1980. 288 p. Illustrated.

DONAHUE, PHIL. Ent.

311. Bonderoff, Jason. *Donahue!* New York: Zebra, 1980. Paperbound. ***

312. Donahue, Phil. *Donahue, My Own Story.* New York: Simon and Schuster, 1979. 247 p. Illustrated.

313. Wadler, Joyce. *Phil Donahue, a Man for All Women: An Unauthorized Biography.* New York: Jove Publications, 1980. 187 p. Illustrated. Paperbound.

DOWNS, HUGH. Ent.

314. Downs, Hugh. *On Camera: My 10,000 Hours on Television.* New York: Putnam, 1986. 253 p. Illustrated.

DURANTE, JIMMY. Ent. 1/29/80

315. Adler, Irene. *I Remember Jimmy: The Life and Times of Jimmy Durante.* Westport, CT: Arlington House, 1980. 189 p. Illustrated. Filmography.

FOXX, REDD. Ent.

316. *Redd Foxx, B. S. (Before Sanford).* Edited by Joe X. Price. Chicago: Contemporary Books, 1979. 144 p. Index.

FRANCIS, ARLENE. Ent.

317. Francis, Arlene, and Rome, Florence. *Arlene Francis: A Memoir.* New York: Simon and Schuster, 1978. 204 p. Illustrated. Index.

GLEASON, JACKIE. Ent. 6/24/87

318. Bacon, James. *How Sweet It Is: The Jackie Gleason Story.* New York: St. Martin's Press, 1985. 214 p. Illustrated. Videography. Filmography. Index.

GRIFFIN, MERV. Ent.

319. Griffin, Merv, and Barsocchini, Peter. *Merv, an Autobiography.* New York: Simon and Schuster, 1980. 287 p. Illustrated. Index.

HOPE, BOB. Ent.

320. Faith, William Robert. *Bob Hope, a Life in Comedy.* New York, Putnam, 1982. 416 p. Illustrated. Bibliography. Filmography. Index.

321. Hope, Bob. *Bob Hope and His Friends [Sound Recording].* North Hollywood, CA: Bob Hope Record Collection, 1979. 3 sound discs, 33 1/3 rpm, 12 in.

Summary: Includes material from radio shows, television specials, records, movies, personal appearances, and Hope's own private library. The record container holds a forty-eight page biography with program notes.

322. Hope, Bob, and Thomas, Bob. *The Road to Hollywood: My 40-Year Love Affair with the Movies.* Garden City, NY: Doubleday, 1977. 271 p. Illustrated.

323. Thompson, Charles. *Bob Hope: Portrait of a Superstar.* New York: St. Martin's Press, 1981. Illustrated. Index.

KAYE, DANNY. Ent. 3/2/87

324. Freedland, Michael. *The Secret Life of Danny Kaye.* New York: St. Martin's Press, 1985. 261 p. Illustrated.

KELLY, GENE. Ent.

325. Hirschhorn, Clive. *Gene Kelly: A Biography.* New York: St. Martin's Press, 1984. 296 p. Illustrated. Filmography. Index.

KING, LARRY. Ent.

326. King, Larry, and Yoffe, Emily. *Larry King.* New York: Simon and Schuster, 1982. 207 p.

327. King, Larry, and Occhiogrosso, Peter. *Tell It to the King.* New York: Putnam, 1988. 285 p. ***

LETTERMAN, DAVID. Ent.

328. Latham, Caroline. *The David Letterman Story.* New York: F. Watts, 1987. 214 p. Illustrated.

LEWIS, JERRY. Ent.

329. Lewis, Jerry, and Gluck, Herb. *Jerry Lewis, in Person.* New York: Atheneum, 1982. 310 p. Illustrated.

LINKLETTER, ART. Ent.

330. *Linkletter, Art, and Bishop, George. Hobo on the Way to Heaven.* Elgin, IL: D. C. Cook, 1980. 212 p. Illustrated.

331. Linkletter, Art, and Bishop, George. *I Didn't Do It Alone: The Autobiography of Art Linkletter as told to George Bishop.* Ottawa, IL: Caroline House, 1980. 208 p. Illustrated.

MARCEAU, MARCEL. Ent.

332. Marceau, Marcel. *Marceau Talks! [Sound Recording].* Los
     Angeles: Pacifica Radio Archive, 1983. 1 sound cassette,
     57 min., analog.

     Summary: Interviewed by Richard Schechner in April,
     1970, Marceau discusses his art, his social attitudes, and his
     politics. He also talks about contemporary theater, both avant-
     garde and traditional, and the joys and frustrations of creation.

333. *Pantomime: The Language of the Heart [Motion Picture].*
     The Art of Silence: Pantomimes with Marcel Marceau.
     Encyclopaedia Britannica Educational Corp., 1975. 10
     min., sd., col., 16mm.

     Summary: Marceau discusses his career, analyzes the
     value of pantomime, and describes the creation of his famous
     character, Bip. Includes short sequences from various routines
     featuring Bip.

MARTIN, DEAN. Ent.

334. Freedland, Michael. *Dino: The Dean Martin Story.*
     London: W. H. Allen, 1984. 208 p. Illustrated. ***

MARTIN, STEVE. Ent.

335. Daly, Marsha. *Steve Martin: An Unauthorized (*Well
     Excuuuse Us!) Biography.* New York: New American
     Library, Signet, 1980. 197 p. Illustrated. Paperbound.

336. Lenburg, Greg; Skretvedt, Randy; and Lenburg, Jeff. *Steve
     Martin, the Unauthorized Biography.* New York: St.
     Martin's Press, 1980. 139 p. Illustrated. Discography.
     Paperbound.

MARX, GROUCHO. Ent. 8/19/77

337. Arce, Hector. *Groucho.* New York: Putnam, 1979. 541 p. Illustrated. Bibliography. Index.

338. Chandler, Charlotte. *Hello, I Must Be Going: Groucho and His Friends.* Garden City, NY: Doubleday, 1978. 568 p. Illustrated.

339. *The Groucho Marx Scrapbook* [*Videorecording*]. Los Angeles: Opening Night Productions, 1984, 1 (VHS) cassette, b&w, 1/2 in.

Summary: Highlights of Groucho in the "You Bet Your Life" television quiz program, a TV interview with Groucho at home, film clips from Marx brothers movies, commercials featuring Groucho, Harpo, and Chico, and a midget car race pitting the Marx brothers against child star Jackie Cooper.

340. Marx, Groucho. *The Groucho Phile: An Illustrated Life.* Introduction by Hector Arce. New York: Pocket Books, Wallaby, 1977. 384 p. Illustrated. Index.

MERMAN, ETHEL. Ent. 2/15/84

341. Merman, Ethel, and Eells, George. *Merman.* New York: Simon and Schuster, 1978. 320 p. Playlist. Filmography. Index.

342. Thomas, Bob. *I Got Rhythm!: The Ethel Merman Story.* New York: Putnam, 1985. 239 p. Illustrated. Playography. Filmography. Index.

MIDLER, BETTE. Ent.

343. Baker, Rob. *Bette Midler.* Rev. ed. New York: Fawcett, 1979. 256 p. Illustrated. Paperbound.

344. Bego, Mark. *Bette Midler, Outrageously Divine: An Unauthorized Biography.* New York: New American Library, Signet, 1987. 190 p. Illustrated. Discography. Filmography. Videography. Bibliography. Paperbound.

345. Midler, Bette. *A View from a Broad.* Photography by Sean Russell. New York: Simon and Schuster , 1980. 150 p. Illustrated.

346. Spada, James. *The Divine Bette Midler.* New York: Collier Books; London: Collier Macmillan, 1984. 214 p. Illustrated. Paperbound.

MILLER, ANN. Ent.

347. Connor, Jim. *Ann Miller, Tops in Taps: An Authorized Pictorial History.* Introduction by Hermes Pan. New York: F. Watts, 1981. 221 p. Illustrated. Paperbound.

MINNELLI, LIZA. Ent.

348. d'Arcy, Susan. *The Films of Liza Minnelli.* St. Paul, MN: Greenhaven Press, 1978. 46 p. Illustrated. Filmography.

349. Petrucelli, Alan W. *Liza! Liza!: An Unauthorized Biography of Liza Minnelli.* New York, Princeton: Karz-Cohl, 1983. 174 p. Illustrated. Filmography. Playography. Videography. Discography. Bibliography. Index. Paperbound.

350. Spada, James, and Swenson, Karen. *Judy and Liza*. Garden City, NY: Doubleday, 1983. 216 p. Illustrated. Bibliography.

MINNIE PEARL. Ent.

351. Minnie Pearl, and Dew, Joan. *Minnie Pearl, an Autobiography.* New York: Simon and Schuster, 1980. 256 p. Illustrated.

MISTER ROGERS. Ent., See: ROGERS, FRED. Ent.

NEWHART, BOB. Ent.

352. Sorensen, Jeff. *Bob Newhart.* New York: St. Martin's Press, 1988. 192 p. Illustrated. Discography. Filmography. Index. ***

ONO, YOKO. Ent.

353. Hopkins, Jerry. *Yoko Ono.* New York: Macmillan; London: Collier Macmillan, 1986. 271 p. Illustrated. Index.

354. Lennon, John. *The Lennon Tapes: John Lennon and Yoko Ono in Conversation with Andy Peebles, 6 December, 1981.* Foreword by Paul Williams. London: British Broadcasting Corporation, 1981. 95 p. Paperbound.

355. Lennon, John. *The Playboy Interviews with John Lennon and Yoko Ono.* Conducted by David Sheff. Edited by G. Barry Golson. New York: Playboy Press, 1981. 207 p. Illustrated.

PAAR, JACK. Ent.

356. Paar, Jack. *P.S. Jack Paar.* Garden City, NY: Doubleday, 1983. 360 p. Illustrated. Index.

357. Paar, Jack. *P.S. Jack Paar [Sound Recording].* Downsview, Ontario, Canada: Listen for Pleasure, 1986. 2 sound cassettes, 120 min., analog.

Summary: Abridged version of *P.S. Jack Paar* (above), read by Paar.

PARTON, DOLLY. Ent.

358. Berman, Connie. *The Official Dolly Parton Scrapbook.* Foreword by Dolly Parton. New York: Grosset & Dunlap, 1978. 95 p. Illustrated. Discography. Paperbound.

359. Caraeff, Ed, and Amdur, Richard. *Dolly: Close up/up Close.* New York: Delilah Books, 1983. 90 p. Illustrated. Paperbound.

360. Nash, Alanna. *Dolly.* Los Angeles: Reed Books, Country Music Magazine, 1978. 275 p. Illustrated. Discography.

PEARL, MINNIE. Ent. See: MINNIE PEARL. Ent.

PRYOR, RICHARD. Ent.

361. Haskins, James. *Richard Pryor, a Man and His Madness: A Biography.* New York: Beaufort Books, 1984. 227 p. Illustrated. Index.

362. Nazel, Joseph. *Richard Pryor: The Man Behind the Laughter.* Los Angeles: Holloway House, 1981. 205 p. Paperbound.

363. Robbins, Fred, and Ragan, David. *Richard Pryor: This Cat's Got 9 Lives.* New York: Delilah Books, 1982. 159 p. Illustrated. Discography. Filmography. Paperbound.

364. Rovin, Jeff. *Richard Pryor: Black and Blue.* Toronto, New York: Bantam Books, 1984. 248 p. Illustrated.

RIVERS, JOAN. Ent.

365. Rivers, Joan, and Meryman, Richard. *Enter Talking.* New York: Delacorte Press, 1986. 398 p. Illustrated. Index.

366. Rivers, Joan, and Meryman, Richard. *Enter Talking [Sound Recording].* Beverly Hills, CA: Dove Audio, 1986. 2 sound cassettes, 142 min., analog.

Summary: Rivers reads her autobiography (above).

ROGERS, GINGER. Ent.

367. Croce, Arlene. *The Fred Astaire & Ginger Rogers Book.* New York: Vintage Books, 1977. 191 p. Illustrated. Paperbound.

SHORE, DINAH. Ent.

368. Cassiday, Bruce. *Dinah!: A Biography.* New York: F. Watts, 1979. 212 p. Illustrated.

SINATRA, FRANK. Ent.

369. Adler, Bill. *Sinatra, the Man and the Myth: An Unauthorized Biography.* New York: New American Library, Signet, 1987. 281 p. Illustrated. Bibliography. Discography. Filmography. Index. Paperbound.

370. Frank, Alan G. *Sinatra.* New York: Leon Amiel Publisher, 1978. 176 p. Illustrated. Filmography. Discography. Bibliography. Index.

371. Goldstein, Norm. *Frank Sinatra, Ol' Blue Eyes.* New York: Holt, Rinehart, and Winston, 1982. 152 p. Illustrated. Filmography. Discography. Paperbound.

372. Howlett, John. *Frank Sinatra.* New York: Simon and Schuster, Wallaby, 1979. 176 p. Illustrated. Filmography. Discography. Bibliography.

373. Jewell, Derek. *Frank Sinatra: A Celebration.* Film commentary by George Perry. Boston, Toronto: Little, Brown, 1985. 192 p. Illustrated. Discography. Filmography.

374. Kelley, Kitty. *His Way: The Unauthorized Biography of Frank Sinatra.* Toronto, New York: Bantam Books, 1986. 575 p. Illustrated. Discography. Filmography. Bibliography. Index.

375. *The Original Frank Sinatra Scrapbook.* [California?]: Golden State Music, 1984. Unpaged. Illustrated.

376. Peters, Richard; O'Brien, Ed; and Sayers, Scott P. Jr. *The Frank Sinatra Scrapbook: His Life and Times in Words and Pictures; Incorporating the Sinatra Sessions, a Complete Listing of All His Recording Sessions, 1939-1982.* New York: St. Martin's Press, 1982. 158 p. Illustrated. Table. Filmography. Paperbound.

377. Rockwell, John. *Sinatra: An American Classic.* New York: Random, Rolling Stone Press, 1984. 251 p. Illustrated. Bibliography. Index.

378. Scaduto, Tony. *Frank Sinatra.* London: Sphere Books, 1977. 159 p. Illustrated. Paperbound.

379. Shaw, Arnold, and Allan, Ted. *Sinatra, the Entertainer.* New York: Delilah Books, 1982. 155 p. Illustrated. Discography. Filmography.

380. Sinatra, Frank. *Sinatra in His Own Words.* Compiled by Guy Yarwood. Art directed by Mike Bell. Designed by John Gordon. New York: Delilah/Putnam, 1983. ***

381. Sinatra, Nancy. *Frank Sinatra, My Father.* New York: Pocket Books, 1986. 388 p. Illustrated. Filmography. Discography. Paperbound.

382. Turner, John Frayn. *Frank Sinatra: A Personal Portrait.* Tunbridge Wells, Kent, England: Midas Books; New York: Hippocrene Books, 1983. 160 p. Illustrated. Discography. Filmography. Index.

SKELTON, RED. Ent.

383. Marx, Arthur. *Red Skelton.* New York: E. P. Dutton, 1979. 325 p. Illustrated. Bibliography. Index.

STREISAND, BARBRA. Ent.

384. *Barbra Streisand Story [Videorecording].* All-Star Video, 1980. 1 videocassette, 120 min., sd., col., 1/2 in.
    Summary: Contains Streisand's television appearances between 1962 and 1976, as well as her performances on the

Ed Sullivan and Jack Paar shows. Includes her two television specials: "My Name Is Barbra," and "Color Me Barbra."

385. Brady, Frank. *Barbra Streisand: An Illustrated Biography.* New York: Grosset & Dunlap, 1979. 151 p. Illustrated. Paperbound.

386. Castell, David. *The Films of Barbra Streisand.* St. Paul, MN: Greenhaven Press, 1978. 45 p. Illustrated. Filmography.

387. Considine, Shaun. *Barbra Streisand: The Woman, the Myth, the Music.* New York: Delacorte Press, 1985. 335 p. Illustrated. Bibliography.

388. *I Remember Barbra [Motion Picture].* Allston, MA: Third Degree Productions, 1981. 1 film reel, 22 min., sd., col., 16mm.

Summary: Candid, funny, and often touching impressions by residents of Brooklyn, N.Y., of one of their most famous former neighbors, Barbra Streisand. Also available as a videorecording.

389. Spada, James, and Nickens, Christopher. *Streisand, the Woman and the Legend.* Garden City, NY: Doubleday, 1981. 249 p. Illustrated.

390. Swenson, Karen. *Barbra, the Second Decade.* Secaucus, NJ: Citadel, 1986. 255 p. Illustrated.

391. Zec, Donald, and Fowles, Anthony. *Barbra: A Biography of Barbra Streisand.* New York: St. Martin's Press, 1981. 253 p. Illustrated. Filmography. Index.

SULLIVAN, ED. Ent. 10/10/74

392. Bowles, Jerry. *A Thousand Sundays: The Story of the Ed Sullivan Show.* New York: Putnam, 1980. 229 p. Illustrated. Index.

WEST, MAE. Ent. 11/22/80

393. Cashin, Fergus. *Mae West: A Biography.* London: W. H. Allen, 1981. 197 p. Illustrated. Playography. Filmography. Index.

394. Eells, George, and Musgrove, Stanley. Mae West: A Biography. New York: Morrow, 1982. 351 p. Illustrated. Playography. Filmography. Index.

395. *Mae West [Sound Recording].* Mark 56 Records, 1974. 1 disc, 33 1/3 rpm, 12 in.

Summary: Presents four radio appearances by West, an Adam and Eve skit from the Edgar Bergan and Charlie McCarthy Show in 1937, starring West and Don Ameche; singing Frankie and Johnny on the Rudy Vallee Show; and two interviews with Frank Bresee done for the American Forces Radio Network's Christmas shows for 1971 and 1972.

WESTHEIMER, RUTH. Ent.

396. Westheimer, Ruth. *All in a Lifetime.* New York: Warner Books, 1987. 225 p. Illustrated. ***

Chapter 9
Books about Celebrity, Fame

397. Boorstin, Daniel J. *The Image: Or, What Happened to the American Dream.* New York: Atheneum, 1962. 315 p. Bibliography. Index.

Writing over a quarter century ago, Boorstin observed that Americans are unable to accept reality, or even recognize it. The popular culture, given predominance in our lives through what he calls the Graphic Revolution, has been a major contributor in the evolution of a synthetic lifestyle. The ways Americans experience life are delusions; our experiences are but pseudo-events. We mistake tourism for travel, substitute reading for literature, and confuse celebrity-worship with hero-worship. ". . . By doing so we come dangerously close to depriving ourselves of all real models." Boorstin on celebrity: "Two centuries ago when a great man appeared, people looked for God's purpose in him; today we look for his press agent" (p. 45).

398. Braudy, Leo. *The Frenzy of Renown: Fame and Its History.* New York: Oxford University Press, 1986. 649 p. Illustrated. Bibliography. Index.

Braudy argues that fame has a past as well as a present. His work identifies "the major routes and important byways of this constant theme in the history of Western society." The nature of fame is defined by its historical and contemporary context; the desire for it is a culturally adaptive trait. The examples chosen range from classical times through the present, and document Braudy's thesis that everyone's persona and private character can be traced back to some precedent.

399. Margolis, Susan. *Fame*. San Francisco: San Francisco Book Co., 1977. 214 p. Illustrated.

In the first chapter of her book, Margolis quotes Daniel Boorstin's working definition of fame: "Being well-known for being well-known." She bemoans fame's degradation from its former honor, glory and immortality to something now indistinguishable from the simple notion of celebrity. In her view, however, true fame is "an award, a reputation, a place in history, and a denial of death." She explores fame's private goal system, its unwritten rules, politics, and arenas (Hollywood, New York, Washington, D.C.). Differences between fame and power are examined, as are the meanings of fame as royalty, myth, and religion. The "high priest" of fame? Johnny Carson.

400. Monaco, James, comp. *Celebrity, the Media as Image Makers*. New York: Dell, Delta, 1978. 258 p. Illustrated. Index. Paperbound.

For this anthology, Monaco has chosen thirty-four fiction and non-fiction pieces which explore and illustrate the phenomenon of media-hyped celebrity. He begins with some general comments on the "State of the Art" of celebrityhood— "before we had celebrities we had heroes"— followed by sections such as "The Medium Connection," with essays describing the function of media-generated fame, and "Victims," discussing three recent sacrifices in ". . . the mode that stretches back to Valentino and Charles Lindbergh." The "rhinestone centerpiece" section is entitled "For Farrah, With Lust and Artifice."

401. Rein, Irving J.; Kotler, Philip; and Stoller, Martin R. *High Visibility*. New York: Dodd, Mead, 1987. 366 p. Index.

"The fact is that everyone is involved in either producing or consuming celebrities." (Preface.) Despite its impact, celebrity is poorly understood. This book, written by communications and marketing experts for a lay audience, is meant to clarify the ambiguity surrounding the celebrity culture and to instruct in achieving "high visibility." Four observations on the realities of celebrity: it pays in terms of money, privilege, and power; it is not the fruit of grace, but of informed drive; it is manufactured and marketed by a sophisticated industry; and, its worship is in an explosive growth phase.

402. Schickel, Richard. *Intimate Strangers: The Culture of Celebrity.* Garden City, NY: Doubleday, 1985. 299 p.

"The power of celebrity and how it works on those who have it, on those who want it, and on a society like ours, which places a large and thoughtless value on it," is the central theme of Schickel's critical essay. His premise is that celebrity is paramount in selling any idea—social, political, aesthetic, or moral, and "famous people are used as symbols for these ideas, or become famous for being symbols of them." Dwight Eisenhower, Merv Griffin, Marlon Brando, Marina Oswald, and many others are discussed in this context. The nonpareil example of the mix of show biz and politics, Ronald Reagan, lends credence to Schickel's thesis.

403. Smith, Robert Ellis. *Celebrities and Privacy.* Washington, DC: Privacy Journal, 1985. 58 p. Bibliography. Paperbound.

In a report describing the legal trends affecting celebrities' privacy and publicity, Smith discusses the "right to privacy" (encompassing the "right to publicity") incorporated in the legal definitions of immortality, misappropriation, and false light. Other sections address attitudes on photography, and public disclosure of private facts. The report concludes with statements by Warren Beatty, Alan Alda, Lauren Bacall, Burt Reynolds, and others about their sensitivity concerning public inspection of their private lives.

PART II
FILM AND TELEVISION CELEBRITIES SOURCES

Chapter 10
Reference Books

Section 1
Bibliographies and Guides

404. *Annotated Bibliography of New Publications in the Performing Arts. Schoolcraft, Ralph Newman, comp.* New York: Drama Bookshop, no. 1-, 1971-. (Quarterly)

This is a serial compilation of new books within the following categories: theatre and drama, technical works in the performing arts, motion pictures, television, radio, general works in the mass media, plays and recordings. It is a supplement to Schoolcraft's *Performing Arts Books in Print: An Annotated Bibliography* (1973). Each entry gives author, title, publisher, date, pagination, price, and an annotation of circa 100 words. Publication was suspended with issue number forty-two, Winter, 1980. However, bibliographic continuum is provided by *The Macmillan Film Bibliography* (1982), and *The Film Yearbook* (1982-).

405. Archer, Stephen M., and Hewitt, Bernard. *American Actors and Actresses: A Guide to Information Sources*. Gale Information Guide Library. Performing Arts Information Guide Series, no. 8. Detroit, MI: Gale Research, 1983. 710 p. Index.

This book is a bibliography of major published sources of information about American actors and actresses from the beginning of professional theatre in this country to the present. Items are listed in seven categories: general references; bibliographies and indexes; histories, surveys, and regional studies; general sources—books; general sources—serials; and collective biographies and autobiographies. The seventh, and by far largest category, is a listing of almost 300 performers, with relevant citations alphabetically by author, each with a brief, critical annotation.

406. Armour, Robert A. *Film: A Reference Guide*. American Popular Culture. Westport, CT: Greenwood Press, 1980. 251 p. Index.

Intended for students, librarians, and interested lay-persons, this bibliography and information guide has almost 1,500 entries on all aspects of American film. Chapters contain a short introductory essay, a critical narrative bibliography, and end with an enumerative bibliography. The chapters entitled "Major Actors," and "Major Directors and Other Production Personnel," list biographical books.

407. *Arts in America: A Bibliography*. Edited by Bernard Karpel. Washington, D.C.: Smithsonian Institution Press, 1979. 4 vols. Index.

Volume three of this comprehensive annotated compilation contains citations to biographical reference works in music, and to reference sources and individual biographies in the field of film. The 403 entries for the individual biographies are arranged by biographee, with publication dates ranging from the early years of this century to the mid 70s. Volumes one and two in the set contain citations to materials in the non-performance creative and decorative arts. Volume four is the index.

408. Brady, Anna; Wall, Richard; and Weiner, Carolynn Newitt, eds. *Union List of Film Periodicals: Holdings of Selected American Collections.* Westport, CT: Greenwood Press, 1984. 316 p. Index.

Intended primarily as a finding tool, this list ". . . represents the most current and detailed information on actual holdings for the periodicals represented as well as the only really comprehensive union listing by subject." (Preface.) Only libraries and research centers with considerable holdings were selected for participation. A typical listing gives title, publication date, notes on title variations, subsequent title changes, and library holdings. There are two indexes: title changes, and country of publication.

409. Ellis, Jack C.; Derry, Charles; and Kern, Sharon. *The Film Book Bibliography, 1940-1975.* Metuchen, NJ: Scarecrow Press, 1979. 752 p. Index.

A classified, largely unannotated listing of English-language books published from 1940 to 1975. Part VI, "Biography, Analysis, and Interview," is a section citing 1764 individual and collective biographies.

410. Fisher, Kim N. *On the Screen: A Film, Television, and Video Research Guide.* Reference Sources in the Humanities Series. Littleton, CO: Libraries Unlimited, 1986. 209 p. Index. ***

411. McCavitt, William E., comp. *Radio and Television: A Selected, Annotated Bibliography.* Metuchen, NJ: Scarecrow Press, 1978. 229 p. Index.

The base volume and supplement (covering the period 1977-1981, and published in 1982), selectively present about 1,600 listings of books and other printed materials associated with all aspects of broadcasting. A bibliography of biography and autobiography is part of the chapter titled: "History."

412. Manz, H. P. *International Motion-Picture Bibliography 1979-80.* International Film Bibliography, New Series, Vol.

1. Munich, Germany: Filmland Presse, 1981. 165 p.
Illustrated. Index.

The 1709 entries in this volume cover reference works,
the film in literature, history, biography, theory and criticism,
scripts, technique, technology, education, the industry, and film
periodicals. With 646 entries, the biography section constitutes
a substantial part of the book.

413. Meyer, William R. *The Film Buff's Catalog.* New Rochelle,
NY: Arlington, 1978. 432 p.

The Film Buff's Catalog is an attempt to distinguish the
good from the bad in the vast field of film, or to at least list what
exists . . ." (Introduction.) Among the 12 information categories
are bibliographies of film books and magazines; an international
list of films; and, directories of distributors, schools,
bookshops, fan clubs, and research collections.

414. *Performing Arts Books, 1876-1981: Including an
International Index of Current Serial Publications.* New
York, London: Bowker, 1981. 1656 p. Index.

Nearly 50,000 titles, representing 106 years of publishing
in all the performing arts, including peripheral subjects. The
bibliography was produced from the computerized files of the
American Book Publishing Record, and the *Bowker Serials
Bibliography Data Base.* Main entries for books or serials are
given in the subject index. Additional access is through author
and title indexes.

415. Rehrauer, George. *The Macmillan Film Bibliography.* New
York: Macmillan, 1982. 2 vols. Index.

Some of the material from Rehrauer's earlier bibliography,
Cinema Booklist, (Metuchen, NJ: Scarecrow Press, 1972;
supplements, 1974 and 1977), has been incorporated into this
work. When used in conjunction with *The Film Yearbook,* one
commands fairly powerful access to the publishing universe,
retrospective and current, for English-language materials in film.
Included are biographies (collective and individual) reference
works, criticism, published scripts, histories; excluded are film

novelizations, and fiction having Hollywood or film themes. The list is alphabetical, by title. Most of the 6762 entries include critical annotations, and are often quite lengthy. Volume two contains three detailed indexes: subject, author and script. The index entry for "biographies, collective" is followed by over 250 titles. Biographical material may be accessed by surname in the subject index.

416. Slide, Anthony. *A Collector's Guide to Movie Memorabilia, with Prices.* Des Moines, IA: Wallace-Homestead, 1983. 104 p. Bibliography. Index. Paperbound.

"Star quality" is the dominant factor in the collectability of movie memorabilia. Thus, major emphasis is given to materials concerning the super stars of film—especially original (and often high priced) paper collectables: photographs, publicity materials, posters, books, autographs, sheet music, programs, and lobby cards.

417. Slide, Anthony, ed. *International Film, Radio, and Television Journals.* Historical Guides to the World's Periodicals and Newspapers. Westport, CT: Greenwood Press, 1985. 428 p. Bibliography. Index.

The entries in this volume have several elements: critical/historical overview; information sources (indexing, reprint editions available and locations) and publication history. Two-hundred periodicals are listed by type and country, with further references to 100 more in the appendices. Among the inclusions are fan club newsletters, fanzines, national film journals and in-house journals.

Section 2
Biographical Dictionaries

418. *American Screenwriters.* Edited by Robert E. Morsberger, Stephen O. Lesser, and Randall Clark. Dictionary of

108 *Film and Television Celebrities Sources*

Literary Biography, vol. 26. Detroit, MI: Gale Research, Bruccoli Clark, 1984. 382 p. Illustrated. Bibliography. Index.

Sixty-five of Hollywood's most important screenwriters are presented in this biographical dictionary. Not every important figure is in this volume, which is considered by the author to be a sampling (a second volume is in progress). ". . . Only writers who wrote primarily for the screen—or those who wrote in other media but had noteworthy film achievements—are included." Each biography is written by a different author and contains: surname, birthdate, death date (if applicable), motion picture and television credits, bibliography, and career studies. Movie stills illustrate the work.

419. Aylesworth, Thomas G., and Bowman, John S. *The World Almanac Who's Who of Film*. Foreword by Douglas Fairbanks, Jr. New York: World Almanac, 1987. 448 p. Illustrated. ***

420. Bergan, Ronald. *A-Z of Movie Directors*. London, New York: Proteus Books, 1982. 160 p. Illustrated.

This is an international biographical dictionary in which are listed "those directors [and animators] whose work has been widely shown in the English-speaking world." (Author's note.) Entries give birth/death dates, education, any non-directorial occupation, career capsule, descriptions of major works, and a selective filmography.

421. Bogle, Donald. *Blacks in American Films and Television: An Encyclopedia*. Garland Reference Library of the Humanities, Vol. 604. New York: Garland, 1988. 510 p. Illustrated. Bibliography. Index. ***

422. *Contemporary Theatre, Film, and Television: A Biographical Guide Featuring Performers, Directors, Writers, Producers, Designers, Managers, Choreographers, Technicians, Composers, Executives, Dancers, and Critics in the United States and Great*

Britain. Detroit, MI: Gale Research, vol. 1-, 1984-. Illustrated. (Irregular?)

This work, currently in its fourth volume, is a continuation of *Who's Who in the Theatre* (17th ed., Gale Research, 1981). The title and subtitle indicate coverage. Emphasis is on contemporary people in the field, although there are some sketches on outstanding people nearing the end of their career. Moreover, there are some posthumous sketches of personalities deceased since 1960. Updated versions of previously published biographies are supplied in cases where the subject is particularly active. There are some 1,000 entries per volume. The format is patterned after Gale's *Contemporary Authors,* and includes: personal data; career information; writings; recordings; awards; memberships; sidelights; and addresses. A cumulative index contains references to *Who's Who in the Theatre,* and *Who Was Who in the Theatre.*

423. Coursodon, Jean Pierre, and Sauvage, Pierre. *American Directors.* New York: McGraw-Hill, 1983. 2 vols. Filmography. Index.

"Within certain self-imposed limitations, all but a very few of the filmmakers with a claim to the serious film student's attention have been included." (Preface.) The focus is on the sound era, with directors excluded who were inactive after 1940, whose output remains predominantly non-American, or whose career consists of fewer than three pictures. Of the 118 director essays, seventy-six were written by the authors. All share the "auteurist" approach to film criticism.

424. *Creative Canada: A Biographical Dictionary of Twentieth-Century Creative and Performing Artists.* Compiled by Reference Division, McPherson Library, University of Victoria. Victoria, B.C., Canada: McPherson Library, University of Victoria; Toronto: University of Toronto Press, vol. 1-, 1971-. Index. (Irregular)

Describes those artists who have contributed as individuals to Canada's culture in this century, and who have had this contribution recognized in print. Inclusion is limited to authors, artists and sculptors, musicians, and performers (ballet, modern dance, radio, theater, television, and motion pictures), and directors, designers, and producers in theater, cinema (including cartoonists and animators), radio, television and dance. Each volume has about 500 sketches with standardized information: name, date/place of birth, parents, spouse, children, education, religion, address, career synopsis, awards/honors, and writings/credits/exhibitions. Cumulative index.

425. Dolmatovskaia, Galina, and Shilova, Irina. *Who's Who in the Soviet Cinema.* Translated from the Russian. Moscow: Progress, 1979. 684 p. Illustrated. Filmography. ***

426. *Film Dope.* London: Film Dope, no. 1-, 1972-. Illustrated. (Irregular) ***

   Film Dope is a serialized biographical dictionary masquerading as a film magazine. Biographical information is arranged alphabetically through the issues, i.e., no. 1: A-., no. 2: B-, etc. Indexed by: *Film Literature Index.*

427. Finler, Joel W. *The Movie Directors Story.* London: Octopus, 1985. 272 p. Illustrated. Index.

   "This book is devoted to the directors of the popular, mainstream Anglo-American cinema, with special emphasis on Hollywood." (Preface.) Coverage is from the silent years through the present. Arrangement is chronological, with major figures balanced by the inclusion of secondary genre or generalist directors. The approximately 125 entries vary in length from one to three pages, with liberal use of film stills and other illustrations, some in color. The sketches give birth date and place, death date, and considerable career information incorporated into a critical, narrative filmography.

428. Franklin, Joe. *Joe Franklin's Encyclopedia of Comedians.* Secaucus, NJ: Citadel, 1979. 347 p. Illustrated.

   Composed of short (from a paragraph to a page or two) biographies of comedians who ". . . have to be creators and originators of comedy." Franklin's definition covers Bob Hope, but not, for example, The Fonz, since the latter works from a script prepared by outside writers. This is confusing and unnecessary in a work of this kind. Selected portraits are included.

429. Gifford, Denis. *The Illustrated Who's Who in British Films.* London: Batsford, 1978. 334 p. Illustrated. Bibliography.

About 1,000 stars, supporting actors, and directors flourishing between 1895 and 1977 are described in this dictionary. Writers and producers are included only when their careers overlap into acting or directing. Entry information: surname, title/honors, real name, work within film industry, birth place/date, death date, original profession, career comment, work in Hollywood (if any), family details, list of any biographies, and a complete (British) filmography.

430. Hogan, David J. *Who's Who of the Horrors and Other Fantasy Films: The International Personality Encyclopedia of the Fantastic Film.* San Diego, CA: A. S. Barnes; London: Tantivy Press, 1980. 279 p. Illustrated. Index.

People from all the film crafts fall within the scope of this book. Coverage is from the 1890s to 1980, with each individual given a descriptive (sometimes critical) paragraph of varying length, but with the basic data of birth/death dates, nationality, craft, and credits.

431. *The Illustrated Who's Who of the Cinema.* Edited by Ann Lloyd, Graham Fuller, and Arnold Desser. Introduction by Jack Lodge. New York: Macmillan, 1983. 480 p. Illustrated.

A selective, international biographical dictionary listing many hundreds of people who have worked either before or behind the camera. The entries are based on "facts compiled by a research team," each being a critical biographical sketch of about 150 words including birthdate and place, death date, and important credits. For virtually every sketch there is an illustration, many in color.

432. *The International Dictionary of Films and Filmmakers.* Edited by Christopher Lyon, et al. Chicago, London: St. James Press, 1984-1988. 5 vols. Bibliography. Index.

The British edition of this dictionary is published as: *The Macmillan Dictionary of Films and Filmmakers* (London: Macmillan, 1984-1987). The volumes are separately titled: Films (vol. 1), Directors/Filmmakers (vol. 2), Actors and Actresses (vol. 3), Writers and Production Artists (vol. 4), Title Index (vol. 5). Individuals profiled in Directors/Filmmakers are persons considered to have had the principal creative responsibility for a substantial body of work, and to have been active in the American, British, or Continental film industry. The actors and actresses chosen for volume three are meant to represent as wide a spectrum as possible, ranging from early cinema to the present, and including all countries. Entries are of varying length (averaging about a page in small type). They contain a chronological profile, critical career summation, current address, filmography, and a bibliography.

433. Katz, Ephraim. *The Film Encyclopedia.* New York: Crowell, 1979. 1266 p.

As explained in his preface, Katz has attempted to be both comprehensive and give a "good balance of American, United Kingdom and international subjects." Biographical material preponderates. These entries give name, nationality, expertise within the industry, birth place/date, death date, education, career summary, critical comment, and complete or partial credits. There are no individual film title entries.

434. Langman, Larry. *Encyclopedia of American Film Comedy.* Garland Reference Library of the Humanities, Vol. 744. New York: Garland, 1987. 639 p. Bibliography. ***

435. Marx, Kenneth S., and Eckert, Geraldine Gonzales. *Star Stats: Who's Whose in Hollywood.* Los Angeles: Price Stern Sloan, 1979. 436 p. Paperbound.

The great motion picture performers, past and present, are listed in computer print-out format. Entries give screen name, real name, birthdates and places, family members, romances, marriages, divorces, residence, screen credits, awards, and more. An astrological calendar, a listing of performers by birthdate, and a breakdown of major studio hierarchies complete the work.

436. Monaco, James, et al. *Who's Who in American Film Now.* 2d ed. New York: Zoetrope, 1987. 388 p. Illustrated.

A product of the computerized service, Baseline, this listing covering the period 1975-1986 and including some influential foreign filmmakers, gives the names and credits of some 11,000 personnel within thirteen major craft categories: writer, producer, director, actor, production designer, costume designer, cinematographer, sound, choreographer, stunts, music, special effects, and editor. No biographical information is provided.

437. *The Movie Stars Story.* Edited by Robyn Karney. New York: Crescent Books, 1984. 287 p. Illustrated. Index.

"We have apportioned our five hundred stars to seven decades in an attempt to give each of them their place in an appropriate social and historical cinematic context." (Preface.) The 500 include the undisputed giants, with the balance being chosen on the basis of box office status, "special achievements," or for an unusual talent. The biographies of four to six or more paragraphs are written by five contributors, with each headed by professional name, real name, birth date/place, and death date. A short essay introduces each decade.

438. Palmer, Scott. *A Who's Who of British Film Actors.* Metuchen, NJ: Scarecrow Press, 1981. 561 p. Bibliography.

Lists 1,400 British and Commonwealth-born actors, plus some others doing their main work in Britain. Entries are brief (4-5 lines) with year of birth, death date and credits.

439. Parish, James Robert, et al. *Film Actors Guide: Western Europe.* Metuchen, NJ: Scarecrow Press, 1977. 606 p. Illustrated. Index.

Listed in this register are film actors, exclusive of Scandanavia, based in Western Europe who have appeared in feature films. If their major reputation was first obtained in Europe, actors who later made films in the United States are included. One entry line is provided for name, birthdate and place of birth. The remainder of the entry is a credit listing of films made, release name in English, distributor and release date.

440. Parish, James Robert, et al. *Hollywood Character Actors.* New Rochelle, NY: Arlington House, 1978. 542 p. Illustrated.

About 370 character actors, of whom a few like Sir Cedric Hardwicke and Lee J. Cobb also have solid credentials as principals, are described in this volume. Each entry is illustrated, giving surname, birthdate/place, spouse, children, death date/place (if applicable), character type, career data, short quote from a film, and dated credits.

441. Pickard, Roy. *Who Played Who in the Movies: An A-Z.* New York: Schocken Books, 1981. 248 p. Illustrated. Index.

The American reprint of an edition first published in 1979, by F. Muller, London, this dictionary is a listing, by character, of individuals (real and fictional) who have been portrayed in movies. Entries are prefaced with a descriptive paragraph about the character, followed by listings (actor, film, director, country of origin, release year) detailing the film portrayals.

442. Quinlan, David. *The Illustrated Directory of Film Stars.* New York: Hippocrene Books, 1981. 497 p. Illustrated. Bibliography.

About 1,600 brief biographies and extensive filmographies form the contents of this work for which Quinlan has chosen mostly British and American players, and some from elsewhere who are known internationally. Each entry gives name, birth date, film dates, awards, and film listings. Each entry has a photograph "from the player's peak period, or as he or she is best remembered."

443. Quinlan, David. *The Illustrated Guide to Film Directors.*
Totowa, NJ: Barnes & Noble, 1983. 334 p. Illustrated.
Bibliography.

Comparatively brief (200-300 words, with directors of
Hitchcock stature in excess of this), the over 550 career
summaries in this volume manage to be both perceptive and
thorough, focusing on "the journeyman working director of
mainline feature films, whether he be auteur, genius or artisan."
(Introduction.) Quinlan's choices ignore nationality, and include
filmmakers whether alive or dead. Information provided: name;
birth date; death date; career summary; filmography (with
original title first, and including shorts, documentaries and TV
movies); film copyright date; and awards won.

444. Ragan, David. *Movie Stars of the Forties: A Complete
Reference Guide for the Film Historian or Trivia Buff.*
Englewood Cliffs, NJ: Prentice-Hall, Spectrum, 1985. 242
p. Index.

See entry below for annotation.

445. Ragan, David. *Movie Stars of the Thirties: A Complete
Reference Guide for the Film Historian or Trivia Buff.*
Englewood Cliffs, NJ: Prentice-Hall, Spectrum, 1985. 181
p. Index.

Stars chosen for inclusion in the two Ragan volumes cited
immediately above are those strongly identified with the decade
in question. Each actor is described in a page-length sketch with
the following elements of information: name, professional name,
birthdate/place, death date (if applicable), career and personal
narrative, and "movie highlights" (credits).

446. Ragan, David. *Who's Who in Hollywood, 1900-1976.*
New Rochelle, NY: Arlington House, 1977. 864 p.

In two main sections, Ragan describes several thousand
screen performers in a few biographical lines intermingled with
(dateless) credits. The length of the material varies as to the
importance and career duration of the actor. Citations for living
players give surname, place of present residence, career and

personal data. Similar information is given for deceased players (with birth and death dates substituted for residence). The book concludes with three lists: "Players Who Died in 1975 and 1976," "'Lost' Players," and "'Lost' Child Players."

447. Shipman, David. *The Great Movie Stars: The Golden Years.* Rev. ed. New York: Hill and Wang, 1979. 592 p. Illustrated. Bibliography. Index.

A companion volume to Shipman's work listed immediately below, and including actors flourishing prior to WW II. "The choice [for inclusion] has been guided by the box-office figures, by popularity polls and by the reputation that remains." (Introduction.) The biographical sketches average two pages in length and contain reference information in sufficient detail for most non-research needs. There is an index to title changes.

448. Shipman, David. *The Great Movie Stars: The International Years.* Rev. ed. New York: Hill and Wang, 1980. 646 p. Illustrated. Index.

More than 230 sketches on ". . . those performers whose names would be known in most households in the US and Britain." The biographies are illustrated with stills from representative movies. The book is a sequel to *The Great Movie Stars: The Golden Years* (rev. ed., 1979, above), and covers the post WW II period. First editions of both volumes were published between 1970 and 1972. Credits using the original names of films and their dates are interspersed throughout the career narrative. There is an index to title changes.

449. Skinner, John Walter, comp. *Who's Who on the Screen.* Worthing, Sussex, England: Madeleine Productions, 1983. 127 p. Illustrated.

Career details of 830 contemporary film actors. Each is accorded a paragraph of varying length containing birth date and place, career background, personal/career highlights or observations, marital information, "important" stage and television credits, and selected citations of biographies. A photograph accompanies the narrative.

450. Stewart, William T.; McClure, Arthur F.; and Jones, Ken D. *International Film Necrology*. Garland Reference Library of the Humanities, vol. 215. New York, London: Garland, 1981. 328 p.

A comprehensive record giving professional name, real name, name known by, occupation, birth date and place, and death date of people in all phases of the film industry. Accuracy was verified by cross-checking in several sources including files of the California Department of Public Health. Most Polish and Czechoslovakian players were excluded.

451. Thomson, David. *A Biographical Dictionary of Film*. 2d ed. New York: Morrow, 1981. 682 p. Index.

Material in the nearly 900 paragraph-length biographical sketches focuses on the artist's work with a "sharp expression of personal taste; jokes; digressions; insults and eulogies." (Introduction.) Selected credits document the author's career observations. Some entries have references to further reading.

452. Truitt, Evelyn Mack. *Who Was Who on Screen*. 3rd. ed. New York: Bowker, 1983. 788 p. Bibliography.

This third edition lists over 13,000 before-the-camera film personalities (mainly American, British, French, and German) who died between 1905 and 1981. Entries are limited to name/varient name; birth and death dates/places; well-known spouses, parents, or children; a brief identifying description; and full screen credits (excluding films made for television).

453. *Variety International Showbusiness Reference*. Edited by Mike Kaplan. Garland Reference Library of the Humanities, vol. 292. New York: Garland, 1981. 1135 p.

Showbusiness in this case includes the people and the product of motion pictures, television, legitimate theater, stage entertainment and the recording industry. Information has been "selected on the basis of possible reference need, judged by the queries which the publication [*Variety*] receives daily. . . ." (Foreword.) There is a lengthy section of some 6,000 biographical sketches also available as a separate publication, *Variety Who's Who in Show Business.* (See below.) Film, TV, and play credits give condensed data for productions from the years 1976 to 1980, and indicate the date when a review appeared in *Variety.* There are tabulations of winners and nominees of Oscars, Emmys, Tonys and Grammys; lists of Pulitzer Prize and long-running plays; festivals, markets, and conventions; platinum records; and a 1976-1980 necrology.

454. *Variety Obituaries, 1905-1986.* Edited by Chuck Bartelt and Barbara Bergeron. New York: Garland, 1988. 11 vols. Index. ***

Over 90,000 facsimile reproduced obituaries are contained in this source. It covers all people in the entertainment field, including business and support personnel. Updates are planned biennially. (Description based on advertising flyer.) Jeb Perry's, *Variety Obits,* published in 1980 (see below in the index section), is a less-comprehensive and less-convenient (but far less-expensive) alternative access tool to the material, providing a full backfile of *Variety* is available.

455. *Variety Who's Who in Show Business.* Rev. ed. Edited by Mike Kaplan. New York: Garland, 1985. 372 p. Paperbound.

This important reference contains over 6,500 entries. Persons in any entertainment-related occupation, and from all countries, now living or having died between January 1, 1983, and June 30, 1985, are listed. Descriptive paragraphs give the following data: craft, birth date/place, education, career notes, awards, and credits. This information expands and updates that in the *Variety International Showbusiness Reference.*

456. *Who's Who in Canadian Film and Television.* Edited by Chapelle Jaffe. Toronto: Academy of Canadian Cinema & Television, 1985-. Paperbound. (Annual)

Fourteen-hundred individuals: writers, producers, directors, production managers, cinematographers, art directors, editors, and composers (but not actors), submitted the information for this directory. The data are presented in a standardized format, and in either English or French depending on the language of submission: name, union/guild membership, addresses, phone numbers, types of production and categories, genres, biography (two-four lines), filmography, and awards.

457. *Who's Who in Television and Cable.* Edited by Steven H. Scheuer. New York: Facts on File, 1983. 579 p. Illustrated. Index.

In addition to television and cable, coverage embraces the video industries, on-tape motion pictures included. Over 2,000 notables are listed.

458. *Who's Who on Television: A Fully Illustrated Guide to 1000 Best Known Faces on British Television.* Rev. ed. London: ITV Books, 1982. 272 p. Illustrated. Paperbound.

Capsule biographies (about 150 words each) of an international group of actors. Birthdate, credits, address, astrological sign, and a photograph constitute the core of each entry.

459. Wicking, Christopher, and Vahimagi, Tise. *The American Vein: Directors and Directions in Television.* New York: E. P. Dutton, 1979. 261 p. Videography. Index.

Presented herein are biographical sketches of approximately 250 television directors who have worked in the medium since the late 1940s. Each entry (about a page in length) includes surname, birthdate (usually), television credits, and career and critical information.

460. Wlaschin, Ken. *The Illustrated Encyclopedia of the World's Great Movie Stars and Their Films.* New York: Harmony Books, Salamander, 1979. 233 p. Illustrated. Index.

Four hundred international film stars of all times and places were selected on the basis of personality, persona, popularity, lasting reputation, and critical prestige. The biographies are arranged by period: Silent, Classic, and Modern. Each entry of several columns length has a critical career and personal synopsis appended with a filmography of the star's "Ten Best." Photographs, posters, and memorabilia (many in color) profusely illustrate the volume.

461. *World Film Directors.* Edited by John Wakeman. New York: H. W. Wilson, 1987-. 2 vols.

First in a planned two-volume work, this book covers directors born before 1920 and working in the field before 1950. Volume two, expected late in 1988, will profile 219 directors whose films brought them to prominence after 1950. Essays range between 1,500-8,000 words and offer film summaries; an examination of early development and influences; criticism; film discussion; casting and production details; a complete filmography; a bibliography of biographical material; and, a list of published screenplays. Directors include: Luis Bunuel, Sergei Eisenstein, Robert J. Flaherty, D.W. Griffith, Alfred Hitchcock, John Huston, Fritz Lang, Yasujiro Ozu, Roberto Rossellini, and Jean Vigo.

Section 3
Encyclopedias

462. Brown, Les. *Les Brown's Encyclopedia of Television.* 2d ed. New York: Zoetrope, 1982. 496 p. Illustrated. Table. Bibliography.

In this expanded edition of the *New York Times Encyclopedia of Television* (1977), Brown brings together history, technology, programs, artists, executives, networks, and other relevant television topics. The celebrities and lesser-known talents in the medium are described in short biographies ranging from a single sentence to several paragraphs. Main credits are given.

463. Halliwell, Leslie. *Halliwell's Filmgoer's Companion.* 8th ed. New York: Scribner, 1985. 1150 p. Bibliography. Paperbound.

This edition of a comprehensive work (7,000 new or revised entries through 1983), presents brief data on American, French, English, Russian, and Italian actors, directors and writers; synopsis of selected films; and a glossary of film terms. In a paragraph or two, the biographies give name, birth/death dates, capsule description, summation of film career, autobiographies (if any) and credits. There is a "List of Recommended Books."

464. Halliwell, Leslie, and Purser, Philip. *Halliwell's Television Companion.* 3rd ed. London: Grafton Books, 1986. 941 p. Illustrated.

While having most of the attributes of *Halliwell's Filmgoers' Companion* (above), this encyclopedia of 12,000 items has a far less international character, covering only English-language television entertainment. The cut-off date for inclusion is 1985, with some programs from the beginning of 1986. These entries contain title, country/year of origin, running time, credits, synopsis, appraisal, and principal cast. In addition to programs, one finds entries for: ". . . people who have made significant creative contributions (plus a few who simply appear a lot);" companies and networks; technical and trade terms; general subjects; and books on television. The biographical material is brief.

465. *The New York Times Encyclopedia of Film.* Edited by Gene Brown. Introduction by Harry M. Geduld. New York: Times Books, 1984. 13 vols. Illustrated. Index.

Because of its coverage of virtually the total history of the medium, this collection of reprinted facsimile articles from *The New York Times* comprises an impressive reservoir of secondary source material about motion pictures. The coverage is from 1896 to 1979, with volumes 9-12 containing articles from the 70s. Volume 13 is a comprehensive index.

466. Robertson, Patrick. *Guinness Film Facts and Feats.* Rev. ed. Enfield, Middlesex, England: Guinness Superlatives, 1985. 240 p. Filmography. Index. Paperbound.

Encyclopedic information on the history, economics, artistry and technology of the film industry. Of special note is the chapter, "Performers," wherein is listed among other items: "Biopics of Screen Stars;" film stars who have played themselves; non-actors who have played themselves; and nonactors who have played roles other than themselves. This is the revised edition of: *Guinness Book of Film Facts and Feats,* 1980.

467. Schemering, Christopher. *The Soap Opera Encyclopedia.* New York: Ballantine Books, 1985. 358 p. Illustrated. Bibliography. Index. Paperbound.

Alphabetical program listings of all the televised shows, daytime and primetime since their beginnings in the 1940s, are featured in this source. Entries give premiere and cancellation dates, story synopsis, reviews, cast lists, and anecdotal sidelights. Part two is entitled, "Who's Who in Soap Opera," and presents thirty-one biographical sketches of celebrities of the genre. These profiles average two pages in length, give birth dates/places, credits, and describe the star's on- and off-screen persona. Several appendices listing awards, ratings, and guest stars, blacks, and famous graduates of daytime drama conclude the work.

468. Stewart, John. *An Encyclopedia of Australian Film.* Frenchs Forest, NSW, Australia: Reed Books, 1984. 304 p. Illustrated. Index.

"This is a book mainly about the people of the Australian film industry, with the emphasis on feature film makers and modern film. Most of the modern directors and stars have entries of their own, as do a great many of the more recent producers, directors of photography, editors, composers, writers, and soundmen." (Introduction.) Entries give name, birthdate, deathdate where appropriate, real name, occupation within the industry, and filmography including relevant television work (with dates of release). Under the entry, "Americans in Australia," is a listing, by decade, of U.S. citizens who have gone to Australia to film, with their Australian credits. An index lists Australian motion pictures year by year.

Section 4
Yearbooks

469. *The Film Yearbook.* Edited by Al Clark. New York: St. Martin's Press, vol. 1-, 1982-. Illustrated. Paperbound. (Annual)

This is a film reference work of multiple dimension, readability, and utility. It is, therefore, regrettable that the new editor of the 1988 volume chose to lessen the latter two attributes by altering the bibliographic format and largely neutralizing the acid content of the critical annotations. The opening section presents film credits, short reviews, and stills from the year's feature films, followed by one or two-page reviews of best and worst films. Next is a section of actor biographies, including portraits. An extensive listing of critically annotated film books, many of which are biographies, fulfills a need for bibliographic continuum, particularly in view of the 1980 suspension of the *Annotated Bibliography of New Publications in the Performing Arts,* and the 1982 publication date of *The Macmillan Film Bibliography.* Of note are the obituaries, which include a full-page portrait upon the death of an important personage.

470. *International Television & Video Almanac.* 32d ed. New York: Quigley, vol. 1-, 1956-. Illustrated. Index. (Annual)

With this edition, the title was changed from *International Television Almanac,* to reflect increasing coverage and importance of the home video market. Approximately half of this publication is devoted to biographical sketches of performers, presented in an abbreviated format, with selected credits listed under headings: pictures, television, stage, and concerts. Other sections of the compendium: home video data; directories of TV stations, agencies, services, distributors; feature releases; and world TV market data.

471. *Magill's Cinema Annual*. Edited by Frank N. Magill. Englewood Cliffs, NJ: Salem Press, v. 1-, 1982-. Index. (Annual)

Serves as a yearly supplement to *Magill's Survey of Cinema*. The volume examined (1985) describes selected films and film books of the previous year. Other categories are: "More films of 1984," "Retrospective films," and "List of awards." Of biographical note are three interviews of film personalities and an obituaries section. Nine separate indexes provide access. The subject index, cumulative since volume 1, is of special help in identifying filmed biography. Under the heading "biography," 30 films are listed.

472. *The Motion Picture Almanac: Pictures and Personalities*. New York: Quigley, vol. 1-, 1929-. Illustrated. (Annual)

Name, vocation, birthdate/place, filmographies, and videographies are listed in a major chapter titled, "Who's Who in Motion Pictures and Television." Other chapters: credits for the year's feature films; theater directory; trade publications; and organizations. Title varies: *Motion Picture Almanac* (1929-36); *International Motion Picture Almanac* (1937-49); *Motion Picture and Television Almanac* (1952-55).

473. *The Motion Picture Annual. 1988-*. Evanston, IL: Cinebooks, 1988-. (Annual) ***

"People to Watch (33 rising industry stars), and Obituaries (117 US actors and technical personnel) provide hard-to-find biographical data." (Publisher's brochure.)

474. *The Motion Picture Guide*. Chicago: Cinebooks, 1985-. (Annual) ***

"People to Watch (33 rising industry stars), and Obituaries (376 international actors and technical personnel) provide hard-to-find biographical data." (Publisher's brochure.)

475. *Screen International Film and Television Yearbook, 1986-87.* 35th ed. London: King Publication, vol. 1-, 1945-. Illustrated. (Annual)

"British Directory," "International Directory," and "International Who's Who," are the major parts of this book. The latter section is the one with biographical sketches of international notables and a listing of credits. Former title: *British Film and Television Yearbook.*

Section 5
Indexes

476. *Film Literature Index.* Albany, NY: Filmdex vol. 1-, 1973-. (Quarterly)

Author-subject index to over 300 international periodicals that treat, either in whole or in part, film (Section 1) and television (Section 2). *"FLI"* excludes fan magazines and totally technical journals, and is published quarterly with an annual cumulation. "In addition to the author's name and over one thousand subject headings, articles are indexed under the names of individual screenwriters, performers, directors, cinematographers, professional societies, and corporations." (Preface.) Entries indicate the presence of filmographies, credits, biographical data or interviews. Potentially useful is the grouping of all individuals indexed in the volume by occupational category, e.g., Actors and Actresses. See also: Abdulov, Aleksander; Abraham, F. Murray, etc. Under the subject heading "Biography," look by year for book reviews of biographies about film personalities.

477. *International Index to Film Periodicals: An Annotated Guide.* London: International Federation of Film Archives; New York: Bowker, vol. 1-, 1972-. (Annual)

An index for approximately eighty periodicals, this source is the precursor and companion to *International Index to Television Periodicals* (below). Any items on film in the "TV" periodicals index are included in this index, and overlap articles are found in both. Entries are arranged in eleven sections, among which are those for general subjects, individual films, and biography. Book reviews are listed. Additional indexing is by author director, and subject.

478. *International Index to Television Periodicals: An Annotated Guide.* Edited by Michael Moulds. London: International Federation of Film Archives, vol. 1-, 1983-. Paperbound. (Biennial)

Companion to the *International Index to Film Periodicals* (above). Any items on television in the film periodicals index are included in this index, and overlap articles are found in both. "The items indexed are chosen [from about 100 periodicals] as being of lasting interest from a social, economic, political, critical or aesthetic point of view. News and other items of ephemeral concern are generally not included." (Preface.) The index is divided in four parts: (1) general subjects; (2) individual programmes and TV films; (3) biography; and (4) author index. A single, descriptive sentence constitutes the annotation.

479. Kidd, Charles. *Debrett Goes to Hollywood.* New York: St. Martin's Press, 1986. 144 p. Illustrated. Bibliography. Index. ***

480. Lieberman, Susan, and Cable, Frances, comps. *Memorable Film Characters: An Index to Roles and Performers, 1915-1983.* Bibliographies and Indexes in the Performing Arts, no. 1. Westport, CT: Greenwood Press, 1984. 291 p. Bibliography.

On-film biography can be identified with this index by checking entries under main character, or biographee. Terse descriptions of about 1,500 characters are found in this main section. Indexes by film and actor.

481. *NewsBank. Review of the Arts: Film and Television.* New Canaan, CT: Newsbank, 1975-. Microfiche. (Monthly)

An information service providing articles, on microfiche, from newspapers published in over 100 U.S. cities. Other parts of this service: *NewsBank. Names in the News* (above), *NewsBank. Review of the Arts: Performing Arts* (below). The April, 1986 issue contained in-depth interviews with Whoopi Goldberg and Bess Armstrong, plus an article remembering the life and career of James Cagney. An index, cumulated every four months, accompanies each issue. The CD-ROM product, *NewsBank Electronic Index,* is an on-disc index to the full-text microfiche.

482. *Performing Arts Biography Master Index: A Consolidated Index to over 270,000 Biographical Sketches of Persons Living and Dead, as They Appear in over 100 of the Principal Biographical Dictionaries Devoted to the Performing Arts.* 2d ed. Edited by Barbara McNeil, and Miranda C. Herbert. Gale Biographical Index Series, no. 5. Detroit, MI: Gale Research, 1981. 701 p.

The first edition, edited by Dennis Le Beau, is titled: *Theatre, Film, and Television Biographies Master Index.* Coverage in this second edition broadens to include music, dance, puppetry, magic, theater, film and television. As with the others within this Gale series of biographical indexes, entries are ordered alphabetically with birth and death dates, followed by one or more title codes to the biographical dictionaries analyzed.

483. Perry, Jeb H. *Variety Obits: An Index to Obituaries in Variety, 1905-1978.* Metuchen, NJ: Scarecrow Press, 1980. 311 p.

Many lesser-known individuals who worked in the production-related areas of motion pictures, television, radio, the legitimate stage, minstrelsy and vaudeville are listed in this index. Main entries are professional names (real, married, maiden, and alternate professional names are in parentheses). Names are followed by age at death, death date, principal professional title(s), and date/page of the *Variety* issue in which the obituary appears. See *Variety Obituaries, 1905-1986* (in the biographical dictionaries section, above), for extended index coverage and facsimile reproductions of the obituaries.

484. *TV Guide Index*. Radnor, PA: Triangle Publications, vol. 1-, 1953-. (Annual,with Quinquennial Cumulations)

The first issue of this index to the largest-selling magazine in America is called, *TV Guide 25 Year Index* (1953-1977), with the quinquennial issue for 1978-1982, called also *TV Guide, Cumulative Supplement*, and annual issues since 1981 called also *TV Guide, Supplement*. Organizing and recording virtually every article published since the magazine's beginning makes this a particularly rich source for identifying information about personalities appearing on television throughout its history. Arrangement is in a combined, alphabetical author and subject sequence, with indexing and pagination based on the New York Metropolitan edition (complete backfile available on microfilm).

Section 6
Directories

485. *Academy Players Directory*. Beverly Hills, CA: Academy of Motion Picture Arts and Sciences, vol. 1-, 1937?-. Illustrated. Index. (3 issues/year)

The intent of this work is to present pictures of the artists and names of their agents as a reference for studios, producers and casting agents. The current four-part issue lists over 16,200 people. Indexing is by name; race or ethnic group; and disability, if any. Similar in purpose and arrangement to the *Players' Guide* below.

486. *Christensen's Ultimate Movie, TV, and Rock Directory*. 3d ed. Edited by Roger Christensen, and Karen

Christensen. Cardiff-by-the-Sea, CA: Cardiff-by-the-Sea Publishing, 1988? Illustrated.

Offering more than 50,000 entries in the form of artist addresses, autograph facsimiles, fan club addresses, fan magazines, memorabilia listings, and photograph sources, this publication's audience is unmistakably the celebrity buff and collector.

487. *The Hollywood Reporter Studio Blu-Book Directory.* Hollywood, CA: Hollywood Reporter, v. 1-. 1978-. Illustrated. Index. Paperbound. (Annual)

A spiral binding, tabbed dividers and heavy paper are indications of the hard use for which this "industrial tool" has been designed. Organization is alphabetical by 324 subjects— from "Actor and celebrity contacts" to "Youth in film awards." The directory sections are offered as the meat in an information sandwich consisting of 60% advertising. An index provides cross references. Continues: *Studio Blu-Book Directory.*

488. Mehr, Linda Harris, ed. *Motion Pictures, Television and Radio: A Union Catalogue of Manuscript and Special Collections in the Western United States.* Reference Publication in Film. Boston: G. K. Hall, 1977. 201 p. Index.

"The Catalogue itself was designed to locate, identify and describe research collections currently available for use in established institutions, libraries, museums, and historical societies in the eleven western United States [AZ, CA, CO, ID, MT, NV, NM, OR, UT, WA, WY]." There is a general index and an occupation index.

489. *Performing Arts Resources.* New York: Drama Book Specialists, vol. 1-, 1974-. (Annual)

Issued by the Theatre Library Association. "Each annual volume of *Performing Arts Resources* is envisioned then as a collection of articles which will enable the performing arts student, scholar, and archivist to locate, identify, and classify information about theatre, film, broadcasting, and popular entertainments." (Preface.) Selected articles describing collections containing popular biographical materials which have appeared in several of the ten volumes published to date: "Film/Broadcasting Resources in the Los Angeles Area;" "The Belknap Collection for the Performing Arts: University of Florida Libraries;" and, "The Popular Culture Library and Audio Center" (all in vol. 1). "A Descriptive Catalogue of the Filmic Items in the Gernsheim Collection" (vol. 2). "The Cinema Library at the University of Southern California" (vol. 3). "The Museum of Broadcasting" (vol. 6). "Twentieth-Century Fox Corporate Archive at the UCLA Theater Arts Library;" and, "The Warner Brothers Collection at Princeton" (both in vol. 10). Articles in this series are indexed selectively by: *MLA International Bibliography of Books and Articles on the Modern Languages and Literatures.*

490. Perry, Jim. *The Stars Beyond: A Biographical Graveside Guide to Hollywood's Greats.* Manhattan Beach, CA: J. E. Perry, 1978. 88 p. Illustrated. Paperbound.

"In this book, I have tried to provide the sincere admirer of the cinema and its stars, a respectful and efficient compilation of the highlights of careers, and final resting places of some of their screen favorites." (Author's notes.) Around sixty stars' burial sites are identified in twelve cemeteries/mausoleums located in the greater Los Angeles area.

491. *Players' Guide: The Annual Pictorial Directory for Stage, Screen, Radio and Television.* Edited by Paul L. Ross, and Marion J. Ross. New York: Players' Guide, vol. 1-, 1953-. Illustrated. (Annual)

The 1977-1978 issue examined lists actors and other performing artists in classifications such as: leading women; character men—comedians; and directors-choreographers. Name, union affiliation, address, credits, and a photograph constitute the information on each person. Similar in arrangement and purpose to the *Academy Players Directory* (above).

492. Singer, Michael. *Film Directors: A Complete Guide.* 4th ed. Beverly Hills, CA: Lone Eagle, 1986. 485 p. Illustrated. Index.

    More than 1000 filmmakers, domestic and foreign, currently working in the industry (plus a very few retired greats) compose the main portion of this directory. Television feature film directors are included. The listings give name, birthdate/place, current contact (address of director or agent) credits. The edition reviewed contained interviews with seven prominent directors: Joe Dante, Marisa Silver, Wayne Wang, Patrick Bailey, Harry Winer, Michael Apted, and Martin Brest. Indexes: Director, Film title, Agent.

493. Slide, Anthony; Hanson, Patricia King; and Hanson, Stephen L., comps. *Sourcebook for the Performing Arts: A Directory of Collections, Resources, Scholars, and Critics in Theatre, Film, and Television.* New York: Greenwood Press, 1988. 227 p. Bibliography. Index. ***

Section 7
Individual Celebrity Sources

ALTMAN, ROBERT. Dir.

494. Wexman, Virginia Wright, and Bisplinghoff, Gretchen. *Robert Altman: A Guide to References and Resources.* Reference Publication in Film. Boston: G. K. Hall, 1984. 243 p. Illustrated. Index.

    This is the first film director bibliography (alphabetically speaking) in the already extensive and continuing G. K. Hall series. The series has a rigid formula for scope and arrangement to which the individual authors carefully adhere. This work is no different, with chapters for biographical background; a critical survey; credits, notes, and synopsis of films; writings about Altman; television work and related film activity; sources for further research. There is a film distributor directory, and indexes for titles and authors.

BERGMAN, INGMAR. Dir.

495. Manvell, Roger. *Ingmar Bergman, an Appreciation.* Dissertations on Film Series, 1980. New York: Arno Press, 1980. 114 p. Illustrated. Bibliography. Filmography.

Of the fourteen chapters in this book, thirteen are concerned with criticism of Bergman's films. However, the first chapter is a short biography. Appendices contain a list of principal translators of Bergman's scripts into English; filmographies of Bergman works and those scripted by Bergman for other directors; and Bergman's principal cinematographers and performers.

496. Steene, Birgitta. *Ingmar Bergman: A Guide to References and Resources.* A Reference Publication in Film. Boston: G. K. Hall, 1987. 342 p. Illustrated. Index.

Beginning with a biographical essay ". . . aimed at conveying the psychological and social ambiance of [Bergman's] childhood and youth and its continuous importance to him as a filmmaker," this guide follows closely the established G. K. Hall series pattern with chapters for: critical survey; film synopsis, credits, notes, reviews and critical commentary; writings by and about Bergman; other professional activities; archival sources; and a film distributor directory.

CAPRA, FRANK. Dir.

497. Wolfe, Charles. *Frank Capra: A Guide to References and Resources.* A Reference Publication in Film. Boston: G. K. Hall, 1987. 464 p. Illustrated. Index.

This work opens with a twenty-page Capra biography, and a critical survey of his work. Conforming in arrangement with other books in this series, subsequent sections offer: credits, notes, and plot synopsis of fifty-six films; a bibliography of writings by and about the director; interviews; other film-related activity; and archives and non-theatrical distributor guides.

COPPOLA, FRANCIS FORD. Dir.

498. Johnson, Robert K. *Francis Ford Coppola.* Twayne's Theatrical Arts Series. Boston: Twayne, 1977. 199 p. Illustrated. Bibliography. Filmography. Index.

Chapter 1, "A Fantasy World," is a twenty-four page biography of Coppola, although there is much more on the director's life found interspersed with the comment and criticism regarding his films in the remaining nine chapters. Films from *Dementia 13* (1963), through *The Godfather, Part II* (1974), are examined.

499. Zuker, Joel Stewart. *Francis Ford Coppola: A Guide to References and Resources.* A Reference Publication in Film. Boston: G. K. Hall, 1984. 241 p. Illustrated. Index.

Part I of Zuker's book is a biography with notes. Subsequent parts include a critical narrative, synopsis, credits and notes on Coppola's films, and a lengthy annotated bibliography. The final parts list other resources.

COSTA-GAVRAS, HENRI. Dir.

500. Michalczyk, John J. *Costa-Gavras, the Political Fiction Film.* Philadelphia, PA: Art Alliance Press; London: Associated University Presses, 1984. 296 p. Illustrated. Filmography. Bibliography. Index.

This is foremost a work of film criticism, the Costa-Gavras biography in a chapter of twenty-two pages notwithstanding. Michalczyk examines such political screen thrillers as: *Z*, *The Confession*, *State of Siege*, and *Missing*.

DE SICA, VITTORIO. Dir. 11/13/74

501. Darretta, John. *Vittorio De Sica: A Guide to References and Resources*. Reference Publication in Film. Boston: G. K. Hall, 1983. 340 p. Illustrated. Index.

Another title in the extensive G. K. Hall series on directors. Seventeen pages of biography are followed by a critical survey; films synopsis, credits and notes; bibliography of works about De Sica; reviews in American magazines; writings, performances, and other film-related activity; archives, and film distributor directory. Author and film-title indexes.

FELLINI, FEDERICO. Dir.

502. Price, Barbara Anne, and Price, Theodore. *Federico Fellini: An Annotated International Bibliography*. Metuchen, NJ: Scarecrow Press, 1978. 282 p. Index.

Covered herein are primary and secondary sources published through February, 1978. Annotations are descriptive/informative, and give "insights" about the films. The primary sources are Fellini screenplays, other fiction, essays, drawings, photographs, interviews, a discography and a filmography. Secondary sources include: published book-length criticism, sections of books, dissertations, articles, reviews, and audio-visual material.

503. Stubbs, John Caldwell; Markey, Constance D.; and Lenzini, Marc. *Federico Fellini: A Guide to References and Resources*. A Reference Publication in Film. Boston: G. K. Hall, 1978. 346 p. Index.

Sixteen pages of biographical background begin this work. Established series format is followed with the standardized chapters: critical survey of oeuvre; synopsis, credits and notes on the films; writings about Fellini; writings, performances and other film related activity; archival sources; and, film distributors list. Author and film title index.

FONTANNE, LYNN. Act. 7/30/83

504. Runkel, Phillip M. *Alfred Lunt and Lynn Fontanne: A Bibliography.* Waukesha, WI: Carroll College Press, 1978. 40 p. Illustrated. Index. Paperbound.

Contains unannotated bibliographical citations to books, articles and play reviews. There are no entries for references in encyclopedias, biographical dictionaries, newspapers, or for reviews of early plays and silent movies. All other published sources are listed comprehensively. The introduction is a two-page biographical sketch of Lunt and Fontanne. Appendix: "Films, Radio and Television Appearances, and Recordings."

FUGARD, ATHOL. Dir.

505. Hauptfleisch, Temple; Viljoen, Wilma; and Van Greunen, Celeste, comps. *Athol Fugard: A Source Guide.* Publication of the Centre for S.A. Theatre Research, No. 7. Johannesburg, South Africa: Donker, 1982. 126 p.

". . . The Guide contains enough material on and by Fugard to serve a useful purpose in guiding and stimulating research. . . ." (Introduction.) The compilers have chosen reviews, articles, books and other information from the period between 1959 and 1979, with a few references to events of 1980. Brief biographical notes on Fugard, and a list of names and works of selected other South African playwrights complete the volume.

506. Vandenbroucke, Russell, comp. *Athol Fugard: Bibliography, Biography, Playography.* Theatre Checklist, No. 15. London: TQ Publications, 1977. 16 p. Illustrated. Paperbound.

"Biographical Notes," (descriptive sentences in chronological order), and, "Stage Plays," (synopsis, cast, performance, and published source notes), are the first sections of this brief work. Other parts: television and film scenarios; article, essay, interview and secondary literature sources.

GODARD, JEAN-LUC. Dir.

507. Lesage, Julia. *Jean-Luc Godard: A Guide to References and Resources.* A Reference Publication in Film. Boston: G. K. Hall, 1979. 438 p. Index.

As do the many others in this series, this bibliographic study provides annotated entries of critical writings, published interviews, and criticism, introduced by a short biography. Other chapters supply film credits, notes and synopsis, archival resources, and a distributor directory.

KAZAN, ELIA. Dir.

508. Michaels, Lloyd. *Elia Kazan: A Guide to References and Resources.* A Reference Publication in Film. Boston: G. K. Hall, 1985. 168 p. Index.

The introductory biographical chapter, at nineteen pages, is longer than the norm for this series. The other parts conform to the series formula: critical survey; synopsis, credits and notes on the films; writings about Kazan; reviews and references; writings, performances, and other film-related activity; archival sources; and list of film distributors.

KUBRICK, STANLEY. Dir.

509. Coyle, Wallace. *Stanley Kubrick: A Guide to References and Resources.* A Reference Publication in Film. Boston: G. K. Hall, 1980. 155 p. Illus. Index.

This work, adhering to the guidelines of its series, begins with a biographical sketch of nine pages, followed by a critical survey of the Kubrick oeuvre, films synopsis, extensive bibliography, and other resources.

LEAN, DAVID. Dir.

510. Castelli, Louis P., and Cleeland, Caryn Lynn. *David Lean: A Guide to References and Resources.* A Reference Publication in Film. Boston: G. K. Hall, 1980. 134 p. Illustrated. Index.

This bio-bibliography continues the arrangement and scope of the others in this series: biographical background; critical survey of the oeuvre; synopsis and criticism of the films; and other resources.

LESTER, RICHARD. Dir.

511. Rosenfeldt, Diane. *Richard Lester: A Guide to References and Resources.* A Reference Publication in Film. Boston: G. K. Hall, 1978. 152 p. Index.

Fifteen pages of Lester biography are presented in the opening two chapters. This is followed by sixteen film synopses with credits, an annotated bibliography of 642 writings about Lester (1960-1977), and various archival sources.

LUMET, SIDNEY. Dir.

512. Bowles, Stephen E. *Sidney Lumet: A Guide to References and Resources.* A Reference Publication in Film. Boston: G. K. Hall, 1979. 151 p. Illustrated. Index.

   One of the earlier works in the continuing series on film directors, containing a biography of 34 pages. Remaining chapters consist of criticism and discussion of Lumet's films.

PENN, ARTHUR. Dir.

513. Zuker, Joel Stewart. *Arthur Penn: A Guide to References and Resources.* A Reference Publication in Film. Boston: G. K. Hall, 1980. 201 p. Illustrated. Index.

   Author's Preface: "The purpose of the book is twofold: first, to trace Penn's career as a filmmaker; second, to identify significant references about Penn and indicate what the material contains." Chapter 1 is a critical biography.

POLANSKI, ROMAN. Dir.

514. Bisplinghoff, Gretchen, and Wexman, Virginia Wright. *Roman Polanski: A Guide to References and Resources.* A Reference Publication in Film. Boston: G. K. Hall, 1979. 116 p. Illustrated. Index.

   As with others in this series, the book is primarily a bibliography of film criticism with a prefatory biography. Of special note is the list of archival locations in Europe and America.

RUSSELL, KEN. Dir.

515. Rosenfeldt, Diane. *Ken Russell: A Guide to References and Resources.* A Reference Publication in Film. Boston: G. K. Hall, 1978. 140 p. Index.

Another in the G. K. Hall series, this guide offers an introductory five-page Russell biographical background. This is succeeded by several longer chapters: critical survey of oeuvre, film synopsis and credits, writings about the director (annotated; seventy-three pages) and other film work and writings. Archival sources, a listing of film distributors, and an author and film title index conclude the work.

SCORSESE, MARTIN. Dir.

516. Weiss, Marion. *Martin Scorsese: A Guide to References and Resources.* A Reference Publication in Film. Boston: G. K. Hall, 1987. 137 p. Illustrated. Index.

A nineteen-page biography traces those specific life experiences which make the cliché, "art imitates life" so appropriate when discussing Scorsese. The biography is followed by the chapters: "Critical Survey," "The Films," "Writings about Martin Scorsese, 1968-1985," "Writings, Performances, and Other Film-Related Activity," "Archival Sources," and "Film Distributors." Indexes are by film title and author.

TRUFFAUT, FRANÇOIS. Dir. 10/21/84

517. Walz, Eugene P. *François Truffaut: A Guide to References and Resources.* A Reference Publication in Film. Boston: G. K. Hall, 1982. 319 p. Index.

This guide opens with a biographical chapter followed by other chapters addressing themes and characters, and synopsis and notes of Truffaut's films. There is a bibliography of works by and about the director. Indexes are organized by author, film title, and auteur.

VISCONTI, LUCHINO. Dir. 3/17/76

518. Mancini, Elaine. *Luchino Visconti: A Guide to References and Resources.* A Reference Publication in Film. Boston: G. K. Hall, 1986. 357 p. Index.

Visconti's film work has been emphasized, "although his theater, opera, and ballet productions, as well as important sources discussing his personal life, have been included." (Preface.) Chapters: biographical background; critical survey; credits, synopsis and notes on the films; writings about and by Visconti (annotated and arranged chronologically); interviews; scripts, screenplays, treatments, unfilmed scripts, libretti; other works; archival sources; and, a list of film distributors.

WILDER, BILLY. Dir.

519. Seidman, Steve. *The Film Career of Billy Wilder.* Reference Publication in Film. Pleasantville, NY: Redgrave Publishing, 1977. 175 p. Bibliography. Index. Paperbound.

A twenty-two page biography begins this reference work of Wilder sources. Following this are chapters addressing criticism of his oeuvre (using the auteur approach), synopsis and reviews of his films, a list of writings about him, archival sources, and film distributors.

Chapter 11
Collective Biographies

520. Agan, Patrick. *The Decline and Fall of the Love Goddesses.* Los Angeles: Pinnacle Books, 1979. 286 p. Illustrated. Filmography. Paperbound.

The ten women portrayed in this volume are yesterday's celebrated film stars who through weakness or circumstance suffered career and personal misfortune. Included are: Rita Hayworth, Jayne Mansfield, Betty Hutton, Linda Darnell, Veronica Lake, Betty Grable, Susan Hayward, Dorothy Dandridge, Frances Farmer, and Marilyn Monroe.

521. Allen, Steve. *Funny People.* New York: Stein and Day, 1981. 323 p. Illustrated. Paperbound.

"The entertainers I write about in this study are not necessarily the best, or even my personal favorites . . . they are simply those concerning whom I find myself with something to say." (Introduction.) Biographical information and comedic criticism are dispensed in equal measure about: Woody Allen, Billy Crystal, Sid Caesar, Richard Pryor, Tom Dreesen, Lily Tomlin, Robin Williams, Jimmy Durante, Andy Kaufman, George Burns, Jonathan Winters, Peter Sellers, Steve Martin, Lenny Bruce, Mel Brooks, Groucho Marx, and Bill Cosby. In the final section are "Comedy's Tough Guys: Don Rickles, Jack Carter, Jan Murray, Buddy Hackett, Red Buttons, Shecky Green, Henny Youngman, and Rodney Dangerfield.

522. Aylesworth, Thomas G. *Hollywood Kids: Child Stars of the Silver Screen from 1903 to the Present.* New York: E. P. Dutton, 1987. 288 p. Illustrated. Filmography. Index.

Aylesworth traces the changing fortunes of the child film star and the careers of individual actors from Mary Pickford"s *Little Lord Fauntleroy*, in 1921, to *The Breakfast Club* (1985), with Molly Ringwald and Anthony Michael Hall. Selected other Hollywood kids profiled: Linda Blair, Robert Blake, Jackie Cooper, Sandra Dee, Laura Dern, Brandon De Wilde, Patty Duke, Jodie Foster, Annette Funicello, Judy Garland, Leo Gorcey, Mitzi Green, Ron Howard, Roddy McDowall, Hayley Mills, Rick Nelson, Margaret O'Brien, Mickey Rooney, Brooke Shields, Russ Tamblyn, Elizabeth Taylor, Shirley Temple, and Natalie Wood.

523. Bego, Mark, ed. *The Best of Modern Screen.* Foreword by Debbie Reynolds. New York: St. Martin's Press, 1986. 224 p. Illustrated. Paperbound.

This is an anthology of biographical articles photographically reproduced from original issues of *Modern Screen* magazine published from 1930 to 1960.

524. Bonderoff, Jason. *Soap Opera Babylon.* New York: Perigee, 1987. 144 p. Illustrated. Paperbound.

In the mold of Kenneth Anger (*Hollywood Babylon II*, above), Bonderoff writes about the indiscretions of a number of television soap opera actors. "Theme chapters" group titillating biographical vignettes on the themes of sex, ambition, AIDS, and drugs, which star, among others: Rock Hudson, Linda Evans, Tony Geary, Lorenzo Lamas, James Farentino, Victoria Principal, Gloria Loring, Susan Lucci, Diahann Carroll, and Joan Collins.

525. Borns, Betsy. *Comic Lives: Inside the World of American Stand-Up Comedy.* New York: Simon and Schuster, Fireside, 1987. 304 p. Illustrated. Paperbound.

Interviews, some of which appeared earlier in *Interview* magazine, provide the background for these sketches on some fifty of today's brightest and most entertaining comics (plus club owners, television producers, managers, etc.). Among those included are: Jay Leno, Steven Wright, Jerry Seinfeld, Paul Reiser, Emo Philips, Judy Tenuta, George Carlin, Phyllis Diller, David Brenner, Carol Leifer, Alan King, and Gilbert Gottfried.

526. Brown, Peter H., and Brown, Pamela Ann. *The MGM Girls: Behind the Velvet Curtain.* New York: St. Martin's Press, 1983. 288 p. Illustrated. Bibliography. Index.

Louis B. Mayer built his film production kingdom largely on a sorority of actresses beginning with the long forgotten Anita Stewart, whom he lured from the Vitagraph company, and continuing through the "survivors:" Ann Miller, Debbie Reynolds, Cyd Charisse, and Jane Powell. "Promise them anything, but give them only what you have to," was Mayer's philosophy. True to this doctrine, he became sensitized to the welfare of his employees only when his ego or his wallet were at issue. Other MGM survivors such as Shirley MacLaine and Elizabeth Taylor emerged from the Mayer autocracy as superstars—and relatively unscathed, while Jean Harlow, Hedy Lamarr, Barbara LaMarr, Mae Murray, Alma Rubens and Judy Garland were destroyed by his system.

527. Brown, Peter H. *Such Devoted Sisters: Those Fabulous Gabors.* New York: St. Martins Press, 1985. 287 p. Illustrated. Index.

In 1935, mother Jolie promised her three daughters ". . . that you will all be rich, famous, and marry kings." As the world knows, this was remarkably close to being prophetic given the limited number of available and willing kings. Zsa Zsa, Eva and Magda, fairly attractive and fairly talented, made a phenomenally successful business of marrying wealth. The sisters have always been close and like-minded, and while their paths to celebrity and fortune differed, each led to the same place.

528. Cahn, William, and Cahn, Rhoda. *The Great American Comedy Scene.* New York, Monarch Press, 1978. 187 p. Illustrated. Index.

Difficult to categorize since it is at once history, humor analysis, and collective biography, the Cahns' book has over 300 index entries for people who have made Americans laugh through the years in vaudeville and burlesque houses, movie theatres, Catskill resorts, Las Vegas casinos, and before millions of television screens. It is a new version of *A Pictorial History of the Great Comedians*, published in 1970.

529. Carr, Larry. *More Fabulous Faces: The Evolution and Metamorphosis of Dolores Del Rio, Myrna Loy, Carole Lombard, Bette Davis, and Katharine Hepburn.* Garden City, NY: Doubleday, 1979. 264 p. Illustrated.

This chiefly pictorial work is a sequel to Carr's *Four Fabulous Faces*, published in 1970. The book presents hundreds of black and white portraits, stills and snapshots of five women "who remain lasting symbols of a glamorous [recent] past when Hollywood was at its peak. . . ." (Introduction.) The five were chosen because they had faces which endured but also changed with the times.

530. Castell, David. *Screen Stars of the '70s.* Godalming, Surrey, England: LSP Books, 1981. 141 p. Illustrated. Paperbound.

The sixty-four film celebrities selected (all from the U.S. or the U.K.) are each described in a paragraph or so of biographical information interwoven with a narrative filmography covering their work during the decade. There are photographs with each sketch, and a section of sixteen color portraits.

531. *Close-up: The Contemporary Director.* Edited by Jon Tuska, Vicki Piekarski, and David Wilson. Metuchen, NJ: Scarecrow Press, 1981. 431 p. Illustrated. Filmography. Index.

Combined with its predecessors: *Close-up: The Hollywood Director* (below), and *Close-up: The Contract Director* (1976), this conclusion to the trilogy combines with the others to present career studies of the greatest filmmakers of the last seven decades. The ten biographies, averaging about twenty-five pages, are written by the three editors, and others. Covered are: Sidney Pollack, Sam Fuller, Sam Peckinpah, George Roy Hill, Robert Altman, Dick Richards, Hal Ashby, Peter Bogdanovich, Martin Scorsese, and Roman Polanski.

532. *Close-Up: The Hollywood Director.* Edited by Jon Tuska, Vicki Piekarski, and David Wilson. Metuchen, NJ: Scarecrow Press, 1978. 444 p. Illustrated. Filmography. Index.

Close-Up offers a definitive impression of the careers of nine directors by eleven cinema critics/historians. Each study was specially commissioned with the intent to reveal ". . . the personality of the director. . .silhouetted by his cinematic enterprises." (Introduction.) The directors: Billy Wilder, Henry King, Frank Capra, Spencer Gordon Bennet, William Wyler, William Wellman, John Huston, Douglas Sirk, and Alfred Hitchcock.

533. Cohen, Daniel, and Cohen, Susan. *Young and Famous.* New York: Pocket Books, 1987. 121 p. Illustrated. Paperbound.

Molly Ringwald, Rob Lowe, Demi Moore, Michael J. Fox, Laura Dern, Emilio Estevez, Lisa Bonet, Tom Cruise, Alyssa Milano, Ralph Macchio, Ally Sheedy, Anthony Michael Hall, Phoebe Cates, and Helena Bonham Carter are among the television and film actors described in this volume. Sketches average six pages, and each is illustrated.

534. Cole, Gerald, and Farrell, Wes. *The Fondas.* New York: St. Martin's Press, 1984. 192 p. Illustrated.

This, of course, is a collective biography about Henry, Jane and Peter Fonda, and provides a composite examination of this family of acclaimed actors. The book is lavishly illustrated with stills from their major motion pictures.

535. Collier, Denise, and Beckett, Kathleen. *Spare Ribs: Women in the Humor Biz.* New York: St. Martin's Press, 1980. 240 p. Illustrated.

Nineteen interviews with comediennes, writers, actresses, producers, and a cartoonist, each with portrait, compose this collection. Some of the women are solid successes (Phyllis Diller, Joan Rivers, Stockard Channing, Gilda Radner, Penny Marshall, Swoosie Kurtz) and others are just gaining a public following or still struggling for recognition (Zora Rasmussen, Suzanne Rand, Marjorie Gross, Marilyn Sokol, Andrea Martin). A further funny business category is that of women in non-public roles: Lynn Roth—Executive for comedy development; Judy Pioli Ervin and Eugenie Ross-Leming—Producers; Deanne Stillman, Anne Beatts, Rosie Schuster, and Gail Parent—Writers; Lee Marrs—Cartoonist.

536. Crist, Judith. *Take 22: Moviemakers on Moviemaking.* Interviews co-edited by Shirley Sealy. New York: Viking Press, 1984. 496 p. Filmography. Index.

A volume composed of twenty-two selections from taped interviews Crist has conducted during her "Film Weekends." In it, she questions directors, actors and actresses, writers and producers about their work and that part of their life away from public scrutiny. Among those interviewed: Julie Andrews, Bette Davis, Richard Dreyfuss, Blake Edwards, Burt Lancaster, Walter Matthau, Paul Newman, Sidney Pollack, Steven Spielberg, and Joanne Woodward.

537. Edmonds, I. G., and Mimura, Reiko. *The Oscar Directors.* London: Tantivy Press; San Diego, CA: A. S. Barnes, 1980. 253 p. Illustrated. Index.

Evaluations of directorial style and career biographies are given for fifty-three filmmakers awarded the annual Academy of Motion Picture Arts and Sciences "Oscar" for best director. Since the beginning of the awards in 1927, the winning pictures have shown no pattern regarding subject, message, or technique. The single, unifying element in the winning films is that they each tell a good story. The sketches are presented in chronological order from Frank Borzage for *Seventh Heaven* (1927-1928), to Robert Benton, *Kramer vs Kramer* (1979). Each has a full-page portrait of the director and is illustrated with stills from some representative films. Besides Benton, other winners from the 1970s are: Franklin J. Schaffner, *Patton*; William Friedkin, *The French Connection*; Bob Fosse, *Cabaret*; George Roy Hill, *The Sting*; Francis Ford Coppola, *The Godfather II*; Milos Forman *One Flew over the Cuckoo's Nest*; John Avildsen, *Rocky*; Woody Allen, *Annie Hall*; Michael Cimino, *The Deer Hunter*.

538. Farber, Stephen, and Green, Marc. *Hollywood Dynasties*. New York: Delilah Books, 1984. 365 p. Bibliography.

This collective biography of the powerful and influential "ruling families" in the film industry is divided into three parts and eleven chapters: from the Mayer-Selznick-Goetz clan and the Zanucks, through "the age of celebrity" (the Fondas, Ladds and Douglases) to "La Famiglia," the Coppolas. The authors write in their preface that "[their] intention is not to recapitulate [earlier] biographies but to zero in on family relationships and their impact on careers."

539. Gottfried, Martin. *In Person: The Greatest Entertainers*. New York: Abrams, 1985. 263 p. Illustrated. Bibliography. Index.

This history of entertainment serves equally well as collective biography, with information on individuals made readily accessible through the name index. Chapters are organized by either period or, most often, genre, e.g., Entertainment Stages, The First Funny Talkers, The Ziegfield Follies, Radio and the Invisible Audience, The Sex Queens, The Stand-ups, International Glitter, Popular Music and Pop Stars, Nightclub City.

540. *Great Film Directors: A Critical Anthology*. Edited by Leo Braudy and Morris Dickstein. New York: Oxford University Press, 1978. 778 p. Paperbound.

In this work, the careers of twenty-three film directors are evaluated by important critics of the medium. The number of critical essays per director ranges from two to five, with the editors providing a brief introductory biography of each, plus bibliographical references to published works, criticism and biography. Among the directors are: Robert Bresson, Frank

Capra, Charles Chaplin, Carl Theodor Dreyer, Sergei Eisenstein, Robert Flaherty, D. W. Griffith, Howard Hawks, Buster Keaton, Akira Kurosawa, Fritz Lang, and Josef von Sternberg.

541. Higham, Charles. *Celebrity Circus.* New York: Delacorte Press, 1979. 334 p. Illustrated.

This collection of interviews with film people includes twenty-three actors and twenty directors. Most of the pieces have been published previously. Each is introduced by a paragraph or two setting the interview scene or containing some fitting anecdote.

542. *Hollywood in the 1940's: The Stars' Own Stories.* Edited by Ivy Crane Wilson. Foreword by Liz Smith. New York: Frederick Ungar, 1980. 159 p. Illustrated.

Autobiographical sketches, popular with the movie-going public (and celebrity press agents), during Hollywood's "golden age," are reprinted in this book. Among the thirty-three personalities profiled are: Ronald Reagan, Ray Milland, Maureen O'Hara, Rod Cameron, Humphrey Bogart, Evelyn Keyes, Shirley Temple Agar, Burt Lancaster, Peter Lawford, Anne Blyth, Loretta Young, Irene Dunne, Johnny Weissmuller, Walt Disney, Joan Bennett, Lew Ayres, Greer Garson, Dana Andrews, Betty Grable, and Joan Crawford. "Looking back, I can only smile, which is what this book will make you do," writes Liz Smith in the Foreword.

543. Jacobson, Laurie. *Hollywood Heartbreak: The Tragic and Mysterious Deaths of Hollywood's Most Remarkable Legends.* New York: Simon and Schuster, Fireside, 1984. 248 p. Illustrated. Bibliography.

Progressing chronologically from the 1920s into the 1980s, Jacobson reviews the lives and untimely deaths (occasionally gruesome), of over thirty Hollywood celebrities.

544. Kanin, Garson. *Together Again!: The Stories of the Great Hollywood Teams.* Designed by William McCaffery. Garden City, NY: Doubleday, 1981. 255 p. Illustrated. Index.

Containing short, bountifully illustrated resumés of mostly familiar film personalities, this collective biography is a veritable super bowl of love teams (Greta Garbo—John Gilbert) song teams (Jeanette MacDonald—Nelson Eddy) comedy teams (Laurel and Hardy) buddy teams (Bob Hope—Bing Crosby) dance teams (Fred Astaire—Ginger Rogers) and new breed intellectual teams (Woody Allen—Diane Keaton). There are fourteen others, plus Kanin's choices for dream, wrong, crazy and tomorrow's teams.

545. Keylin, Arleen, and Fleischer, Suri, eds. *Hollywood Album: Lives and Deaths of Hollywoods Stars from the Pages of the New York Times.* New York: Arno Press, 1977-1979. 2 vols. Illustrated. Filmography.

Perhaps a more accurate title for this book would have been *Hollywood Obituaries,* since it is composed of over 200 death notices (often poorly reproduced from 35 mm microfilm) which originally appeared in the *New York Times.* Volume two, published in 1979, was not inspected.

546. Kobal, John. *People Will Talk.* New York: Knopf, 1985. 728 p. Illustrated. Index.

Forty-one recorded interviews with influential people in the cinema, have been transcribed for inclusion. Among these are: Gloria Swanson, Lewis Milestone, Mae West, Anita Loos, Joan Blondell, Joan Crawford, Joel McCrea, Irene Dunne, Katharine Hepburn, Loretta Young, Ann Sheridan, Joan Fontaine, Ingrid Bergman, Howard Hawks, Barbara Stanwyck, Hermes Pan, Tallulah Bankhead and Kim Stanley.

547. Lamparski, Richard. *Whatever became of — ?, All New Tenth Series: 100 Profiles of the Most Asked about Movie Stars and TV Personalities: Hundreds of Never Before Published Facts, Dates, Etc., over 200 Then-and-Now Photographs of Celebrities.* New York: Crown Publishers, 1986. 214 p. Illustrated. Paperbound.

Each individual in this "all new tenth series," is described in a two-page narrative. Each narrative is embellished with a "then," and "now" portrait. Volumes in this series have been published since 1967.

548. Maltin, Leonard. *The Great Movie Comedians: Updated Edition from Charlie Chaplin to Woody Allen.* New York: Harmony Books, 1982. 238 p. Illustrated. Filmography. Index. Paperbound.

Maltin has chosen the twenty-two movie comedians he considers unique. They possess that quality of humanity which sets them apart "from all their cut-rate colleagues." Only the final five selections may be called contemporary comedians: Bob Hope, Danny Kaye, Red Skelton, Jerry Lewis and Woody Allen. Each biographical sketch is about ten pages, including photographs and filmography. This "updated" edition is identical to the first edition of 1978.

549. Meyer, William R. *Warner Brothers Directors: The Hard-Boiled, the Comic, and the Weepers.* New Rochelle, NY: Arlington House, 1978. 381 p. Illustrated. Filmography. Index.

From the silents to films made through 1977, the careers and private lives of nineteen Warner directors are detailed in this book. The biographies are illustrated with appropriate stills and other photographs. Each concludes with a filmography. The directors: Lloyd Bacon, Busby Berkeley, Curtis Bernhardt, Alan Crosland, Michael Curtiz, Delmer Daves, William Dieterle, Peter Godfrey, Edmund Goulding, Howard Hawks, John Huston, William Keighley, Mervyn LeRoy, Anatole Litvak, Jean Negulesco, Irving Rapper, Vincent Sherman, Raoul Walsh, and William Wellman.

550. Miller, Lee O. *The Great Cowboy Stars of Movies & Television.* Introduction by Joel McCrea. New Rochelle, NY: Arlington House, 1979. 384 p. Illustrated. Index.

Only the most important actors doing significant work in the genre are corralled in this round-up. The biographies are about five pages, with photographs and credits. George O'Brien, Col. Tim McCoy, Lash LaRue, William "Hopalong Cassidy" Boyd, Tom Mix, Henry Fonda, Roy Rogers, Lorne

Greene, James Garner, Gary Cooper, and John Wayne are among the forty-three included.

551. Miller, Lynn F. *The Hand That Holds the Camera: Interviews with Women Film and Video Directors*. Garland Reference Library of the Humanities, Vol. 688. New York: Garland, 1988. 271 p. Index. ***

552. Miller, Robert Milton. *Star Myths: Show Business Biographies on Film*. Metuchen, NJ: Scarecrow, 1983. 405 p. Illustrated. Bibliography. Filmography. Index.

Over 125 theatrical and television biographies, screened between 1930-1982 and depicting the lives of American show business celebrities, have been analyzed according to several criteria. Eschewing aesthetics-based evaluation of the films, Miller supplies considerable biographical content through his historical and critical comparisons. A filmography and a celebrity and motion picture index increase reference capability.

553. Moore, Dick. *Twinkle, Twinkle, Little Star: But Don't Have Sex or Take the Car*. New York: Harper & Row, 1984. 303 p. Illustrated. Index.

Moore, himself a little star in the *Our Gang* comedies and other films, has written of his experiences and those of thirty-one other Hollywood child actors in what Jane Powell said was ". . . a catharsis for [Moore] and possibly for the rest of us." Among those profiled: Jackie Coogan, Jackie Cooper, Peggy Ann Garner, Lillian Gish, Spanky McFarland, Margaret O'Brien, Donald O'Connor, Mickey Rooney, Ann Rutherford, Dean Stockwell, Shirley Temple, Jane Withers, and Natalie Wood.

554. Mordden, Ethan. *Movie Star: A Look at the Women Who Made Hollywood*. New York: St. Martin's Press, 1983. 296 p. Illustrated. Bibliography. Index.

This collective biography presents sixty-nine women whom Mordden sees ". . . as unique for a variety of reasons." The author has grouped together many of the actresses, resulting in twelve composite biographies, and four which stand alone: Bette Davis, Janet Gaynor, Katharine Hepburn and Mae West.

555. Mostel, Kate, et al. *170 Years of Show Business*. New York: Random House, 1978. 175 p. Illustrated.

The years to which the title refers are the combined total accumulated by long-time show business and personal friends, the Mostels (Kate and Zero) and the Gilfords (Madeline and Jack). While this is a two-family, four-person chronicle, the wives were its inspiration; all four contributed, and Kate Mostel was author and spokesperson. Publication was postponed, almost abandoned, at the death of Zero Mostel, September 8, 1977.

556. Norman, Barry. *The Film Greats*. Sevenoaks, Kent, Eng.: Hodder and Stoughton; London: British Broadcasting, 1985. 262 p. Illustrated. Index.

Five superstar actors, one superstar mogul, and an anecdotal appraisal of Hollywood today are the subjects of this work based on the BBC TV series, *The Hollywood Greats*. Precursors, also based on Norman's BBC documentaries are his: *The Hollywood Greats* and, *The Movie Greats* (below). Presented in this volume are: David Niven, Steve McQueen, Henry Fonda, John Wayne, Bing Crosby, and Cecil B. de Mille.

557. Norman, Barry. *The Hollywood Greats*. New York: F. Watts, 1979. 272 p. Illustrated. Index.

Based on the BBC TV series of the same title, this volume contains ten short biographies of film stars of the "Golden Age" (1920 to 1950). (Sequels, *The Film Greats*, and *The Movie Greats*, also by Norman, and also adapted from his television documentaries, are described above and below.) The book's subjects are all deceased, in keeping with Norman's premise that ". . . when the star is not only great but also late, a much closer approximation to the truth emerges." In the order of their appearance: Clark Gable, Errol Flynn, Spencer Tracy, Gary Cooper, Humphrey Bogart, Joan Crawford, Ronald Colman, Jean Harlow, Judy Garland, and Charles Laughton.

558. Norman, Barry. *The Movie Greats*. Sevenoaks, Kent, Eng.: Hodder and Stoughton; London: British Broadcasting, 1981. 319 p. Illustrated. Index.

Nine film stars, some British, some American but all owing their stardom to having worked in Hollywood, are featured in this work—based on and developed from BBC TV documentaries by Norman. (Entries for two other Norman adaptations, *The Hollywood Greats*, and *The Film Greats* are above.) The length of the sketches, including illustrations, is about thirty pages. The biographees: Marilyn Monroe, Peter Finch, Groucho Marx, Jack Hawkins, Edward G. Robinson, Robert Donat, Gracie Fields, Leslie Howard, and Charlie Chaplin.

559. Parish, James Robert, et al. *The Forties Gals*. Westport, CT: Arlington House, 1980. 463 p. Illustrated. Index.

The lives and careers of seven women who achieved their greatest film success in the 1940s, are discussed in lengthy, illustrated sketches, each concluding with a detailed filmography. The actresses in the (alphabetical) order used in the book: Lauren Bacall, Susan Hayward, Ida Lupino, Virginia Mayo, Ann Sheridan, Esther Williams, and Jane Wyman.

560. Parish, James Robert, et al. *The Funsters*. New Rochelle, NY: Arlington House, 1979. 752 p. Illustrated. Index.

The sixty-odd funsters chosen for this work are the people who, unfailingly, have made movie audiences laugh. Each has a chapter with photographs and details about personal life, career, and a complete listing of feature films giving studio and year of release. In addition to the comedic greats such as Charles Chaplin, Buster Keaton, W. C. Fields, Lucille Ball, Milton Berle, Jack Benny, Phyllis Diller, Danny Kaye, and Woody Allen, are the lesser-knowns: Mischa Auer, Mary Boland, Judy Canova, Arthur Lake, Harry Langdon, Thelma Todd, S. Z. Sakall, Charlie Ruggles, Ben Turpin, George Sidney, Mabel Normand, Edna Mae Oliver, and Polly Moran.

561. Parish, James Robert; Mank, Gregory W.; and Stanke, Don E. *The Hollywood Beauties*. Research associates,

John Robert Cocchi, et al. New Rochelle, NY: Arlington House, 1978. 476 p. Illustrated. Filmography. Index.

Another among several Parish biographies of film stars (see above/below), *The Hollywood Beauties* presents seven of the screen's loveliest actresses in lengthy, illustrated sketches averaging seventy pages. Time coverage is from the 20s through the 70s. Each sketch concludes with a meticulous filmography. The beauties: Dolores Del Rio, Kay Francis, Ava Gardner, Jean Harlow, Grace Kelly, Elizabeth Taylor, and Lana Turner.

562. Peary, Danny, ed. *Close-Ups: Intimate Profiles of Movie Stars by Their Co-Stars, Directors, Screenwriters and Friends.* New York: Workman Publishing, 1978. 606 p. Illustrated. Filmography. Index. Paperbound.

In this collective biography, there are over 160 profiles ranging in length from two to five pages. Each is illustrated with several photographs, usually movie stills. An appendix contains a complete filmography for each star.

563. Pettigrew, Terence. *British Film Character Actors: Great Names and Memorable Moments.* London: David & Charles; Totowa, NJ: Barnes & Noble, 1982. 208 p. Illustrated. Index.

Pettigrew's work is comprised of illustrated sketches, each approximately four pages long, in which one finds career information on some sixty (male) British actors. The author makes a distinction between "actors" and "characters": Alec Guinness, John Mills, Denholm Elliott, Richard Attenborough, Laurence Olivier, Peter Sellers, and Peter Ustinov exemplify the former, while his "characters" are players ". . . who give us in film after film minor variations of the same persona": Harry Andrews, Ian Carmichael, Trevor Howard, and Alastair Sim, among others. Each of the sketches concludes with a filmography.

564. Pitts, Leonard, Jr. *The Glamour Girls of Hollywood.* Edited by Mary J. Edrei. Cresskill, NJ: Sharon Starbook, 1984. 95 p. Illustrated. Paperbound.

Short biographies of a dozen screen beauties are presented. Each sketch is illustrated with publicity portraits and movie stills. The glamour girls in chapter order: Greta Garbo, Gloria Swanson, Ava Gardner, Marlene Dietrich, Betty Grable, Mae West, Lana Turner, Ingrid Bergman, Marilyn Monroe, Elizabeth Taylor, Grace Kelly, and Natalie Wood.

565. Pitts, Michael R. *Horror Film Stars*. Jefferson, NC: McFarland, 1981. 324 p. Bibliography. Index.

Fifteen "stars" and twenty-eight "players" are profiled in this collective biography. Each sketch contains a listing of the player's theatrical and television films. The stars: Lionel Atwill, John Carradine, Lon Chaney Sr., Lon Chaney Jr., Peter Cushing, Boris Karloff, Christopher Lee, Peter Lorre, Bela Lugosi, Paul Naschy, Vincent Price, Claude Rains, Basil Rathbone, Barbara Steele and, George Zucco.

566. Pye, Michael, and Myles, Lynda. *The Movie Brats: How the Film Generation Took over Hollywood*. New Yory: Holt, Rinehart and Winston, 1979. 273 p. Illustrated. Filmography. Bibliography.

The authors have examined the careers and films of several of the successful new generation of cine-literate American filmmakers within a historical, industrial and sociological context. Pye was film critic for the Edinburgh *Scotsman*, and Myles is director of the Edinburgh Film Festival. The biographees are: Francis Coppola, George Lucas, Brian DePalma, John Milius, Martin Scorsese, and Steven Spielberg.

567. Reed, Rex. *Travolta to Keaton*. New York: Morrow, 1979. 222 p. Illustrated.

Thirty-three show folk, Lassie, and a city (Las Vegas), are treated in this Reed read. Selected people in the order of their appearance: Geraldine Fitzgerald, Marthe Keller, Liza Minnelli, Melina Mercouri, Jacqueline Bisset, Susan Sarandon, Burt Lancaster, Geraldine Page, Lauren Hutton, and Jon Voight.

568. Robinson, Jeffrey. *Teamwork*. London, New York: Proteus Books, 1982. 127 p. Illustrated.

In the 1950s, comedy teams were highly popular with movie patrons, and this collective work includes a selection of the best. A film was yet another vehicle for a previously established team, such as Laurel & Hardy or The Marx Brothers. Some were strictly "movie" teams: Hope, Crosby & Lamour, and Lemmon & Matthau. The biographies are about a dozen pages long, embellished by many illustrations (stills and posters, some in color) and a concluding filmography. Teams not previously mentioned: The Ritz Brothers, Abbott & Costello, and Martin & Lewis.

569. Rothel, David. *The Singing Cowboys*. South Brunswick, NJ, New York: A. S. Barnes, 1978. 272 p. Illustrated. Bibliography. Index.

Rothel limits the scope of this collective biography to the singing cowboy stars of feature films. His top three: Gene Autry, Roy Rogers, and Rex Allen. Others in the OK Corral are Tex Ritter, Eddie Dean, Jimmy Wakely, and Monty Hale. Each sketch is fairly lengthy, well-illustrated, and concludes with a filmography and discography. "The Unsung Singing Cowboys," is a chapter of short sketches about individuals who never achieved wide popularity.

570. Rovin, Jeff. *TV Babylon*. New York: New American Library, Signet, 1984. 253 p. Illustrated. Paperbound.

Several dozen television personalities are given the sensationalized *Hollywood Babylon* treatment in this collection. Some of the chosen Babylonians are: Joan Collins, Inger Stevens, Nick Adams, Freddie Prinze, John Belushi, Brenda Benet, George Reeves, Dave Garroway, Peter Duel, Ernie Kovacs, Bruce Lee, Sal Mineo, Farrah Fawcett, James Garner, Daniel J. Travanti, Sid Caesar, Erik Estrada, Pernell Roberts, Lorne Greene, Johnny Carson, John Travolta, and Suzanne Somers.

571. St. Johns, Adela Rogers. *Love, Laughter, and Tears: My Hollywood Story*. Garden City, NY: Doubleday, 1978. 342 p. Illustrated.

St. Johns, many years a Hollywood columnist, contributes anecdotal recollections about, among others: Marion Davies, William Randolph Hearst, Greta Garbo, John Gilbert, Ingrid Bergman, Gary Cooper, Jean Harlow, William Powell, Mary Pickford, Gloria Swanson, Clark Gable, Douglas Fairbanks, Charles Chaplin, and Cary Grant.

572. Silverman, Stephen M. *Public Spectacles*. New York: E. P. Dutton, 1981. 241 p. Index.

Public Spectacles is a picaresque tale of entertainment reporter Silverman's encounters with dozens of the celebrated of Hollywood and Broadway. Since the chapters are unstructured, the index is most useful in discovering anecdotal sketches about: Woody Allen, Robert Redford, Bette Midler, Lily Tomlin, John Travolta, Bob Fosse, Yul Brynner, and Miss Piggy.

573. Sinyard, Neil. *Directors: The All-Time Greats*. New York: Gallery Books, 1985. 94 p. Illustrated.

"Guided by a sense of film history, which necessitates certain inclusions, and by personal taste," Sinyard divides his chosen directors by category: pioneers (up to 1929), stylists and storytellers (1930-1960), artists (since 1960), and new voices (since 1980). There are approximately forty sketches averaging two illustrated pages in length and describing the career, development, film themes/styles, and filmmaking strengths and weaknesses. Included, among others: King Vidor, Erich von Stroheim, Charles Chaplin, D. W. Griffith, Nicholas Ray, George Cukor, Howard Hawks, Joseph L. Mankiewicz, William Wyler, Akira Kurosawa, Joseph Losey, Luchino Visconti, Werner Herzog, Nagisa Oshima, Nicolas Roeg, and Steven Spielberg.

574. Smith, Dian G. *American Filmmakers Today*. New York: Julian Messner, 1983. 166 p. Illustrated. Bibliography. Index.

Smith makes the distinction between "director" and "filmmaker"; the latter exercises control of the picture from conception to release, while the former functions as little more than a studio hired hand. There are nine contemporary Hollywood filmmakers whose stories are told: Woody Allen, Robert Altman, Mel Brooks, Francis Coppola, Brian De Palma, George Lucas, Paul Mazursky, Martin Scorsese, and Steven Spielberg. The book concludes with observations concerning the slow acceptance of women and blacks into the filmmaking ranks.

575. Smith, Ron. *The Stars of Stand-Up Comedy: A Bibliographical Encyclopedia.* Garland Reference Library of the Humanities, Vol. 564. New York: Garland, 1986. 227 p. Illustrated.

Approximately 100 comedians/comediennes, individuals and teams, are presented in sketches of a page or two, ". . . balancing biography, jokes, facts, insight and evaluation." Stand-up comedians are defined as those who practice the ". . . art of getting up in front of people and being funny." At the conclusion of each sketch is a list of the subject's credits in the various media, and a bibliography. Since they only did an occasional solo sketch or monologue, Jackie Gleason, Sid Caesar, and Danny Kaye were excluded.

576. *Soap Stars: America's 31 Favorite Daytime Actors Speak for Themselves.* Edited by Dianna Whitley, and Ray Manzella. Photographs by Dianna Whitley. Garden City, NY: Doubleday, Dolphin, 1985. 186 p. Illustrated. Paperbound.

The televised soap opera became acceptable, legitimate drama around 1980, when the actors on these shows began to receive corresponding critical notice and wide publicity. Those chosen for inclusion ". . . have proven themselves as the most popular in the genre." The autobiographical sketches are three to four pages in length, with portraits.

577. Strait, Raymond. *Hollywood's Children.* New York: St. Martin's Press, 1982. 209 p. Illustrated.

In this collective biography, Strait has assembled material on the lives of 12 children of celebrity parents: Tracy Keenan Wynn, Suzanne LaCock, Peter Ford, Patricia Johnston Towers, Michael Riva, Julia Warren, Marty Haggard, Jack Haley Jr., Diana Markes, Perry Anthony, Margaret Whiting, and William Katt.

578. Strait, Raymond. *Star Babies*. New York: St. Martin's Press, 1979. 255 p. Illustrated.

This is the first of Strait's collective biographies of children of celebrity parents. The book contains 14 biographies, each about 20 pages including photographs, on the following: Colleen Lanza, Lorna Luft, Perry Damone, Laury Boone, Betty Mix, Tommy Howard, Danny Selznick, Chris Costello, Maura Dhu Greaves, Jeff Bridges, Meredith MacRae, Miguel Ferrer, Ellen Geer, and Alicia Previn.

579. Strick, Philip. *Great Movie Actresses*. Foreword by John Russell Taylor. New York: Beech Tree Books, 1985. 256 p. Illustrated. Index.

The popular Japanese movie magazine, *Star* is the source for the hundreds of studio-supplied black and white portraits and stills which constitute the raison d'être for this collective biography of some 270 international female stars. Arrangement is by decade with occasional digressions, i.e., "Pin-Up Parade," "New Faces," and "Pick of the Tops." Strick's (14) picks: Greta Garbo, Marlene Dietrich, Ingrid Bergman, Katharine Hepburn, Vivien Leigh, Sophia Loren, Claudia Cardinale, Audrey Hepburn, Diane Keaton, Jean Seberg, Anouk Aimée, Monica Vitti, Elizabeth Taylor, and Marilyn Monroe. The biographical sketches, little more than amplified picture captions, provide historical background and an assessment of each actress's career.

580. Sweet, Jeffrey. *Something Wonderful Right Away*. New York: Avon, Discus, 1978. 383 p. Illustrated. Paperbound.

Sweet attempts to answer the question, "why does having performed with an improvisational comedy troupe seem to increase one's chances of artistic and commercial achievement?" The careers of dozens of successful graduates of The Compass, and The Second City troupes are explored. Acknowledged omissions include Peter Boyle, John Belushi, and Elaine May.

581. Vadim, Roger. *Bardot, Deneuve, Fonda.* Translated from the French by Melinda Camber Porter. New York: Simon and Schuster, 1986. 328 p. Illustrated.

    ·   "Brigitte, Catherine and Jane: three modern fairy-tale princesses. But fairy tales are also tales of cruelty, although fortunately they usually have happy endings. I want to speak of these adolescents, these young girls, and who they were before they became fairy-tale princesses." (From Vadim's Preface.)

582. Wanamaker, Marc, ed. *The Hollywood Reporter Star Profiles.* New York: Gallery Books, 1984. Illustrated. Index.

    From yesterday's idols to current superstars, in this book the lives and careers of ninety-one major film personalities are presented in candid biographical sketches and hundreds of photographs.

583. Weis, Elisabeth, ed. *The National Society of Film Critics on the Movie Star.* New York: Viking Press, 1981. 402 p. Illustrated. Index.

    About seventy stars are included in the main biographical section. This part is preceded by one on the business and craft of stardom. All the material has previously appeared in film reviews, book reviews, obituaries and other pieces by the various members of the society. The biographies average four pages in length, and many have photographs.

584. Welch, Julie. *Leading Men.* Design by Louise Brody. Foreword by Jane Russell. New York: Villard Books, 1985. 224 p. Illustrated. Index.

This sumptuously illustrated work (photographs from the Kobol collection) is arranged by period: "The Silent Era," "The War Years," "Modern Times." It profiles in a page or two, dozens of Hollywood's best-loved lovers. A selection of these men, in reverse chronological order: Sean Penn, Matt Dillon, Jeremy Irons, Donald Sutherland, Warren Beatty, James Dean, Burt Lancaster, Errol Flynn, Charles Boyer, Leslie Howard, James Cagney, John Barrymore, Douglas Fairbanks Sr., and Rudolph Valentino.

585. Wilkerson, Tichi, and Borie, Marcia. *The Hollywood Reporter: The Golden Years*. New York: Coward-McCann, 1984. 356 p. Illustrated. Index.

Based on stories, reviews, gossip items, and features contained in over 7,800 issues of *The Hollywood Reporter*, as published between September 3, 1930, and December 31, 1959. This material is augmented by reporters' files and interviews. Finally, there are reprints of forty-seven celebrity byline pieces written by the stars exclusively for *The Reporter's* special editions, beginning in 1930.

586. Wilkie, Jane. *Confessions of an Ex-Fan Magazine Writer*. Garden City, NY: Doubleday, 1981. 280 p. Illustrated. Index.

Wilkie, a feature writer for over thirty-five years for such fan magazines as *Photoplay, Modern Screen,* and *Motion Picture*, writes about the private lives of scores of stars. She explains her sometimes devious methods of obtaining celebrity interviews. Among those included: Lucille Ball, Katharine Hepburn, Bette Davis, Clark Gable, Rock Hudson, June Allyson, Ronald Reagan, Tony Curtis, John Wayne, Jane Fonda, and Elizabeth Taylor.

Chapter 12
Periodicals

587. *After Dark*. New York: Dance Magazine, Inc., vol. 1-, 1968-. (Monthly)

Continues: *Ballroom Dance Magazine* (1960-1968). Covers all the performing arts. Indexed selectively by: *Media Review Digest*.

588. *American Film*. New York: American Film Institute and the AMS Foundation for the Arts, Sciences and Humanities, vol. 1-, 1975-. (10 yearly)

Coverage of current motion pictures and personalities. Indexed (some selectively) by: *Art Index, Film Literature Index, Humanities Index, Magazine Index, Book Review Index, Index to Book Reviews in the Humanities, Media Review Digest, Magazine Article Summaries*.

589. *The Best of Daytime TV*. New York: Sterlings' Magazines, vol. 1-, 1981?-. (5 issues yearly)

Contains two-page, illustrated biographical sketches. "Bonus color pin-ups," of soap opera stars.

590. *The Best of Soap Opera People*. New York: Tempo Publishing Co., no. 1-, 1987-. (Irregular)

In the initial issue seen, there were sixteen interviews with actors, plus complete cast lists for the soap operas.

591. *The Big Bopper.* Burbank, CA: Lauffer Publishing, vol. 1-, 1988(?)-. (Monthly)

A new sibling of Lauffer's *Bop* (below), this teen magazine publishes short biographical articles on this month's "hot" actors and musicians. Two departments in the August, 1988 issue: "We've got your number" (entertainers' addresses), and "Hollywood heartbeat" (news notes and gossip.)

592. *Black Beat.* New York: Lexington Library, vol. 14-, 1983-. (Monthly)

See entry 1433, for annotation.

593. *Bright Lights.* Los Angeles: G. Morris, vol. 1-, 1977-. (Quarterly)

Primarily criticism, but includes American filmmakers. Indexed by: *Film Literature Index.*

594. *Cineaste.* New York: G. Crowdus, vol. 1-, 1967-. (Quarterly)

Every issue has several interviews with people in the motion picture industry. Indexed (some selectively) by: *Film Literature Index, Alternative Press Index, Media Review Digest.*

595. *Cinema Canada.* Montreal: Canadian Society of Cinematographers, no. 32-, 1967-. (Bimonthly)

Continues: *Canadian Cinematography* (1961-1967). Has supplement: *Cinema Canada News Update.* A typical issue will have interviews with individuals in the industry. Indexed (some selectively) by: *Magazine Index, Film Literature Index, Canadian Periodical Index, Media Review Digest.*

596. *Cinema Journal.* Champaign, IL: University of Illinois Press, 1979?-. (Quarterly)

Continues: *Journal of the Society of Cinematologists* (1966/67-1978), and is the official publication of the Society for Cinema Studies. Contains scholarly critical and historical material, sometimes on individual filmmakers. Indexed (some selectively) by: *Arts and Humanities Citation Index,*

International Index to Film Periodicals, Art Index, Film Literature Index, Writings on American History.

597. *Cinema Papers.* North Melbourne, Victoria, Australia, Cinema Papers, vol. 1-, 1974-. (Bimonthly)

Provides coverage of Australian, and some international film industry news and features, including interviews with directors, actors and screenwriters. Indexed (some selectively) by: *Film Literature Index, APAIS, Australian Public Affairs Information Service, Media Review Digest.*

598. *Classic Images.* Muscatine, IA: Muscatine Journal, no. 67?-, 1980-. (Bimonthly)

Continues *Classic Film/Video Images* (1978-1980?), *Classic Film Collector* (1966-1978), and *8mm Collector.* Contains information on the home entertainment field, including pieces on film personalities, and the collection of movie memorabilia. Indexed (some selectively) by: *Film Literature Index, Media Review Digest.*

599. *Continental Film & Video Review.* Essex, England, Bellbright Investments, vol. 27-, 1980-. (Monthly)

Continues: *Continental Film Review* (1952-1980). Publication status is currently unknown. An amalgam of sometimes titillating photographs and intelligent articles about cinema in Europe.

600. *Daily Variety.* Hollywood, CA: Daily Variety, Ltd., vol. 1-, 1933-. (Daily)

"News of the show world." No connection with the weekly, *Variety* (below). Similarities in frequency, content, and place of publication with *The Hollywood Reporter* (below). Publishes news and features about the people and business of entertainment.

601. *Daytime Digest Plus Night-Time.* New York: Sterlings' Magazines, vol. 1-, 1987?-. (Monthly)

In the June, 1987 issue examined, there were sixteen "real life interviews" of soap opera actors, and an in-depth look at the show and stars of "General Hospital."

602. *Daytime TV.* New York: Sterlings' Magazines, vol. 1-, 1970-. (Frequency varies)

Has feature biographies, and a regular department: "Confidential Close-ups."

603. *Daytime TV Presents.* New York: Sterlings' Magazines, vol. 1-, 1982?-.

Unable to determine the frequency of publication. Sections in the May, 1987 issue examined (the "Super Special") contained biographical information about soap opera actors, color pin-ups, stories about the various shows, and guides to the exploits of the characters.

604. *Drama-Logue.* Hollywood, CA: Bill Bordy Enterprises, vol. 1-, 1969-. (Weekly)

This is a service which reports who is casting whom, and other news of people in the entertainment industry.

605. *Emmy.* Burbank, CA: Academy of Television Arts & Sciences, vol. 1-, 1979-. (Bimonthly)

Running title: *Emmy Magazine.* Contains interviews and profiles, eschewing the fanzine-type items. Indexed by: *Access.*

606. *Film.* London: British Federation of Film Societies, vol. 1-, 1954-. (Monthly)

Contains critical articles about cinema genres and filmmakers. Indexed (some selectively) by: *Film Literature Index, Media Review Digest.* "Self" indexed: 1954-1961.

607. *Film Bill.* New York: George Fenmore Associates, Film Bill, vol. 1-, 1970-. (Monthly)

Publishes stories about movie stars, filmmakers, memorabilia, trends, and individual films.

608. *Film Comment.* New York: Lorien Productions, vol. 1-, 1962-. (Bimonthly)

Continues: *Vision* (1962). This is a publication of the Film Society of Lincoln Center containing a broad spectrum of articles in the field including interviews/profiles. Indexed (some selectively) by: *Magazine Index, Film Literature Index, Readers' Guide to Periodical Literature, Art Index, Magazine Article Summaries, Book Review Index, Media Review Digest.*

609. *Films and Filming.* London: Brevet Publishing, Ltd. vol. 1-, 1954-. (Monthly)

Absorbed: *Focus on Film.* Illustrated features on (preponderantly British and American) actors and/or directors. Indexed in: *Film Literature Index.*

610. *Films in Review.* New York: National Board of Review of Motion Pictures, vol. 1-, 1950-. (10 issues yearly)

Supersedes: *New Movies.* Comprehensive biographical articles on stars (including detailed filmographies) appear in each issue. Indexed (some selectively) by: *Film Literature Index, Art Index, Book Review Index, Reference Sources, Index to Book Reviews in the Humanities, Media Review Digest.* "Self" indexed: 1950-1969.

611. *The Hollywood Reporter.* Hollywood, CA: Hollywood Reporter, Inc., vol. 1-, 1930-. (Daily)

Frequency and content invite some comparison with the *Daily Variety* (above). Contains news, columns, film and television movie reviews, gross film receipts, and obituaries.

612. *The Hollywood Reporter TV Special.* Hollywood, CA: Hollywood Reporter, Inc., vol. 1-, 1979-.

Continues: *TeleVisions.* Cover title: *TV Special.*

613. *Hollywood Studio Magazine.* Studio City, CA: R. B. Productions, vol. 1-, 1957-. (Monthly)

"Then and Now," inscribed on the cover of this glossy, heavily-illustrated magazine indicates its nostalgic predisposition—particularly for the 1920s through the 1950s. Occasional special numbers are dedicated to an actor. A large classified section and "Collector's Corner" provides useful locations for, and some indication of value of movie memorabilia.

614. *The Journal of Popular Film and Television: JPF&T.* Bowling Green, OH: The Journal, vol. 7-, 1978-. (Quarterly)

Continues: *Journal of Popular Film* (1972-1977). A scholarly journal covering commercial motion pictures and television, including the creative people in these media. Indexed (some selectively) by: *Art Index, Film Literature Index, America: History and Life, Book Review Index, Historical Abstracts, Media Review Digest, Reference Sources, Writings on American History.*

615. *Modern Screen.* Dunellen, NJ: Syndicate Publishing Co., vol. 1-, 1930-. (Monthly)

Continues *Modern Screen Magazine* (1930). Provides a popular approach to film stars and other motion picture news.

616. *Movie Collector's World.* Iola, WI: Krause Publications, no. 200-, 1984-. (Biweekly)

Continues *Movie and Film Collector's World,* (1983-1984), and *Film Collector's World* (1983). Tabloid format for an audience of film and video collectors. Issues contain interviews and profiles.

617. *Movie Mirror.* New York: Sterling's Magazines, 1979-. (Bimonthly)

Continues: *Movie Mirror* (193?-1941). Continues in part: *Photoplay Combined with Movie Mirror* (Macfadden, 1941-1946). Popular features on movies and movie people. The "special collector's edition" examined (May, 1987), contained a 1937-1987 retrospective of the magazine.

618. *Movietone News.* Seattle, WA: Seattle Film Society, no. 18-, 1972-. (10 issues yearly)

Publication status is in question. Presents thoughtful pieces on current film topics, including directors and actors. Indexed by: *Film Literature Index.*

619. *On Cable.* Norwalk, CT: On Cable Publications, vol. 1-, 1980-. (Monthly)

On Cable is the program guide for cable television viewers. It is similar to *TV Guide* (below), in that it includes listings of programs, reviews, letters, and articles about the medium and its stars.

620. *On Film.* Santa Barbara, CA: Film Society of the University of California, Santa Barbara, vol. 1-, 1970-. (Quarterly)

Imprint varies: Los Angeles: College of Fine Arts, UCLA. Scholarly content concerning all aspects of film study, including interviews with creative people in and outside the field. Indexed by: *Film Literature Index.*

621. *Photoplay.* New York: Macfadden Publications, vol. 10-, 1916-. (Monthly)

Continues: *Photoplay Magazine* (1911-1913). Publication suspended, 1913-1916. Continues: *Photoplay*, Chicago (1916-1940). Continues in part: *Photoplay Combined with Movie Mirror* (1941-1946). Split from: *Movie Mirror.* Continues: *Photoplay* (1946), (1946-1977). Merged with *TV Mirror*, to form: *Photoplay with TV Mirror*, (1977-1980?-). Split from: *TV Mirror* in 1980?-. Throughout its long and trend-sensitive history, *Photoplay* has continued publication of fan-type feature articles on movie stars; biographies and the latest news about screen personalities.

622. *Photoplay Movies & Video.* London: Photoplay/M.A.P. Ltd., vol. 1-, 1950-. (Monthly)

Absorbed: *Films Illustrated.* Running title: *Photoplay.* "The Cinema and Home Screen Monthly." Articles have an emphasis on commercial (most often, American) cinema and television.

Biographical articles focus on major, contemporary stars, e.g., Eddie Murphy, Tom Selleck. Indexed by: *Film Literature Index.*

623. *Photo Screen.* New York: Sterlings' Magazines, vol. 1-, 1965-. (Bimonthly)

In each issue, *Photo Screen* has several illustrated articles on film stars and "wanna-be" stars.

624. *Premier.* New York: Premier Publishing, vol. 1-, 1987-. (Monthly)

From publishing colossus Rupert Murdoch comes this slick English-language version of the French movie magazine of the same name. Its intent is to provide general audience coverage of feature films and videos. To this end there are features on making and financing movies, story origins, and casting. There are also thoughtful articles about movie people, e.g., "Cher, Seriously," and "Louis Malle," in the February, 1988 issue. Indexed by: *Access.*

625. *Prevue.* Reading, PA: Prevue Entertainment, vol. 1-, 1981-. (5 issues yearly)

Variant title: *Mediascene Preview.* Continues: *Mediascene* (1976?-1980), and *Comixscene* (1972-1976?). The issue examined has nine interviews with film actors (established stars and lesser names), and four motion picture previews—all lavishly illustrated in color. Curiously, this worthy material, much of it written by editor/publisher/designer, James Steranko, is found interspersed with scores of titillating illustrated advertisements for "Fabulous foreign femme-filled foto books"; and "A pulsing parade of pin-ups and paperdolls." These kinds of publications are the only products advertised in the magazine.

626. *Right On!* Teaneck, NJ: D.S. Magazines, Inc., vol. 1-, 1971-. (Monthly)

See entry 1475, for annotation.

627. *Screen Actor Hollywood.* Los Angeles, CA: Screen Actors' Guild, vol. 7-, 1986-. (Quarterly)

Continues: *Screen Actor* (1959-1986). This official publication of the Screen Actors' Guild covers the film industry from a practitioner perspective. Indexed by: *Film Literature Index.*

628. *Screen International.* London: King Publication, no. 1-, 1912-. (Weekly)

Continues: *Screen International & Cinema TV Today,* and *Cinema TV Today.* "The paper of the entertainment industry," presenting reviews, news, and comment on British show business via the electronic media.

629. *Screen Stars.* New York: Interstate Publishing, vol. 1-, 1944-. (Monthly)

Illustrated (some color) star biographies and general film news and publicity hyperbole for the fan.

630. *Show Business.* New York: Leo Schull Publications, 1950- . (Weekly)

Formerly: *Actors Cues* (1941-1949). Subtitle: "The Entertainment Weekly." Contains feature articles, book and play reviews.

631. *Sight and Sound.* London: British Film Institute, vol. 1-, 1932-. (Quarterly)

Thorough, scholarly articles, news reports, film reviews, and much more concerning the international film milieu. Includes in-depth interviews. Indexed (some selectively) by: *Art Index, Film Literature Index, Humanities Index, Book Review Index, Index to Book Reviews in the Humanities, Media Review Digest.*

632. *Soap Opera Digest.* New York: Network Publishing, vol. 1-, 19??-. (Biweekly)

Prevalence of articles/interviews about daytime (and nighttime) personalities, and tie-in features, i.e., health or beauty with soap opera personalities. Each issue brings story synopsis, special interest features, and industry news.

633. *Soap Opera People.* New York: Tempo Publishing Co., vol. 1-, 19(?)-. (Monthly)

Features short interviews with the actors in daytime drama. These are in combination with full-color pin-ups and black and white photographs. The July, 1988 issue examined contained interviews with James Depaiva, Noelle Beck, Melanie Smith, Beth Ehlers, and twelve others.

634. *Soap Opera Stars.* New York: Sterlings' Magazines , vol. 1-, 1984-. (Bimonthly)

Another star-studded Sterling fan magazine containing features on soap opera actors. The March, 1988 issue featured a piece titled: "Daytime Dynamite Dozen" (of TV "hunks").

635. *Soap Opera Update.* New York: Soap Opera Update Magazine, vol. 1-, 1988-. (Triweekly)

The contents of the premier number include articles on the actors, Charles Keating and Susan Lucci. Regular features: "Scene Around Town," and soap plots synopsis.

636. *The Soap Set: The Best of Daytime and Nighttime.* Beverly Hills, CA: Coast to Coast, vol. 1-, 1986?-. (6 issues yearly)

The television soap opera fan will find articles, regular departments, and stories (with pinup pictures) about the actors.

637. *Splice.* New York: Ira Friedman, Inc., no. 1-, 1987?-. (Bimonthly)

Targeting the hip adolescent and early adult audience, *Splice* offers articles and interviews with entertainers, e.g., Kiefer Sutherland, Michael J. Fox, and Phoebe Cates in the January, 1988 issue.

638. *Teen Beat.* New York: Macfadden Publications, vol. 1-, 1976-. (Monthly)

"Hunk of the month," "Interview of the month," and "Starviews: hot personality profiles," are regular departments of this teen fan magazine. There are short, heavily illustrated feature bios of younger (mostly male) film and television stars.

639. *Tiger Beat.* Cresskill, NJ: D.S. Magazines, Inc., vol. 1-, 1965-. (Monthly)

See entry 1485, for annotation.

640. *Tiger Beat Special.* Cresskill, NJ: D.S. Magazines, Inc., vol. 1-, 1987?-. (Quarterly)

See entry 1486, for annotation.

641. *Tiger Beat Star.* Cresskill, NJ: D.S. Magazines, Inc., vol. 1-, 1983-.

See entry 1487, for annotation.

642. *TV and Movie Screen.* New York: Sterlings' Magazines, vol. 1-, 1957-. (Bimonthly)

Contents include popular-audience stories about the stars of films and television.

643. *TV Radio Mirror.* Chicago: Macfadden Publications, vol. 1-, 1933-. (Monthly)

Title varies: *Radio Mirror* (1933-1939), *Radio and Television Mirror* (1939-1942; 1948-1951), *Radio Romances* (1945), *Radio Television Mirror* (1951), and *TV Mirror* (1951-1954). Women or homemakers compose the audience for this media magazine covering network radio and TV and its personalities. It also offers other feature stories and regular advice departments.

644. *TV Star Parade.* New York: Ideal Publishing, vol. 1-, 1951-. (Bimonthly)

Serves as a guide to the shows and personalities in the television industry.

645. *TV Superstar.* New York: Sterlings' Magazines, vol. 1-, 19??-. (Bi-monthly)

TV Superstar is yet another popular fan magazine published by Sterling. Among its staple offerings are short, illustrated biographies.

646. *Variety.* New York: Variety Publishing, vol. 1-, 1905-. (Weekly)

A principal showbusiness tabloid, with news stories, reviews, and features on the people and events within the entertainment milieu. No connection with *Daily Variety* (above). Indexed (some selectively) by: *Magazine Index, Film Literature Index, Media Review Digest, Music Index, Magazine Article Summaries.*

647. *Velvet Light Trap.* Madison, WI: Velvet Light Trap, no. 1-, 1971-. (Quarterly)

Intended for the serious student of the cinema, and addressing any topic dealing with some aspect of the medium (including occasional interviews). Indexed by: *Film Literature Index.*

648. *Video Times: For Home Viewing on Tape & Disc.* Skokie, IL: Publications International, vol. 1-, 1985-. (Monthly)

Continues: *Video Movies* (1984-1985). Specializes in movie themes (including some interview/profile features), and videotape reviews.

649. *Wow.* New York: Pilot Communications, vol. 1-, 19(?)-. (Monthly)

A teen-audience fan magazine containing feature stories, each about two pages long, on young film, television and music personalities. The June, 1988 issue contains a fan club directory, and the department: "Big mouth" (star gossip).

Chapter 13
Computerized Databases

650. *Arts Documentation Service*. North Sydney, NSW, Australia: Australia Council Library.

Subject: biography. Contents: some 27,000 citations to clippings from major Australian newspapers on Australian personalities in the arts. Coverage: 1974-. Updates at the rate of 800 items monthly. Address: P.O. Box 302, 168 Walker St., North Sydney, NSW, 2060 Australia. Telephone: 61 (2) 923-3333.

651. *Baseline*. New York: Baseline.

Subjects: films, television, entertainment, publishing, literature. Contents: several databases in the entertainment industry with the names of some 200,000 people with their credits, industry news, 35,000 film, TV and theatrical titles listings. Coverage: 1900-. This file is continuously updated, adding 20,000 records yearly. Corresponding print sources: *Who's Who in Television; Movies Made for Television, 1964-1984; Encyclopedia of Television Series, Plots and Specials*. Address: 80 E. 11th St., New York, NY 10003. Telephone: (212) 254-8235.

652. *Electric Bank, Performance Bank*. Des Moines, IA: The Electric Bank.

Subjects: art, performing arts, entertainment. Contents: all performance proposals and originating artist realized performances. Coverage: the file contains about 7,000 irregularly updated records since 1979, with historical data from 1970. Corresponding print source: *Biennial Report of the Performance Bank*. Address: 4225 University, Des Moines, IA 50311. Telephone: (515) 277-6185.

653. *ESI Street*. Los Angeles: Entertainment Systems International.

Subject: the entertainment industry. Contents: news wire stories about the entertainment business, plus other stories and data. Coverage: current information, updated continuously. Address: 183 North Martel Ave., Suite 205, Los Angeles, CA 90036. Telephone: (213) 937-0347.

654. *Hollywood Hotline*. Burbank, CA: Hollywood Hotline.

Subjects: entertainment, films, music industry, television, communications. Contents: features and news including all the popular media, the celebrities, the business of entertainment, daily soap opera summaries, movie reviews, and fan mail services. Full text files cover 1983 to the present. They are updated daily. Address: P.O. Box 1945, Burbank, CA 91507. Telephone: (818) 843-2837.

Chapter 14
Organizations

655. ACADEMY OF MOTION PICTURE ARTS AND SCIENCES
The Margaret Herrick Library
8949 Wilshire Blvd.
Beverly Hills, CA 90211
(213) 278-8990

Holdings: clipping-file biography collection, 360 shelf-feet. Hedda Hopper Collection from the 1950s and 1960s (her files and interviews). MGM Studios biographies and photographs. Services: operates the National Film Information Service, offering biographical and other information by telephone or mail; on-site use by the public; reference service and photocopying.

656. ADULT FILM ASSOCIATION
1654 Cordova St.
Los Angeles, CA 90007
(213) 731-7236

Purpose: information exchange for distributors and exhibitors of sexually explicit adult films. No known library holdings, but a hall of fame is maintained. Publication: monthly bulletin.

657. AMERICAN BROADCASTING COMPANIES, INC.
ABC News Information Center
1926 Broadway

New York, NY 10023

(212) 887-3796

Holdings: 5,000 books and 300 periodicals subscriptions to support the network news operation; clippings file. Services: interlibrary loans and on-site use, subject to restrictions.

658. AMERICAN FILM INSTITUTE

Center for Advanced Film Studies
Charles K. Feldman Library
501 Doheny Rd.
Beverly Hills, CA 90212
(213) 278-8777

Holdings: clipping files and biographical information on film and television personalities. Restricted holdings: periodicals, reference books, film and TV scripts, oral histories, seminar transcripts, and other special collections.

659. ANTHOLOGY FILM ARCHIVES

80 Wooster St.
New York, NY 10002

Purpose: primarily a film archive with screenings of classic and avant-garde films. Library holdings: 3,000 books and 125 periodical subscriptions on cinema history, video, avant-garde filmmaking, and performing; biographical files on directors and critics; stills files. Services: public use by appointment. Publication: *Film Culture Magazine.*

660. BRITISH FILM INSTITUTE, NATIONAL FILM ARCHIVE

Information and Documentation Dept.
81 Dean St.
London W1V 6AA
England
(Tel.) 01-437-4355

Holdings: large collection of books, periodicals, screenplays, stills, and clippings. Services: most materials in this special collection are available for on-site use; reference services and photocopying. Still photographs may be mail ordered. Publications: brochures descriptive of the collection.

661. CALIFORNIA INSTITUTE OF THE ARTS

   The Library
   24700 McBean Pkwy.
   Valencia, CA 91355
   (805) 255-1050

   Holdings: over 60,000 books and 7,000 periodicals in all arts disciplines. Services: public access for reference purposes only; interlibrary loan; photocopying. Publications: handbook of the library.

662. CENTER FOR ADVANCED FILM STUDIES (See: AMERICAN FILM INSTITUTE, above.)

663. CINEMATHEQUE QUEBECOISE

   Centre de Documentation Cinématographique
   335 Blvd. de Maisonneuve E.
   Montreal PQ H2X 1K1
   Canada
   (514) 842-9763

   Holdings: 30,000 books and 125,000 bound periodical volumes, stills, 300,000 clippings on actors and filmmakers, original scripts and other manuscript and archival film materials in the fields of film television, photography and mass media. Services: restricted public on-site use; photocopying.

664. DANSKE FILMMUSEUM

   St. Sondervoldstraede
   1419 Copenhagen
   Denmark
   (Tel.) ASTA 6500

   Holdings: a motion picture archive and library of printed materials and stills.

665. DEUTSCHES INSTITUT FÜR FILMKUNDE

   Postfach 5129
   6200 Wiesbaden 12
   Germany

(Tel.) 69074-75

Holdings: of the DIF (German Institute for Film Studies) Library include clipping files, stills, program notes, books, and publicity material.

666. FILMOTEKA POLSKA
   Pulawska Nr. 61
   Warsaw 12
   Poland
   (Tel.) 45 50 74

Holdings: film books, periodicals, posters, stills, and reviews from Polish periodicals.

667. FUNDACION CINEMATECA ARGENTINA
   LaValle 2168-1-37
   Buenos Aires
   Argentina
   (Tel.) 49-6306

Holdings: film books, periodicals, pressbooks, and clipping files of reviews and articles.

668. HOLLYWOOD STUDIO COLLECTORS CLUB
   3960 Laurel Canyon Blvd., Suite 450
   Studio City, CA 91604
   (818) 990-5450

Purpose: to encourage the collecting of movie memorabilia; conduct research on film history. Holdings: biographical archive on film personalities. Publication: *Hollywood Studio Magazine.*

669. INDEPENDENT BROADCASTING AUTHORITY
   Information Office/Library
   70 Brompton Road
   London SW3 1EY
   England
   (Tel.) 01-584-7011

Formerly the Independent Television Authority. Holdings: books and periodicals on broadcasting; clippings file. Services: inquire. Publication: *Broadcasting: A Selected Bibliography.*

670. INDIANA UNIVERSITY

Lilly Library
Bloomington, IN 47401
(812) 337-2452

Holdings: cinema books, periodicals, scripts, pressbooks, and stills.

671. ISRAEL FILM ARCHIVE/CINEMATHEQUE

43 Jabotinsky St.
Jerusalem
Israel
(Tel.) 67131

Purpose: presents film festivals. Holdings: books, periodicals, film prints and scripts.

672. KENT STATE UNIVERSITY LIBRARIES

Special Collections Dept.
Kent, OH 44242
(216) 672-2270

Major holdings: Open Theater Archives; Collection of Motion Picture & Television Performing Arts; papers of Joseph Chaikin, Gerald Mast, Jean-Claude van Itallie, Dorothy Fuldheim, James Robert Parish, Andy Purman, Lois Wilson. Also holds "vast collections of clippings and photographs of actors, and playbills."

673. THE LIBRARY OF CONGRESS

Motion Picture, Broadcasting and Recorded Sound Div.
Madison Bldg., Room 336
Washington, DC 20540
(202) 287-1000

Holdings: film and TV collections include over 100,000 titles. Screening (with certain restrictions) is permitted upon application. Film and TV printed materials are available in the reading room. There is a vast collection of sound recordings (recorded since 1890 on: wire, wax, aluminum, zinc, glass, rubber, and plastic). Services: listening facilities are provided. Research is conducted in the Recorded Sound Reference Center.

674. METRO-GOLDWYN-MAYER/UNITED ARTISTS
    Picture Research Dept.
    10202 West Washington Blvd.
    Culver City, CA 90230
    (213) 558-5518

    Holdings: 25,000 film books and periodicals; large photograph and clippings collection. Services: use of the collection is limited to production companies.

675. MOTION PICTURE ASSOCIATION OF AMERICA
    The Library
    522 Fifth Ave.
    New York, NY 10036
    (212) 840-6161

    Holdings: 3,000 volumes and 20 periodicals subscriptions in the areas of film history, biography, and business. Services: telephone and mail requests only.

676. MUSEO NAZIONALE DEL CINEMA
    Piazza San Giovanni 2
    Torino 10122
    Italy
    (Tel.) 510-370

    Library holdings: books, pamphlets, periodicals, stills and posters.

677. THE MUSEUM OF BROADCASTING
    1 E. 53rd St.
    New York, NY 10022
    (212) 752-4690

Purpose: dedicated to the history of radio and television broadcasting. Holdings: specialized books and periodicals (1,000 volumes); off-takes from broadcasts over a fifty-year period including war propaganda by the Axis during WW II; television programs from the first years of the medium. Services: on-site library use by the public; public use broadcast study consoles and other listening/viewing facitities. Publication: newsletter.

678. MUSEUM OF MODERN ART

Film Library
11 W. 53rd St.
New York, NY 10019
(212) 956-7236

Holdings: a large number of films, books, periodicals, screenplays, posters, stills, and pressbooks. Services: materials may be used in the Library by application; film viewing by prior appointment (fee).

679. NATIONAL FILM ARCHIVE, NATIONAL LIBRARY OF AUSTRALIA

Canberra, A.C.T. 2600
Australia
(Tel.) 62-1111

Holdings: extensive collection of books, periodicals, 35mm motion picture prints, and stills. Services: on-site use of the collection; reference; photocopying.

680. NATIONAL FILM INFORMATION SERVICE (See: ACADEMY OF MOTION PICTURE ARTS AND SCIENCES, above.)

681. NATIONAL FILM SOCIETY

8340 Mission Rd., Suite 106
Prairie Village, KS 66206
(913) 341-1919

Purpose: preserve early American films, artifacts, and movie theatres. Selected individuals in the film industry receive an annual NFS award. The Society has been recently inactive.

682. NATIONAL MUSEUM OF COMMUNICATIONS

6305 N. O'Connor, Suite 123
Irving, TX 75039
(214) 556-1234

Purpose: to exhibit artifacts and memorabilia relating to the history of recorded, radio and television communications in North America. Holdings: 30,000-volume library of books, films, video, recordings, etc. Services: on-site and interlibrary loan of most materials; photocopying. Publication: newsletter.

683. NEW YORK PUBLIC LIBRARY, LINCOLN CENTER

Library and Museum of the Performing Arts
Lincoln Center at 111 Amsterdam Ave.
New York, NY 10023
(212) 799-2200

See entry 190, for annotation.

684. NORSK FILMINSTITUTT

Aslakveien 14 B, Postboks 5
Oslo 7
Norway
(Tel.) 24 29 94

Holdings: films, books, periodicals and a still photograph collection. Services: on-site use of collection.

685. NORTHWEST FILM & VIDEO CENTER

1219 S.W. Hood St.
Portland, OR 97201
(503) 221-1156

Purpose: regional media arts resource and service organization founded to encourage the study, appreciation and utilization of the moving arts, foster their artistic excellence and help create a climate in which they may flourish. Holdings and services: circulating film library with classic feature films, files with reviews, celebrity photographs, and film stills.

686. PRINCETON UNIVERSITY

William Seymour Theatre Collection
Firestone Library
Princeton, NJ 08544
(609) 452-3223

See entry 1516, for annotation.

687. PUBLIC ARCHIVES OF CANADA, NATIONAL FILM, TELEVISION & SOUND ARCHIVES

Documentation and Public Services Div.
395 Wellington St.
Ottawa, ON K1A 0N3
Canada
(613) 995-1311

Holdings: 9,000 books and periodical volumes; 450 periodicals subscriptions; clippings files about motion pictures, TV, and recorded sound. Services: on-site use by public; reference; interlibrary loan; photocopying. Publications: collection bibliography.

688. SOUTHERN METHODIST UNIVERSITY LIBRARY

McCord Theater Collection
Dallas, TX 75275
(214) 692-2400

Holdings: clippings files, photographs, artifacts about the performing arts including cinema, radio, and TV. Services: public use by appointment; photocopying.

689. STATE UNIVERSITY OF NEW YORK, ALBANY, FILM AND TELEVISION DOCUMENTATION CENTER

1400 Washington Ave.
Albany, NY 12222
(518) 442-5745

Purpose: to promote research in film and television documentation. Publication: *Film Literature Index* (above).

690. SVENSKA FILMINSTITUTET

Filmhuset Box 27
Stockholm 27
Sweden
(Tel.) 63 05 10

Holdings: international collection of film prints and stills; program notes and pressbooks in various languages. Services: reference; film viewing; photocopying.

691. UNIVERSAL CITY STUDIOS

Research Dept. Library
100 Universal City Plaza
Universal City, CA 91608
(213) 985-4321

See entry 194, for annotation.

692. UNIVERSITY OF CALIFORNIA, BERKELEY

Bancroft Library, Theater Collection
Berkeley, CA 94720
(415) 642-6481

Holdings: extensive, non-circulating collection of books, manuscripts, pictures, maps, etc. Services: public access to the widely dispersed materials on stage productions and actors is through the library's card and computer catalogs; on-site, telephone and mail reference inquiries.

693. UNIVERSITY OF CALIFORNIA, DAVIS

Special Collections Dept.
Davis, CA 95616
(916) 752-1621

Biography holdings: books, clippings, photographs, artifacts. There are more than seventy theater archives, personal papers, and ephemera collections—the emphasis here is on actors with a stage reputation. Services: on-site use by public; reference.

694. UNIVERSITY OF CALIFORNIA, LOS ANGELES

Theater Arts Library
22478 University Research Library
Los Angeles, CA 90024
(213) 825-4880

Holdings: over 190,000 motion picture production stills, 800 posters, and files on individuals including, among many others, Hugh O'Brian, Marilyn Monroe, and Carol Burnett. Other files with significant biographical content: the CBS clippings files, National Academy of Motion Picture Arts and Sciences collection, and a miscellaneous file of 263,900 clippings about the entertainment industry. Services: use by public on-site; reference; photocopying.

695. UNIVERSITY OF SOUTHERN CALIFORNIA LIBRARY

Archives of Performing Arts
University Park
Los Angeles, CA 90007
(213) 743-6362

Purpose: to acquire, preserve and make available to students and scholars all possible research materials in motion pictures and television. Holdings: large collection of film and TV books, periodicals, screenplays, stills, memorabilia of individuals (200 actors, writers, directors, producers and composers), and studio files. Services: in-house use by the public; reference; photocopying of clippings files; stills photograph copying.

696. WARNER BROTHERS

The Library
75 Rockefeller Plaza
New York, NY 10020
(212) 484-6359

Holdings: movie stills archive. Services: telephone requests answered by a researcher; on-site visits by appointment; photograph reproduction service.

697. WISCONSIN CENTER FOR FILM AND THEATER RESEARCH   University of Wisconsin

6039 Vilas Hall
Madison, WI 53706
(608) 262-9706

Purpose: to collect, preserve and make available for serious research primary source materials documenting the performing arts in the twentieth century. Holdings: 14,000 motion picture and television programs; 2,000,000 stills and negatives of performers and production personnel; 250 manuscript and/or feature films collections from individuals and organizations involved with contemporary performing arts and mass media (the largest being those of United Artists Corporation, Warner Brothers, RKO, and Monogram); photograph and clippings files on about 8,000 individuals. Services: public use of Center (film archive use by qualified individuals); reference; photocopying and duplication of stills. Publications: collection guide; film lists.

Chapter 15
Commercial Sources and Services

698. ALDREDGE BOOK STORE (Bookstore, Collector Source)
2506 Cedar Springs
Dallas, TX 75201
(214) 748-2043

For sale: movie books; movie collectables.

699. ANDREWSKI, GENE (Collector Source)
165 West 91st St.
New York, NY 10024

For sale: movie stills; posters.

700. ANG & LIL'S COLLECTOR'S CORNER (Collector Source)
12-14 Bennington Dr.
Rochester, NY 14616
(716) 621-8930

For sale: movie memoribilia.

701. BARBOUR, ALAN (Collector Source)
P.O. Box 154
Kew Gardens, NY 11415

For sale: mail order movie stills; posters.

702. THE BETTMAN ARCHIVE (Collector Source)
136 East 57th St.

New York, NY 10022
(212) 758-0362

For sale: a massive collection of quality movie photographs.

703. BIJOU SOCIETY (Collector Source)

7800 Conser Pl.
Shawnee Mission, KS

For sale: movie memorabilia.

704. BIOSCOPE BOOKS LIMITED (Bookstore, Collector Source)

27 Trafalgar St.
Brighton, East Sussex BN1 4ED
England
(Tel.) 0273 684754

For sale: movie books; movie stills; posters.

705. BLEECKER STREET FILM BOOKSHOP (Bookstore, Collector Source)

144 Bleecker St.
New York, NY 10012
(212) 674-2560

For sale: movie books; periodicals; stills; posters.

706. BOOK NICHE (Bookstore)

2008 Mt. Vernon Ave.
Alexandria, VA 22301
(202) 548-3466

For sale: movie books.

707. BOULEVARD BOOKS (Bookstore)

P.O. Box 89
Topanga, CA 90290
(213) 455-1036

For sale: drama books.

708. (EDDY) BRANDT'S MEMORY SHOP (Bookstore, Collector Source)

    P.O. Box 3232
    North Hollywood, CA 91069
    (213) 769-9043

    For sale: movie books; posters.

709. CHEROKEE BOOK SHOP (Bookstore, Collector Source)

    6638 Hollywood Blvd.
    Hollywood, CA
    (213) 463-6090

    For sale: movie books; stills.

710. CINEMA ATTIC (Collector Source)

    P.O. Box 7772, Dept. MT
    Philadelphia, PA 19101

    For sale: mail order movie memorabilia.

711. CINEMABILIA (Bookstore, Collector Source)

    10 West 13th St.
    New York, NY 10011
    (212) 989-8519

    For sale: extensive collection of movie books; periodicals; stills; transparencies; press books, etc.

712. CINEMA BOOKSHOP (Bookstore)

    13-14 Great Russell St.
    London WC1B 3NH
    England
    (Tel.) 01 637-0206

    For sale: large stock of movie books.

713. CINEMA CITY (Collector Source)

    P.O. Box 7406
    Ann Arbor, MI 48107

    For sale: mail order movie posters; pressbooks, etc.

714. CINEMA SHOP (Bookstore, Collector Source)
      526 O'Farrell
      San Francisco, CA 94102
      (415) 885-6785
      For sale: movie books; periodicals; stills.

715. CINEMEDIA BOOKS (Service)
      108 Beaumont Rd.
      P.O. Box 4331
      Silver Spring, MD 20904
      (301) 384-8833
      For sale: mail order movie and moviemaking books.

716. CINE REVUE (Collector Source)
      5 Rue de Danemark
      060 Brussels
      Belgium
      (Tel.) 538 12 76
      For sale: photographs from the magazine, *International Cinema*.

717. (GEOFFREY) CLIFTON'S THEATRE BOOKSHOP (Books)
      Piccadilly Plaza
      York St.
      Manchester M1 4AH
      England
      (Tel.) 061-236-2537
      For sale: movie and broadcasting books; magazines.

718. COLLECTORS' BOOKSTORE (Bookstore, Collector Source)
      6763 Hollywood Blvd.
      Hollywood, CA 90028
      (213) 467-6950
      For sale: movie memorabilia; books; posters; stills.

719. COLLECTORS' EDITIONS (Bookstore, Collector Source)
     P.O. Box 899
     Tiburon, CA 94920

     For sale: mail order movie periodicals; photographs of stars; scrapbooks; posters.

720. CORNHILL MAGAZINE & BOOK CO. (Bookstore, Collector Source)
     94 South St.
     Boston, MA. 02135
     (617) 542-3262

     For sale: movie books; stills.

721. CROFTER'S BOOKS (Bookstore)
     P.O. Box 226
     Washington, CT 06793

     For sale: mail order movie and television books; television.

722. DALBY, RICHARD (Service)
     4 Westbourne Park
     Scarborough, North Yorkshire YO12 4AT
     England
     (Tel.) 0723 77049

     For sale: mail order movie books.

723. DOMINIC PHOTOGRAPHY (Collector Source)
     9a Netherton Grove
     London SW10 9TQ
     England
     (Tel.) 01 352 6118

     For sale: movie and television photographs.

724. DOWN MEMORY LANE (Collector Source)
     2417 Classen

Oklahoma City, OK 73106
(405) 521-9338
For sale: movie posters.

725. DRAMA BOOKSHOP (Bookstore)

150 West 52nd St.
New York, NY 10019
(212) 582-1037
For sale: movie and theater books; periodicals.

726. (LARRY) EDMUND'S BOOKSHOP (Bookstore, Collector Source)

6658 Hollywood Blvd.
Hollywood, CA 90028
(213) 463-3273
For sale: thousands of movie books; stills; posters; memorabilia.

727. (ANNE M.) ELLIS SALES (Bookstore)

P.O. Box 854
Kentfield, CA 94914
For sale: mail order movie and television books.

728. FILM FAVORITES (Collector Source)

P.O. Box 133
Canton, OK 73724
For sale: a multitude of inexpensive movie stills by mail order.

729. FILMHISTORISCHES BILDARCHIVE DR. KARKOSCH (Collector Source)

Greigstrasse 7
8000 Munich 40
Germany
(Tel.) 089 35 54 28
For sale: photographs of German and foreign movie stars.

730. GOLD DIGGERS OF 1933 (Collector Source)

143 Pearl
Cambridge, MA
(617) 868-1933
For sale: movie memorabilia.

731. GOTHAM BOOK MART (Bookstore)

41 West 47th St.
New York, NY 10036
(212) 757-0367
For sale: movie and television books; magazines.

732. THE GRAND ILLUSION (Bookstore)

608 Lincoln Blvd.
Venice, CA 90291
For sale: movie books.

733. HAMPTON BOOKS (Bookstore, Collector Source)

Box 76
Newberry, SC 29108
(803) 276-6870
For sale: mail order thousands of movie books; stills.

734. HERITAGE RECORDING SERVICE (Collector Source)

340 Parker St.
Newton Center, MA 02159
For sale: thousands of movie soundtracks.

735. HOBBYVILLE (Collector Source)

433 West 34th St.
New York, NY 10001
(212) 868-9344
For sale: movie stills; memorabilia.

736. HOLLYWOOD DREAM FACTORY (Bookstore, Collector Source)

    1842 W. Sylvania Ave.
    Toledo, OH 43613
    (419) 474-3065

    For sale: movie and moviemaking books; magazines; biography; posters.

737. THE HOLLYWOOD REVIEW (Collector Source)

    1523 North La Brea
    Hollywood, CA 90028
    (213) 876-9206

    For sale: movie stills.

738. JAY BEE MAGAZINES (Collector Source)

    776 Eighth Ave.
    New York, NY 10036
    (212) 757-6923

    For sale: movie stills.

739. LANGLY ASSOCIATES (Collector Source)

    5728 Schaefer Rd.
    Dearborn, MI 48126

    For sale: large collection of movie stills; posters.

740. LAWS, LARRY (Bookstore)

    831 Cornelia Ave.
    Chicago, IL 60657
    (312) 477-9247

    For sale: movie and television books; magazines.

741. LIMELIGHT BOOKSTORE (Bookstore)

    1803 Market St.
    San Francisco, CA 94103
    (415) 864-2265

    For sale: movie books.

742. MADELEINE PRODUCTIONS (Collector Source, Service)
     15 Wallace Ave.
     Worthing, West Sussex BN11 5RA
     England
     (Tel.) 0903 503551

     For sale: movie books; movie biography; movie photographs.

743. (GEOFFREY H.) MAHFUZ—PAPER CINEMA (Bookstore, Collector Source)
     P.O. Box 40, Prudential Center Sta.
     Boston, MA 02199
     (617) 267-0012

     For sale: movie and television books; memorabilia.

744. MEMORY SHOP (Collector Source)
     109 East 12th St.
     New York, NY 10003
     (212) 473-2404

     For sale: thousands of movie stills; memorabilia.

745. MEMORY SHOP WEST (Collector Source)
     2324 Market St.
     San Francisco, CA 94114
     (415) 626-4873

     For sale: thousands of movie stills; posters; lobby cards.

746. METRO-GOLDEN-MEMORIES (Bookstore, Collector Source)
     5941 W Irving Park Rd.
     Chicago, IL 60634
     (312) 736-4133

     For sale: movie and moviemaking books; radio and television; memorabilia; posters; phonograph records.

747. MOVIE MADNESS (Bookstore)
     141 W 6th

Cincinnati, OH 45202
(513) 241-9856
For sale: movie books.

748. MOVIE MEMORABILIA SHOP OF HOLLYWOOD
(Collector Source)
P.O. Box 29027
Los Angeles, CA
For sale: mail order movie memorabilia; magazines.

749. MOVIE STAR NEWS (Collector Source)
212 East 14th St.
New York, NY 10003
(212) 777-5564
For sale: huge quantity of movie stills.

750. MOVIE STILL ARCHIVES (Collector Service)
P.O. Box 627, Canal Street Sta.
New York, NY 10003
(212) 925-8952
For sale: photographs of movie and television stars.

751. NOSTALGIA ENTERPRISES (Collector Source)
11702 Venice Blvd.
Los Angeles, CA 90066
(213) 390-6564
For sale: movie posters; stills.

752. NOSTALGIAPHON (Collector Source)
P.O. Box 13205
Whitehall, OH 43213
For sale: mail order movie soundtracks.

753. NOSTALGIA SHOP (Bookstore, Collector Source)
534 North Clark
Chicago, IL 60610

(312) 751-9163

For sale: movie books; stills.

754. OLD NEW YORK BOOK SHOP (Bookstore)

1069 Juniper St. NE
Atlanta, GA 30309
(404) 881-1285

For sale: movie books.

755. PACKAGE   PUBLICITY   SERVICE,   BOOK   DEPT.
(Bookstore, Service)

27 W 24th St., Suite 402
New York, NY 10010
(212) 255-2872

For sale: mail order movie and moviemaking books.

756. PASSAIC BOOK CENTER (Bookstore, Collector Source)

594 Main Ave.
Passaic, NJ 07055
(201) 778-6646

For sale: movie books; memorabilia.

757. PERCEPTION PLUS (Bookstore, Service)

P.O. Box 283
Arlington, MA 02174

For sale: mail order movie and television books; out of
print book searching.

758. PERSONALITY PHOTOS INC. (Collector Source)

P.O. Box 50
Brooklyn, NY 11230
(212) 645-9181

For sale: large collection of mail order photographs of
movie and television personalities.

759. PHOTO ARCHIVES (Collector Source)
1472 Broadway, Room 709
New York, NY 10036
For sale: thousands of movie photographs.

760. PICKWICK BOOKSHOP (Bookstore)
6743 Hollywood Blvd.
Hollywood, CA
(213) 469-8191
For sale: movie books; magazines.

761. ROGOFSKY, HOWARD (Bookstore, Service)
Box 107-FC
Glen Oaks, NY 11004
For sale: movie and television books; magazines; conducts a photograph and magazine research service.

762. SALLY, STEPHEN (Collector Source)
339 West 44th St.
New York, NY 10036
(212) 987-0061
For sale: movie stills; memorabilia.

763. SAN FRANCISCIANA (Collector Source)
Cliff House
1900 Pt. Lobos Ave.
San Francisco, CA 94121
(415) 751-7222
For sale: photographs; posters; prints; movie and fan magazines; postcards; other ephemera.

764. (PAUL) SARYAN, NOSTALGIA (Collector Source)
P.O. Box 265
Staten Island, NY
For sale: mail order movie memorabilia; stills; posters, etc.

765. SCRIPTORIUM (Bookstore, Collector Source)

427 North Canon Dr.
Beverly Hills, CA 90210

For sale: autographs; manuscripts; movie and fan magazines.

766. SILVER SCREEN (Collector Source)

1192 Lexington Ave.
New York, NY 10028
(212) 737-3167

For sale: movie stills; posters; artifacts.

767. SPREAD EAGLE BOOKSHOP (Bookstore)

8 Nevada St., Greenwich
London SE10
England
(Tel.) 01 692-1618

For sale: movie books.

768. STAR TIMERS (Collector Source)

P.O. Box 39555
Los Angeles, CA 90039

For sale: mail order movie posters; stills; scrapbooks; films.

769. SUPERIOR PHOTOTECH (Collector Source)

32 West 45th St.
New York, NY 10036
(212) 246-5110

For sale: thousands of movie stills.

770. VAGABOND BOOKS (Bookstore)

2076 Westwood Blvd.
Los Angeles, CA 90025
(213) 475-2700

For sale: movie and television books.

771. WORDS AND MUSIC (Collector Source)

Box 534
Galion, OH 44833

For sale: mail order movie soundtracks.

772. YESTERDAY (Collector Source)

174-A Ninth Ave.
New York, NY 10011
(212) 691-1615

For sale: movie stills; posters.

773. YESTERDAY'S MEMORIES (Bookstore, Collector Source)

5406 West Center
Milwaukee, WI 53210
(414) 444-6210

For sale: movie books; memorabilia.

Chapter 16
Fan Clubs (FC)

774. ANN-MARGRET.

   Ann-Margaret FC
   c/o Theresa Ann Swedick
   Winnipeg General P.O. Box 2165
   Winnipeg, MB R3C 3RS
   Canada

775. BALL, LUCILLE.

   We Love Lucy FC
   P.O. Box 480216
   Los Angeles, CA 90048

776. BATES, ALAN.

   Alan Bates FC
   c/o Gary Lee
   2416 E. 4th St.
   Tucson, AZ 85719

777. BROSNAN, PIERCE.

   Pierce Brosnan FC
   c/o Kim Grant
   P.O. Box 25858
   Los Angeles, CA 90025

778. CARTER, LYNDA.

  Lynda Carter International FC
  P.O. Box 1235
  Beverly Hills, CA 90213

779. COLLINS, JOAN.

  Joan Collins FC
  c/o Madge Duhon
  P.O. Box 30
  Paris, AR 72855

780. EASTWOOD, CLINT.

  Clint Eastwood FC
  c/o Chris Thrasher
  R.R. 2
  Abilene, KS 67410

781. FIELD, SALLY.

  Sally Field National FC
  c/o Sandi Kremi
  P.O. Box 26610 No. 313
  Sacramento, CA 95826

782. FORD, HARRISON.

  The Official Fandom of Harrison Ford
  c/o Kathy Jentz
  18132 Kitchen House Ct.
  Germantown, MD 20874

783. GARNER, JAMES.

  James Garner FC
  c/o Pat Persico
  33 Woodbury Rd.
  Edison, NJ 08830

784. GIBSON, MEL.

  The Mel Gibson FC
  c/o Marlene Bratach

P.O. Box 172
Colinia, NJ 07067

785. GRIFFITH, ANDY.

The Andy Griffith Show Rerun Watchers Club
c/o Jim Clark
1313 21st Ave. S.
Nashville, TN 37212

The Andy Griffith Appreciation Society
c/o Stanley J. Meroney
P.O. Box 330
Clemmons, NC 27012

786. HAMILL, MARK.

Mark Hamill FC
P.O. Box 5276
Orange, CA 92667-0276

787. HAMILTON, GEORGE.

George Hamilton FC
c/o Dolores Merrill
Rt. 1, Box 60
Tenstrike, MN 56683

788. KEACH, STACY.

Stacy Keach FC
c/o Susan M. Brunot
R.D. 1, Box 801
Greensburg, PA 15601

Stacy Keach FC
c/o Shari Carr
P.O. Box 704
Beverly Hills, CA 90210

789. KERR, DEBORAH.

Deborah Kerr FC
c/o Bridget Watson
10 Barrett Rd.

Holt, Norfolk
England

790. KRISTOFFERSON, KRIS.

Kris Kristofferson FC
c/o Ginny Alifragis
1 Happ Rd.
Wilmette, IL 60091

Kris Kristofferson FC
c/o Jeri Smith
200 Crescent Dr.
Littlefield, TX 79339

791. MARX, GROUCHO.

The (Groucho) Marx Brotherhood
c/o Paul G. Wesolowski
28 Darien St.
New Hope, PA 18938

792. MIDLER, BETTE.

The Best of Bette
P.O. Box 1010
Bayonne, NJ 07002
Los Angeles, CA 90036

793. NIMOY, LEONARD.

The Leonard Nimoy FC
c/o Sandra Keel
Rt. 3, Box 48
LaFayette, AL 36862

Leonard Nimoy FC
Barbara Walker, President
17 Gateway Dr.
Batavia, NY 14020

Spotlight on Leonard Nimoy
c/o Wendy Downes

96 B. Broadway
Bexleyheath, Kent, DA6 7DE
England

794. REDFORD, ROBERT.

Robert Redford FC
c/o Trudy Hoffman
517 William St.
Dunmore, PA 18510

795. REYNOLDS, BURT.

Burt Reynolds FC
c/o Harriett Mullins
80 Broadmeadows, No. 5450
Columbus, OH 43214

796. REYNOLDS, DEBBIE.

Friends of Debbie Reynolds FC
c/o Jeabbe Bilyeu
5713 Rosario Blvd.
N. Highlands, CA 95660

797. ROGERS, ROY; and EVANS, DALE.

Roy Rogers/Dale Evans FC
c/o Jim Wilson
P.O. Box 1166
Portsmouth, OH 43227

798. SELLECK, TOM.

Tom Selleck FC
177 Park St.
New Haven, CT 06511

Tom Selleck FC
c/o Phyllis Schooley
1115 Brewster Dr.
El Cerrito, CA 94530

799. SHATNER, WILLIAM.
     William Shatner Fellowship
     P.O. Box 1366
     Hollywood, CA 90078

800. SHIELDS, BROOKE.
     Brooke Shields FC
     P.O. Box 777
     Mt. Morris, IL 61054

801. SPIELBERG, STEVEN.
     Steven Spielberg Film Society
     c/o Archer Hubbard
     4126 E. 32nd St.
     Tucson, AZ 85711

802. STALLONE, SYLVESTER.
     Sylvester Stallone FC
     582 Rt. 9
     Waretown, NJ 08758

803. TAYLOR, ELIZABETH.
     Elizabeth Taylor FC
     c/o Alan F. Berg
     2125 Lockport St.
     Niagara Falls, NY 14305

804. TRAVOLTA, JOHN.
     John Travolta FC
     c/o CMC
     8899 Beverly Blvd., Suite 906
     Los Angeles, CA 90048

805. WEST, MAE.
     International Mae West Society
     c/o Robert Howard
     P.O. Box 2623
     Beverly Hills, CA 90213

806. WHITE, BETTY.
     Betty White FC
     c/o Kay Daly
     3552 Federal Ave.
     Los Angeles, CA 90069

807. YORK, MICHAEL.
     Michael York FC
     c/o Justine Banevicius
     3425 Knox Pl., No. 38
     Bronx, NY 10467

Chapter 17
Individual Biographies

ALDA, ALAN. Act.

808. Bonderoff, Jason. *Alan Alda, an Unauthorized Biography.* New York: New American Library, Signet, 1982. 246 p. Illustrated. Paperbound.

809. Strait, Raymond. *Alan Alda: A Biography.* New York: St. Martin's Press, 1983. 250 p.

ALLEN, WOODY. Dir.

810. Allen, Woody. *Woody Allen* [*Sound Recording*]. Washington, DC: Tapes for Readers, 1978. 1 sound cassette.
Summary: An interview with Allen.

811. Brode, Douglas. *Woody Allen: His Films and Career.* Secaucus, NJ: Citadel, 1985. 255 p. Illustrated.

812. Guthrie, Lee. *Woody Allen, a Biography.* New York: Drake Publishers, 1978. 183 p. Illustrated. Filmography. Index.

813. Hirsch, Foster. *Love, Sex, Death, and the Meaning of Life: Woody Allen's Comedy.* New York McGraw-Hill, 1981. 231 p. Bibliography. Filmography. Index. Paperbound.

814. Jacobs, Diane. *The Magic of Woody Allen.* London: Robson Books, 1982. 176 p. Illustrated. Filmography. Playography. Bibliography. Index.

815. McKnight, Gerald. *Woody Allen: Joking Aside.* London: W. H. Allen, Star Book, 1982. 205 p. Illustrated. Index. ***

816. Palmer, Myles. *Woody Allen, an Illustrated Biography.* London, New York: Proteus Books, 1980. Illustrated. Filmography. Paperbound.

817. *Woody Allen: An American Comedy [Motion Picture].* Films for the Humanities, 1977. sd., 16mm.

Summary: The director discusses how and why he writes comedy. He reveals what he reads, and excerpts from his films illustrate his style.

ALTMAN, ROBERT. Dir.

818. Kass, Judith M. *Robert Altman: American Innovator.* Popular Library Film Series. New York: Popular Library, 1978. 282 p. Illustrated. Filmography. Paperbound.

819. Plecki, Gerard. *Robert Altman.* Twayne's Filmmakers Series. Boston: Twayne, 1985. 159 p. Illustrated. Bibliography. Filmography. Index.

JULIE ANDREWS. Act.

820. Windeler, Robert. *Julie Andrews: A Biography*. New York: St. Martin's Press, 1983. 223 p. Illustrated. Filmography. Discography. Index.

ASHCROFT, PEGGY. Act.

821. Tanitch, Robert. *Ashcroft*. London: Hutchinson, 1987. 160 p. Illustrated. Playography. Filmography. Videography. Radiography. Discography. Index.

ASTIN, PATTY DUKE. Act.

822. Astin, Patty Duke, and Duran, Kenneth. *Call Me Anna: The Autobiography of Patty Duke*. Toronto, New York: Bantam Books, 1987. 298 p. Illustrated.

ATTENBOROUGH, RICHARD. Dir.

823. Attenborough, Richard. *In Search of Gandhi*. Piscataway, NJ: New Century Publishers, 1982. 229 p. Illustrated. Index.

824. Castell, David. *Richard Attenborough: A Pictorial Film Biography*. London: Bodley Head, 1984. 128 p. Illustrated. Filmography. Index.

BACALL, LAUREN. Act.

825. Bacall, Lauren. *Lauren Bacall by Myself*. New York: Knopf, 1979. 377 p. Illustrated.

826. Greenberger, Howard. *Bogey's Baby*. New York: St. Martin's Press, 1978. 216 p. Illustrated.

827. Quirk, Lawrence J. *Lauren Bacall: Her Films and Career*. Secaucus, NJ: Citadel, 1986. 192 p. Illustrated.

BALL, LUCILLE. Act.

828. Andrews, Bart, and Watson, Thomas. *Loving Lucy: An Illustrated Tribute to Lucille Ball*. Foreword by Gale Gordon. Photographs from the Howard Frank Archives. New York: St. Martin's Press, 1980. 226 p. Illustrated. Index.

829. Higham, Charles. *Lucy: The Life of Lucille Ball*. New York: St. Martin's Press, 1986. 261 p. Illustrated. Filmography. Videography. Index.

830. Morella, Joe, and Epstein, Edward Z. *Forever Lucy: The Life of Lucille Ball*. Secaucus, NJ: Lyle Stuart, 1986. 267 p. Illustrated. Index.

BANCROFT, ANNE. Act.

831. Holtzman, William. *Seesaw, a Dual Biography of Anne Bancroft and Mel Brooks*. Garden City, NY: Doubleday, 1979. 300 p. Illustrated. Index.

BARDOT, BRIGITTE. Act.

832. Frischauer, Willi. *Bardot: An Intimate Biography*. London: Michael Joseph, 1978. 222 p. Illustrated. Filmography. Index.

833. Haining, Peter. *The Legend of Brigitte Bardot.* London: W. H. Allen, Comet Book, 1983. 224 p. Illustrated. Paperbound. ***

834. Roberts, Glenys. *Bardot.* New York: St. Martin's Press, 1984. 290 p. Illustrated. Filmography. Bibliography. Index.

BEATTY, WARREN. Act.

835. Kercher, John. *Warren Beatty.* London, New York: Proteus Books, 1984. 127 p. Illustrated. Filmography. Paperbound.

836. Munshower, Suzanne. *Warren Beatty—His Life, His Loves, His Work.* New York: St. Martin's Press, 1983. 165 p. Illustrated. Index.

837. Quirk, Lawrence J. *The Films of Warren Beatty.* Secaucus, NJ: Citadel, 1979. 222 p. Illustrated.

838. Thomson, David. *Warren Beatty and Desert Eyes: A Life and a Story.* Garden City, NY: Doubleday, 1987. 399 p. Illustrated. Filmography. Index.

BERGEN, CANDICE. Act.

839. Bergen, Candice. *Knock Wood.* New York: Linden Press; Simon and Schuster, 1984. 354 p. Illustrated.

Film and Television Celebrities Sources

BERGMAN, INGMAR. Dir.

840. *The Art of the Film: Two by Bergman [Filmstrip].* Educational Dimensions, 1972. 2 filmstrips, b&w., 35mm, and 2 phonodiscs, 20 min. each, 12 in., 33 1/3 rpm.

Summary: Photographs and narrative sequences from Bergman's films, *The Virgin Spring,* and *The Magician* are used to show how his philosophy of life is revealed through his films.

841. Bergman, Ingmar. *The Magic Lantern: An Autobiography.* Translation from the Swedish. New York: Viking Press, 1988. ***

842. Cowie, Peter. *Ingmar Bergman: A Critical Biography.* New York: Scribner, 1982. 397 p. Illustrated. Bibliography. Filmography. Playography. Index.

BERGMAN, INGRID. Act. 8/29/82

843. Bergman, Ingrid, and Burgess, Alan. *Ingrid Bergman: My Story.* New York: Delacorte Press, 1980. 504 p. Illustrated. Filmography. Playography. Videography. Index.

844. *Ingrid Bergman.* Introduction by Sheridan Morley. Series edited by John Kobal. Photographs from the Kobal Collection. Boston: Little, Brown, 1985. 143 p. Illustrated. Paperbound.

845. *Ingrid [Videorecording].* Directed by Gene Feldman. Ossining, NY: Wombat Productions, 1984. 2 videocassettes, 70 min., sd., col., 3/4 in.

Summary: Narrated by John Gielgud and in standard documentary form, this work includes interviews with co-workers such as Liv Ullman, Coleen Dewhurst, Jose Ferrer, and Anthony Quinn; clips from films such as *Intermezzo,*

Spellbound, and *Autumn Sonata*; and visuals of personal events. Issued also as a motion picture.

846. Leamer, Laurence. *As Time Goes By: The Life of Ingrid Bergman*. New York: Harper & Row, 1986. 423 p. Illustrated. Filmography. Playography. Videography. Bibliography. Index.

847. Taylor, John Russell. *Ingrid Bergman*. Photographs from the Kobal Collection. New York: St. Martin's Press, 1983. 127 p. Illustrated.

BERTOLUCCI, BERNARDO. Dir.

848. Kolker, Robert Phillip. *Bernardo Bertolucci*. New York: Oxford University Press, 1985. 258 p. Illustrated. Filmography. Bibliography. Index.

BLONDELL, JOAN. Act. 12/25/79

849. Blondell, Joan. *Hollywood in the 30's [Sound Recording]*. Avid Reader Series. New York: Norton, 1972? 1 sound cassette, 55 min.

Summary: Blondell talks about her book, *Center Door Fancy*, and how it relates to her life. She discusses her movies and acting career. Included are out-takes of productions in which she starred.

BLOOM, CLAIRE. Act.

850. Bloom, Claire. *Limelight and After: The Education of an Actress*. New York: Harper & Row, 1982. 187 p. Illustrated.

BOGARDE, DIRK. Act.

851. Bogarde, Dirk. *Backcloth.* Harmondsworth, Middlesex, England, Viking Press, Penguin, 1986. 313 p. Illustrated. Index.

852. Bogarde, Dirk. *An Orderly Man.* New York: Knopf, 1983. 291 p. Illustrated. Index.

853. Bogarde, Dirk. *A Postillion Struck by Lightning.* New York: Holt, Rinehart and Winston, 1977. 268 p. Illustrated. Index.

854. Bogarde, Dirk. *Snakes & Ladders.* New York: Holt, Rinehart and Winston, 1978. 341 p. Filmography. Index.

BOGDANOVICH, PETER. Dir.

855. Bogdanovich, Peter. *The Killing of the Unicorn: Dorothy Stratten (1960-1980).* New York: Morrow, 1984. 186 p. Illustrated.

856. *Pieces of Time: Peter Bogdanovich [Videorecording].* Paul Joyce Productions, 1988? 1 videocassette, 30 min., col., VHS.

Summary: An interview with the famed director in which he recounts his rise from the Roger Corman "stable" of exploitation filmmakers to the top of his craft.

BOYER, CHARLES. Act. 8/26/78

857. Swindell, Larry. *Charles Boyer: The Reluctant Lover.* Garden City, NY: Doubleday, 1983. 280 p. Illustrations. Filmography. Index.

BRANDO, MARLON. Act.

858. Braithwaite, Bruce. *The Films of Marlon Brando.* Heroes of the Movies. New York, Toronto: Beaufort Books, 1982. 94 p. Illustrated. Filmography. Paperbound.

859. Braithwaite, Bruce. *The Films of Marlon Brando.* St. Paul, MN: Greenhaven Press, 1978. 45 p. Illustrated. Filmography.

860. Brando, Anna Kashfi, and Stein, E. P. *Brando for Breakfast.* New York: Crown Publishers, 1979. 273 p.

861. Carey, Gary. *Marlon Brando: The Only Contender.* New York: St. Martin's Press, 1985. 276 p. Illustrated. Filmography. Index.

862. Downing, David. *Marlon Brando.* New York: Stein & Day, 1984. 216 p. Illustrated. Filmography. Index.

863. Frank, Alan G. *Marlon Brando.* The Screen Greats. New York: Exeter Books, 1982. 80 p. Filmography.

864. Higham, Charles. *Brando: The Unauthorized Biography.* New York, Scarborough, ON: New American Library, 1987. 330 p. Illustrated. Index.

865. Nickens, Christopher. *Brando: A Biography in Photographs.* Garden City, NY: Doubleday, Dolphin, 1987. 141 p. Illustrated. Paperbound.

866. Shaw, Sam. *Brando in the Camera Eye.* London, New York: Hamlyn, 1979. 160 p. Illustrated.

BRONSON, CHARLES. Act.

867. Downing, David. *Charles Bronson.* New York: St. Martin's Press, 1983. 156 p. Illustrated. Index.

868. Vermilye, Jerry. *The Films of Charles Bronson.* Secaucus, NJ: Citadel, 1980. 254 p. Illustrated. Videography.

BROOKS, MEL. Dir. See: BANCROFT, ANNE. Act.

BRYNNER, YUL. Act. 10/10/85

869. Robbins, Jhan. *Yul Brynner: The Inscrutable King.* New York: Dodd, Mead, 1987. 212 p. Illustrated. Playography. Filmography. Index.

BUÑUEL, LUIS. Dir. 7/29/83

870. Buñuel, Luis. *My Last Sigh.* Translated by Abigail Israel. New York: Knopf, 1983. 256 p. Illustrated.

871. Higginbotham, Virginia. *Luis Buñuel.* Twayne's Theatrical Arts Series. Boston: Twayne, 1979. 222 p. Illustrated. Bibliography. Filmography. Index.

BURTON, RICHARD. Act. 8/5/84

872. Alpert, Hollis. *Burton.* New York: Putnam, 1986. 270 p. Illustrated.

873. Bragg, Melvyn. *Rich: The Life of Richard Burton.* London: Hodder and Stoughton, 1988. 533 p. Illustrated. Playography. Filmography. Discography. Index.

874. David, Lester, and Robbins, Jhan. *Richard & Elizabeth.* New York: Funk & Wagnalls, 1977. 242 p. Illustrated. Index.

875. Ferris, Paul. *Richard Burton.* New York: Berkley Books, 1982. 328 p. Illustrated. Bibliography. Index. Paperbound.

876. Jenkins, Graham, and Turner, Barry. *Richard Burton, My Brother.* London: M. Joseph, 1988. 247 p. Illustrated. ***

877. Junor, Penny. *Burton: The Man Behind the Myth.* New York: St. Martin's Press, 1985. 210 p. Illustrated. Index.

CAGNEY, JAMES. Act.

878. Clinch, Minty. *Cagney: The Story of His Film Career.* London, New York: Proteus Books, 1982. 126 p. Illustrated. Filmography.

879. *James Cagney, That Yankee Doodle Dandy [Videorecording].* New York: MGM/UA Home Video, 1981. 1 videocassette, 73 min., sd., col., with b&w sequences, 1/2 in.

Summary: Produced, written and directed by Richard Schickel, this video offers interviews with Cagney as well as with his friends and fellow actors. These scenes are interspersed with clips from *Public Enemy, A Midsummer Night's Dream, Angels with Dirty Faces, The Strawberry Blonde, White Heat,* and *Yankee Doodle Dandy.*

880. McGilligan, Patrick. *Cagney, the Actor as Auteur.* Rev. ed. San Diego, CA: A. S. Barnes, 1982. 320 p. Illustrated. Filmography. Bibliography. Index.

881. Schickel, Richard. *James Cagney: A Celebration.* Boston, Toronto: Little, Brown, 1985. 192 p. Illustrated. Filmography.

882. Warren, Doug, and Cagney, James. *James Cagney, the Authorized Biography.* New York: St. Martin's Press, 1983. Illustrated. Filmography. Index.

CAINE, MICHAEL. Act.

883. Andrews, Emma. *The Films of Michael Caine.* St. Paul, MN: Greenhaven Press, 1978. 47 p. Illustrated. Filmography.

884. Hall, William. *Raising Caine: The Authorized Biography.* Englewood Cliffs, NJ: Prentice-Hall, 1981. 246 p. Illustrated. Filmography. Index.

885. Hunter, Allan. *Michael Caine: The Man and His Movies.* New York: St. Martin's Press, 1986. ***

886. Judge, Philip. *Michael Caine.* Tunbridge Wells, Kent, England: Spellmount; New York: Hippocrene Books, 1985. Illustrated. Filmography.

CAPRA, FRANK. Dir.

887. Maland, Charles J. *Frank Capra.* Twayne's Theatrical Arts Series. Boston: Twayne, 1980. 218 p. Illustrated. Bibliography. Filmography. Index.

888. Scherle, Victor, and Levy, William Turner, eds. *The Films of Frank Capra.* Introduction by William O. Douglas. Secaucus, NJ: Citadel, 1977. 278 p. Illustrated. Index.

CARLISLE, KITTY. Act.

889. Hart, Kitty Carlisle. *Kitty: An Autobiography.* New York: Doubleday, 1988. 263 p. Illustrated. Index.

CHRISTIE, JULIE. Act.

890. Callan, Michael Feeney. *Julie Christie.* New York: St. Martin's Press, 1985. 192 p. Illustrated. Index.

COLBERT, CLAUDETTE. Act.

891. Quirk, Lawrence J. *Claudette Colbert: An Illustrated Biography.* New York: Crown Publishers, 1985. 212 p. Illustrated. Filmography. Index.

COLEMAN, GARY. Act.

892. Davidson, Bill, et al. *Gary Coleman, Medical Miracle.* New York: Coward, McCann & Geoghegan, 1981. 236 p. Illustrated.

COLLINS, JOAN. Act.

893. Collins, Joan. *Past Imperfect: An Autobiography.* New York: Simon and Schuster, 1984. 358 p. Illustrated. Filmography.

894. David, Jay. *Inside Joan Collins: A Biography.* New York: Carroll & Graf, 1988. 253 p. Illustrated. Bibliography. ***

895. Levine, Robert. *Joan Collins, Superstar: A Biography.* New York: Dell, 1985. 192 p. Illustrated. Paperbound.

896. Rovin, Jeff. *Joan Collins, the Unauthorized Biography.* Toronto, New York: Bantam Books, 1984. 223 p. Illustrated. Paperbound.

897. Sanderson, Eddie. *Joan Collins: Portrait of a Star.* Introduction by Joan Collins. New York: Simon and Schuster, Fireside, 1987. 128 p. Illustrated. Paperbound.

CONNERY, SEAN. Act.

898. Andrews, Emma. *The Films of Sean Connery.* St. Paul, MN: Greenhaven Press, 1978. 46 p. Illustrated. Filmography.

899. Callan, Michael Feeney. *Sean Connery.* Introduction by John Boorman. New York: Stein & Day, 1983. 295 p. Illustrated. Filmography. Index.

900. Passingham, Kenneth. *Sean Connery: A Biography.* New York: St. Martin's Press, 1983. 160 p. Illustrated. Filmography. Index.

COPPOLA, FRANCIS FORD. Dir.

901. Chaillet, Jean-Paul, and Vincent, Elizabeth. *Francis Ford Coppola*. Translated from the French by Denise Raab Jacobs. New York: St. Martin's Press, 1985. 124 p. Illustrated. Filmography. Paperbound.

902. *Filmmaker, a Personal Diary [Motion Picture]*. Los Angeles: Direct Cinema, 1983. 1 film reel, 33 min., sd., col., 16mm.

Summary: This is George Lucas' documentary film on the making of Coppola's *Rain People*, combining insights into the business of filmmaking with acting, cinematography, editing, and associated creative activities.

CORMAN, ROGER. Dir.

903. Corman, Roger. *The Movie World of Roger Corman*. Edited by J. Philip di Franco, and Karyh G. Browne. Designed by Peter Davis. New York: Chelsea House, 1979. 237 p. Illustrated. Filmography.

904. *Roger Corman, Hollywood's Wild Angel [Videorecording]*. MPI Home Video, 1985. 1 videocassette, 58 min., sd., col., VHS.

Summary: This video is a semi-irreverent appreciation of the films and influence of Corman, prolific "B" movie maker. Interviews with his directors, his actors, and Corman, himself, reveal his philosophy of filmmaking.

CORNELL, KATHARINE. Act. 6/9/74

905. Mosel, Tad, and Macy, Gertrude. *Leading Lady: The World and Theatre of Katharine Cornell*. Foreword by

Martha Graham. Boston, Toronto: Little, Brown, Atlantic Monthly Press Book, 1978. 534 p. Illustrated. Index.

CRAWFORD, JOAN. Act. 5/13/77

906. Castle, Charles. *Joan Crawford: The Raging Star.* London: New English Library, 1977. 188 p. Illustrated. Bibliography. Filmography. Index. ***

907. Crawford, Christina. *Mommie Dearest.* New York: Morrow, 1978. 286 p. Illustrated.

908. Houston, David. *Jazz Baby.* New York: St. Martin's Press, 1983. 203 p. Illustrated. Bibliography.

909. Crawford, Christina. *Survivor.* New York: D. I. Fine, 1988. 268 p. Illustrated. ***

910. *Mommie Dearest [Videorecording].* Hollywood, CA: Paramount Home Video, 1981. 1 videocassette, 129 min., sd., col., 1/2 in.

Summary: This feature-length video was originally issued as a motion picture in 1981. It tells the story of Crawford's struggles for her career and the torments of her private life. The public Crawford was strong-willed, glamorous, but the private Crawford was desperate to be a mother, adopting her children when she was single. Cast: Faye Dunaway, Steve Forrest, Diana Scarwid, Mara Hobel, Xander Berkeley. Directed by Frank Perry.

911. Newquist, Roy. *Conversations with Joan Crawford.* Introduction by John Springer. Secaucus, NJ: Citadel, 1980. 175 p. Illustrated.

912. Raeburn, Anna. *Joan Crawford.* Photographs from the Kobal Collection. Boston: Little, Brown, 1986. 109 p. Illustrated. Paperbound.

913. Thomas, Bob. *Joan Crawford, a Biography*. New York: Simon and Schuster, 1978. 315 p. Illustrated. Filmography. Bibliography. Index.

914. Walker, Alexander. *Joan Crawford: The Ultimate Star*. London: Weidenfeld and Nicolson, 1983. 192 p. Illustrated. Filmography. Bibliography. Index.

CUKOR, GEORGE. Dir.

915. Phillips, Gene D. *George Cukor*. Twayne's Filmmakers Series. Boston: Twayne, 1982. 211 p. Bibliography. Filmography. Index.

CURTIS, TONY. Act.

916. Hunter, Allan. *Tony Curtis: The Man and His Movies*. New York: St. Martin's Press, 1985. 162 p. Illustrated. Bibliography. Index.

917. Munn, Michael. *Kid from the Bronx: The Life of Tony Curtis*. London: W. H. Allen, 1984. 248 p. Illustrated. ***

DAVIS, BETTE. Act.

918. Davis, Bette, and Herskowitz, Michael. *This 'n That*. New York: Putnam, 1987. 207 p. Illustrated.

919. Higham, Charles. *Bette, the Life of Bette Davis*. New York: Macmillan, 1981. 316 p. Illustrated. Playography. Filmography. Index.

920. Hyman, B. D. *My Mother's Keeper*. New York: Morrow, 1985. 348 p. Illustrated.

921. Hyman, B. D., and Hyman, Jeremy. *Narrow Is the Way.* New York: Morrow, 1987. 285 p.

922. Nickens, Christopher. *Bette Davis: A Biography in Photographs.* Garden City, NY: Doubleday, 1985. 215 p. Illustrated. ***

923. Ringgold, Gene. *Bette Davis, Her Films and Career.* Rev. ed. Foreword by Henry Hart. Secaucus, NJ: Citadel, 1985. 208 p. Illustrated.

924. Robinson, Jeffrey. *Bette Davis: Her Film & Stage Career.* London, New York: Proteus Books, 1982. 127 p. Illustrated. Filmography. Playography. Videography. Paperbound.

925. Walker, Alexander. *Bette Davis: A Celebration.* Picture research by the Kobal Collection. Boston, Toronto: Little, Brown, 1986. 192 p. Illustrated. Filmography.

DAY, DORIS. Act.

926. Gelb, Alan. *The Doris Day Scrapbook.* New York: Grosset & Dunlap, 1977. 159 p. Illustrated. Filmography. Index.

927. Young, Christopher. *The Films of Doris Day.* Secaucus, NJ: Citadel, 1977. 253 p. Illustrated.

DE HAVILLAND, OLIVIA. Act.

928. Higham, Charles. *Sisters: The Story of Olivia de Havilland and Joan Fontaine.* New York: Coward-McCann, 1984. 257 p. Illustrated. Index.

929. Thomas, Tony. *The Films of Olivia de Havilland.* Foreword by Bette Davis. Secaucus, NJ: Citadel, 1983. 254 p. Illustrated.

DEL RIO, DOLORES. Act. 4/11/83

930. Woll, Allen L. *The Films of Dolores Del Rio.* New York: Gordon Press, 1978. 129 p. Illustrated. Filmography. Videography. Bibliography.

DE NIRO, ROBERT. Act.

931. McKay, Keith. *Robert De Niro: The Hero Behind the Masks.* New York: St. Martin's Press, 1986. 195 p. Illustrated. Playography. Filmography. Index.

DIETRICH, MARLENE. Act.

932. Higham, Charles. *Marlene: The Life of Marlene Dietrich.* New York: Norton, 1977. 319 p. Illustrated. Index.

933. Spoto, Donald. *Falling in Love Again, Marlene Dietrich.* Boston, Toronto: Little, Brown, 1985. 154 p. Illustrated.

934. Walker, Alexander. *Dietrich.* Illustrations from the Kobal Collection. New York: Harper & Row, 1984. 207 p. Illustrated. Filmography. Bibliography. Index.

DOUGLAS, KIRK. Act.

935. Douglas, Kirk. *The Ragman's Son.* New York: Simon and Schuster, 1988. ***

936. Munn, Michael. *Kirk Douglas.* New York: St. Martin's Press, 1985. 192 p. Illustrated. Filmography. Index.

DUNAWAY, FAYE. Act.

937. Hunter, Allan. *Faye Dunaway.* New York: St. Martin's Press, Thomas Dunne, 1986. 256 p. Illustrated. Filmography. Playography. Videography. Bibliography. Index.

DUVALL, ROBERT. Act.

938. Slawson, Judith. *Robert Duvall: Hollywood Maverick.* New York: St. Martin's Press, 1985. 198 p. Illustrated. Index.

EASTWOOD, CLINT. Act.

939. Cole, Gerald, and Williams, Peter. *Clint Eastwood.* London: W. H. Allen, 1983. 224 p. Illustrated.

940. Downing, David, and Herman, Gary. *Clint Eastwood, All-American Anti-Hero: A Critical Appraisal of the World's Top Box Office Star and His Films.* New York: Quick Fox, 1977. 144 p. Illustrated. Filmography.

941. Frank, Alan. *Clint Eastwood.* New York: Exeter Books, 1982. 80 p. Illustrated. Filmography.

942. Guerif, Francois. *Clint Eastwood.* Translated from the French by Lisa Nesselson. New York: St. Martin's Press, 1986. 186 p. Illustrated. Bibliography. Paperbound.

943. Johnstone, Iain. *The Man with No Name*. New York: Morrow, Quill Paperbacks, 1981. 144 p. Illustrated. Filmography. Paperbound.

944. Ryder, Jeffrey. *Clint Eastwood*. New York: Dell, 1987. 189 p. Illustrated. Bibliography. Filmography. Paperbound.

945. Whitman, Mark. *The Films of Clint Eastwood*. Heroes of the Movies. New York: Confucian Press, Beaufort Books, 1982. 93 p. Illustrated. Filmography. Paperbound.

946. Zmijewsky, Boris, and Pfeiffer, Lee. *The Films of Clint Eastwood*. Secaucus, NJ: Citadel, 1982. 223 p. Illustrated. Table.

EVANS, EDITH. Act. 10/14/76

947. Batters, Jean. *Edith Evans: A Personal Memoir*. London: Hart-Davis MacGibbon, 1977. 159 p. Illustrated. Index.

948. Forbes, Bryan. *Ned's Girl: The Authorized Biography of Dame Edith Evans*. London: Elm Tree Books, 1977. 297 p. Illustrated. Index.

EVANS, LINDA. Act.

949. Freedland, Michael. *Linda Evans*. New York: St. Martin's Press, 1986. 127 p. Illustrated. Index.

FAIRBANKS, DOUGLAS, JR. Act.

950. Fairbanks, Douglas. *The Salad Days: An Autobiography of Douglas Fairbanks, Jr.* Garden City, NY: Doubleday, 1988. Index. ***

FAWCETT-MAJORS, FARRAH. Act.

951. Burstein, Patricia. *Farrah: An Unauthorized Biography of Farrah Fawcett-Majors.* New York: New American Library, Signet, 1977. 159 p. Illustrated. Paperbound.

FELLINI, FEDERICO. Dir.

952. Alpert, Hollis. *Fellini, a Life.* New York: Atheneum, 1986. 337 p. Illustrated. Filmography. Bibliography. Index.

953. Betti, Liliana. *Fellini.* Translated from the Italian by Joachim Neugroschel. Boston: Little, Brown, 1979. 249 p. Illustrated.

954. *Ciao Federico! [Motion Picture].* Macmillan Films, 1972. 55 min., sd., col., 16mm.
Summary: This is a study of the internationally acclaimed director filmed during the making of his *Satyricon.*

955. Fellini, Federico. *Fellini on Fellini.* Edited by Anna Keel and Christian Strich. Translated from the Italian by Isabel Quigley. New York: Dell, Delta, 1977. 180 p. Illustrated. Filmography. Bibliography. Index. Paperbound.

956. *Fellini: The Director as Creator [Motion Picture].* RAI, Rome, 1967. 29 min., sd., b&w., 16mm.

Summary: Fellini is shown behind and before the camera as he creates the film, *Juliet of the Spirits*, revealing his cinematic philosophy, craft, and personality.

957. Murray, Edward. *Fellini the Artist.* 2d ed. New York: Frederick Ungar, 1985. 282 p. Illustrated. Filmography. Bibliography. Index.

FIELD, SALLY. Act.

958. Bonderoff, Jason. *Sally Field.* New York: St. Martin's Press, 1987. 224 p. Illustrated. ***

FONDA, HENRY. Act. 8/12/82

959. Fonda, Afdera, and Thurlow, Clifford. *Never Before Noon: An Autobiography.* New York: Weidenfeld & Nicolson, 1987. 177 p. Illustrated. ***

960. Fonda, Henry, and Teichmann, Howard. *Fonda: My Life.* New York: New American Library, Signet, 1981. 399 p. Illustrated. Index. Paperbound.

961. Goldstein, Norm, and the Associated Press. *Henry Fonda.* New York: Holt, Rinehart and Winston, Owl, 1982. 123 p. Illustrated. Filmography. Paperbound.

962. Roberts, Allen, and Goldstein, Max. *Henry Fonda: A Biography.* Jefferson, NC: McFarland, 1984. 199 p. Illustrated. Index.

963. Thomas, Tony. *The Films of Henry Fonda.* Secaucus, NJ: Citadel, 1983. 255 p. Illustrated.

234

FONDA, JANE. Act.

964. Freedland, Michael. *Jane Fonda*. New York: St. Martin's Press, 1987. ***

965. Guiles, Fred Lawrence. *Jane Fonda: The Actress in Her Time*. New York: Pinnacle Books, 1983. 354 p. Illustrated. Bibliography. Index. Paperbound.

966. Haddad-Garcia, George. *The Films of Jane Fonda*. Secaucus, NJ: Citadel, 1981. 254 p. Illustrated.

967. Herman, Gary, and Downing, David. *Jane Fonda: All American Anti-Heroine*. Designed by Perry Neville. New York: Quick Fox, 1980. 144 p. Illustrated. Filmography. Paperbound.

968. *Jane [Motion Picture]*. The Living Camera. New York: Time-Life Films, 1970. 54 min., sd., b&w, 16mm.
Summary: Follows Fonda as she prepares for her Broadway début by appearing in a new play in Baltimore, Wilmington, and Philadelphia.

969. Kiernan, Thomas. *Jane Fonda: Heroine for Our Time*. New York: Delilah/Putnam, 1982. 320 p. Illustrated. Filmography. Paperbound.

970. Spada, James. *Fonda, Her Life in Pictures*. Garden City, NY: Doubleday, Dolphin, 1985. 229 p. Illustrated. Paperbound.

FONTAINE, JOAN. Act.

971. Fontaine, Joan. *No Bed of Roses*. New York: Morrow, 1978. 319 p. Illustrated. Index.

FONTANNE, LYNN. Act. 7/30/83

972. Brown, Jared. *The Fabulous Lunts: A Biography of Alfred Lunt and Lynn Fontanne*. Foreword by Helen Hayes. New York: Atheneum, 1986. 523 p. Illustrated. Bibliography.

FORD, HARRISON. Act.

973. Clinch, Minty. *Harrison Ford: A Biography*. London: New English Library, 1987. 214 p. Illustrated. Filmography. Bibliography. Index. ***

974. McKenzie, Alan. *The Harrison Ford Story*. New York: Arbor House, Priam, 1984. 109 p. Illustrated. Filmography. Paperbound.

975. Vare, Ethlie Ann, and Toledo, Mary. *Harrison Ford*. New York: St. Martin's Press, 1988. 127 p. Illustrated. Filmography. Paperbound. ***

FORD, JOHN. Dir. 8/31/73

976. Anderson, Lindsay. *About John Ford*. London: Plexus, 1981. 256 p. Illustrated. Filmography. Index.

977. Bogdanovich, Peter. *John Ford*. Rev. ed. Movie Paperbacks. Berkeley: University of California Press, 1978. 149 p. Filmography. Bibliography. Paperbound.

978. *Directed by John Ford [Motion Picture]*. American Film Institute, 1972. 3 motion pictures, 102 min., sd., col., 16mm.
Summary: This documentary reviews the achievements of Ford in a series of reminiscences by actors and technicians,

with comments by Ford himself, and with excerpts from his films.

979. Ford, Dan. *Pappy: The Life of John Ford.* Englewood Cliffs, NJ: Prentice-Hall, 1979. 324 p. Illustrated. Index.

980. Ford, Dan. *The Unquiet Man.* London: William Kimber, 1982. 324 p. Illustrated. Index.

981. Gallagher, Tag. *John Ford: The Man and His Films.* Berkeley: University of California Press, 1986. 572 p. Illustrated. Filmography. Bibliography. Index.

982. Sinclair, Andrew. *John Ford.* New York: Dial Press/J. Wade, 1979. 305 p. Illustrated. Filmography. Index.

983. Stowell, Peter. *John Ford.* Twayne's Filmmakers Series. Boston: Twayne, 1986. 168 p. Illustrated. Bibliography. Filmography. Index.

FORMAN, MILOS. Dir.

984. *Meeting Milos Forman [Motion Picture].* Macmillan Films, 1973. 30 min., sd., col., 16mm.

Summary: Presents an interview with the Czech filmmaker, Forman, including filmclips of his work. Forman explains his reasons for using nonprofessional actors, tells anecdotes about his discoveries of talent, and comments on the artistry of performers.

985. Slater, Thomas J. *Milos Forman: A Bio-bibliography.* Bio-bibliographies in the Performing Arts, no. 1. New York: Greenwood Press, 1987. 193 p. Filmography. Index. ***

FOX, MICHAEL J. Act.

986. Daly, Marsha. *Michael J. Fox, on to the Future*. New York: St. Martin's Press, 1985. 112 p. Illustrated. Paperbound.

987. Kasbah, Mimi. *The Michael J. Fox Scrapbook*. New York: Ballantine Books, 1987. 78 p. Illustrated. Paperbound.

FUGARD, ATHOL. Dir.

988. Fugard, Athol. *Notebooks, 1960-1977*. Introduction by Mary Benson. New York: Knopf, 1983. 238 p.

GARBO, GRETA. Act.

989. Sands, Frederick, and Broman, Sven. *The Divine Garbo*. New York: Grosset & Dunlap, 1979. 243 p. Illustrated. Index.

990. Walker, Alexander. *Garbo: A Portrait*. New York: Macmillan, 1980. 191 p. Illustrated. Filmography. Bibliography. Index.

GARDNER, AVA. Act.

991. Daniell, John. *Ava Gardner*. New York: St. Martin's Press, 1982. 221 p. Illustrated. Bibliography. Filmography. Index.

992. Flamini, Roland. *Ava: A Biography*. New York: Coward, McCann & Geoghegan, 1983. 269 p. Illustrated.

993. Kass, Judith M. *Ava Gardner: An Illustrated History of the Movies*. New York: Jove Publications, Harvest/HBJ Book, 1977. 158 p. Illustrated. Bibliography. Filmography. Index. Paperbound.

GARNER, JAMES. Act.

994. Strait, Raymond. *James Garner*. New York: St. Martin's Press, 1985. 388 p. Illustrated. Index.

GEARY, ANTHONY (TONY). Act.

995. Blumenthal, John. *Anthony Geary*. New York: Simon and Schuster, Wallaby, 1982. 93 p. Illustrated.

GEORGE, (CHIEF) DAN. Act. 9/23/81

996. *Dan George Special [Motion Picture]*. Edmonton, Alberta, Canada: Alberta Native Communications Society, 1975. 1 reel, 28 min., sd., col., 16mm.

Summary: A shorter version (21 min.) released under the title: *Chief Dan George Speaks*. Credit: Produced and directed by Jeff Howard. Features George reading his poems and talking about the Indian people in a changing society.

997. Mortimer, Hilda, and George, Dan. *You Call Me Chief: Impressions of the Life of Chief Dan George*. Toronto: Doubleday Canada; Garden City, NY: Doubleday, 1981. 182 p. Illustrated.

GERE, RICHARD. Act.

998. Davis, Judith. *Richard Gere: An Unauthorized Biography.* New York: New American Library, Signet, 1983. 190 p. Illustrated. Filmography. Paperbound.

GIBSON, MEL. Act.

999. Hanrahan, John. *Mel Gibson.* Milwaukee, WI: Heroic! Publishing, 1986. 88 p. Illustrated. Filmography. Playography. Videography. Paperbound.

1000. McKay, Keith. *Mel Gibson.* New York: Doubleday, Dolphin, 1986. 95 p. Filmography. Paperbound.

1001. Ragan, David. *Mel Gibson.* New York: Dell, 1985. 172 p. Illustrated. Paperbound.

GIELGUD, JOHN. Act.

1002. *The Ages of Gielgud.* Edited by Ronald Harwood. New York: Limelight Editions, 1984. 182 p. Illustrated. Tables. Index.

1003. Brandreth, Gyles. *John Gielgud: A Celebration.* Boston: Little, Brown, 1984. 186 p. Illustrated. Playography. Filmography. Videography. Bibliography. Index.

1004. Gielgud, John; Miller, John; and Powell, John. *An Actor and His Time.* London: Sidgwick & Jackson, 1979. 253 p. Illustrations. Table. Index.

1005. Gielgud, John. *An Actor in His Time [Sound Recording].* Downsview, Ontario, Canada: Listen for Pleasure, 1981. 2 sound cassettes, 120 min., mono.

Summary: This is an abridged version (read by Gielgud) of the BBC broadcasts of *An Actor and His Time*, by Gielgud, John Miller, and John Powell (above).

GISH, LILLIAN. Act.

1006. *Lillian Gish*. Foreword by Eileen Bowser. New York: Museum of Modern Art, 1980. 32 p. Illustrated. Filmography. Paperbound.

GODARD, JEAN-LUC. Dir.

1007. Kreidl, John. *Jean-Luc Godard*. Twayne's Theatrical Arts Series. Boston: Twayne, 1980. 273 p. Illustrated. Bibliography. Filmography. Index.

1008. MacCabe, Colin; Eaton, Mick; and Mulvey, Laura. *Godard: Images, Sounds, Politics*. British Film Institute Cinema Series. Photography by Eric Sargent. London: Macmillan, 1980. 175 p. Illustrated. Filmography. Videography. Bibliography.

GODDARD, PAULETTE. Act.

1009. Morella, Joe, and Epstein, Edward Z. *Paulette: The Adventurous Life of Paulette Goddard*. New York: St. Martin's Press, 1985. 240 p. Illustrated. Index. Filmography.

GORDON, RUTH. Act. 8/28/85

1010. Gordon, Ruth. *Ruth Gordon, an Open Book.* Garden City, NY: Doubleday, 1980. 395 p. Index.

GRABLE, BETTY. Act. 7/2/73

1011. Pastos, Spero. *Pin-up: The Tragedy of Betty Grable.* New York: Putnam, 1986. 175 p. Illustrated.

1012. Warren, Doug. *Betty Grable, the Reluctant Movie Queen.* New York: St. Martin's Press, 1981. 237 p. Illustrated. Filmography. Index.

GRANT, CARY. Act. 11/29/86

1013. Britton, Andrew. *Cary Grant: Comedy and Male Desire.* Edited by Sheila Whitaker. Newcastle upon Tyne, England: Tyneside Cinema, 1983. 24 p. Paperbound. ***

1014. *Cary Grant: In the Spotlight.* New York: Galley Press, 1980. 156 p. Illustrated.

1015. *Cary Grant: The Leading Man [Videorecording].* New York: Wombat Film & Video, 1988? 1 videocassette, 60 min., col., 1/2 in.

Summary: Containing clips from many Grant films, this documentary includes interviews with eight of his co-stars and directors.

1016. Godfrey, Lionel. *Cary Grant: The Light Touch.* New York: St. Martin's Press, 1981. 224 p. Illustrated. Bibliography. Filmography. Index.

1017. Guthrie, Lee. *The Life and Loves of Cary Grant: A Biography.* New York: Drake Publishers, 1977. 239 p. Illustrated. Filmography. Index.

1018. Harris, Warren G. *Cary Grant: A Touch of Elegance.* Garden City, NY: Doubleday, 1987. 296 p. Illustrated. Filmography. Index.

1019. McIntosh, William Currie, and Weaver, William. *The Private Cary Grant.* London: Sidgwick & Jackson, 1983. 158 p. Illustrated. Index.

1020. Schickel, Richard. *Cary Grant: A Celebration.* Boston: Little, Brown, 1983. 190 p. Illustrated. Filmography.

1021. Trescott, Pamela. *Cary Grant.* Washington, DC: Acropolis Books, 1987. Index. ***

1022. Wansell, Geoffrey. *Haunted Idol: The Story of the Real Cary Grant.* New York: Morrow, 1984. 336 p. Illustrated. Filmography. Index.

GUINNESS, ALEC. Act.

1023. *The Art of Film: Volume 8, Performance in Depth, the Many Roles of Alec Guinness [Videorecording].* Northbrook, IL: Coronet Films & Video, 1978. 1 videocassette, 28 min., sd., col., with b&w sequences, 1/2 in.
    Credits: Written and directed by Saul J. Turell, and Jeff Lieberman. Narrated by Douglas Fairbanks, Jr. Summary: A look at the career of Alec Guinness, with scenes from his movies.

1024. Guinness, Alec. *Blessings in Disguise.* New York: Knopf, 1986. 238 p. Illustrated. Index.

1025. Taylor, John Russell. *Alec Guinness: A Celebration.* Boston: Little, Brown, 1984. 184 p. Illustrated. Index.

HAGMAN, LARRY. Act.

1026. Adams, Leon. *Larry Hagman: A Biography.* New York: St. Martin's Press, Thomas Dunne, 1987. 134 p. Illustrated. Index.

HARRISON, REX. Act.

1027. Eyles, Allen. *Rex Harrison.* Secaucus, NJ: Lyle Stuart, 1986. 220 p. Illustrated. ***

1028. Moseley, Roy; Masheter, Philip; and Masheter, Martin. *Rex Harrison: A Biography.* New York: St. Martin's Press, 1987. 350 p. Illustrated. Bibliography. Playography. Filmography. Index.

HART, KITTY CARLISLE. Act. See: CARLISLE, KITTY. Act.

HAWN, GOLDIE. Act.

1029. Berman, Connie. *Solid Goldie: An Illustrated Biography of Goldie Hawn.* New York: Simon and Schuster, Fireside, 1981. 125 p. Illustrated. Paperbound.

1030. Haining, Peter. *Goldie.* London: W. H. Allen, 216 p. Illustrated. Filmography.

HAYES, HELEN. Act.

1031. Barrow, Kenneth. *Helen Hayes, First Lady of the American Theatre*. Garden City, NY: Doubleday, Dolphin, 1985. 216 p. Illustrated. Playography. Filmography. Radiography. Videography. Index.

1032. *Helen Hayes—Portrait of an American Actress [Motion Picture]*. Phoenix Films, 1973. 90 min., sd., col., 16mm.
Summary: Helen Hayes reminisces about her life and acting career on the stage and screen.

1033. Robbins, Jhan. *Front Page Marriage*. New York: Putnam, 1982. 224 p. Illustrated. Bibliography. Index.

HAYWORTH, RITA. Act. 5/14/87

1034. Hill, James. *Rita Hayworth: A Memoir*. New York: Simon and Schuster, 1983. 238 p. Illustrated.

1035. Kobal, John. *Rita Hayworth: The Time, the Place, and the Woman*. New York: Norton, 1977. 328 p. Illustrated. Bibliography. Index.

1036. Morella, Joe, and Epstein, Edward Z. *Rita: The Life of Rita Hayworth*. New York: Dell, 1983. 261 p. Illustrated. Filmography. Paperbound.

HEPBURN, AUDREY. Act.

1037. Higham, Charles. *Audrey: The Life of Audrey Hepburn*. New York: Macmillan, 1984. 228 p. Illustrated. Filmography. Index.

1038. Latham, Caroline. *Audrey Hepburn*. London, New York: Proteus, 1984. 127 p. Illustrated. Filmography. Paperbound.

1039. Woodward, Ian. *Audrey Hepburn*. New York: St. Martin's Press, 1984. 318 p. Illustrated. Filmography. Paperbound.

HEPBURN, KATHARINE. Act.

1040. Andersen, Christopher. *Young Kate*. New York: H. Holt, Hutter Book, 1988. 270 p. Illustrated. Bibliography. Index. ***

1041. Britton, Andrew. *Katharine Hepburn, the Thirties and After*. Newcastle upon Tyne, England: Tyneside Cinema, 1984. 134 p. Bibliography. Filmography. Index.

1042. Carey, Gary. *Katharine Hepburn: A Hollywood Yankee*. Rev. ed. New York: St. Martin's Press, 1983. 284 p. Illustrated. Filmography. Index.

1043. Edwards, Anne. *A Remarkable Woman: A Biography of Katharine Hepburn*. New York: Morrow, 1985. 512 p. Illustrated. Filmography. Playography. Videography. Radiography. Bibliography. Index.

1044. Freedland, Michael. *Katharine Hepburn*. London: W. H. Allen, 1984. 250 p. Illustrated. Filmography. Index.

1045. Grisolia, Cynthia, ed. *Hepburn*. The Screen Greats, Vol. 6. New York: Starlog Press, 1982. 82 p. Illustrated. Filmography. Paperbound.

1046. Higham, Charles. *Kate: The Life of Katharine Hepburn*. New York: New American Library, Signet, 1981. 238 p. Illustrated. Index. Paperbound.

1047. Latham, Caroline. *Katharine Hepburn: Her Film and Stage Career*. Proteus Reels Series. London, New York: Proteus Books, 1982. 127 p. Illustrated. Filmography. Playography. Videography.

1048. Morley, Sheridan. *Katharine Hepburn*. Picture research by the Kobal Collection. Boston: Little, Brown, 1984. 190 p. Illustrated. Filmography.

1049. Spada, James. *Hepburn, Her Life in Pictures*. New York: Doubleday, Dolphin, 1984. 212 p. Illustrated. Paperbound.

HESTON, CHARLTON. Act.

1050. Crowther, Bruce. *Charlton Heston, the Epic Presence*. London: Columbus Books, 1986. 192 p. Illustrated. Bibliography. Filmography. Index. Paperbound.

1051. Heston, Charlton. *The Actor's Life: Journals, 1956-1976*. Edited by Hollis Alpert. New York: E. P. Dutton, A Henry Robbins Book, 1978. 482 p. Illustrated.

1052. Munn, Michael. *Charlton Heston*. New York: St. Martin's Press, 1986. 224 p. Illustrated. Filmography. Playography. Videography. Index.

1053. Rovin, Jeff. *The Films of Charlton Heston*. Secaucus, NJ: Citadel, 1977. 224 p. Illustrated.

1054. Williams, John. *The Films of Charlton Heston*. 2d ed. Bembridge, England: BCW Publishing, 1977. 47 p. Illustrated. Filmography. ***

HITCHCOCK, ALFRED. Dir. 4/29/80

1055. *Alfred Hitchcock [Videorecording]*. MPI Home Video, 1985. 1 videocassette, 55 min., col., VHS.

Summary: Alfred Hitchcock talks about his work; what it was he was saying, and how he illustrated his themes. This discussion is accompanied by segments from several of his more famous movies including: *North by Northwest, Psycho, The Birds*, and *Frenzy*.

1056. Freeman, David. *The Last Days of Alfred Hitchcock: A Memoir Featuring the Screenplay of "Alfred Hitchcock's The Short Night."* Woodstock, NY: Overlook Press, 1984. 281 p. Illustrated.

1057. Haley, Michael. *The Alfred Hitchcock Album*. Englewood Cliffs, NJ: Prentice-Hall, 1981. 177 p. Illustrated. Filmography. Bibliography. Index.

1058. Phillips, Gene D. *Alfred Hitchcock*. Twayne's Filmmakers Series. Preface by Andrew Sarris. Boston: Twayne, 1984. 211 p. Illustrated. Bibliography. Filmography. Index.

1059. Spoto, Donald. *The Dark Side of Genius: The Life of Alfred Hitchcock*. Boston: Little, Brown, 1983. 594 p. Illustrated. Bibliography. Filmography. Index.

1060. Taylor, John Russell. *Hitch: The Life and Times of Alfred Hitchcock*. New York: Pantheon Books, 1978. 320 p. Illustrated. Index.

HOFFMAN, DUSTIN. Act.

1061. Brode, Douglas. *The Films of Dustin Hoffman*. Secaucus, NJ: Citadel, 1983. 224 p. Illustrated.

1062. Johnstone, Iain. *Dustan Hoffman.* Film and Theatre Stars Series. Tunbridge Wells, Kent, England: Spellmount; New York: Hippocrene Books, 1984. 94 p. Illustrated. Filmography.

1063. Lenburg, Jeff. *Dustin Hoffman, Hollywood's Anti-Hero.* New York: St. Martin's Press, 1983. 172 p. Illustrated. Filmography. Bibliography. Index.

HOLDEN, WILLIAM. Act. 11/16/81

1064. Quirk, Lawrence J. *The Complete Films of William Holden.* Secaucus, NJ: Citadel, 1986. 285 p. Illustrated. Paperbound.

1065. Thomas, Bob. *Golden Boy: The Untold Story of William Holden.* New York: St. Martin's Press, 1983. 276 p. Illustrated. Filmography. Index.

HOUSEMAN, JOHN. Act. 10/30/88

1066. Houseman, John. *Final Dress.* New York: Simon and Schuster, 1983. 559 p. Illustrated. Index.

1067. Houseman, John. *Front and Center.* New York: Simon and Schuster, 1979. 512 p. Illustrated. Bibliography. Index.

1068. Houseman, John. *Unfinished Business: A Memoir.* London: Chatto & Windus, 1986. 498 p. Illustrated. ***

HOWARD, TREVOR. Act. 1/7/88

1069. Knight, Vivienne. *Trevor Howard: A Gentleman and a Player.* New York: Beaufort Books, 1986. Filmography. Bibliography. ***

HUDSON, ROCK. Act. 10/2/85

1070. Bego, Mark. *Rock Hudson, Public and Private: An Unauthorized Biography.* New York: New American Library, Signet, 1986. 189 p. Illustrated. Filmography. Videography. Playography. Discography. Bibliography. Paperbound.

1071. Gates, Phyllis, and Thomas, Bob. *My Husband, Rock Hudson: The Real Story of Rock Hudson's Marriage to Phyllis Gates.* Garden City, NY: Doubleday, 1987. 232 p. Illustrated.

1072. Hudson, Rock, and Davidson, Sara. *Rock Hudson, His Story.* New York: Morrow, 1986. 311 p. Illustrated.

1073. Oppenheimer, Jerry, and Vitek, Jack. *Idol Rock Hudson: The True Story of an American Film Hero.* New York: Villard Books, 1986. 273 p. Illustrated. Filmography. Index.

HURT, WILLIAM. Act.

1074. Goldstein, Toby. *William Hurt, the Man, the Actor.* New York: St. Martin's Press, 1987. 170 p. Index.

HUSTON, JOHN. Dir. 8/28/87

1075. Hammen, Scott. *John Huston.* Twayne's Filmmakers Series. Boston: Twayne, 1985. 163 p. Illustrated. Bibliography. Filmography. Index.

1076. Huston, John. *An Open Book.* New York: Knopf, 1980. 389 p. Illustrated. Index.

1077. Kaminsky, Stuart M. *John Huston, Maker of Magic.* Boston: Houghton Mifflin, 1978. 237 p. Illustrated. Filmography. Bibliography. Index.

1078. Madsen, Axel. *John Huston.* Garden City, NY: Doubleday, 1978. 280 p. Illustrated. Filmography. Bibliography. Index

1079. Pratley, Gerald. *The Cinema of John Huston.* South Brunswick, NJ: A. S. Barnes; London: Tantivy Press, 1977. 223 p. Illustrated.

JACKSON, GLENDA. Act.

1080. Nathan, David. *Glenda Jackson.* Film and Theatre Stars. Tunbridge Wells, Kent, England: Spellmount; New York: Hippocrene Books, 1984. 95 p. Illustrated. Filmography. Playography.

1081. Woodward, Ian. *Glenda Jackson: A Study in Fire and Ice.* New York: St. Martin's Press, 1985. 225 p. Illustrated. Filmography. Index.

JONES, JAMES EARL. Act.

1082. *James Earl Jones: Actor [Filmstrip].* Black Experience in the Arts. Pleasantville, NY: Warren Schloat Productions, 1971. 68 fr., col., 35mm., and phonodisc, 33 1/3 rpm.
    Credits: Producer and editor, Lilla Brownstone. Summary: Jones discusses his early reasons for going into the theater, his experiences, and his hopes for the future.

KAZAN, ELIA. Dir.

1083. Pauly, Thomas H. *An American Odyssey: Elia Kazan and American Culture.* Philadelphia, PA: Temple University Press, 1983. 282 p. Illustrated. Bibliography. Index.

KEATON, DIANE. Act.

1084. Munshower, Suzanne. *The Diane Keaton Scrapbook.* New York: Grosset & Dunlap, 1979. 95 p. Illustrated. Paperbound.

KERR, DEBORAH. Act.

1085. Braun, Eric. *Deborah Kerr.* New York: St. Martin's Press, 1978. 264 p. Illustrated. Bibliography. Filmography. Discography. Index.

KORDA, MICHAEL. Dir.

1086. Korda, Michael. *Charmed Lives: A Family Romance.* New York: Random House, 1979. 498 p. Illustrated. Index.

KRAMER, STANLEY. Dir.

1087. Spoto, Donald. *Stanley Kramer, Film Maker.* New York: Putnam, 1978. 367 p. Illustrated. Filmography. Index.

KRISTOFFERSON, KRIS. Act.

1088. Kalet, Beth. *Kris Kristofferson.* New York: Quick Fox, 1979. 96 p. Illustrated. Discography. Paperbound.

LANCASTER, BURT. Act.

1089. Clinch, Minty. *Burt Lancaster.* New York: Stein & Day, 1984. 198 p. Illustrated. Filmography. Bibliography. Index.

1090. Hunter, Allan. *Burt Lancaster: The Man and His Movies.* New York: St. Martin's Press, 1984. 160 p. Illustrated. Index.

1091. Windeler, Robert. *Burt Lancaster.* New York: St. Martin's Press, 1984. 217 p. Illustrated. Index.

LANDON, MICHAEL. Act.

1092. Daly, Marsha. *Michael Landon.* New York: St. Martin's Press, 1987. ***

1093. *Sam's Son [Videorecording].* Worldvision Home Video, 1985. 1 videocassette, 107 min., sd., col., 1/2 in., VHS.
Credits: Written and directed by Michael Landon; produced by Kent McCray. Cast: Eli Wallach, Timothy Patrick Murphy, Anne Jackson, Hallie Todd, Alan Hayes, and Jonna Lee. Summary: Landon relates the dramatic story of his own teenage years. Also issued as a motion picture.

LANGE, JESSICA. Act.

1094. Jeffries, J. T. *Jessica Lange: A Biography.* New York: St. Martin's Press, 1986. 158 p. Illustrated. Filmography.

LANSBURY, ANGELA. Act.

1095. Bonanno, Margaret Wander. *Angela Lansbury: A Biography.* New York: St. Martin's Press, 1987. 225 p. Illustrated. Filmography. Playography. Videography. Discography. Bibliography. Index.

LEMMON, JACK. Act.

1096. Baltake, Joe. *Jack Lemmon, His Films and Career.* Rev. ed. Tribute by Walter Matthau. Foreword by Judith Crist. Secaucus, NJ: Citadel, 1986. 286 p. Illustrated. Paperbound. ***

1097. Freedland, Michael. *Jack Lemmon*. New York: St. Martin's Press, 1985. 177 p. Illustrated. Index.

1098. Holtzman, William. *Jack Lemmon*. A Pyramid Illustrated History of the Movies. New York: Pyramid Publications, 1977. 160 p. Illustrated. Bibliography. Filmography. Index. Paperbound.

1099. Widener, Don. *Lemmon: A Biography*. London: W. H. Allen, 1977. 247 p. Illustrated. Index.

LESTER, RICHARD. Dir.

1100. Sinyard, Neil. *The Films of Richard Lester*. Totowa, NJ: Barnes & Noble, 1985. 174 p. Illustrated. Filmography. Index.

LOGAN, JOSHUA. Dir. 7/12/88

1101. Logan, Joshua. *Movie Stars, Real People, and Me*. New York: Delacorte Press, 1978. 368 p. Illustrated. Playography. Filmography. Index.

LOREN, SOPHIA. Act.

1102. Hotchner, A. E. *Sophia, Living and Loving: Her Own Story*. New York: Morrow, 1979. 256 p. Illustrated. Filmography.

1103. Levy, Alan. *Forever, Sophia: An Intimate Portrait*. New York: St. Martin's Press, 1986. 264 p. Illustrated. Index.

1104. Shaw, Sam. *Sophia Loren in the Camera Eye*. New York: Exeter Books, 1979. 160 p. Illustrated. Filmography.

LOSEY, JOSEPH. Dir. 6/22/84

1105. Hirsch, Foster. *Joseph Losey.* Twayne's Theatrical Arts Series. Boston: Twayne, 1980. 256 p. Illustrated. Bibliography. Filmography. Index.

1106. Losey, Joseph, and Ciment, Michel. *Conversations with Losey.* London, New York: Methuen, 1985. 436 p. Illustrated. Filmography. Index.

LOY, MYRNA. Act.

1107. Kay, Karyn. *Myrna Loy.* A Pyramid Illustrated History of the Movies. New York: Pyramid Publications, 1977. 160 p. Illustrated. Bibliography. Filmography. Index. Paperbound.

1108. Kotsilibas-Davis, James, and Loy, Myrna. *Myrna Loy: Being and Becoming.* New York: Knopf, 1987. 372 p. Illustrated. Index.

1109. Quirk, Lawrence J. *The Films of Myrna Loy.* Secaucus, NJ: Citadel, 1980. 254 p. Illustrated.

LUCAS, GEORGE. Dir.

1110. Pollock, Dale. *Skywalking: The Life and Films of George Lucas.* New York: Harmony Books, 1983. 304 p. Illustrated. Filmography. Bibliography. Index.

LUCCI, SUSAN. Act.

1111. Siegel, Barbara, and Siegel, Scott. *Susan Lucci*. New York: St. Martin's Press, 1986. 154 p. Illustrated. Index.

McCOWEN, ALEC. Act.

1112. McCowen, Alec. *Double Bill*. New York: Atheneum, 1980. 197 p. Illustrated.

1113. McCowen, Alec. *Young Gemini*. New York: Atheneum, 1979. 111 p.

McKELLEN, IAN. Act.

1114. Gibson, Joy Leslie. *Ian McKellen*. London: Wiedenfeld & Nicolson, 1986. 190 p. Illustrated. Bibliography. Index.

1115. McKellen, Ian. *Acting Shakespeare [Sound Recording]*. IBM, 1982. 1 sound cassette.

Issued in conjunction with a television program of the same title, April 26, 1982. Gives excerpts from and commentary on McKellen's one-man show, "Acting Shakespeare." Contents: An interview with McKellen (seventeen minutes); Highlights from the performance (twenty minutes).

MacLAINE, SHIRLEY. Act.

1116. Denis, Christopher. *The Films of Shirley MacLaine*. Secaucus, NJ: Citadel, 1980. 217 p. Illustrated.

1117. Erens, Patricia. *The Films of Shirley MacLaine.* South Brunswick, NJ: A. S. Barnes; London: Thomas Yoseloff, 1978. 202 p. Illustrated. Filmography. Bibliography. Index.

1118. Freedland, Michael. *Shirley MacLaine.* Manchester, NH: Salem House, 1986. 236 p. Illustrated.

1119. MacLaine, Shirley. *Dancing in the Light.* Toronto, New York: Bantam Books, 1985. 421 p.

1120. MacLaine, Shirley. *Out on a Limb.* Toronto, New York: Bantam Books, 1984. 367 p. Paperbound.

1121. MacLaine, Shirley. *It's All in the Playing.* Toronto, New York: Bantam Books, 1987. 338 p.

1122. Pickard, Roy. *Shirley MacLaine.* Tunbridge Wells, Kent, England: Spellmount; New York: Hippocrene Books, 1985. 95 p. Illustrated. Filmography. Bibliography.

1123. Spada, James. *Shirley & Warren.* New York: Macmillan, 1985. 214 p. Illustrated. Bibliography.

MacLEOD, GAVIN. Act.

1124. MacLeod, Gavin; MacLeod, Patti; and Chapian, Marie. *Back on Course.* Old Tappan, NJ: F. H. Revell, 1987. 183 p. Illustrated.

McQUEEN, STEVE. Act. 11/7/80

1125. Campbell, Joanna. *The Films of Steve McQueen.* St. Paul, MN: Greenhaven Press, 1978. 46 p. Illustrated. Filmography.

1126. Nolan, William F. *McQueen*. New York: Berkley Books, 1984. 241 p. Illustrated. Index. Paperbound.

1127. Ragsdale, Grady Jr. *Steve McQueen, the Final Chapter*. Foreword by Billy Graham. Ventura, CA: Vision House, 1983. 198 p. Illustrated.

1128. St. Charnez, Casey. *The Films of Steve McQueen*. Secaucus, NJ: Citadel, 1984. 255 p. Illustrated.

1129. Spiegel, Penina. *McQueen: The Untold Story of a Bad Boy in Hollywood*. Garden City, NY: Doubleday, 1986. 367 p. Illustrated. Playography. Videography. Filmography.

1130. *Steve McQueen: Man on the Edge [Videocassette]*. Wombat Productions, 1966. 1 videocassette, 60 min., sd., col., VHS/Beta.

Summary: A thorough look at the career and personality (including rare home movie footage) of the Hollywood star. Credit: Narrated by James Coburn.

1131. Toffel, Neile McQueen. *My Husband, My Friend*. New York: Atheneum, 1986. 327 p. Illustrated. ***

MANKIEWICZ, JOSEPH. Dir.

1132. Geist, Kenneth L. *Pictures Will Talk: The Life and Films of Joseph L. Mankiewicz*. Introduction by Richard Burton. New York: Scribner, 1978. 443 p. Illustrated. Filmography. Videography. Index.

MARVIN, LEE. Act. 8/29/87

1133. Zec, Donald. *Marvin: The Story of Lee Marvin.* New York: St. Martin's Press, 1980. 252 p. Illustrated. Filmography. Index.

MASON, JAMES. Act. 7/27/84

1134. Mason, James. *Before I Forget: Autobiography and Drawings.* London: H. Hamilton, 1981. 345 p. Illustrated. Index.

MATTHAU, WALTER. Act.

1135. Hunter, Allan. *Walter Matthau.* New York: St. Martin's Press, 1984. 208 p. Illustrated. Filmography. Playography. Videography. Bibliography. Index.

MAZURSKY, PAUL. Dir.

1136. *Word into Image: Screenwriter, Paul Mazursky [Videorecording].* Santa Monica, CA: American Film Foundation, 1984. 1 videocassette, 30 min., sd., col., U-matic, Beta, or VHS.

Credits: Producer-directors Freida Lee Mock, and Terry Sanders. Summary: An interview with Mazursky. He talks about his early work and his progression from serious writer to performer to television comedy writer to screenwriter-director. Clips from his films show how he speaks to the changes people face, yet never fails to remain the entertainer.

MILLER, JONATHAN. Dir.

1137. *Jonathan Miller [Motion Picture]*. Toronto: Canadian Broadcasting Corporation, 1972. 30 min., sd., col., 16mm.

   Credits: Producer-director, Sam Levene. Summary: Reviews the career of writer, director, and actor Jonathan Miller.

1138. *Jonathan Miller's London [Motion Picture]*. New York: Learning Corporation of America, 1980. 1 film reel, 26 min., sd., col., 16mm.

   Also in a videocassette version (VHS, 51 minutes). Credits: Producer-director, John McGreevy. Summary: Miller takes the viewer on a tour of London, highlighting his childhood, which was spent in the city.

MR. T. Act.

1139. Mr. T. *Mr. T, the Man with the Gold: An Autobiography*. New York: St. Martin's Press, 1984. 276 p. Illustrated.

MITCHUM, ROBERT. Act.

1140. Downing, David. *Robert Mitchum*. London: W. H. Allen, 1985. 220 p. Illustrated. ***

1141. Eells, George. *Robert Mitchum: A Biography*. New York: F. Watts, 1984. 328 p. Illustrated. Filmography. Index.

1142. Malcolm, Derek. *Robert Mitchum*. Film and Theatre Stars. Tunbridge Wells, Kent, England: Spellmount; New York: Hippocrene Books, 1984. 95 p. Illustrated. Filmography.

1143. Marill, Alvin H. *Robert Mitchum on the Screen.* South Brunswick, NJ: A. S. Barnes, 1978. 246 p. Illustrated. Radiography. Videography. Index.

MONTALBAN, RICARDO. Act.

1144. Montalban, Ricardo, and Thomas, Bob. *Reflections: A Life in Two Worlds.* Garden City, NY: Doubleday, 1980. 164 p. Illustrated.

MOORE, DUDLEY. Act.

1145. Lenburg, Jeff. *Dudley Moore: An Informal Biography.* New York: Delilah Communications, 1982. 143 p. Illustrated. Filmography. Discography. Paperbound.

MOORE, MARY TYLER. Act.

1146. Bonderoff, Jason. *Mary Tyler Moore.* New York: St. Martin's Press, 1986. 200 p. Illustrated. Index.

1147. Bryars, Chris. *The Real Mary Tyler Moore.* New York: Pinnacle Books, 1977. 164 p. Illustrated. Paperbound.

1148. Stefoff, Rebecca. *Mary Tyler Moore: The Woman Behind the Smile: An Unauthorized Biography.* New York: New American Library, Signet, 1986. 190 p. Illustrated. Paperbound.

MOORE, ROGER. Act.

1149. Donovan, Paul. *Roger Moore.* London: W. H. Allen, Comet Books, 1983. 224 p. Illustrated. Filmography. Index. Paperbound.

1150. Moseley, Roy; Masheter, Philip; and Masheter, Martin. *Roger Moore: A Biography.* London: New English Library, 1985. 249 p. Illustrated. Filmography. Index. ***

1151. Williams, John. *The Films of Roger Moore.* St. Paul, MN: Greenhaven Press, 1978. 46 p. Illustrated. Filmography.

MORLEY, ROBERT. Act.

1152. Morley, Margaret. *Robert Morley: Larger Than Life.* London: Coronet Books, 1980. 208 p. Illustrated. Bibliography. Index. Paperbound.

1153. Morley, Robert. *The Best of Robert Morley.* London: Robson Books, 1981. 378 p.

1154. Morley, Robert. *More Morley.* London: Hodder and Stoughton, 1978. 224 p. Paperbound. ***

1155. Morley, Robert. *Morley Marvels: Memoirs, Notes, and Essays of the Famed Actor, Raconteur, Collector, Hotel Guest and Man of Leisure.* Edited by Sheridan Morley. Preface by William Davis. South Brunswick, NJ: A. S. Barnes, 1979. 192 p.

MURPHY, EDDIE. Act.

1156. Ruuth, Marianne. *Eddie: Eddie Murphy from A to Z.* Los Angeles: Holloway House, 1985. 192 p. Illustrated. Paperbound.

1157. Sova, Dawn B. *Eddie Murphy.* New York: Kensington, Zebra, 1985. Illustrated. Paperbound.

NEAL, PATRICIA. Act.

1158. Neal, Patricia, and DeNeut, Richard. *As I Am: An Autobiography.* New York: Simon and Schuster, 1988. 384 p. Illustrated. Index. ***

NEWMAN, PAUL. Act.

1159. *Driven [Videorecording].* Aspen, CO: New Visions, 1983. 1 videocassette, 23 min., sd., col., 3/4 in., or Beta 1/2 in., or VHS 1/2 in.
  Credits: Camera, Peter Seller; editor, Doug Smith. Summary: Focuses on Newman's 1982 racing season, with insights into the man who acts, directs motion pictures, and drives race cars with equal intensity and enjoyment.

1160. Godfrey, Lionel. *Paul Newman, Superstar: A Critical Biography.* New York: St. Martin's Press, 1978. 208 p. Illustrated. Bibliography. Filmography. Index.

1161. Landry, J. C. *Paul Newman.* McGraw-Hill Paperbacks. New York: McGraw-Hill, 1983. 144 p. Illustrated. Bibliography. Filmography. Index. Paperbound.

1162. Morella, Joe, and Epstein, Edward Z. *Paul & Joanne: A Biography of Paul Newman and Joanne Woodward.* New York: Delacorte Press, 1988. Index. ***

1163. Quirk, Lawrence J. *The Films of Paul Newman.* Rev. ed. Secaucus, NJ: Citadel, 1981. 256 p. Illustrated. Playography.

1164. Thompson, Kenneth. *The Films of Paul Newman.* St. Paul, MN: Greenhaven Press, 1978. 46 p. Illustrated. Filmography.

NICHOLSON, JACK. Act.

1165. Braithwaite, Bruce. *The Films of Jack Nicholson.* St. Paul, MN: Greenhaven Press, 1978. 45 p. Illustrated. Filmography.

1166. Brode, Douglas. *The Films of Jack Nicholson.* Secaucus, NJ: Citadel, 1987. 256 p. Illustrated. ***

1167. Downing, David. *Jack Nicholson: A Biography.* London: W. H. Allen, 1983. 192 p. Illustrated. Filmography. Index.

1168. Sylvester, Derek. *Jack Nicholson.* New York: Proteus Books, 1982. 96 p. Illustrated. Filmography. Paperbound.

NIVEN, DAVID. Act. 7/29/83

1169. Francisco, Charles. *David Niven, Endearing Rascal.* New York: St. Martin's Press, 1986. 303 p. Illustrated. Filmography. Paperbound.

1170. Haining, Peter. *The Last Gentleman: Tribute to David Niven.* London: W. H. Allen, 1984. 224 p. Illustrated. ***

1171. Hutchinson, Tom. *Niven's Hollywood*. Introduction by Peter Ustinov. Afterword by David Niven, Jr. Salem, NH: Salem House, 1984. 192 p. Illustrated. Filmography. Index.

1172. Morley, Sheridan. *The Other Side of the Moon: The Life of David Niven*. New York: Harper & Row, 1985. 300 p. Illustrated. Bibliography. Filmography. Index.

1173. Niven, David. *Bring on the Empty Horses [Sound Recording]*. Downsview, Ontario, Canada: Listen for Pleasure, 1981. 2 sound cassettes, ca. 150 min., mono.

Summary: This is a reading, by Niven, of one of his partial autobiographies. It has been abridged for recording purposes by Graham Goodwin.

1174. Niven, David. *The Moon's a Balloon; Bring on the Empty Horses*. London: Octopus, 1984. 632 p.

1175. Niven, David. *The Moon's a Balloon [Sound Recording]*. Downsview, Ontario, Canada: Listen for Pleasure, 1981. 2 sound cassettes, mono.

Summary: This is a reading, by Niven, of one of his partial autobiographies. It has been abridged for recording purposes by Chris Barlas.

1176. *The Other Side of the Moon [Sound Recording]*. Beverly Hills, CA: Dove Books-on-Tape, 1985. 2 sound cassettes, 170 min., analog.

Summary: Sheridan Morley reads his biography of Niven, which in one reviewer's opinion, is "more accurate than Niven's own accounts of his life, but less fun."

OBERON, MERLE. Act. 11/23/79

1177. Higham, Charles, and Moseley, Roy. *Merle, a Biography of Merle Oberon.* Sevenoaks, Kent, England: New English Library, 1983. 227 p. Illustrated. Filmography. Index.

1178. Higham, Charles, and Moseley, Roy. *Princess Merle; The Romantic Life of Merle Oberon.* New York: Coward-McCann, 1983. 317 p. Illustrated. Index.

OLIVIER, LAURENCE. Act.

1179. Barker, Felix. *Laurence Olivier: A Critical Study.* Film and Theatre Stars Series. Tunbridge Wells, Kent, England: Spellmount; New York: Hippocrene Books, 1984. 95 p. Illustrated. Playography. Filmography. Bibliography.

1180. Bragg, Melvyn. *Laurence Olivier.* London: Hutchinson, 1984. 144 p. Illustrated.

1181. Daniels, Robert L. *Laurence Olivier, Theater and Cinema.* San Diego, CA: A. S. Barnes; London: Tantivy Press, 1980. 319 p. Illustrated. Filmography. Bibliography. Index.

1182. Hirsch, Foster. *Laurence Olivier.* Twayne's Theatrical Arts Series. Boston: Twayne, 1979. 190 p. Illustrated. Filmography. Bibliography. Index.

1183. Kiernan, Thomas. *Sir Larry: The Life of Laurence Olivier.* New York: Times Books, 1981. 302 p. Illustrated. Bibliography. Index.

1184. Lasky, Jesse, Jr., and Silver, Pat. *Love Scene: The Story of Laurence Olivier and Vivien Leigh.* New York: Crowell, 1978. 256 p. Illustrated. Bibliography. Index.

1185. Morley, Margaret, and Powell, Dilys. *The Films of Laurence Olivier*. Foreword by Michael Caine. Secaucus, NJ: Citadel, 1977. 208 p. Illustrated. Filmography. Bibliography.

1186. O'Connor, Garry. *Darlings of the Gods: One Year in the Lives of Laurence Olivier and Vivien Leigh*. London: Hodder and Stoughton, 1984. 192 p. Illustrated. Bibliography. Index.

1187. *Olivier, in Celebration*. Edited by Garry O'Connor. London, Toronto: Hodder and Stoughton, 1987. 236 p. Illustrated. Index. ***

1188. Olivier, Laurence. *Confessions of an Actor: An Autobiography*. New York: Simon and Schuster, 1982. 348 p. Illustrated.

1189. Olivier, Laurence. *On Acting*. New York: Simon and Schuster, 1986. 397 p. Illustrated. Playography. Filmography. Videography. Index.

1190. Tanitch, Robert. *Olivier: The Complete Career*. New York: Abbeville Press, 1985. 191 p. Illustrated. Index.

O'TOOLE, PETER. Act.

1191. Freedland, Michael. *Peter O'Toole: A Biography*. New York: St. Martin's Press, 1982. 237 p. Illustrated. Index.

1192. Wapshott, Nicholas. *Peter O'Toole: A Biography*. New York: Beaufort Books, 1983. 239 p. Illustrated. Filmography. Index.

PARKS, GORDON. Dir.

1193. Parks, Gordon. *To Smile in Autumn: A Memoir*. New York, London: Norton, 1979. 249 p. Illustrated.

1194. *They Have Overcome—Gordon Parks [Slides]*. Warren Schloat Productions, 1967. 93 slides, col., with phonodisc: 12 in., 33 1/3 rpm., and phonotape: 1 reel, 7 1/2 ips., and 1 cassette, 14 min.

Summary: Describes the early life of author, photographer, composer, and director Parks, revealing his first interest in photography, his early failures, and his struggle to overcome racial prejudice.

1195. *The Weapons of Gordon Parks [Motion Picture]*. Contemporary Films, 1967. 28 min., sd., col., 16 mm.

Summary: Presents a biography of *Life* magazine photographer-journalist, and film director Parks, emphasizing how he used his will and his talents to overcome racial bias.

PECK, GREGORY. Act.

1196. Freedland, Michael. *Gregory Peck: A Biography*. New York: Morrow, 1980. 250 p. Illustrated.

1197. *Gregory Peck: His Own Man [Videorecording]*. New York: Wombat Film & Video, 1988? 1 videocassette, 60 min., col., VHS.

Summary: With clips from Peck's most important films, this biography also contains interviews with Jane Fonda, Audrey Hepburn, Liza Minnelli, Anthony Quinn, Lee Remick, Lauren Bacall, Jack Lemmon, and directors J. Lee Thompson and Robert Mulligan.

1198. Griggs, John. *The Films of Gregory Peck.* Introduction by Judith Crist. Secaucus, NJ: Citadel, 1984. 239 p. Illustrated.

1199. Thomas, Tony. *Gregory Peck.* Pyramid Illustrated History of the Movies. New York: Pyramid Publications, 1977. 160 p. Illustrated. Bibliography. Filmography. Index. Paperbound.

PECKINPAH, SAM. Dir. 12/28/84

1200. McKinney, Doug. *Sam Peckinpah.* Twayne's Theatrical Arts Series. Boston: Twayne, 1979. 266 p. Illustrated. Bibliography. Filmography. Index.

1201. Simmons, Garner. *Peckinpah: A Portrait in Montage.* Austin: University of Texas Press, 1982. 260 p. Illustrated. Index.

PICKFORD, MARY. Act. 5/29/79

1202. Herndon, Booton. *Mary Pickford and Douglas Fairbanks: The Most Popular Couple the World Has Ever Known.* New York: Norton, 1977. 324 p. Illustrated. Bibliography. Index.

POITIER, SYDNEY. Act.

1203. Keyser, Lester J., and Ruszkowski, Andre H. *The Cinema of Sidney Poitier: The Black Man's Changing Role on the American Screen.* San Diego, CA: A. S. Barnes, 1980. 192 p. Illustrated. Filmography. Bibliography. Index.

1204. Marill, Alvin H. *The Films of Sidney Poitier.* Introduction by Frederick O'Neal. Secaucus, NJ: Citadel, 1978. 224 p. Illustrated. Playography. Videography.

1205. Poitier, Sidney. *This Life.* New York: Knopf, 1980. 374 p. Illustrated.

POLANSKI, ROMAN. Dir.

1206. Kiernan, Thomas. *The Roman Polanski Story.* New York: Grove Press, Delilah, 1980. 262 p. Illustrated.

1207. Leaming, Barbara. *Polanski, the Filmmaker as Voyeur: A Biography.* New York: Simon and Schuster, 1981. 220 p. Illustrated. Filmography. Index.

1208. Polanski, Roman. *Roman.* New York: Morrow, 1984. 461 p. Illustrated. Index.

PREMINGER, OTTO. Dir.

1209. Preminger, Otto. *Preminger: An Autobiography.* Garden City, NY: Doubleday, 1977. 208 p. Illustrated. Filmography. Index.

PRICE, VINCENT. Act.

1210. McAsh, Iain F. *The Films of Vincent Price.* St. Paul, MN: Greenhaven Press, 1978. 46 p. Illustrated. Filmography.
***

REDFORD, ROBERT. Act.

1211. Castell, David. *The Films of Robert Redford*. St. Paul, MN: Greenhaven Press, 1978. 46 p. Illustrated. Filmography.

1212. Crowther, Bruce. *Robert Redford*. Tunbridge Wells, Kent, England: Spellmount; New York: Hippocrene, 1985. 95 p. Illustrated. Filmography. Bibliography.

1213. Downing, David. *Robert Redford*. New York: St. Martin's Press, 1982. 224 p. Illustrated. Index. Paperbound.

1214. Spada, James. *The Films of Robert Redford*. Rev. ed. Secaucus, NJ: Citadel, 1984. 269 p. Illustrated. Paperbound.

REEVE, CHRISTOPHER. Act.

1215. Steinberg, Margery. *The Christopher Reeve Scrapbook*. New York: Tempo Books, 1981. 141 p. Illustrated. Table. Paperbound.

REYNOLDS, BURT. Act.

1216. Eliot, Marc. *Burt!: The Unauthorized Biography*. New York: Dell, Hitzig McDonell, 1982. 224 p. Illustrated. Paperbound.

1217. Hurwood, Bernhardt J. *Burt Reynolds*. New York: Quick Fox, 1979. 112 p. Illustrated. Filmography. Table. Discography. Paperbound.

1218. Latham, Caroline. *Burt Reynolds: Superstar.* New York: Delilah/Putnam, 1985. ***

1219. Resnick, Sylvia Safran. *Burt Reynolds: An Unauthorized Biography.* New York: St. Martin's Press, 1983. 137 p. Illustrated. Index.

1220. Streebeck, Nancy. *The Films of Burt Reynolds.* Foreword by Orson Welles. Afterword by Joe Baltake. Secaucus, NJ: Citadel, 1982. 256 p. Illustrated.

1221. Whitley, Dianna. *Burt Reynolds, Portrait of a Superstar.* New York: Grosset & Dunlap, 1979. 112 p. Illustrated. Paperbound.

RICHARDSON, RALPH. Act. 10/10/83

1222. O'Connor, Garry. *Ralph Richardson, an Actor's Life.* London: Hodder and Stoughton, 1982. 260 p. Illustrated. Playography. Filmography. Bibliography. Index.

1223. *Ralph Richardson: A Tribute.* Compiled by Robert Tanitch. London: M. Evans, 1982. 128 p. Illustrated. Playography. Filmography. Videography. Radiography. Index.

ROBERTS, RACHEL. Act. 11/25/80

1224. Roberts, Rachel. *No Bells on Sunday: The Rachel Roberts Journals.* Edited with a documentary biography by Alexander Walker. New York: Harper & Row, 1984. 246 p. Illustrated.

ROBERTSON, CLIFF. Act.

1225. McClintick, David. *Indecent Exposure: A True Story of Hollywood and Wall Street.* New York: Morrow, 1982. 544 p. Illustrated. Index.

ROGERS, ROY. Act.

1226. Rogers, Roy; Evans, Dale; and Stowers, Carlton. *Happy Trails: The Story of Roy Rogers and Dale Evans.* Waco, TX: Word Books, 1979. 213 p. Illustrated. Filmography.

1227. Rogers, Roy, Jr., and Wojahn, Karen Ann. *Growing Up with Roy and Dale.* Ventura, CA: Regal Books, 1986. 206 p. Illustrated.

ROONEY, MICKEY. Act.

1228. Marx, Arthur. *The Nine Lives of Mickey Rooney.* New York: Stein and Day, 1986. 320 p. Illustrated. Index.

RUSSELL, ROSALIND. Act. 11/28/76

1229. Russell, Rosalind, and Chase, Chris. *Life Is a Banquet.* Preface by Frederick Brisson. New York: Random House, 1977. 260 p. Illustrated. Index.

SAYLES, JOHN. Dir.

1230. Sayles, John. *John Sayles Interview with Kay Bonetti [Sound Recording].* Columbia, MO: American Audio

Prose Library, 1982. 1 sound cassette, 82 min., analog, mono.

Summary: Sayles discusses his career as a writer, director, actor, and editor in films and television and on stage.

SCHWARZENEGGER, ARNOLD. Act.

1231. Schwarzenegger, Arnold, and Hall, Douglas Kent. *Arnold: The Education of a Bodybuilder.* New York: Simon and Schuster, 1977. 256 p. Illustrated.

SCORSESE, MARTIN. Dir.

1232. Kelly, Mary Pat. *Martin Scorsese, the First Decade.* Introduced by Francis Ford Coppola and Michael Powell. Pleasantville, NY: Redgrave Publishing, 1980. 206 p. Illustrated. Filmography.

SELLECK, TOM. Act.

1233. Bonderoff, Jason. *Tom Selleck: An Unauthorized Biography.* New York: New American Library, Signet, 1983. 184 p. Illustrated. Paperbound.

SELLERS, PETER. Act. 7/23/80

1234. Sellers, Michael; Sellers, Sarah; and Sellers, Victoria. *P.S. I Love You: An Intimate Portrait of Peter Sellers.* New York: E. P. Dutton, 1982. 238 p. Illustrated.

1235. Sylvester, Derek. *Peter Sellers*. London, New York: Proteus Books, 1981. 128 p. Illustrated. Filmography. Paperbound.

1236. Walker, Alexander. *Peter Sellers, the Authorized Biography*. Preface by Lynne Frederick Sellers. New York: Macmillan, 1981. 281 p. Illustrated. Filmography. Index.

SHATNER, WILLIAM. Act.

1237. Shatner, William; Marshak, Sondra; and Culbreath, Myrna. *Shatner, Where No Man: The Authorized Biography of William Shatner*. New York: Grosset & Dunlap, Tempo, 1979. 327 p. Illustrated. ***

SHIELDS, BROOKE. Act.

1238. Bonderoff, Jason. *Brooke*. New York: Zebra, 1981. ***

1239. Shields, Brooke. *The Brooke Book*. Rev. ed. New York: Simon and Schuster, Wallaby, 1982. 150 p. Illustrated. Paperbound.

SIGNORET, SIMONE. Act. 9/30/85

1240. Signoret, Simone. *Nostalgia Isn't What It Used to Be*. New York: Harper & Row, 1978. 403 p. Index.

SOMERS, SUZANNE. Act.

1241. Somers, Suzanne. *Keeping Secrets*. New York: Warner Books, 1988. 297 p. Illustrated.

SPACEK, SISSY. Act.

1242. Emerson, Mark, and Pfaff, Eugene E., Jr. *Country Girl: The Life of Sissy Spacek.* New York: St. Martin's Press, 1988. ***

SPIELBERG, STEVEN. Dir.

1243. Crawley, Tony. *The Steven Spielberg Story.* New York: Quill, 1983. 159 p. Illustrated. Paperbound.

1244. Mott, Donald R., and Saunders, Cheryl McAllister. *Steven Spielberg.* Twayne's Filmmakers Series. Boston: Twayne, 1986. 199 p. Bibliography. Filmography. Index.

STACK, ROBERT. Act.

1245. Stack, Robert, and Evans, Mark. *Straight Shooting.* New York: Macmillan, 1980. 292 p. Illustrated. Index.

STALLONE, SYLVESTER. Act.

1246. Daly, Marsha. *Sylvester Stallone: An Illustrated Life.* New York: St. Martin's Press, 1984. 127 p. Illustrated. Paperbound.

1247. Rovin, Jeff. *Stallone! a Hero's Story: An Unauthorized Biography.* New York: Pocket Books, 1985. 254 p. Illustrated. Paperbound.

STANWYCK, BARBARA. Act.

1248. Dickens, Homer. *The Films of Barbara Stanwyck.* Foreword by Frank Capra. Secaucus, NJ: Citadel, 1984. 288 p. Illustrated. Filmography. ***

1249. DiOrio, Al. *Barbara Stanwyck.* New York: Coward-McCann, 1983. 249 p. Illustrated. Filmography.

1250. Smith, Ella. *Starring Miss Barbara Stanwyck.* Updated ed. New York: Crown Publishers, 1985. 370 p. Illustrated. Filmography. Index.

1251. Wayne, Jane Ellen. *Stanwyck.* New York: Arbor House, 1985. 220 p. Illustrated. Filmography.

STAPLETON, JEAN. Act.

1252. *A Simple Matter of Justice [Motion Picture].* Wilmette, IL: Films Inc., 1978. 1 reel, 26 min., sd., col., 16mm.

Credits: A film by Ann Hassett. Summary: Follows actress, Jean Stapleton, from the taping of her television show in Hollywood to the 1978 International Women's Conference in Houston, where she meets other women advocates for passage of the Equal Rights Amendment.

STEVENS, GEORGE. Dir. 3/8/75

1253. *George Stevens, a Filmmaker's Journey [Motion Picture].* Washington, DC: Creative Film Center, 1984. 6 reels, 112 min., sd., col., 35mm.

Also issued as a videocassette (1/2 inch, VHS). Credits: Produced, written, directed, and narrated by George Stevens, Jr. Summary: Presents the story of one of the great filmmakers of Hollywood's golden age through scenes from many of

Stevens' most famous films, in personal reminiscences of stars and directors who knew him, and in recently discovered color film of World War II.

STEWART, JAMES. Act.

1254. Eyles, Allen. *James Stewart.* New York: Stein and Day, 1984. 264 p. Illustrated. Filmography. Bibliography. Index.

1255. Hunter, Allan. *James Stewart.* Tunbridge Wells, Kent, England: Spellmount; New York: Hippocrene Books, 1985. 96 p. Illustrated. Filmography. Videography. Playography. Bibliography.

1256. Robbins, Jhan. *Everybody's Man: A Biography of Jimmy Stewart.* New York: Putnam, 1985. 192 p. Illustrated. Filmography. Index.

STRASBERG, LEE. Act. 2/17/82

1257. Adams, Cindy. *Lee Strasberg, the Imperfect Genius of the Actor's Studio.* Garden City, NY: Doubleday, 1980. 398 p. Illustrated. Index.

1258. *Old Friends—New Friends, Lee Strasberg [Videorecording].* Pittsburgh, PA: Family Communications, 1980. 1 videocassette, 28 min., sd. col., 3/4 in.
    Summary: Portrays Lee Strasberg as an intuitive, but intense and demanding, coach of novice and professional actors. Includes scenes of Strasberg talking about his sources of inspiration and motivation, and shows him teaching relaxation techniques.

STREEP, MERYL. Act.

1259. Maychick, Diana. *Meryl Streep: The Reluctant Superstar.* New York: St. Martin's Press, 1984. 166 p. Illustrated. Index.

1260. Pfaff, Eugene E., Jr., and Emerson, Mark. *Meryl Streep: A Critical Biography.* Jefferson, NC: McFarland, 1987. 148 p. Filmography. Bibliography. Index.

1261. Smurthwaite, Nick. *The Meryl Streep Story.* New York: Beaufort Books, 1984. 128 p. Illustrated. Filmography. Index. Paperbound.

1262. *The Women of "Out of Africa:" Isak Dinesen and Meryl Streep [Videorecording].* Seattle: Shoreline Community College, 1986. 1 videocassette, 60 min., sd., col., 1/2 in., VHS.

Credits: Produced by the Shoreline Community College Women's Student Network. Presented by Inga Wiehl. Summary: Wiehl, an instructor at Yakima Community College and a native of Denmark, discusses the lives of the author of *Out of Africa,* and the actress who portrayed her in the movie of the same title.

STRITCH, ELAINE. Act.

1263. Stritch, Elaine. *Am I Blue?: Living with Diabetes and, Dammit, Having Fun!* Foreword by Doreen Gluckin. New York: M. Evans, 1984. 132 p. Illustrations. Tables. Bibliography. Index.

SWANSON, GLORIA. Act. 4/4/83

1264. Madsen, Axel. *Gloria and Joe.* New York: Arbor House/William Morrow, 1988. Bibliography. Index. ***

1265. Quirk, Lawrence J. *The Films of Gloria Swanson.* Secaucus, NJ: Citadel, 1984. 256 p. Illustrated.

1266. Swanson, Gloria. *Swanson on Swanson.* New York: Random House, 1980. 535 p. Illustrated. Index.

T, MR. Act. See: MR. T. Act.

TAYLOR, ELIZABETH. Act.

1267. Adler, Bill. *Elizabeth Taylor, Triumphs & Tragedies.* New York: Ace Books, 1982. 278 p. Paperbound. ***

1268. D'Arcy, Susan. *The Films of Elizabeth Taylor.* Heroes of the Movies. New York: Confucian Press; Beaufort Books, 1982. 94 p. Illustrated. Paperbound.

1269. Hutchinson, Tom. *Elizabeth Taylor.* New York: Exeter Books, 1982. 80 p. Illustrated. Filmography.

1270. Kelley, Kitty. *Elizabeth Taylor, the Last Star.* New York: Simon and Schuster, 1981. 448 p. Illustrated. Bibliography. Filmography. Index.

1271. Maddox, Brenda. *Who's Afraid of Elizabeth Taylor?* New York: M. Evans, 1977. 252 p. Illustrated. Filmography.

1272. Morley, Sheridan. *Elizabeth Taylor: A Celebration.* London: Pavilion Books, 1988. 192 p. Illustrated. Filmography.

1273. Nickens, Christopher. *Elizabeth Taylor: A Biography in Photographs.* Garden City, NY: Doubleday, Dolphin, 1984. 186 p. Illustrated. Paperbound.

1274. Taylor, Elizabeth. *Elizabeth Takes Off.* New York: Putnam, 1987. ***

TIEGS, CHERYL. Act., Mod.

1275. Tiegs, Cheryl, and Lindner, Vicki. *The Way to Natural Beauty.* New York: Simon and Schuster, 1980. 284 p. Illustrated.

TRAVOLTA, JOHN. Act.

1276. Munshower, Suzanne. *The John Travolta Scrapbook: An Illustrated Biography.* New York: Sunridge Press, 1978. 121 p. Illustrated.

1277. Norbom, Mary Ann. *John and Diana: A Love Story.* New York: Bantam Books, 1979. 179 p. Illustrated. Paperbound.

1278. Reeves, Michael. *Travolta!: A Photo Bio.* New York: Jove Publications, 1978. 272 p. Illustrated. Paperbound.

TRUFFAUT, FRANÇOIS. Dir. 10/21/84

1279. Allen, Don. *Finally Truffaut.* New York: Beaufort Books, 1985. 240 p. Illustrated. Filmography. Paperbound.

TURNER, KATHLEEN. Act.

1280. Stefoff, Rebecca. *Kathleen Turner.* New York: St. Martin's Press, 1987. 184 p. Illustrated. Filmography. Paperbound.

TURNER, LANA. Act.

1281. Crane, Cheryl, and Jahr, Cliff. *Detour: A Hollywood Story.* New York: Arbor House/William Morrow, 1988. 334 p. Illustrated.

1282. Pero, Taylor, and Rovin, Jeff. *Always, Lana.* Toronto, New York: Bantam Books, 1982. 274 p. Paperbound.

1283. Turner, Lana. *Lana: The Lady, the Legend, the Truth.* New York: E. P. Dutton, 1982. 311 p. Illustrated.

ULLMANN, LIV. Act.

1284. Outerbridge, David, comp. *Without Makeup, Liv Ullmann: A Photo-Biography.* New York: Morrow, 1979. 160 p. Illustrated.

1285. Ullmann, Liv. *Changing.* Translated from the Norwegian by the author in collaboration with Gerry Bothmer and Erik Friis. New York: Knopf, 1977. 244 p.

1286. Ullmann, Liv. *Changing [Sound Recording].* New York: Bantam Audio, 1987. 1 sound cassette. 60 min.

Summary: This cassette contains the translation from the Norwegian, *Forandringen,* an autobiographical work written and performed by Ullmann.

1287. Ullmann, Liv. *Choices.* New York: Knopf, 1984. 193 p.

USTINOV, PETER. Act.

1288. Ustinov, Peter. *Dear Me.* Boston: Little, Brown, Atlantic Monthly Press, 1977. 374 p. Illustrated. Index.

VISCONTI, LUCHINO. Dir. 3/17/76

1289. Servadio, Gaia. *Luchino Visconti, a Biography.* London: Weidenfeld & Nicolson, 1981. 262 p. Illustrated. Bibliography. Playography. Filmography. Index.

1290. Stirling, Monica. *A Screen of Time: A Study of Luchino Visconti.* New York, London: Harcourt Brace Jovanovich, A Helen and Kurt Wolff Book, 1979. 295 p. Illustrated. Bibliography. Index.

WAGNER, ROBERT. Act.

1291. Maychick, Diana, and Borgo, L. Avon. *Heart to Heart with Robert Wagner.* New York: St. Martin's Press, 1986. 173 p. Illustrated. Index.

WARHOL, ANDY. Dir. 2/22/87

1292. Ultra Violet. *Famous for 15 Minutes: My Years with Andy Warhol.* San Diego, CA: Harcourt Brace Jovanovich, 1988. 274 p. Illustrated.

1293. Warhol, Andy, and Hackett, Pat. *POPism: The Warhol '60s.* New York: Harcourt Brace Jovanovich, 1980. 310 p. Illustrated. Index.

WARNER, JACK. Dir. 9/9/78

1294. Freedland, Michael. *The Warner Brothers.* London: Harrap, 1983. 240 p. Illustrated. Index.

WAYNE, JOHN. Act. 6/11/79

1295. Bishop, George. *John Wayne, the Actor, the Man.* Ottawa, IL: Caroline House, 1979. 254 p. Illustrated. Filmography. Index.

1296. Boswell, John, and David, Jay. *Duke: The John Wayne Album: The Legend of Our Time.* Foreword by Richard Schickel. New York: Ballantine Books, 1979. 160 p. Illustrated. Filmography. Paperbound.

1297. Carpozi, George Jr. *The John Wayne Story.* New Rochelle, NY: Arlington House, 1979. 366 p. Illustrated. Filmography. Index.

1298. Eyles, Allen. *John Wayne.* Memorial ed. Introduction by Louise Brooks. South Brunswick, NJ: A. S. Barnes; London: Tantivy Press, 1979. 333 p. Illustrated. Filmography.

1299. Goldstein, Norm. *John Wayne: A Tribute.* Foreword by James Stewart. New York: Holt, Rinehart and Winston, 1979. 159 p. Illustrated. Filmography.

1300. Hanna, David. *The Life and Times of John Wayne.* New York: Harrison House, 1979. 80 p. Illustrated. Filmography.

1301. *John Wayne: Duke's Own Story.* Edited by Bessie Little. New York: Reliance, 1979. 96 p. Illustrated. Filmography.

1302. Kieskalt, Charles John. *The Official John Wayne Reference Book.* Secaucus, NJ: Citadel, 1985. 224 p. Illustrated. Bibliography.

1303. Levy, Emanuel. *John Wayne: Prophet of the American Way of Life.* Metuchen, NJ: Scarecrow Press, 1988. Bibliography. Index. ***

1304. Roberson, Chuck, and Thoene, Bodie. *The Fall Guy: 30 Years as the Duke's Double.* Foreword by John Wayne. North Vancouver, BC: Hancock House, 1980. 288 p. Illustrated.

1305. Shaw, Sam. *John Wayne in the Camera Eye.* Afterword by Dore Schary. New York: Exeter Books, 1979. 160 p. Illustrated. Filmography.

1306. Shepherd, Donald; Slatzer, Robert; and Grayson, Dave. *Duke, the Life and Times of John Wayne.* Garden City, NY: Doubleday, 1985. 372 p. Illustrated. Bibliography. Filmography. Index.

1307. Stacy, Pat, and Linet, Beverly. *Duke, a Love Story: An Intimate Memoir of John Wayne's Last Years.* New York: Atheneum, 1983. 233 p. Illustrated.

1308. Wayne, Pilar, and Thorleifson, Alex. *John Wayne: My Life with the Duke.* New York: McGraw-Hill, 1987. 287 p. Illustrated. Index.

1309. Zmijewsky, Steven; Zmijewsky, Boris; and Ricci, Mark. *The Complete Films of John Wayne.* Rev. ed. Secaucus, NJ: Citadel, 1983. 320 p. Illustrated. Paperbound.

WELCH, RAQUEL. Act.

1310. Haining, Peter. *Raquel Welch: Sex Symbol to Super Star.* New York: St. Martin's Press, 1984. 224 p. Illustrated. Filmography.

1311. Latham, Caroline. *Raquel: Brains and Beauty.* New York: Delilah/Putnam, 1985. ***

WELLES, ORSON. Dir.

1312. Bazin, André. *Orson, Welles: A Critical View.* Foreword by François Truffaut. Profile by Jean Cocteau. Translated from the French by Jonathan Rosenbaum. London: Elm Tree Books, 1978. 138 p. Illustrated. Index.

1313. France, Richard. *The Theatre of Orson Welles.* Foreword by Robert W. Corrigan. Lewisburg, PA: Bucknell University Press; London: Associated University Presses, 1977. 212 p. Illustrated. Playography. Radiography. Bibliography. Index.

1314. Higham, Charles. *Orson Welles, the Rise and Fall of an American Genius.* New York: St. Martin's Press, 1985. 373 p. Illustrated. Table. Filmography. Discography. Bibliography. Index.

1315. Leaming, Barbara. *Orson Welles, a Biography.* New York: Viking Press, 1985. 562 p. Illustrated. Bibliography. Index.

1316. McBride, Joseph. *Orson Welles, Actor and Director.* An Illustrated History of the Movies. New York: Harvest/HBJ Books, 1977. 159 p. Illustrated. Bibliography. Filmography. Index. Paperbound.

1317. Naremore, James. *The Magic World of Orson Welles.* New York: Oxford University Press, 1978. 339 p. Illustrated. Bibliography. Filmography. Index.

1318. Taylor, John Russell. *Orson Welles: A Celebration.* Picture research by the Kobal Collection. Boston: Little, Brown, 1986. 176 p. Illustrated. Bibliography. Filmography.

WERTMULLER, LINA. Dir.

1319. Ferlita, Ernest, and May, John R. *The Parables of Lina Wertmuller.* An Exploration Book. New York: Paulist Press, 1977. 104 p. Illustrated. Filmography. Bibliography. Index. Paperbound.

WHITE, BETTY. Act.

1320. White, Betty. *Betty White, in Person.* Garden City, NY: Doubleday, 1987. 201 p.

WILDER, BILLY. Dir.

1321. Dick, Bernard F. *Billy Wilder.* Twayne's Theatrical Arts Series. Boston: Twayne, 1980. 188 p. Illustrated. Bibliography. Filmography. Index.

1322. Zolotow, Maurice. *Billy Wilder in Hollywood.* New York: Putnam, 1977. 364 p. Illustrated. Index.

WINGER, DEBRA. Act.

1323. Cahill, M. J. *Debra Winger: Hollywood's Wild Child.* New York: St. Martin's Press, 1984. 96 p. Illustrated. Filmography. Paperbound.

WINKLER, HENRY. Act.

1324. Green, Jonathon. *The Fonz & Henry Winkler: His Real-Life Story Packed with Dozens of Great Photographs.* Paradise Press, Bunch, 1978. 62 p. Illustrated.

WINTERS, SHELLEY. Act.

1325. Winters, Shelley. *Shelley: Also Known As Shirley.* New York: Morrow, 1980. 511 p. Illustrated.

WOOD, NATALIE. Act. 11/29/81

1326. Nickens, Christopher. *Natalie Wood: A Biography in Photographs.* Garden City, NY: Doubleday, 1986. 202 p. Illustrated. ***

1327. Wood, Lana. *Natalie: A Memoir by Her Sister.* New York: Putnam, 1984. 240 p. Illustrated.

WYMAN, JANE. Act.

1328. Morella, Joe, and Epstein, Edward Z. *Jane Wyman: A Biography.* New York: Delacorte Press, 1985. 257 p. Illustrated. Index.

1329. Quirk, Lawrence J. *Jane Wyman, the Actress and the Woman: An Illustrated Biography.* New York: Dembner Books, 1986. 216 p. Illustrated. Filmography. Index.

YOUNG, LORETTA. Act.

1330. Morella, Joe, and Epstein, Edward Z. *Loretta Young: An Extraordinary Life.* New York: Delacorte Press, 1986. 302 p. Illustrated.

ZANUCK, DARRYL. Dir. 12/22/79

1331. Gussow, Mel. *Darryl F. Zanuck: Don't Say Yes until I Finish Talking.* New epilogue by the author. New York: Da Capo Press, 1980. 322 p. Illustrated. Filmography. Index. Paperbound.

1332. Mosley, Leonard. *Zanuck: The Rise and Fall of Hollywood's Last Tycoon.* Boston: Little, Brown, 1984. 424 p. Illustrated. Filmography. Index.

ZEFFIRELLI, FRANCO. Dir.

1333. Zeffirelli, Franco. *Zeffirelli: The Autobiography of Franco Zeffirelli.* New York: Weidenfeld & Nicolson, 1986. 358 p. Illustrated. Index.

PART III
MUSIC CELEBRITIES SOURCES

Chapter 18
Reference Books

Section 1
Bibliographies and Guides

1334. *Arts in America: A Bibliography.* Edited by Bernard Karpel. Washington, DC: Smithsonian Institution Press, 1979. 4 vols. Index.

See entry 407, for annotation.

1335. Hoffmann, Frank. *The Literature of Rock,1954-1978.* Metuchen, NJ: Scarecrow Press, 1981. 337 p. Illustrated. Discography. Bibliography. Index.

See entry below for annotation.

1336. Hoffmann, Frank; Cooper, B. Lee; and Hoffmann, Lee Ann. *The Literature of Rock, II,1979-1983: With Additional Material for the Period 1954-1978.* Metuchen, NJ: Scarecrow Press, 1986. 2 vols. Index.

The two Hoffmann works cited above comprise a three-volume selective, annotated bibliography of books, articles, and other documents which span the years from 1954 to 1983. The intent is to identify, promote access, and evaluate the utility of rock music sources for the serious student and enthusiast. Arrangement is by genre/period, e.g., Doo-Wop (1954-57), New Wave (1975-) etc.; relevant topics not amenable to a chronological pattern (drugs, festivals, mass media, etc.) are grouped at the end. The historical development of rock music literature is discussed in the introduction. An annotated list of periodicals, and a "stock list" of recordings conclude the work. Indexing is by artist, genre, concept, and trend.

1337. *Musicians in Canada: A Bio-bibliographical Finding List.* Edited by Kathleen M. Toomey, and Stephen C. Willis. Publications of the Canadian Association of Music Libraries, 1. Ottawa, ON: The Association, 1981. 185 p. Index.

The scope of this work embraces those musicians who were, have been, or are currently active in Canada. Some 218 sources were searched for biographical content. These are keyed from the main alphabetical listing by individual or group name. There are indexes by musical pursuit, e. g. , performer, composer, teacher, etc.

1338. *Performing Arts Books, 1876-1981: Including an International Index of Current Serial Publications.* New York, London: Bowker, 1981. 1656 p. Index.

See entry 414, for annotation.

1339. Sandahl, Linda J. *Rock Films: A Viewer's Guide to Three Decades of Musicals, Concerts, Documentaries and Soundtracks 1955-1986.* New York: Facts on File, 1987. 239 p. Illustrated. Index.

Rock Films was first published in England by Blanford Press in 1986 as: *Encyclopedia of Rock Music on Film.* Some 400 rock feature films (at least fifty minutes long, and in English) are divided into three categories: musicals, concerts/documentaries, and soundtracks. Musicals are films in which actors perform musically (or seem to), and in which musicians also act; concerts/documentaries are filmed performances; soundtracks are films with rock scores, and those with scores written or performed by rock musicians. Entries give original titles, alternative titles, release date, country, company, length, credits, songs performed, availability of copies, and a brief plot synopsis. Performer, song title, and film title indexes.

Section 2
Biographical Dictionaries

1340. *ASCAP Biographical Dictionary.* 4th ed. Foreword by Hal David. New York: Bowker, 1980. 589 p.

Continues: *ASCAP Biographical Dictionary of Composers, Authors and Publishers.* Over 8,000 individual members of the American Society of Composers, Authors and Publishers are profiled in the main section followed by a listing of some 7,000 publisher members. The arrangement is alphabetical by given name, and cross-referenced by professional pseudonym. Entry content: name, professional category, birthplace and date, study and training, career outline, chief collaborators, major published works.

1341. Baker, Theodore. *Baker's Biographical Dictionary of Musicians.* 7th ed. Revised by Nicholas Slonimsky. New York: Schirmer Books; London: Collier Macmillan, 1984. 2577 p. Bibliography.

A standard work listing musicians of all times and places, this revision contains for the first time selected listings ". . . of rock-'n'-roll musicians, crooners, songstresses, movie stars who occasionally sang, in fact, everyone with an operative larynx. . . ." (Preface.) Biographies are compact, varying from a few lines to several pages. Some conclude with citations to other biographical sources. Published irregularly (with

occasional supplements) since 1900. The preceding edition
appeared in 1978.

1342. Bane, Michael. *Who's Who in Rock.* Researched by
      Kenny Kertok. New York: Facts on File, 1981. 259 p.
      Illustrated. Index.

Bane's selection criteria for biographees as stated in the
introduction are: "How a person or group fits into the overall
scheme of rock; what are they famous for or best remembered
for; how did that affect the music and ultimately, how did that
affect me?" The sketches are anecdotal, ranging from a
sentence to a column or more in length. Most include birth date
and place, but not all. There is an index to artists and album
titles.

1343. Carr, Ian; Fairweather, Digby; and Priestley, Brian. *Jazz:
      The Essential Companion.* London: Grafton Books, 1987.
      562 p. Illustrated.

The authors of this dictionary are musicians who have
written the critical biographical sketches ". . . which [give]
answers to fundamental questions about artistic value." The
scope is international with the biographees either having gained
fame as jazz artists, or via some distinctive musical contribution.
Sketches have selective discographies. Jazz glossary included.

1344. Case, Brian, and Britt, Stan. *Illustrated Encyclopedia of
      Jazz.* 3d ed. Revised and updated by Crissie Murray.
      New York: Harmony Books, Salamander Book, 1987.
      208 p. Illustrated. Discography. Index.

"In this book, we've tried to show that there are no
frontiers to the directions jazz has taken or, indeed, can take."
(Introduction.) Therefore, one finds biographical and other
listings in all the many tributaries of mainstream jazz, i.e., jazz
fusion, blues, etc. Scope has been broadened since publication
of the first edition (*The Illustrated Encyclopedia of Jazz,* 1978).
Included now are many more artists from outside the United
States. Further, there has been concerted effort ". . . to redress
the imbalance regarding women musicians. . . ." Coverage, as
previously, includes both living and dead musicians. Other

subject entries, such as the one on British jazz, are also new to this edition. The sketches are brief, giving name (professional and real) birth date/place, career summary, influences, and death date. Illustrations (some in color) are interspersed throughout. Each entry has a selective discography.

1345. Chilton, John. *Who's Who of Jazz: Storyville to Swing Street.* 4th ed. Foreword by Johnny Simmen. New York: Da Capo Press, 1985. 375 p. Illustrated. Bibliography.

"This is an anthology of biographies detailing the careers of over 1,000 musicians whose names are part of jazz history. All the musicians and vocalists given individual entries were born before 1920. Only musicians born or raised in the U.S.A. are included in this volume." (Introduction.) The basic data for each entry: name, real name, jazz specialty, birthplace/date, and death date. The number of lines in the sketches vary, however Chilton cautions this should not be misconstrued as an indication of the importance of a particular biographee.

1346. Claghorn, Charles Eugene. *Biographical Dictionary of Jazz.* Englewood Cliffs, NJ: Prentice-Hall, 1982. 377 p.

A reference work, without geographical or time boundaries, offering concise identification of jazz composers, musicians and vocalists. There are over 3,400 entries giving name, birth place/date, artist's associates, career highlights, and comments from critics and peers. An "Index of Jazz and Various Small Groups," is less an index than it is a descriptive list.

1347. Clifford, Mike. *The Harmony Illustrated Encyclopedia of Rock.* 4th ed. Foreword by Eric Burdon. New York: Harmony Books, Salamander, 1983. 272 p. Illustrated. Index. Paperbound.

In the edition examined (there is a 5th ed. , published in 1986), performer biographies occupy 238 pages with the remainder of the book containing profiles of management and promotion personnel, and descriptions of record companies and instruments. Rock groups are included in the biography section. There are over 700 entries, each with name, country of origin, talent description, birth date/place, real name, career, awards, and discography. Group entries show year/place founded, and original members. Hundreds of photographs illustrate the text.

1348. Coupe, Stuart, and Baker, Glenn A. *The New Rock 'n' Roll.* Foreword by [Barry] Miles. New York: St. Martin's Press, 1983. 192 p. Illustrated. Index. Paperbound.

In an attempt to provide a reference to the dynamic rock music scene since the 1977 punk explosion, the authors provide some 450 illustrated (many in color)biographical pieces of about 400 words. The focus of these pieces is mainly on professional rather than personal matters. There are no separate discographies, although important albums are italicized within the text. Particular emphasis is given to Japanese and Australian "New Music."

1349. Craig, Warren. *Sweet and Lowdown: America's Popular Songwriters.* Foreword by Milton Ager. Metuchen, NJ: Scarecrow Press, 1978. 645 p. Bibliography. Index.

The artistic output of noted Broadway and other critically recognized composers and lyricists is presented in the form of "digests" (a paragraph of career highlights followed with an extensive listing of song credits). Only Broadway or independent songs having lyrics were considered. Excluded are country, western, and rock songwriters. Indexed by song title, production, and name.

1350. *Creative Canada: A Biographical Dictionary of Twentieth-Century Creative and Performing Artists.* Compiled by Reference Division, McPherson Library, University of Victoria. Victoria, B.C., Canada: McPherson Library, University of Victoria; Toronto: University of Toronto Press, vol. 1-, 1971-. Index. (Irregular)

See entry 424, for annotation.

1351. Dellar, Fred; Thompson, Roy; and Green, Douglas B. *The Illustrated Encyclopedia of Country Music.* Foreword by Roy Acuff. New York: Harmony Books, Salamander Book, 1977. 256 p. Illustrated. Index.

Country and western music artists and acts are described in entries of several paragraphs. There are over 450 entries with selective discographies. The illustrations are a mix of publicity stills, photographs, and over 300 record jackets reproduced in color. An index provides access to those musicians or acts mentioned but not awarded an individual entry in the main list.

1352. Ewen, David. *American Songwriters: An H. W. Wilson Biographical Dictionary.* New York: H. W. Wilson, 1987. 489 p. Index.

Replaces *Popular American Composers* (1962), and *Popular American Composers: First Supplement* (1972). Chosen for inclusion are 146 composers or lyricists who flourished during the past two centuries (emphasis on the last fifty years), and who have a durable place in the history of the American popular song, primarily through their popularity with a mass audience. The book deals exclusively with writers of compositions intended for the voice. Biography is emphasized over criticism. Sketches (several pages in length) include a song performance history. There is a song index.

1353. Feather, Leonard G. *The Encyclopedia of Jazz.* Rev. ed. Appreciations by Duke Ellington, Benny Goodman and John Hammond. London, New York: Quartet Books, 1978. 527 p. Illustrated. Discography. Bibliography.

The main section, "Biographies" (pages 96-473), has over 2, 000 sketches, including those of foreign, blues, and some "cross-over" popular musicians. In addition to name, birth place/date, and specialty, the author attempts to provide information on the artist's background, most important associations, and on what LP recording(s) s/he can be heard. For the most well-known artists, there is a brief delineation of the nature or quality of their work. Sketches average about a paragraph in length. The book begins with a historical survey of the genre; it ends with a series of essays, e.g., "Jazz Overseas," "Jazz and Classical Music."

1354. Given, Dave. *The Dave Given Rock 'n' Roll Stars Handbook: Rhythm and Blues Artists and Groups.* Smithtown, NY: Exposition Press, Exposition-Banner, 1980. 328 p. Discography.

Biographical sketches of a page or so about musicians who achieved stardom in rock music, accompanied by full discographies (single records). The author intends to follow this initial effort with a "matched set of volumes."

1355. Harris, Sheldon. *Blues Who's Who: A Biographical Dictionary of Blues Singers.* New Rochelle, NY: Arlington House, 1979. 775 p. Illustrated. Bibliography. Index.

For this bio-bibliography, Harris selected 571 blues singers who flourished between 1900 and 1977. Information is standardized in the following order: name, birth/death, instruments, biography (work chronology) pertinent notes, personal data, billings, bibliography, songs written, awards, influences, quotations (assessing style) and photographs. Pertinent sub-captions were eliminated when facts were unavailable or undiscovered. Separate indexes are provided: film, radio, television, theater, song, names and places.

1356. Helander, Brock. *The Rock Who's Who: A Biographical Dictionary and Critical Discography Including Rhythm-and-Blues, Soul, Rockabilly, Folk, Country, Easy Listening, Punk, and New Wave.* New York: Schirmer Books; London: Collier Macmillan, 1982. 699 p. Bibliography. Index. Paperbound.

From ABBA to Zappa, about 300 groups and people from rock 'n' roll's honor roll are represented in this work. Each is given a page or more of biographical narrative followed by a discography. The index is essential in locating individuals who are part of a musical group mentioned in the book.

1357. *The Illustrated Encyclopedia of Black Music.* Consultant, Mike Clifford. Authors, Jon Futrell, et al. New York: Harmony Books, Salamander Book, 1982. 224 p. Illustrated. Index.

Black music is defined ". . . as that [music] which has been aimed primarily at a mass black audience."(Introduction.) Therefore, important musicians, producers, songwriters, and recording executives of all races are covered in this volume. Arrangement is first by decade, then by performer or group. The determining factor of placement is the date of the artist's major "breakthrough" into black pop music. Profiles are several paragraphs long. Each concludes with a selective album discography. Many of the illustrations are in color.

1358. Jasper, Tony, et al. *The International Encyclopedia of Hard Rock & Heavy Metal.* New York, Oxford, England: Facts on File, 1983. 400 p.

Within its scope, this rock bio-discography gives essential information on individuals and groups, living or dead. The group or artist name, nationality, group line-up, instrumentation, basic career details, general critical analysis and discography are presented. "When a line-up is not known we have still included the respective entry provided that at the very least we have a working knowledge of their album or other material." (Author's note.)

1359. McRae, Barry. *The Jazz Handbook.* Foreword by Ronnie Scott. Harlow, Essex, England: Longman, 1987. 272 p. Illustrated. Bibliography. Index.

Two hundred entries describing major musicians and groups are arranged by decades—pre-1920s into the 1980s. Entries vary in length according to the relative importance of the musician, and contain: biographical sketch, critique, influences, additional information sources, and a "listening critically" discography. The book concludes with a "Databank" (record label directory, glossary, bibliography, and other information sources).

1360. Marschall, Rick. *The Encyclopedia of Country and Western Music.* New York: Exeter Books, Bison, 1985. 192 p. Illustrated.

A biographical dictionary featuring the great musicians of the genre. It presents descriptive and critical sketches, ranging in length from several paragraphs to a page. Most of the biographies are accompanied by portraits or on-stage candids, many in color. Marschall's admitted bias is toward traditional forms of country and western music, avoiding bluegrass-jazz fusion and pop country.

1361. *MTV Music Television, Who's Who in Rock Video.* Executive editor, Maxim Jakubowski. Editorial director, Judith A. McGrath. Managing editor, Emily White. Text and research by John Tobler. New York: Quill, 1984. 190 p. Illustrated. Index. Paperbound.

A page or so of biography, each with several illustrations, occasional mention of biographical books, and concluding with a brief videography and discography, constitute this work which presents enough material to qualify as collective biography. A round one hundred of rock's greatest stars and groups are represented. The video directors are listed.

1362. *The New Grove Dictionary of American Music.* Edited by H. Wiley Hitchcock, and Stanley Sadie. NewYork: Grove's Dictionaries of Music, 1986. 4 vols. Illustrated. Bibliography. ***

1363. Nite, Norm N. *Rock On: The Illustrated Encyclopedia of Rock n' Roll.* Updated ed. Introduction in volume one by Dick Clark. Introduction in volume two by Wolfman Jack. Introductions in volume three by Nina Blackwood, Mark Goodman, Alan Hunter, J.J. Jackson, and Martha C. Quinn. New York: Harper & Row, 1982-1985. 3 vols. Illustrated. Index.

Contents: The Solid Gold Years (vol. 1, covering the years 1950-1963); The Years of Change, 1964-1978 (vol. 2, New York: Crowell); and, The Video Revolution, 1978-Present (vol. 3, co-written with Charles Crespo). "The book contains primarily rock artists, but it also contains any artist who was on the charts during the fifties and early sixties with a hit record." (Foreword.) Some 2, 500 artists are represented in biographical sketches ranging from a few sentences to several paragraphs.

Each sketch is followed by a complete discography, and includes a photograph, when available.

1364. *The Rolling Stone Encyclopedia of Rock & Roll.* Edited by Jon Pareles, and Patricia Romanowski. New York: Rolling Stone Press, Summit Books, 1983. 615 p. Illustrated. Bibliography. Paperbound.

Although this book is chiefly a guide to the people closely identified with rock 'n' roll, there are entries on country, blues, jazz, and even classical musicians who have influenced rock. A particular effort is made to give in-depth coverage of black music and new music. The encyclopedia also contains definitions, Grammy award listings, and "boxes" (sidebars on rock festivals, rock on Broadway, rock on television, rock stars who have written books and other related information).

1365. Roxon, Lillian. *Lillian Roxon's Rock Encyclopedia.* Compiled by Ed Naha. Rev. ed. New York: Grosset & Dunlap, 1978. 565 p. Index. Paperbound.

An encyclopedia which lists "the contemporary artists as well as the prototypical ravers." (Compiler's introduction.) Hundreds of individual artists and groups are profiled with a sketch and a discography in an alphabetical listing ranging from A&R Men to Z.Z. Top.

1366. Stambler, Irwin, and Landon, Grelun. *The Encyclopedia of Folk, Country & Western Music.* 2d ed. New York: St. Martin's Press, 1983. 902 p. Illustrated. Bibliography.

The comingled coverage of this biographical dictionary reflects the author's premise that there is a strong relationship between folk, country, and western music. This relationship also embraces the generic subgroups of folk rock, folk blues, country rock and bluegrass. The biographies are a page or so in length, and based on questionnaire-generated information and interviews. Entries contain name, musical specialty, birthplace/date, and personal/career data. The narrative contains selective mention (with dates), of songs composed, sung, or played, and recorded works.

1367. Stambler, Irwin. *Encyclopedia of Pop, Rock & Soul.* New York: St. Martin's Press, 1977. 609 p. Illustrated. Bibliography.

Around 500 musical groups and individuals are described in a somewhat more extensive way than in most biographical dictionaries (average length, two columns). Included are several essays, principal of which is that by Bob Edmands entitled, "British Pop and Rock Since the Beatles," complete with a listing of artists. Music award lists are given in three appendices.

1368. *Variety International Showbusiness Reference.* Edited by Mike Kaplan. Garland Reference Library of the Humanities, vol. 292. New York: Garland, 1981. 1135 p.

See entry 453, for annotation.

1369. *Variety Obituaries, 1905-1986.* Edited by Chuck Bartelt and Barbara Bergeron. New York: Garland, 1988. 11 vols. Index ***

See entry 454, for annotation.

1370. *Variety Who's Who in Show Business.* Rev. ed. Edited by Mike Kaplan. New York: Garland, 1985. 372 p. Paperbound.

See entry 455, for annotation.

1371. White, Mark. *"You Must Remember This . . .": Popular Songwriters, 1900-1980.* Foreword by David Jacobs. London: F. Warne, 1983. 304 p. Bibliography. Index.

"This book is not an encyclopedia. It is a personal selection of some of those I consider to be among the all-time greats of the songwriting profession." (Introduction.) Excluded are composers who have written only a few songs, and those who have composed for just their own group (e.g., Mick Jagger, and Keith Richard for The Rolling Stones). Lyric writers have also been excluded, although major figures are mentioned in conjunction with their composer-partners (Alan Jay Lerner/Frederick Loewe). The sketches give birthplace/date, personal and professional biographical notes (including landmark song titles), and a concluding list of additional important songs. Four separate indexes: song titles, composers and lyricists, performers, and musical shows and films.

1372. *Who's Who in Country & Western Music.* Edited by Kenn Kingsbury. Co-edited by Gene Bear, et al. Special contributing editors, William Ivey, Jim Halsey and John Sturdivant. Introduction by Arthur E. "Uncle Art" Satherley. Culver City, CA: Black Stallion Country Press, 1981. 304 p. Illustrated. Bibliography. Index.

Not just the artists but people in all the major fields in the country music business have been included in this dictionary of over 700 biographical sketches. Biographical categories are: artists/entertainers, musicians, songwriters/music publishers, record producers, disc jockeys, agents/managers, and industry related. Sketches contain name, birth place/date, career narrative, and a small black and white portrait. Non-biographical chapters: top ten songs, 1949-1980; organizations; television and films; international country music; award winners; and publications.

1373. York, William. *Who's Who in Rock Music.* Rev. ed. New York: Scribner, 1982. 413 p.

An attempt to gather in a single volume, and in very brief form, the ". . . essential facts about the recording career of every individual and group in the history of rock music." (Preface.) Emphasis is on the comprehensive discography. Only major artists are awarded a sentence or so of career biographical data, although all are identified by rock specialty and group affiliation.

Section 3
Encyclopedias

1374. *Encyclopedia of Music in Canada.* Edited by Helmut Kallmann, Gilles Potvin, and Kenneth Winters. Toronto, Buffalo: University of Toronto Press, 1981. 1076 p. Illustrated. Index.

Addressing itself to the widest audience, this encyclopedia ". . . relates the activities and contributions of Canadian [musicians] . . . and discusses general topics in their Canadian aspects." (Introduction.) For the biographical entries, inclusion criteria were reasonable duration of residence or activity in Canada, musical merit, historical significance, and readers' interest. The sketches combine evaluative material with all the standard elements of factual data. They conclude with bibliographies, discographies and/or filmographies. Length of an essay is no indication of the importance of a person or topic.

1375. *Encyclopedia of Rock.* Edited by Phil Hardy, et al. 2d ed. London, Sydney: Macdonald, Orbis, 1987. 480 p. Illustrated.

Solo stars and super-groups as well as back-up musicians, technicians, producers, songwriters, musical styles, musical places (e.g., Liverpool), and record companies are among the over 1,500 entries presented in this revision of the 1976 edition from Panther Books. The intention is to provide ". . . a balanced, authoritative overview of well over thirty years of rock." (Introduction.) Entry length reflects the editors' estimate of the subject's importance. No discographies are given, although reference is made to "significant" recordings. Illustrations are interspersed throughout.

Section 4
Indexes

1376. *The Music Index: A Subject-Author Guide to Music Periodical Literature.* Detroit, MI: Information Coordinators, vol. 1-, 1949-. (Monthly)

Lists articles published in over 350 periodicals representing twenty countries. The subjects range from past and present personalities to computer produced music. Biographical articles are accessed by surname or subject, i. e. folk singers, jazz musicians. All first performances and obituaries are noted. There is an annual subject heading guide. Cumulations are usually yearly, however an arrearage necessitates biennial cumulations beginning with the most current, 1979-1980.

1377. *NewsBank. Review of the Arts: Performing Arts.* New Canaan, CT: Newsbank, 1975-. Microfiche. (Monthly)

An information service providing articles, on microfiche, from newspapers published in over 100 U.S. cities. Articles are selected from the fields of music, theater, dance, and circus. A title-subject index (cumulated every four months and annually) accompanies each issue. The CD-ROM product, *NewsBank Electronic Index*, is an on-disc index to the full-text microfiche.

1378. *Performing Arts Biography Master Index: A Consolidated Index to over 270,000 Biographical Sketches of Persons Living and Dead, as They Appear in over 100 of the Principal Biographical Dictionaries Devoted to the Performing Arts.* 2d ed. Edited by Barbara McNeil, and Miranda C. Herbert. Gale Biographical Index Series, no. 5. Detroit, MI: Gale Research, 1981. 701 p.

See entry 482, for annotation.

Section 5
Directories

1379. *Christensen's Ultimate Movie, TV, and Rock Directory.* 3d ed. Edited by Roger Christensen, and Karen Christensen. Cardiff-by-the-Sea, CA: Cardiff-by-the-Sea Publishing, 1988? Illustrated.

    See entry 486, for annotation.

1380. Mapp, Edward. *Directory of Blacks in the Performing Arts.* Foreword by Kenn Freeman. Metuchen, NJ: Scarecrow Press, 1978. 428 p. Bibliography. Index.

    A compendium of biographical data on over 850 black performers, alive or deceased, who have received a degree of artistic recognition. Excluded were groups such as The Supremes and The Ink Spots because of their changing composition. However, Diana Ross is included, since she has earned recognition apart from a group. Entries include name, birth date, education, credits (by field of entertainment), honors, current address (when feasible), familial relationship to other black performers, and career/performance information. Classified index by specialty.

1381. *Performing Arts Resources.* New York: Drama Book Specialists, vol. 1-, 1974-. (Annual)

    See entry 489, for annotation.

Section 6
Individual Celebrity Sources

BAEZ, JOAN. Mus.

1382. Swan, Peter. *Joan Baez, a Bio-Disco-Bibliography: Being a Selected Guide to Material in Print, on Record, on*

Cassette and on Film, with a Biographical Introduction. Brighton, Eng.: Noyce, 1977. 23 p. Index. ***

1383. Swanekamp, Joan, comp. *Diamonds & Rust: A Bibliography and Discography on Joan Baez.* Ann Arbor, MI: Pierian Press, 1980. 75 p. Illustrated. Index.

This comprehensive bibliography covers materials on Baez since the beginning of her career in 1960. There are 184 annotated citations, listed chronologically by title. The indexes provide access to authors, titles, periodicals, subjects, song titles and composers. A discography (albums only) is followed by an album chronology, and a listing of songs released as singles.

BASIE, COUNT. Mus. 4/26/84

1384. Sheridan, Chris, comp. *Count Basie: A Bio-Discography.* Discographies, no. 22. New York: Greenwood Press, 1986. 1350 p. Illustrated. Bibliography. Index.

"This is not trying to be a biography," Sheridan writes in his Preface. Despite his disclaimer there is ample biographical material both in the introduction, and inserted as annotation throughout the ten chronologically arranged discographic chapters. Appendices list microgroove issues of performances, and band itinerary. Five separate indexes: films and videos, radio and television programs, arrangers, musicians/vocalists, and songs.

THE BEATLES. Mus.

1385. Fenick, Barbara. *Collecting the Beatles: An Introduction & Price Guide to Fab Four Collectibles, Records & Memorabilia.* Photographs by Rick A. Kolodzie. Chicago: Contemporary Books, 1982. 276 p. Illustrated. Paperbound.

Listings of over 850 items: records (including bootlegs), books, magazines, pamphlets, programs, comics, promotional items, and movie items. Appendices list: manufacturers of Beatles products; auctions of Beatles memorabilia; glossary of terms; and an address list for collectors.

1386. Harry, Bill. *The Beatles Who's Who*. New York: Delilah Books, 1982. 192 p. Illustrated. Index. Paperbound.

Mersey Beat founder, Harry, has selected almost 300 Beatles friends and associates for inclusion in this biographical dictionary. In sketches of varying length, he writes of musicians, wives, lovers, producers, engineers, publishers, parents, and friends whose lives touched those of the "Fab Four."

1387. Harry, Bill. *The Book of Beatle Lists*. Poole, Dorset, England: Javelin Books, 1985. 224 p. Illustrated. Paperbound.

Beatleania (168 separate lists) including: Ringo's films; books by Beatles; The other Moptops; twenty Beatle fanzines; Brit hits; Pepper profiles; movie medley; and, McCartney's menu.

1388. Reinhart, Charles. *The Book of Beatles Lists*. Chicago: Contemporary Books, 1985. 230 p. Illustrated.

A reference miscellany of discography, concert chronologies, radio and television appearances, tours, filmography, bibliography, and plain trivia keyed to the fan and collector.

1389. Terry, Carol D., comp. *Here, There & Everywhere: The First International Beatles Bibliography, 1962-1982*. Foreword by Tom Schultheiss. Rock & Roll Reference Series, Vol. 11. Ann Arbor, MI: Pierian Press, 1985. 282 p. Illustrated.

A comprehensive (emphasis on comprehensive), universal, enumerative bibliography of Beatles information sources from 1962 through 1982. It is divided into fourteen major sections: ten sections of bibliographies grouped by source and type, one of fan magazines and clubs, and three of indexes (separate author, title, and subject). There are about 6, 000 citations to books, parts of books, magazine and newspaper articles. The indexes are extensive, with reference to individual entries.

JACKSON, MICHAEL. Mus.

1390. Machlin, Milton. *The Michael Jackson Catalog: A Comprehensive Guide to Records, Videos, Clothing, Posters, Toys and Millions of Collectible Souvenirs.* New York: Arbor House, Priam, 1984. 128 p. Illustrated. Paperbound.

"This book aspires to give as complete a listing as possible of memorabilia reflecting Michael's phenomenal impact on the world today." (Introduction.) Price ranges are given for "mint condition" collectibles.

1391. Terry, Carol D. *Sequins & Shades: The Michael Jackson Reference Guide.* Rock & Roll Reference Series, No. 22. Foreword by Tom Schultheiss. Ann Arbor, MI: Pierian Press, 1987. 507 p. Illustrated. Index.

A comprehensive bibliography, chronology, discography (including British records), and song list on the life and career of Jackson, supported by author, title, subject, date, publications, and record number indexes totalling a massive 146 pages.

LENNON, JOHN. Mus. 12/8/80

1392. Harry, Bill. *The Book of Lennon.* New York: Delilah/Putnam, 1984. 223 p. Illustrated. Paperbound.

An encyclopedia containing an explanatory paragraph or so about Lennon's friends, relatives, rivals, songs, books, and films. Harry, writer for *Mersey Beat*, and the musician's friend since the 1950s, ". . . has attempted to remind people of the positive side of John's life." The material is arranged alphabetically under boldface headings.

PRESLEY, ELVIS. Mus. 8/16/77

1393. Hammontree, Patsy Guy. *Elvis Presley: A Bio-Bibliography.* Popular Culture Bio-Bibliographies. Westport, CT: Greenwood Press, 1985. 301 p. Filmography. Discography. Index.

"In the Zenith" is the title of the 129-page section of biography with which Hammontree begins. This is followed by an evaluation of Presley's contribution to music and popular culture, and then by excerpts from various interviews with reporters and disc jockeys. Remaining segments: bibliography (books, periodical and newspaper articles); chronology; filmography (with accompanying assessment); and discography.

1394. Sauers, Wendy. *Elvis Presley, a Complete Reference: Biography, Chronology, Concerts List, Filmography, Discography, Vital Documents, Bibliography, Index.* Jefferson, NC: McFarland, 1984. vii, 194 p. Illustrated.

In addition to the contents listed as part of the subtitle, there is a list of memorabilia. Included here are prints, jewelry, and miscellany like the "King of Rock Game." There is some biographical material in short sections titled: "Biography," and "Memories." The bibliographical sections of this work are extensive.

1395. Whisler, John A. *Elvis Presley, Reference Guide and Discography.* Metuchen, NJ: Scarecrow Press, 1981. 258 p. Index.

Intended as a beginning point for research, this guide has a short bibliography (unannotated), two extensive subject indexes to newspaper and periodical articles, a discography listing albums and singles, and a song title index. The subject indexes were compiled from several major indexing services, with additional material cited from the clipping files of the Memphis *Commercial Appeal,* and *Memphis Press-Scimitar.*

ROBESON, PAUL. Mus. 1/23/76

1396. Davis, Lenwood G. , comp. *A Paul Robeson Research Guide: A Selected, Annotated Bibliography.* Foreword by John Henrik Clarke. Westport, CT: Greenwood Press, 1982. 879 p. Illustrated. Index.

This listing of English language printed materials by and about Robeson is the most complete reference source published to date. Part one is comprised of sixteen chapters. The first nine are writings by Robeson: book and pamphlets; forewords; introductions; articles; speeches; remarks and statements; messages and advertisements; letters and telegrams; and greetings. The remaining seven chapters list writings about Robeson: interviews; major books, pamphlets, and booklets; general books, pamphlets, and booklets; dissertations and theses; articles (arranged by decade); book reviews; and, obituaries. Part two (appendices), contains a discography, filmography, performance list, and archival/manuscript locations.

THE ROLLING STONES. Mus.

1397. Dimmick, Mary Laverne. *The Rolling Stones: An Annotated Bibliography.* Rev. ed. Foreword by Jay E. Daily. Pittsburgh: University of Pittsburgh Press, 1979. 159 p. Index.

Features ". . . articles and books that are substantial and informative, but also [cites] those items that, though brief, provide insight or reveal hitherto unknown facets of the group." (Preface.) Sources are listed by title, within chronological groupings. "Highly recommended" items are asterisked. Concludes with a chronology, and periodical and author indexes.

1398.   MacPhail, Jessica Holman Whitehead, comp. *Yesterday's Papers: The Rolling Stones in Print, 1963-1984.* Rock & Roll Reference Series, 19. Ann Arbor, MI: Pierian Press, 1986. 216 p. Illustrated. Index.

With this extensive, but unannotated bibliography, the author attempts to include, ". . . all known U. S. newspaper and magazine articles and books about the Stones from 1962 through 1984." (Introduction.) However, some material from other countries is to be found. Divided into fifteen sections: books; parts of books; fan magazines; magazine articles; newspaper articles; full periodical issues featuring the group; reviews of books, films, and recordings; address directory; and five indexes (author, title, subject, date, and publications).

1399. Weiner, Sue, and Howard, Lisa. *The Rolling Stones A to Z.* Foreword by Karen Rose. New York: Grove Press, Evergreen, 1983. 149 p. Illustrated. Paperbound.

Arranges more than twenty years of the group's history under 3,000 alphabetical entries, answering questions ranging from, "what was the fate of the sixth Stone?," to "who is the nineteen-year-old redhead who changed the Stones' lives?"

Chapter 19
Collective Biographies

1400. Balfour, Victoria. *Rock Wives: The Hard Lives and Good Times of the Wives, Girlfriends, and Groupies of Rock and Roll.* New York: Beech Tree Books, 1986. 270 p. Illustrated.

The subtitle succinctly describes what this book is all about. Seventeen women (and one man) who have lived with rock stars speak candidly about their experiences: Myra Lewis/Jerry Lee Lewis; Lee Angel /Little Richard; Susan Rotolo/Bob Dylan; Claudette Robinson/Smokey Robinson; Linda Lawrence Leitch/Brian Jones, Donovan Leitch; Marilyn Wilson/Brian Wilson; Anita Pallenberg/Brian Jones, Keith Richards; Gail Zappa/Frank Zappa; Patricia Kennealy/Jim Morrison; Monika Dannemann/Jimi Hendrix; Angie Bowie/David Bowie; Ingrid Croce/Jim Croce; Bebe Buell/Todd Rundgren, Rod Stewart, Elvis Costello, Stiv Bators; Leslie Meat Loaf/Meat Loaf; Jo Howard/Ron Wood; Carlene Carter/Nick Lowe; Vera Ramone/Dee Dee Ramone; David Wolff/Cyndi Lauper. Portraits, photographed by Harvey Wang, accompany the sketches.

1401. Balliett, Whitney. *American Singers.* New York: Oxford University Press, 1979. 178 p.

A group of essays about fourteen leading American popular and jazz singers. Balliett's stress is on the subject's career. The singers: Teddi King, Mary Mayo, Barbara Lea, Alberta Hunter, Joe Turner, Helen Humes, Ray Charles, Tony

Bennett, Sylvia Syms, Hugh Shannon, Blossom Dearie, Bobby Short, Mabel Mercer, and Anita Ellis.

1402. Benjaminson, Peter. *The Story of Motown.* New York: Grove Press, 1979. 191 p. Discography. Index. Paperbound.

In 1959, Berry Gordy started the Motown record company with 800 borrowed dollars. Within ten years, it had become the largest black-owned business in America. This history is, essentially, a collective biography of the musicians associated with Motown: Diana Ross, The Supremes, Stevie Wonder, The Temptations, The Four Tops, Marvin Gaye, Gladys Knight & the Pips, and Gordy himself, to list only the best known names.

1403. Berendt, Joachim E. *The Jazz Book: From Ragtime to Fusion and Beyond.* Rev. ed. Translated from the German by H. and B. Bredigkeit, with Dan Morgenstern. Westport, CT: L. Hill, 1982. 436 p. Discography. Index.

Translation of: *Das grosse Jazzbuch.* There have been nine revised editions in sixteen languages since this standard work of history, biography and criticism was first published in 1953. Nine chapters are labeled: the styles of jazz, the musicians of jazz, the elements of jazz, the instruments of jazz, the vocalists of jazz, the big bands of jazz, the jazz combos, and a definition of jazz. There is an extensive discography.

1404. Bigard, Barney. *With Louis and the Duke: The Autobiography of a Jazz Clarinetist.* Edited by Barry Martyn. Introduction by Earl "Fatha" Hines. New York: Oxford University Press, 1986. 152 p. Illustrated. Index.

Bigard played for many years in the bands of Louis Armstrong and Duke Ellington. While it is Bigard's autobiography, in actuality it is a collective biography about three jazz greats.

1405. Bogle, Donald. *Brown Sugar: Eighty Years of America's Black Female Superstars.* Designed by Joan Peckolick.

New York: Harmony Books, 1980. 208 p. Illustrated. Bibliography. Index.

The author has identified ". . . important figures—those women who captured the imagination of millions and became bona fide legends." The period of coverage is from 1900 to the mid-1970s; from Ma Rainey to Donna Summer. Each sketch is from one to eight pages, almost evenly divided between pictorial matter and narrative. About thirty artists are presented, grouped within the period they flourished.

1406. Brown, Charles T. *Music U.S.A.: America's Country & Western Tradition.* Englewood Cliffs, NJ: Prentice-Hall, 1986. 215 p. Illustrated. Discography. Bibliography. Index.

The sketches of eighty-six individual musicians and groups focus on the music itself as opposed to sociological and personal influences. Each piece is about a page long. The book is structured chronologically and by artist or topic. Techniques which may aid in appreciating country/western music are explained.

1407. Busnar, Gene. *Superstars of Country Music.* New York: Julian Messner, 1984. 239 p. Illustrated. Bibliography. Index.

This volume is a collective biography with twenty to thirty-page biographies on nine singers. Each essay includes a black and white portrait and a discography. The singers: Hank Williams, Johnny Cash, Loretta Lynn, Willie Nelson, Charley Pride, Dolly Parton, Kenny Rogers, Jerry Lee Lewis, and Tammy Wynette.

1408. Cohen, Daniel, and Cohen, Susan. *Rock Video Superstars.* New York: Pocket Books, Archway, 1985. 122 p. Illustrated. Paperbound.

Precursor of *Rock Video Superstars II* (below), this book established the format: four-page illustrated biographical sketches of a rock group or single artist emphasizing their video work, and ending with an address for fan contact. Among others, there are sketches of: Cyndi Lauper, Culture Club, Wham!, Eurythmics, Billy Joel, Lionel Richie, Quiet Riot, The Cars, Hall and Oates, Prince, Billy Idol, Police, Pat Benatar, Van Halen, Madonna, Duran Duran, Michael Jackson, "Weird Al" Yankovic, David Bowie, Frankie Goes to Hollywood, Twisted Sister, and Bruce Springsteen.

1409. Cohen, Daniel, and Cohen, Susan. *Rock Video Superstars II*. New York: Pocket Books, Archway, 1987. 115 p. Illustrated. Paperbound.

Rock-MTV megastars of the moment are profiled in this sequel to *Rock Video Superstars* (above). Five-page sketches with photograph(s) and agent's address are supplied for: Phil Collins, Whitney Houston, Heart, Sade, John Cougar Mellencamp, Howard Jones, Belinda Carlisle, Simply Red, El DeBarge, Simple Minds, U2, Tom Petty and the Heartbreakers, Huey Lewis and the News, Mr. Mister, Janet Jackson, Tears for Fears, The Moody Blues, Peter Gabriel, The Fat Boys, a-ha, Dire Straits, Jackson Browne, The Monkees, and George Michael.

1410. Colman, Stuart. *They Kept on Rockin': The Giants of Rock 'n' Roll*. Foreword by Dave Price. Poole, Dorset, England: Blandford Press, 1982. 160 p. Illustrated. Index. Paperbound.

"Original" rock 'n' roll is still with us. This is largely a consequence of the impact and staying power of many of the giants and other pioneers of this music. Some twenty-seven illustrated sketches of these originators and interpreters are found in this book including those of: Bill Haley, Bo Diddley, The Coasters, Buddy Holly, Little Richard, Jerry Lee Lewis, Fats Domino, Cliff Richard, and Billy Fury.

1411. *The Country Music Hall of Fame & Museum*. Nashville, TN: Country Music Foundation, 1983. 48 p. Illustrated. Paperbound.

The first part of this work tells "The Story of Country Music," e.g., old-time traditions, singing cowboys, bluegrass, etc. Illustrations used throughout this section are of the artifacts displayed in the Hall. Part two consists of mini-biographies and color portraits of the members of the Hall: Jimmie Rodgers, Fred Rose, Hank Williams, Roy Acuff, Tex Ritter, Ernest Tubb, Eddy Arnold, James R. Denny, George D. Hay, Uncle Dave Macon, Red Foley, J. L. (Joe) Frank, Jim Reeves, Stephen H. Sholes, Bob Wills, Gene Autry, Original Carter Family, Bill Monroe, Arthur Edward Satherley, Jimmie H. Davis, Chet Atkins, Patsy Cline, Owen Bradley, Frank "Pee Wee" King, Minnie Pearl, Paul Cohen, Kitty Wells, Merle Travis, Grandpa Jones, Hubert Long, Hank Snow, Johnny Cash, Connie B. Gay, Original Sons of the Pioneers, Vernon Dalhart, Grant Turner, Lefty Frizzell, Roy Horton, and Marty Robbins.

1412. Craig, Warren. *The Great Songwriters of Hollywood.* Foreword by Harry Warren. San Diego: A. S. Barnes; London: Tantivy Press, 1980. 287 p. Illustrated. Song listing. Index.

For the two decades beginning in 1928, Hollywood monopolized the services of almost all of the most talented writers of popular songs for its movie musicals (notable exceptions: Cole Porter, George Gershwin, and Richard Rodgers, all of whom have been omitted from this book). Busby Berkeley and Warner Brothers are together credited as the director and studio giving early creative momentum to this cinematic musical form. From the inception of the Oscar for best song in 1934, through 1978, the thirty-two composers and lyricists represented in this book have won twenty-five, while being nominated for 214. Each songwriter, listed desultorily from Irving Berlin to the team of Jay Livingston and Ray Evans, is described in a page-length career biography followed by a song listing arranged by movie and song title. Portraits and other illustrations complete the sketches. Indexing is by name, film and song. In addition to Berlin, the most famous names include: Johnny Mercer, Harold Arlen, Jerome Kern, Ira Gershwin, Jule Styne, and Sammy Cahn.

1413. David, Andrew. *Rock Stars: People at the Top of the Charts.* New York: Exeter Books, 1979. 96 p. Illustrated. Index.

The forty subjects of this book are the rock music superstars of the 1970s as certified by the Record Institute Association of America's sales figures (platinum and gold record awards), the National Academy of Recording Arts and Sciences (Grammy awards), and the *Billboard Magazine* Awards. A page of career biographical narrative with a selective discography is presented for each star. The facing page contains a portrait. Artists having the most platinum records: Kiss (5), Neil Diamond (4), Barry Manilow (4), Paul McCartney & Wings (4), Linda Ronstadt (4), Barbra Streisand (4), The Bee Gees (2), Andy Gibb (1), and Olivia Newton-John (1).

1414. Feather, Leonard. *The Passion for Jazz.* New York: Horizon Press, 1980. 208 p. Illustrated.

Who are the ten top jazz artists? Feather goes where few have dared by offering his choices. There are many additional profiles, and other relevant essays, e.g., "Jazz on Public Radio." The ten gods of the jazz pantheon—in order of importance: Duke Ellington, Louis Armstrong, Art Tatum, Billie Holiday, Dizzy Gillespie, Charlie Parker, Benny Goodman, Coleman Hawkins, Earl "Fatha" Hines, and Joe Venuti.

1415. Gelly, Dave. *The Giants of Jazz.* Drawings by Weef. Introduction by Miles Kington. London: Aurum Press, 1986. 143 p. Illustrated. Index.

A collection of over eighty short biographical narratives accompanied by cartoons are combined with the intent of presenting an uncommon perspective on the personality and artistry of the subject. The sketches are ordered by birthdate, beginning with King Oliver (1885-1938), and proceeding with such celebrated greats as: Jelly Roll Morton, Bessie Smith, Duke Ellington, Louis Armstrong, Fats Waller, Count Basie, Lionel Hampton, Benny Goodman, Dizzy Gillespie, Ella Fitzgerald, et al.

1416. *The Great Jazz Pianists: Speaking of Their Lives and Music.* Interviewed by Len Lyons. Photographs by Veryl Oakland. New York: Morrow, 1983. 321 p. Illustrated. Discography. Index.

The book is in two parts. Part One is a survey of jazz pianists from 1900 to today. Part Two consists of interviews with twenty-seven artists. Each interview consists of a portrait, an introduction of several paragraphs, eight pages or so of questions and answers, and a selected discography. The first ten interviews: Theodore "Teddy" Wilson, Mary Lou Williams, John Lewis, Sun Ra, George Shearing, Dave Brubeck, Ahmad Jamal, Horace Silver, Oscar Peterson, and William "Red" Garland.

1417. Hampton, Wayne. *Guerrilla Minstrels: John Lennon, Joe Hill, Woody Guthrie, Bob Dylan.* Knoxville: University of Tennessee Press, 1986. 306 p. Illustrated. Bibliography. Discography. Index.

The book coalesces around Lennon, Hill, Guthrie, and Dylan, who summarize eras or genres of protest. The four key personalities are important both biographically and politically, as are the other minstrals whose stories complete the history of protest singing in America. A few of the others: the Almanac Singers, Pete Seeger, The Weavers, and Peter, Paul, and Mary.

1418. Lyttelton, Humphrey. *Enter the Giants, 1931-1944.* New York: Taplinger, Crescendo, 1982. 239 p. Illustrated. Bibliography. Discography. Index. ***

1419. McColm, Bruce, and Payne, Doug. *Where Have They Gone?: Rock 'n' Roll Stars.* New York: Tempo Books, 1979. 254 p. Illustrated. Paperbound.

". . . These are the veterans of a revolution in music that has had profound cultural consequences. Even though they're not as visible as they once were, they've seen it all and have plenty to tell." (Introduction.) The lives of thirty musicians are described in sketches of between five and eight pages. Each includes a portrait. Some of those profiled: Brenda Lee, Archie Bell, Bobby Rydell, Del Shannon, Tommy Sands, Dion, Bobby Vee, Sheb Wooley, Dolores Kenniebrew, Gary Lewis, Peter Noone, and Billy Joe Royal.

1420. Miller, Jim, ed. *The Rolling Stone Illustrated History of Rock & Roll.* Rev. ed. New York: Rolling Stone, 1980. 474 p. Illustrated. Discography. Index. Paperbound.

Presents a series of essays on important events and personalities since the beginnings of rock. Motown, Jerry Lee Lewis, Folk Rock, Janis Joplin, New Wave: America, and Anarchy in the U.K. are several representative essays from a total of eighty-three.

1421. Pascall, Jeremy. *The Illustrated History of Rock Music.* Rev. ed. New York: Exeter Books, 1984. 237 p. Illustrated. Bibliography. Index.

The first edition of this book was published in 1978. A satisfactory index to biographical information and illustrations enable this history to function perfectly well as collective biography. The illustrations (mostly in color) share roughly equal space and emphasis with the narrative material.

1422. Placksin, Sally. *American Women in Jazz: 1900 to Present: Their Words, Lives, and Music.* New York: Wideview Books, 1982. 332 p. Illustrated. Discography. Bibliography. Index.

Placksin presents profiles of over sixty women set within the context of their musical and social environment. Much of the material was generated through interviews with the artists. The profiles are grouped by decade, and range in length from one to eight pages. A selected, however extensive, discography concludes the work.

1423. Pollock, Bruce. *When the Music Mattered: Rock in the 1960's.* New York: Holt, Rinehart and Winston, 1984. 243 p. Illustrated. Index.

Seven essays featuring eleven rock musicians representative of the youth cult of the 60s comprise this work. A "playlist" (a selection of song lyrics as poetry) accompanies each chapter introduction. The musicians: Dave Van Ronk, John Kuse, Jiggs Meister, Paul Simon, Roger McGuinn, Tracy

Nelson, Marty Balin, Peter Tork, Tuli Kupferberg, Essra Mohawk, and John Sebastian.

1424. Simon, George T. *The Best of the Music Makers: From Acuff to Ellington to Presley to Sinatra to Zappa and 279 More of the Most Popular Performers of the Last Fifty Years*. Foreword by Dinah Shore. Garden City, NY: Doubleday, 1979. 635 p. Illustrated.

Limited to a selection of ". . . the [284] most important popular music performers of the past fifty years" (introduction), these biographical articles combine anecdotal material, pertinent biographical data, and a representative photograph. About half the sketches are by Simon; the rest, edited by him, are contributions by seventeen popular music journalists.

1425. Simon, George T. *The Big Bands*. 4th ed. Foreword by Frank Sinatra. New York: Schirmer Books; London: Collier Macmillan, 1981. 614 p. Illustrated. Discography. Index.

Popular biography and history are blended in equal measure, resulting in a reading experience apparently so satisfactory that Simon's book is now in its fourth edition. "The Big Bands—Then," "Inside the Big Bands" (individual musicians), and "Big Bandleaders Revisited," are three of the seven chapters. Among the band leader sketches: Count Basie, Benny Goodman, Woody Herman, Harry James, Stan Kenton, Guy Lombardo, and Artie Shaw.

1426. Spitz, Robert Stephen. *The Making of Superstars: Artists and Executives of the Rock Music Business*. Garden City, NY: Anchor Press, Doubleday, 1978. 325 p. Index.

About twenty-five important rock 'n' roll figures, selected ". . . on their credits and on [Spitz'] personal expectations," are profiled in this anecdotal history which easily qualifies as a collective biography. Some of those included: Jim Messina, Don Kirshner, Barry Manilow, Janis Ian, Arif Mardin, Dion DiNucci, Neil Sedaka, Ron Delsener, Peter Frampton, Sid Bernstein, Grace Slick, Jerry Wexler, Peter Knobler, and Barry White.

1427. Tobler, John. *Guitar Heroes*. New York: St. Martin's Press, 1978. 88 p. Illustrated. ***

1428. Ullman, Michael. *Jazz Lives: Portraits in Words and Pictures*. Washington, DC: New Republic Books, 1980. 244 p. Illustrated. Discography.

Two dozen jazz people are profiled in this work which combines biography, criticism, and reviews of recordings. Among the well-known musicians are Earl Hines, Betty Carter, Sonny Rollins, Marian McPartland, Dizzy Gillespie, and Charles Mingus. Also included are several non-musician friends of jazz: promoter Steve Backer, producer John Snyder, manager Maxine Gregg, and lawyer Maxwell Cohen.

1429. White, Timothy. *Rock Stars*. Designed by J. C. Suares. New York: Stewart, Tabori & Chang, 1984. 284 p. Illustrated. Index.

A former senior editor for *Rolling Stone*, White has written sketches describing forty-one rock stars. However, the focal point of his book is its scores of illustrations, many of which are full-page and in color. Some of the stars: Elvis Presley, John Lennon, Paul McCartney, Aretha Franklin, David Bowie, Michael Jackson, Sting, Prince, Diana Ross, James Brown, and Jerry Lee Lewis.

Chapter 20
Periodicals

1430. *After Dark.* New York: Dance Magazine, Inc., vol. 1-, 1968-. (Monthly)

See entry 587, for annotation.

1431. *The Big Bopper.* Burbank, CA: Lauffer Publishing, vol. 1-, 1988(?)-. (Monthly)

See entry 591, for annotation.

1432. *Billboard.* New York: Billboard Publications, vol. 1-, 1963-. (Weekly)

Continues: *Billboard Music Week* (1894-1962). "The international music-record-tape newsweekly." A tabloid-size magazine, paramount in its field, which regularly includes news of music personalities. Indexed (some selectively) by: *Music Index, Trade & Industry Index.*

1433. *Black Beat.* New York: Lexington Library, vol. 14-, 1983-. (Monthly)

Continues: *Soul Teen* (1970-March, 1983). This fan magazine is predominantly concerned with the music scene. However, a few articles spotlight film and TV personalities. Both black and white entertainers are profiled, with emphasis on the former. Departments include: "Gossip beat," and "Heartthrob corner."

1434. *Black Sounds.* Los Angeles: Cambray Publishing, vol. 1-, 19(?)-. (Quarterly)

Its title to the contrary, this music fan magazine does include some material on white performers. Four of the interview articles in the June, 1987 issue: Pointer Sisters, Beastie Boys, Tina Turner, and Bruce Willis.

1435. *Blues & Soul.* London: Napfield, no. 412-, 1984-. (Biweekly)

Continues: *Blues & Soul Music Review* (1966-1984). Contemporary developments, news, reviews, charts, and historical perspective on this popular music genre.

1436. *Blues Unlimited.* London: BU Publications Ltd., no. 1-, 1963-. (Quarterly)

Contains serious, illustrated biographical and historical articles about blues musicians. Indexed (some selectively) by: *Jazz Index, MLA International Bibliography.*

1437. *BMI Music World.* New York: Broadcast Music, vol. 1-, 1988-. (Quarterly)

Formerly: *The Many Worlds of Music/BMI* (1964-1987), *About Music & Writers/BMI* (1964), and *News About Music & Writers* (1961-1964). Rock, pop, jazz, R&B, country, gospel, Latin, concert, theater, film and television music are covered in profusely illustrated features and departments. Dexter Gordon, Michael Jackson, Billy Joel, Rosanne Cash, Thomas Newman are some of those profiled in the winter, 1988 issue. Indexed by: *Music Index.*

1438. *Bomp.* Burbank, CA: Bomp Magazine, vol. 1-, 1985?-. (Bimonthly)

Formerly: *Who Put the Bomp!* (1966-1985?). This former fanzine contains articles and interviews, discographies, and advertisements of rock 'n' roll memorabilia.

1439. *Bop.* Toluca Lake, CA: Laufer Publishing Co., vol. 1-, 1984-. (Monthly)

An illustrated teen-audience publication containing biographical articles about rock music personalities.

1440. *The Cash Box*. New York: Cash Box Publishing Co., vol. 1-, 1942-. (Weekly)

"The international music record weekly." Similar to *Billboard* (above), with an emphasis on the record industry. Presents news and ratings of performers. Indexed by: *Music Index*.

1441. *Circus*. New York: Circus Enterprises Corp., vol. 1-, 1969-. (Monthly)

Supersedes: *Circus Weekly* (1978-1979). This magazine is the early teenage counterpart to *Rolling Stone*, publishing a diversity of articles relevant to its audience, foremost among which are those about rock music and musicians.

1442. *CMA Close-Up*. Nashville, TN: Country Music Association, vol. 1-, 1967-. (Monthly)

Variant titles: *Close-Up, Country Music Close-Up.* Contains news about C&W people and events.

1443. *Country Music*. New York: Silver Eagle, vol. 1-, 1972-. (Bimonthly)

Articles about the country music scene, including interviews of the artists. Indexed by: *Magazine Index.*

1444. *Country Music Review*. London: Country Music Review Ltd., vol. 1-, 1971-. (Monthly)

Running title: *C M R*. This is an authoritative country/western music publication which presents biographical, historical and other articles.

1445. *Country Music Round-Up*. London: Country Music Round-Up Publishing Co., vol. 1-, 1976-. (Monthly)

Biographical pieces and book reviews are among the regular features.

1446. *Country Music World.* Country Music Society, vol. 1-, 1972-. (Monthly)

This is a publication for the Society membership.

1447. *Country Song Roundup.* Derby, CT: Charlton Publications, vol. 1-, 1949-. (Monthly)

Photographs, interviews and articles about country music performers. Also publishes book and record reviews.

1448. *Creem.* Los Angeles: Cambray Publishing, vol. 1-, 1969. (Bimonthly)

Other title: *Creem Magazine.* While indisputably the original rock 'n' roll magazine, it unabashedly calls itself "America's only rock 'n' roll magazine." *Creem Close-up* and *Creem Presents* are related Cambray titles. All contain biographical articles. Indexed (some selectively) by: *Music Index, Media Review Digest.*

1449. *Creem Collector's Series.* Birmingham, MI: Cambray Publishing, vol. 1-, 1987-.

Intended as a continuing publication, although frequency is unknown. Issues are devoted to an individual musician or group. Bruce Springsteen is featured in the issue examined (eighty-six pages of vol. 1, no. 1). The story is heavily illustrated and contains a discography.

1450. *Creem Rock-Shots.* Los Angeles: Cambray Publishing, vol. 1-, 198?-. (Quarterly)

For the adolescent fan, here is yet another *Creem* scion, with heavily illustrated (including posters) stories about popular rock 'n' roll personalities, e.g., "Nothing Like Sting," "The Good, the Bad and Michael Jackson."

1451. *Daily Variety.* Hollywood, CA: Daily Variety, Ltd., vol. 1-, 1933-. (Daily)

See entry 600, for annotation.

1452. *Down Beat.* Elmhurst, IL: Maher Publications, vol. 1-, 1934-. (Monthly)

"The contemporary music magazine" (subtitle). The focus is jazz, and the audience is the musician and the fan. There are articles on jazz personalities. Indexed (some selectively) by: *Jazz Index, Magazine Index, Music Index, Readers' Guide to Periodical Literature, Book Review Index, Magazine Article Summaries, RILM Abstracts.*

1453. *Faces Rocks.* River Edge, NJ: Faces Magazines, vol. 1-, 1984-. (Monthly)

An illustrated rock 'n' roll teenage fan vehicle much like the dozens of other *Creem* clones (above), the March, 1988 issue of this magazine contains articles on Dokken, Aerosmith, Alice Cooper, and Def Leppard.

1454. *Guitar for the Practicing Musician.* Port Chester, NY: Cherry Lane Books, vol. 1-, 1984-. (Monthly)

This magazine contains many pages of guitar and bass scores with intermingled rock music and biographical features. The February, 1988 issue examined contains features about Desmond Child, Adrian Vandenberg, Vinnie Moore, Eric Clapton, and others.

1455. *Guitar Player.* Cupertino, CA: GPI Publications, vol. 1-, 1967-. (Monthly)

Other title: *Guitar Player Magazine.* Contains material on all aspects of (predominantly rock) guitar/bass musicianship, with biographical features on players. The March, 1988 issue has a seventeen-page cover story on Chuck Berry. Indexed (some selectively) by: *Magazine Index, Jazz Index, Music Index, Magazine Article Summaries.*

1456. *Guitar World.* New York: Harris Publications, vol. 1-, 1980-. (11 issues yearly)

The March, 1988 issue examined was devoted to the career and the recordings of Jimi Hendrix. Intermittently, other guitarists are accorded similar special treatment.

1457. *Hard Rock's Metal Studs Superstar Special.* New York: Sterlings' Magazines, vol. 1-, 198(?)-. (Bi-monthly)

Jon Bon Jovi, and Motley Crue are two of the rockers featured in articles with biographical content in the issue seen: "Superstar Special No. 20." "Metal addresses," a fan club directory, appears to be a regular department.

1458. *Hit Parader.* Derby, CT: Charlton Publications, vol. 1-, 1954-. (Monthly)

Among other short articles are those profiling musicians. Recurring departments: "Roots"; "Legends of Rock" (both reminiscences); and, a centerfold, usually of a group. Indexed selectively by: *Magazine Article Summaries.*

1459. *Jazz Digest.* McLean, VA: E. Steane, vol. 1-, 1973-. (Monthly) ***

Supersedes: *Hip: The Jazz Record Digest.*

1460. *Jazz Journal International.* London: Billboard, Ltd., vol. 30-, 1977-. (Monthly)

Continues: *Jazz Journal* (1948-1973; 1974-1977), and *Jazz Journal and Jazz & Blues* (1974). Provides a serious approach to this indigenous American music form, surveying all its aspects. Indexed by: *Jazz Index, Music Index.*

1461. *Jazz Times.* Silver Spring, MD: Jazz Times, vol. ?-, 1980-. (Monthly)

Continues: *Radio Free Jazz.* Concerts, book and recordings reviews, and articles about musicians are among the offerings. Indexed by: *Jazz Index, Music Index.*

1462. *Jazz World.* New York: World Jazz Society, vol. 14-, 1984-. (Monthly)

Continues: *Jazz World Index* (1981-1984), *Jazz Echo* (1979-1981), and *Swinging Newsletter* (1972-1978). "Maximum facts, minimum words." (Title from caption.) Indexed by: *Jazz Index, Music Index.*

1463. *The Journal of Country Music.* Nashville, TN: Country Music Foundation, vol. 2-, 1971-. (Three issues yearly)

Continues: *Country Music Foundation Newsletter* (1970-1971). Contains biographical articles on performers and their career development. Indexed (some selectively) by: *MLA International Bibliography, RILM Abstracts, Reference Sources, Arts and Humanities Citation Index.*

1464. *Keyboard.* Cupertino, CA: GPI Publications, vol. 7-, 1981-. (Monthly)

Formerly: *Contemporary Keyboard* (1975-1981). *Keyboard* covers the personalities, technologies, and methodologies connected with key instruments. Classical, pop, rock, and jazz music are within its purview. The March, 1988 number contains a feature on rock producer and musician, David Foster, and Russian emigre pianist, Vladimir Feltsman. Indexed (some selectively) by: *Music Index, RILM Abstracts.*

1465. *Living Blues.* University, MS: Center for the Study of Southern Culture, The University of Mississippi, no. 1-, 1970-. (Bimonthly)

Has supplement *Living Bluesletter.* "A Journal of the Black American Blues Tradition" (subtitle). This journal is the vehicle for the scholarly study of the history of this American music genre, and its criticism. Indexed (some selectively) by: *Jazz Index, Music Index, MLA International Bibliography, RILM Abstracts.*

1466. *Melody Maker.* London: IPC Specialist and Professional Press, vol. 1-, 1926-. (Weekly)

A tabloid music weekly with European and British emphasis on rock 'n' roll groups and individual stars. Indexed in *Music Index.*

1467. *Metal Mania.* New York: Tempo Publishing Co., vol. 1-, 19(?)-. (Bi-monthly)

Intended for the teen fan, *Metal Mania* (for August, 1988), offers giant color posters of Def Leppard and Ozzy.

Featured interviews are of Saxon, Yngwie Malmsteen, and Billy Sheehan.

1468. *Movie Mirror's Country Music Special.* New York: Lexington Library, Inc., no. 1-, 1981-. (Irregular)

The cover of one issue of this lavishly illustrated (in color) fan magazine promises, "Twelve revealing interviews with Nashville's biggest stars!"

1469. *Music City News.* Nashville, TN: Music City News Publishing Co., vol. 1-, 1963-. (Monthly)

Country and western music news, features, and reviews in a tabloid format.

1470. *Musician.* Gloucester, MA: Amordian Press, no. 42-, 1982-. (Monthly)

Continues: *Musician, Player, and Listener* (1977-1982), and *Music America Magazine* (1976-1977). One issue examined featured an interview with Marvin Gaye, and features on Bryan Ferry and The Kinks. A Paul McCartney interview appears in the February, 1988 number. Indexed by: *Music Index, Jazz Index.*

1471. *New Musical Express.* London: IPC Magazines, Ltd., no. 1-, 1952-. (Weekly)

This British magazine is analogous to *Rolling Stone* (above), however, with far less socio-political content. Emphasis is on pop music (especially interviews with pop stars and groups).

1472. *Nine-O-One Network.* Memphis, TN: Nine-O-One Network, Inc., vol. 1-, 1986?-. (Bimonthly?)

Country-blues-rock music devotees are the audience for this magazine in which the December, 1987 issue contains a Chet Atkins interview, and the article: "B. B. King Looks Back." Quality in content and design set this title apart from the standard mass-market popular music vehicles.

1473. *Popular Music and Society.* Bowling Green, OH: Dept. of Sociology, Bowling Green State University, vol. 1-, 1971-. (Quarterly)

Anything concerning the field of popular music is the concern of this scholarly quarterly, whether song lyrics, song themes, the audience, the business of recording, or interviews with the musicians. Indexed (some selectively) by: *Music Index, RILM Abstracts, Book Review Index, Index to Book Reviews in the Humanities.*

1474. *Record.* New York: Straight Arrow Publishers, vol. 1-, 1981-. (Monthly)

Rock 'n' roll magazine with some biographical content. Indexed by: *Music Index.*

1475. *Right On!* Teaneck, NJ: D.S. Magazines, Inc., vol. 1-, 1971-. (Monthly)

Gossipy articles ("Does Janet Jackson Like Taimak?" and "Jody Watley: is she looking for a new love?"—July, 1987) are found sandwiched among color pin-ups and regular departments containing short news clips. Target audience: black teens.

1476. *Rip.* Los Angeles: L. F. P., Inc., vol. 1-, 1986-. (Monthly)

Hustler's Larry Flynt moves further into publishing's "non-skin" trade with this vehicle. (Other titles from L. F. P.: *Running Times, Men's Look, Supercycle.*) *Rip* is aimed right at a punk and heavy-metal rock music audience. It publishes a number of articles of biographical content each month.

1477. *Rock & Soul.* Derby, CT: Charlton Publications, vol. 28-, 1984-. (Bimonthly)

Continues: *Rock & Soul Songs; Rock and Roll Songs* (1956-1984). Long-running rock magazine with feature stories (including biographies/interviews), song lyrics, and regular departments.

1478. *Rock Poster Magazine*. New York: Starlog Press, vol. 1-, 1983-. (Quarterly)

Biographies (with plentiful illustrations) of rock 'n' roll performers.

1479. *Rock Scene*. New York: Tempo Publishing Co., vol. 1-, 1973-. (Monthly)

In the May, 1987 issue seen, there were interviews with Joan Jett, Alice Cooper, and several other rock artists and groups. Illustrated, chiefly in color.

1480. *Rock Scene Presents (Concert Shots)*. New York: Tempo Publishing Co., no. 1-, 1986?-. (Bimonthly)

Fold-out color posters and rock 'n' roll features. The issue examined (no. 11) had "Liberace Rock," and "Motley Crue Gives Metal a New Wave," as main articles.

1481. *Sing Out*. New York: Sing Out, Inc., vol. 1-, 1950-. (Quarterly)

Covers the world of folk music with a wide variety of articles and essays including musician interviews. Indexed (some selectively) by: *Magazine Index, Music Index, MLA International Bibliography, Alternative Press Index*.

1482. *Song Hits*. Derby, CT: Charlton Publications, vol. 1-, 1987-. (Bimonthly)

Other title: *Song Hits Magazine*. Popular with the teen audience since it contains song lyrics for pop, soul, and country hits. Also presents regular articles about a music star or group.

1483. *Spin*. New York: Spin Magazine, vol. 1-, 1985-. (Monthly)

Edited by Bob Guccione, Jr., this polished new publication covers rock music and the hip scene. The May, 1987 issue has features with biographical content on Julian Copes, Camper van Beethoven, and Joan Jett.

1484. *Star Hits.* New York: Pilot Communications, vol. 1-, 1984-. (Monthly)

Teen audience vehicle with biographical-content articles on David Lee Roth, Rick Astley, Sinead O'Connor, and others (June, 1988). Departments: a (brief) fan club directory, "Chatterbox" (news about rockers), and performer profiles ("Personal file").

1485. *Tiger Beat.* Cresskill, NJ: D.S. Magazines, Inc., vol. 1-, 1965-. (Monthly)

Continues: *Lloyd Thaxton's Tiger Beat.* For the teenager there are illustrated stories about young entertainers, their lives, what they do, their interests.

1486. *Tiger Beat Special.* Cresskill, NJ: D.S. Magazines, Inc., vol. 1-, 1987?-. (Quarterly)

There are special features (with photographs) on Michael J. Fox, Madonna, and Duran Duran, in the spring, 1987 issue examined.

1487. *Tiger Beat Star.* Cresskill, NJ: D.S. Magazines, Inc., vol. 1-, 1983-.

Teen audience fan magazine featuring television, movie, and rock stars. An average issue has twenty feature interviews.

1488. *Trouser Press.* New York: Trans-oceanic Trouser Press, vol. 1-, 19??-. (Irregular)

Continues: *Trans-Oceanic Trouser Press.* Up from the ranks of fanzine, this is an "insider" music magazine containing articles about rock musicians (in one issue, Adam Ant and The Who), and the general youth scene. Indexed by: *Music Index.*

1489. *Variety.* New York: Variety Publishing, vol. 1-, 1905-. (Weekly)

See entry 646, for annotation.

1490. *Wow.* New York: Pilot Communications, vol. 1-, 19(?)-. (Monthly)

See entry 649, for annotation.

Chapter 21
Computerized Databases

1491. *Arts Documentation Service.* North Sydney, NSW, Australia: Australia Council Library.

See entry 650, for annotation.

1492. *Electric Bank, Performance Bank.* Des Moines, IA: The Electric Bank.

See entry 652, for annotation.

1493. *ESI Street.* Los Angeles: Entertainment Systems International.

See entry 653, for annotation.

1494. *Hollywood Hotline.* Burbank, CA: Hollywood Hotline.

See entry 65, for annotation.

1495. *Music Information Service.* Ft. Lauderdale, FL: Music Information Service; Shoemaker's Music.

Subject: music, musicians, and the music industry. Contents: interviews and data relevant to jazz, rock, country, western, pop and other musical genres. Coverage as of early 1986: 500 records updated with weekly frequency. Address: P.O. Box 14012, Ft. Lauderdale, FL 33301. Telephone: (305) 463-2666.

1496. *Rocknet.* La Mesa, CA: Les Tracy.

Subjects: entertainment industry; music and the music industry. Contents: news of the rock music industry; reviews; interviews with rock 'n' roll stars and others in the business. Coverage: 1985-. Updating occurs daily. Address: 9609 Sunset Ave., La Mesa, CA 92041. Telephone: (619) 469-4806.

Chapter 22
Organizations

1497. ACADEMY OF COUNTRY MUSIC

6255 Sunset Blvd., Suite 915
Hollywood, CA 90028
(213) 462-2351

Purpose: to enhance and promote the country music credo throughout the world. Presents annual awards. Produces country music shows. Publications: monthly newsletter; annual awards book.

1498. BLACK MUSIC ASSOCIATION

1500 Locust St., Suite 1905
Philadelphia, PA 19102
(215) 545-8600

Objective: "Preserve, protect, and perpetuate black music on an- international level. . . ." BMA's future plans include a black music institute and museum. Publication: *Innervisions.*

1499. BLUES FOUNDATION

P.O. Box 161272
Memphis, TN 38186
(901) 756-0425

Objective: to perpetuate, preserve and promote blues music. Plans to create a museum, library and theatre. Publication: *Blues Connection.*

1500. BLUES HEAVEN FOUNDATION

    822 Hillgrove Ave.
    Western Springs, IL 60558
    (312) 246-8222

Goal: dedicated to building an organization to preserve and perpetuate blues music through documentation and performance. An audio-visual archive is planned.

1501. CALIFORNIA INSTITUTE OF THE ARTS

    The Library
    24700 McBean Pkwy.
    Valencia, CA 91355
    (805) 255-1050

    See entry 661, for annotation.

1502. COUNTRY MUSIC FOUNDATION, HALL OF FAME, MUSEUM, LIBRARY AND MEDIA CENTER

    4 Music Sq., E.
    Nashville, TN 37203
    (615) 256-1639

Purpose: "The Country Music Foundation is the world's largest and most active research and exhibition center dedicated to a form of popular music." The hall of fame/museum has 20,000 square feet of exhibition space housing the largest collection of country music artifacts anywhere. Library holdings: 120,000 recordings; printed materials (several hundred books, 300 periodical titles, sheet music, song books, photographs). There are many clippings files, and all known biographies of country stars. Publications: a newsletter, a journal, and various monographs, including: *The Country Music Hall of Fame & Museum*, describing the facility.

1503. THE BING CROSBY HISTORICAL SOCIETY MUSEUM

    524 South 11th St.
    Tacoma, WA 98401
    (206) 627-2947

Purpose: a nonprofit organization, established to honor the art and life of Bing Crosby. Objective: to acquire the Tacoma home in which Bing Crosby was born. Holdings: films, photographs, sheet music, personal items and other memorabilia.

1504. DETROIT JAZZ CENTER

Jazz Archive
2628 Webb St.
Detroit, MI 48206
(313) 867-4141

Purpose: intended as a clearinghouse for jazz, DJC embraces a management consulting service, a study program, and an archive with 500 original tape recordings plus printed sources. Other holdings: 1,000 books and periodicals, 1,000 photographs, 1,000 posters and other ephemeral materials. Services: public use by appointment; photocopying.

1505. GRACELAND (ELVIS PRESLEY SHRINE)

3764 Elvis Presley Blvd.
Memphis, TN 38116
(901) 332-3322

Purpose and holdings: to operate and maintain the mansion (Graceland) and grounds belonging to the famed King of Rock 'n' Roll for public viewing. In addition to furnishings, "the world's only shrine equipped with a jungle room . . .," also holds other of Presley's personal possessions.

1506. INTERNATIONAL COUNTRY AND WESTERN MUSIC ASSOCIATION

102 E. Exchange Ave., Suite 302
Ft. Worth, TX 76106
(817) 625-6267

Purpose: to promote and support the study of country and western music throughout the world. Publications: a quarterly newsletter.

1507. INTERNATIONAL FAN CLUB ORGANIZATION

P.O. Box 177
Wild Horse, CO 80862-0177
(303) 962-3543

Purpose: to promote and advance the country music industry, including the grass-roots support organizations (fan clubs). IFCO advises, guides, and assists the operators of fan clubs, monitoring their credibility, and assisting in promotion and advertising. Publication: quarterly newsletter with C & W news, and a rated listing of member clubs.

1508. INTERNATIONAL RHYTHM AND BLUES ASSOCIATION

11616 S. Lafayette Ave.
Chicago, IL 60628
(312) 264-2166

Purpose: to gather information and maintain an extensive library on rhythm and blues for the use of members (musicians, record companies, songwriters and other interested individuals).

1509. INTERNATIONAL ROCK 'N' ROLL MUSIC ASSOCIATION

P.O. Box 50111
Nashville, TN 37205
(615) 247-9072

Holdings: library includes films, books, periodicals, photographs, and audio holdings. Services: use of the library is by request. Publication: annual periodical.

1510. INTERNATIONAL SONGWRITERS' ASSOCIATION

22 Sullane Cresent
Raheen Heights, Limerick
Republic of Ireland
(Tel.) 61-28837

Purpose: international representative body for songwriters and the music industry. Holdings: biographical archives. Services: database on music publishers and musicians. Publications: *Songwriter Magazine*.

1511. JAZZ INTERACTIONS, INC.

P.O. Box 268
Glen Oaks, NY 11004
(718) 465-7500

Purpose: "To foster a greater understanding of jazz, America's only original, indigenous art form." No library, although there is a 24-hour "jazzline" for current information on the New York jazz scene.

1512. JAZZ WORLD SOCIETY

P.O. Box 777, Times Square Station
New York, NY 10108
(201) 939-0836

Purpose: to further international interest in jazz music. Holdings: biographical archives, vertical file materials, phonograph records, books and photographs. Operates a hall of fame. Services: on-site use by prior application; telephone reference or referral. Publication: *Jazz World*.

1513. LIBERACE FOUNDATION FOR THE PERFORMING & CREATIVE ARTS MUSEUM

1775 East Tropicana
Las Vegas, NV 89119
(702) 798-5595

Purpose and collection: to display the costumes, pianos, automobiles and many other artifacts, as well as numerous photographs of Liberace and his family taken throughout their lives.

1514. THE LIBRARY OF CONGRESS

Motion Picture, Broadcasting and Recorded Sound Div.
Madison Bldg., Room 336

Washington, DC 20540
(202) 287-1000

See entry 673, for annotation.

1515. NEW YORK PUBLIC LIBRARY, LINCOLN CENTER

Library and Museum of the Performing Arts
Lincoln Center at 111 Amsterdam Ave.
New York, NY 10023
(212) 799-2200

Museum holdings: artifacts and some related printed materials in dance, drama, music, and film. Library holdings: a large number of performing arts reference and circulating books and periodicals; many uncataloged items (30,000 scrapbooks, 1,000,000 photographs, pressbooks); 800 films and video tapes, etc., including film, television and radio materials in dozens of special collections (e.g., Billy Rose Theatre Collection). Services: a comprehensive reference and research collection offering full library services for on-site use by the public; interlibrary loans; photocopying; photoreproduction.

1516. PRINCETON UNIVERSITY

William Seymour Theatre Collection
Firestone Library
Princeton, NJ 08544
(609) 452-3223

Holdings: 12,000 books; 115 periodicals subscriptions; 3,300 file drawers of programs, pictures, posters, and other paper artifacts in the fields of theater, popular music, film, etc. Services: on-site use for qualified individuals; reference; photocopying.

1517. RHYTHM AND BLUES ROCK AND ROLL SOCIETY

P.O. Box 1949
New Haven, CT 06510
(203) 735-2736

Purpose: education about the "true history" of the Black Americans who created and developed rock 'n' roll. Holdings: biographies, clippings, photographs, and phonograph records.

Services: reference service provided in the evening, in cooperation with the Blues Foundation, Memphis, TN (above).

1518. ROCK AND ROLL HALL OF FAME FOUNDATION
c/o Atlantic Records
75 Rockefeller Plaza
New York, NY 10019
(212) 484-6427

Goal: to honor those having made significant contributions to rock 'n' roll, and to seek funding for construction of a hall of fame (to be located in Cleveland, OH). The hall is to include a library.

Chapter 23
Commercial Sources and Services

1519. ABOUT MUSIC (Bookstore, Service)

357 Grove St.
San Francisco, CA 94102
(415) 621-1634

For sale: music books; performing arts books; out of print book searching.

1520. AMADEUS BOOKS (Bookstore)

P.O. Box 18052
Denver, CO 80218
(303) 377-7509

For sale: mail order music books; performing arts.

1521. ARISTA RECORDS (Collector Source)

6 West 57th St.
New York, NY 10019
(212) 489-7400

For sale: photographs of Arista's artists (rhythm and blues).

1522. BANK, BOBBY (Collector Source)

3025 Ocean Ave.

Brooklyn, NY 11235
(212) 489-7400

For sale: photographs of pop music stars.

1523. (EDDIE) BAXTER BOOKS (Service)

88 Benedict St.
Glastonbury, Somerset BA6 9EZ
England
(Tel.) 0458 31662

For sale: mail order dance band books; jazz.

1524. BLOCK, RAY (Collector Source)

458 West 20th St.
New York, NY 10011
(212) 692-9375

For sale: photographs of jazz musicians.

1525. THE BOOK BAZAAR (Bookstore)

755 Bank St.
Ottawa, ON K1S 3V3
Canada
(613) 233-4380

For sale: music books.

1526. BOOK SEARCH SERVICE (Bookstore, Service)

36 Kensington Rd.
Avondale Estates, GA 30002

For sale: music books; book searching service.

1527. FIRSTBORN BOOKS (Bookstore, Service)

1007 East Benning Rd.
Galesville, MD 20765
(301) 867-7050

For sale: music books; book searching service.

1528. GRAHAM, RON (Bookstore)

    8167 Park Ave.

    Forestville, CA 95436

    For sale: music books.

1529. HOBO PRESS (Bookstore, Service)

    P.O. Box 19 00 62

    800 Munich 19

    Germany

    For sale: Hobo publishes and sells books, and responds to information research queries in the rock 'n' roll genre.

1530. INTERNATIONAL MUSIC SALES (Bookstores)

    210 Bloor St. W.

    Toronto, ON M5S 1T8

    Canada

    (416) 920-3118

    For sale: music books.

1531. INTERNATIONAL MUSIC STORE, LTD. (Bookstore)

    1334 St. Catherine St. W.

    Montreal, PQ H3G 1P6

    Canada

    (514) 878-4485

    For sale: music books.

1532. NICKELODEON (Bookstore, Collector Source)

    13826 Ventura Blvd.

    Sherman Oaks, CA 91423

    For sale: music books; music collectibles.

1533. PHOTO RESERVE (Collector Source)

    842 West Lill Ave.

    Chicago, IL 60614

    (312) 871-7371

    For sale: photographs of rock and jazz musicians.

1534. POTTER, NICHOLAS (Bookstore)

203 East Palace Ave.
Santa Fe, NM 87501
(505) 983-5434

For sale: music books.

1535. (DAVID) REDFERN PHOTOGRAPHY (Collector Source)

83-84 Long Acre
London WC2E 9NG
England
(Tel.) 01 240 1883

For sale: photographs of pop musicians.

1536. SALTY'S RECORD ATTIC (Bookstore, Collector Source, Service)

1326 9th St.
Modesto, CA 95354
(209) 527-4010

For sale: music books; phonograph records; search service.

1537. SCHNASE, ANNEMARIE (Bookstore)

120 Brown Rd., Box 119
Scarsdale, NY 10583
(914) 725-1284

For sale: music books; periodicals.

1538. THE TELEGRAPH/WANTED MAN (Bookstore, Service)

c/o Bob Dylan Information Office
P.O. Box 18
Bury, Lancashire BL9 0XJ
England

For sale: mail order books, information and publications on Bob Dylan.

1539. VI & SI'S ANTIQUES LTD. (Bookstore, Collector Source)

8970 Main St.

Clarence, NY 14031
(716) 634-4488

For sale: phonograph records.

1540. YARDBIRD RECORDS & BOOKS (Bookstore, Service)

2809 Bird Ave.
Miami, FL 33133
(305) 447-9610

For sale: music books; out of print book searching.

Chapter 24
Fan Clubs (FC)

1541. ALABAMA.

Alabama Band FC
P.O. Box 529
Fort Payne, AL 35967

1542. ANKA, PAUL.

Jubilation—A Paul Anka Organization
c/o Margaret Aker
2136 Lincoln Ave., Apt. J
Alameda, CA 94501

Paul Anka FC
c/o Barbara Dwyer
106 Ambassador Ave.
Warwick, RI 02889

Paul Anka FC
c/o Connie Marinucci
124 Terryville Rd.
Port Jefferson Station, NY 11776

1543. ATKINS, CHET.

Chet Atkins Appreciation Society
6715 Park Lake Dr.
Knoxville, TN 37920

1544. BAEZ, JOAN.

Joan Baez FC
c/o CBS Records
1801 Century Park West
Los Angeles, CA 90067

1545. THE BEACH BOYS

Add Some Music, Beach Boys FC
P.O. Box 10405
Elmwood, CT 06110

Beach Boys FC
c/o A. Bainborough
22 Avondale Rd.
Wea Mea HA3 7RE
England

Beach Boys FC
c/o Donald Cunningham
P.O. Box 10405
Elmwood, CT 06110

1546. THE BEATLES. (3 of over 50)

Beatles FC
c/o Hans Nyhlen
P.O. Box 7481
S-103 92 Stockholm,
Sweden

Good Day Sunshine Beatles FC
c/o Charles F. Rosenay
397 Edgewood Ave.
New Haven, CT 06511

The Write Thing (Beatles FC)
3310 Roosevelt Ct.
Minneapolis, MN 55418

1547. BENNETT, TONY.

Tony Bennett FC
c/o Wynn Campbell

104 Blake La.
Bardsley Green
Birmingham B95 QY
England

1548. BOONE, PAT.

National Association of Pat Boone FC's
c/o Chris Bujnovsky
526 Boeing Ave.
Reading, PA 19601

1549. BOWIE, DAVID.

David Bowie FC
c/o Nancy Gardner
94C Glenhove Rd.
Carbrain Cumbernauld, Glasgow
Scotland

1550. BOY GEORGE.

Culture Club FC (Boy George)
c/o Wedge Music
63 Grosvenor St.
London W1
England

Culture Club FC (Boy George)
c/o Zebra
P.O. Box 947
Hollywood, CA 90028

Multicultural Club (Boy George)
P.O. Box 40
Ruislip HA4 7ND
England

1551. CAMPBELL, GLEN.

Glen Campbell FC
c/o Lori Raine
P.O. Box 69500
Hollywood, CA 90069

1552. CASH, JOHNNY; and CASH, JUNE CARTER.

Carter Family FC
P.O. Box 1371
Hendersonville, TN 37077

House of (Johnny) Cash FC
P.O. Box 508
Hendersonville, TN 37075

Johnny Cash/June Carter Cash FC
c/o Curt & Alma Todd
Rt. 12, Box 350
Winston-Salem, NC 27107

1553. CASSIDY, DAVID.

Friends of David Cassidy
c/o Cathy Ortez
P.O. Box 4293
San Diego, CA 92104

1554. COLLINS, PHIL.

Genesis/Phil Collins Information
S. Brad Lentz, President
P.O. Box 12250
Overland Park, KS 66212

1555. CROSBY, BING.

Bing Crosby Historical Society
P.O. Box 216
Tacoma, WA 98401

1556. DAY, DORIS.

Doris Day FC
c/o Michael Doyle
1534 Cambria
E. Lansing, MI 48823

1557. DENVER, JOHN.

The Higher We Fly John Denver FC

c/o Cindy Marx
7304 16th Ave.
Kenosha, WI 53140

John Denver FC
c/o Nancy Barney
5219 Alhambra Dr.
Woodland Hills, CA 91364

Partners in Harmony (John Denver FC)
c/o Nancy Mountz
P.O. Box 945
Jessup, MD 20794-0945

Spirit in the Wind World Family of John Denver FC
c/o Susie Baldwin
11026 32nd Dr. S.E.
Everett, WA 98204

1558. DIAMOND, NEIL.

Friends of Neil Diamond
P.O. Box 3357
Hollywood, CA 90028

1559. DILLON, MATT.

Matt Dillon FC
c/o Karen S. Schwait
100 S. Berkeley
Atlantic City, NJ 08401

1560. DURAN DURAN.

Duran Duran Club
273 Broad St.
Birmingham B1 2DS
England

1561. DYLAN, BOB.

Bob Dylan FC
c/o Mitch Barth
9 Northampton Dr.
Willingsboro, NJ 08046

1562. GOULET, ROBERT.

Robert Goulet FC
c/o Backstage International
12021 Wilshire Blvd.
Los Angeles, CA 90025

1563. HALL & OATES.

The Daryl Hall & John Oates FC
P.O. Box 1760
Grand Central Station
New York, NY 10017

1564. HUMPERDINCK, ENGELBERT. (2 of almost 40)

Engelbert Humperdinck FC
P.O. Box 236
Bou, PQ J4B 5J6
Canada

Engelbert Humperdinck FC
c/o Inge Aulik Adams
751 Beresford Cir., No. 2
Stone Mountain, GA 30083

1565. IGLESIAS, JULIO.

Friends of Julio Iglesias
Isabel Butterfield, President
28 Farmington
Longmeadow, MA 01106

Intenational FC, Amigos de Julio (Iglesias)
4500 Biscayne Blvd., Suite 333
Miami, FL 33137

Julio Iglesias FC
c/o Christine Arren
P.O. Box 57
Wellesley, MA 02181

1566. JACKSON, MICHAEL.

The World of Michael Jackson

P.O. Box 1804
Encino, CA 91426-1804

1567. JENNINGS, WAYLON.

Waylon Jennings FC
P.O. Box 4537
Corpus Christi, TX 78469

Waylon Jennings FC
P.O. Box 11848
Nashville, TN 37211

1568. JOEL, BILLY.

The Root Beer Rags, Ltd. (Billy Joel)
375 N. Broadway
Jericho, NY 11753

1569. JOHN, ELTON.

Elton John FC
211 S. Beverly Dr., Suite 200
Beverly Hills, CA 90212

1570. JONES, QUINCY.

Quincy Jones FC
Mellow Management
6430 Sunset Blvd., Suite 1210
Los Angeles, CA 90028

1571. JONES, TOM. (3 of almost 30)

T. J.'s Fans of Soul
2191 N.W. 58th St.
Miami, FL 33142

Tom Jones FC
c/o Barbara Anderson
669 Shore Dr.
W. Henrietta, NY 14586

Tom Jones FC
c/o Agnes Arrigo

22 Beckett St.
Quincy, MA 02171

1572. LAUPER, CYNDI.

Cindi Lauper FC
Sixty-five West Entertainment Co.
65 W. 55th St.
New York, NY 10019

1573. LEE, PEGGY.

Peggy Lee FC
c/o Ray Richards Allen
133 W. 72nd St., No. 601
New York, NY 10023

Peggy Lee FC
Robert Strom, President
744 Collier Dr.
San Leandro, CA 94577

LENNON, JOHN. (See: THE BEATLES, above.)

1574. LIBERACE.

Liberace FC
c/o Pauline Lachance
1808 E. Nelson Ave.
N. Las Vegas, NV 89030

Liberace FC
c/o Felicia Clark
7461 Beverly Blvd., Apt. A
Los Angeles, CA 90036

1575. LYNN, LORETTA.

Loretta Lynn FC
c/o Johnson Girls
P.O. Box 177
Wild Horse, CO 80862-0177

1576. McCARTNEY, PAUL. (See also: THE BEATLES, above.)

The McCartney Observer
c/o Doylene Kindsvatter
220 E. 12th St.
LaCrosse, KS 67548

Paul McCartney & Wings FC
P.O. Box 4UP
London W1 4UP
England

1577. MADONNA.

Madonna FC
P.O. Box 77505
San Francisco, CA 94107

1578. MANDRELL, BARBARA.

Barbara Mandrell FC
Mary Lynn West, Director
P.O. Box 620
Hendersonville, TN 37075

1579. MANILOW, BARRY. (2 of 10)

Barry All the Time
c/o Ellie Letourneau
521 Pulaski Blvd.
Bellingham, MA 02019

Barry Manilow International FC
P.O. Box 1649
Covina, CA 91722

1580. MARTIN, DEAN.

The Dean Martin Association
48 Brigstock Rd.
Thornton Heath, Surrey CR4 8RX
England

Dean Martin Collectors Club
c/o Dale Neidigh

P.O. Box 113
Milton, FL 32572-0113

1581. MATHIS, JOHNNY. (3 of 6)

Friends of Johnny Mathis
c/o Alice T. Williams
605 Bonnie Meadow Ln.
Ft. Washington, MD 20744

Johnny Mathis FC
P.O. Box 69278
Hollywood, CA 90069

Johnny Mathis FC
c/o Shirley Robinson
200 E. 33rd St.
New York, NY 10016

1582. MENUDO.

Menudo Universal Club
Ponce de Leon Ave. 157
Hato Rey, PR 00917

Las Princesas de Menudo FC
Nereida Lopez Sunnerklint, President
P.O. Box 545
Richmond Hills, NY 11418

1583. MILSAP, RONNIE.

Ronnie Milsap FC
c/o Cheryl LeClair
P.O. Box 23109
Nashville, TN 37202

1584. MINNELLI, LIZA.

Liza Minnelli FC
c/o Suzan Meyer
9000 Fairview, No. 201
San Gabriel, CA 91775

1585. MURRAY, ANN.

Ann Murray FC
c/o Leonard Rambeau
4881 Yonge St., Suite 412
Toronto, ON M2N 5XE
Canada

Ann Murray FC
P.O. Box 1069, Radio City Station
New York, NY 10019

1586. NELSON, WILLIE.

Willie Nelson FC
c/o Jan Coney
P.O. Box 571
Danbury, CT 06810

1587. NEWTON, WAYNE.

Wayne Newton FC
6629 S. Pecos
Las Vegas, NV 89120

1588. NEWTON-JOHN, OLIVIA.

Olivia Newton-John FC
P.O. Box 730
Medina, OH 44256

Olivia Newton-John FC
P.O. Box 2020
Newbury Park, CA 91320

1589. OSMOND, MARIE.

Marie Osmond FC
c/o Jill Simmons
P. O. Box 1629
Provo, UT 84603

1590. PARTON, DOLLY.

Dolly Parton FC

P.O. Box 938
Montrose, CA 91021

Dolly Parton FC
P.O. Box 4499
N. Hollywood, CA 91607

Dolly Parton FC
c/o Cassie Seaver
P.O. Box 1976
Nolensville, TN 37135

1591. PRESLEY, ELVIS. (3 of almost 40)

Friends of Elvis FC
P.O. Box 16969
Memphis, TN 38116

International Federation of Elvis Presley FC's
P.O. Box 16948
Memphis, TN 38116

Elvis Presley FC
P.O. Box 6104
Orlando, FL 32803

1592. PRIDE, CHARLEY.

Charley Pride FC
c/o Maxine Luster
P.O. Box 670507
Dallas, TX 75367-0507

1593. PRINCE.

Prince FC
P.O. Box 10118
Minneapolis, MN 55401

1594. RAWLS, LOU.

Lou Rawls FC
P.O. Box 4475
N. Hollywood, CA 91607

1595. REDDY, HELEN.

> Helen Reddy FC
> c/o James D. Keaton
> P.O. Box 4731
> Arlington, VA 22204

> Helen Reddy FC
> P.O. Box 371
> Southampton, PA 18966

1596. RICHIE, LIONEL.

> Lionel Richie FC
> P.O. Box 1862
> Encino, CA 91426-1862

1597. ROGERS, KENNY.

> Kenny Rogers FC
> c/o Nancy Barney
> 5219 Alhama Dr.
> Woodland Hills, CA 91364

> Special Friends of Kenny Rogers
> 8265 Beverly Blvd.
> Los Angeles, CA 90048

1598. ROLLING STONES. (2 of over 10)

> Einziger Offizieller Rolling Stones FC
> c/o Brigitte Hipmann
> Postfach 320442
> D-4000 Düsseldorf
> Germany

> The Stones FC
> c/o Robert Furrer
> P.O. Box 603
> Suisun City, CA 94585

1599. ROSS, DIANA.

> Diana Ross, VIP
> c/o Larry Kleno

9157 Sunset Blvd.
Los Angeles, CA 90069

1600. SHORE, DINAH.
Dinah Shore FC
c/o Kay Daly
3552 Federal Ave.
Los Angeles, CA 90066

1601. SINATRA, FRANK. (2 OF 7)
Frank Sinatra FC
c/o Yasua Sangu
2-40-13 Honmachi
Shibuya-Ku, Tokyo 151
Japan
The Sinatra Society FC
c/o Gary Doctor
P.O. Box 254
Getzville, NY 14068

1602. SPRINGFIELD, RICK.
Rick Springfield British FC
266 Appleton Ave.
Great Barr, Birmingham B43 5QD
England
Rick Springfield FC
P.O. Box 9418
N. Hollywood, CA 91609

1603. STARR, RINGO. (See also: THE BEATLES, above.)
Ringo Starr FC
416 Chartridge La.
Chesham, Bucks HP5 2SJ
England

1604. STREISAND, BARBRA.
Barbra Streisand FC
c/o Vincent Ricci, Jr.

304 N. Park Ave.
Buffalo, NY 14216

The Barbra Streisand FC
c/o Josette Sang Ajang
Postbus 11113
Amsterdam 1001 GC
Holland

The Scottish Barbra Streisand Association
c/o Shirley Jenkins
17 Dunbar Ln.
Duffus, Elgin, Moray IV30 2 QJ
Scotland

1605. WILLIAMS, ANDY.

Andy Williams FC
P.O. Box 6708
Ft. Worth, TX 76115

1606. WONDER, STEVIE.

Official Stevie Wonder Universal FC
5933 Corvette St.
Commerce, CA 90040

Stevie Wonder's Universal Family
P.O. Box 2128
N. Hollywood, CA 91602

1607. WYNETTE, TAMMY.

Tammy Wynette FC
c/o Pam Stokes
1800 Grand Ave.
Nashville, TN 37212

Chapter 25
Individual Biographies

ALABAMA. Mus. (Jeff Cook, Teddy Gentry, Mark Herndon, Randy Owen)

1608. Morris, Edward. *Alabama*. Chicago: Contemporary Books, 1985. 109 p. Illustrated. Discography. Index. Paperbound.

ALLEN, PETER. Mus.

1609. Smith, David, and Peters, Neal. *Peter Allen: "Between the Moon and New York City."* Introduction by Peter Allen. Design by Lester Glassner and Neal Peters. New York: Delilah Books, 1983. 149 p. Illustrated. Paperbound.

AZNAVOUR, CHARLES. Mus.

1610. Aznavour, Charles. *Yesterday When I Was Young.* London: W. H. Allen, 1979. 202 p. Illustrated. Index.

BAEZ, JOAN. Mus.

1611. Baez, Joan. *And a Voice to Sing With: A Memoir.* New York: Summit Books, 1987. 378 p. Illustrated.

1612. DuBois, Fletcher Ranney. *A Troubador As Teacher, the Concert As Classroom?: Joan Baez, Advocate of Nonviolence and Motivator of the Young: A Study in the Biographical Method.* Studien zur Kinder-und-Jugendmedien-Forschung, Bd. 11. Frankfurt/Main, Ger.: Haag Herchen, 1985. 323 p. Illustrated. Bibliography. Paperbound.

BAKER, JOSEPHINE. Mus. 4/12/75

1613. Baker, Josephine, and Bouillon, Jo. *Josephine.* Translated from the French by Mariana Fitzpatrick. New York: Harper & Row, 1977. 302 p. Illustrated. Index.

1614. Haney, Lynn. *Naked at the Feast: A Biography of Josephine Baker.* New York: Dodd, Mead, 1981. 338 p. Illustrated. Bibliography. Index.

BASIE, COUNT. Mus. 4/26/84

1615. Basie, Count, and Murray, Albert. *Good Morning Blues: The Autobiography of Count Basie.* New York: Random House, 1985. Illustrated. Index.

1616. Dance, Stanley. *The World of Count Basie.* New York: Scribner, 1980. 399 p. Illustrated. Discography. Index.

1617. Morgan, Alun. *Count Basie.* Jazz Masters Series. Tunbridge Wells, Eng.: Spellmount; New York:

Hippocrene Books, 1984. 94 p. Illustrated. Discography. Bibliography.

THE BEACH BOYS. Mus. (Al Jardine, Mike Love, Brian Wilson, Carl Wilson, Dennis Wilson.)

1618. Gaines, Steven. *Heroes and Villains: The True Story of the Beach Boys.* New York, Scarborough, ON: New American Library, NAL Books, 1986. 374 p. Illustrated. Index.

1619. Leaf, David. *The Beach Boys.* Philadelphia, PA: Courage Books, 1985. 208 p. Illustrated.

1620. Milward, John. *The Beach Boys Silver Anniversary.* Introductions by Brian, Carl, and Dennis Wilson, Al Jardine, Mike Love. Design by J. C. Suares. Photographs edited by Ilene Cherna. Production by Caroline Ginesi. Garden City, NY: Doubleday, Dolphin, 1985. 240 p. Illustrated. Discography. Paperbound.

1621. Preiss, Byron. *The Beach Boys.* New York: Ballantine Books, 1979. 160 p. Illustrated. Discography.

1622. Tobler, John. *The Beach Boys.* Secaucus, NJ: Chartwell Books; London: Phoebus, 1978. 96 p. Illustrated. Discography.

THE BEATLES. Mus. (George Harrison, John Lennon 12/8/80, Paul McCartney, Ringo Starr.)

1623. Bacon, David, and Maslov, Norman. *The Beatles' England: There Are Places I'll Remember.* San Francisco: 910 Press, 1982. 139 p. Illustrated. Bibliography. Paperbound.

1624. *The Beatles at Shea Stadium [Videorecording].* 197-? 1 videocassette, 70 min., sd., col., 1/2 in.

Summary: Events leading up to and a recording as it happened of the historic concert in the stadium before 55, 000 enthusiastic fans. Includes comments by the Beatles and their manager, Brian Epstein.

1625. *Beatles in Their Own Words.* Compiled by Barry Miles. Edited by Pearce Marchbank. Designed by Perry Neville. New York, London: Quick Fox, 1978. 125 p. Illustrated. Paperbound.

1626. Bedford, Carol. *Waiting for the Beatles: An Apple Scruff's Story.* Poole, Dorset, England: Blandford Press, 1984. 296 p. Illustrated. Index. Paperbound.

1627. Best, Pete, and Doncaster, Patrick. *Beatle, the Pete Best Story.* New York: Dell, 1985. 192 p. Illustrated. Paperbound.

1628. Blake, John. *All You Needed Was Love: The Beatles after the Beatles.* New York: Putnam, Perigee, 1981. 286 p. Illustrated. Paperbound.

1629. *Braverman's Condensed Cream of Beatles [Motion Picture].* Braverman Productions, 1973. 17 min., sd., col., 16mm.

Summary: Traces the rise and popularity of the Beatles.

1630. Brown, Peter, and Gaines, Steven. *The Love You Make: An Insider's Story of the Beatles.* New York: McGraw-Hill, 1983. 434 p. Illustrated. Index.

1631. Cepican, Robert, and Waleed, Ali. *Yesterday—Came Suddenly: The Definitive History of the Beatles.* New York: Arbor House, 1985. 287 p. Illustrated. Bibliography. Paperbound.

1632. *The Complete Beatles [Videorecording].* New York: MGM/UA Home Video, 1982. 1 videocassette, 119 min., sd., col., with b&w sequences, 1/2 in., VHS.

Credits: Produced by Stephanie Bennett and Patrick Montgomery; Directed by Patrick Montgomery; Written by David Silver; Narrated by Malcolm McDowell. Summary: A musical documentary of the Beatles.

1633. Davies, Hunter. *The Beatles.* 2d rev. ed. New York: McGraw-Hill, 1985. 423 p. Illustrated. Discography. Bibliography. Index. Paperbound.

1634. DiLello, Richard. *The Longest Cocktail Party: An Insider's Diary of the Beatles, Their Million-Dollar Apple Empire and Its Wild Rise and Fall.* Reprint edition with additions. Rock & Roll Remembrances Series, Vol. 2. Ann Arbor, MI: Pierian Press, 1983. 339 p. Illustrated. Discography. Index.

1635. Fulpen, H. V. *The Beatles: An Illustrated Diary.* Translation of: *Beatles Dagbok.* New York: Putnam, Perigee, 1985. 175 p. Illustrated. Paperbound.

1636. Giuliano, Geoffrey. *The Beatles: A Celebration.* Foreword by Tiny Tim. Backword by Neil Innes. Toronto: Methuen, 1986. 223 p. Illustrated.

1637. Howlett, Kevin. *The Beatles at the Beeb, 62-65: The Story of Their Radio Career.* Reprint ed., with additions. Foreword by Jeff Griffin. Ann Arbor, MI: Pierian Press, 1983. 137 p. Illustrated. Radiography. Bibliography. Discography. Index.

1638. Norman, Philip. *Shout!: The Beatles in Their Generation.* New York: Simon and Schuster, Fireside. 414 p. Illustrated. Index. Paperbound.

1639. Tobler, John. *The Beatles*. New York: Exeter Books, 1984. 192 p. Illustrated. Bibliography. Filmography. Discography. Index.

BELAFONTE, HARRY. Mus.

1640. Fogelson, Genia. *Belafonte*. Los Angeles: Holloway House, 1980. 215 p. Discography. Filmography. Paperbound.

BERLIN, IRVING. Mus.

1641. Freedland, Michael. *A Salute to Irving Berlin*. Rev. ed. London: W. H. Allen, 1986. 316 p. Illustrated. Index.

1642. *Irving Berlin [Filmstrip]*. American Musical Theater. Brunswick Productions, 1973. 47 fr., col., 35mm.
    Summary: A captioned survey of the career of the American composer, Irving Berlin.

BOONE, PAT. Mus.

1643. Boone, Pat. *A New Song*. Nashville, TN: Impact Books, 1981. 192 p. Illustrated. Paperbound.

1644. Boone, Pat. *Together: 25 Years with the Boone Family*. Photographs selected by Shirley and Laury Boone. Nashville, TN: Thomas Nelson, 1979. 128 p. Illustrated.

1645. Boone, Shirley, and Boone, Pat. *The Honeymoon Is Over*. Carol Stream, IL: Creation House, 1977. 185 p. Illustrated.

1646. Elwood, Roger. *Blessed By God: The Christian Marriage of Pat & Shirley Boone.* New York: New American Library, Signet, 1978. 168 p. Illustrated. Paperbound.

BOWIE, DAVID. Mus.

1647. Bowie, David. *Bowie in His Own Words.* Compiled by Barry Miles. Designed by Perry Neville. New York, London: Quick Fox, 1981. 127 p. Illustrated.

1648. Cann, Kevin. *David Bowie, a Chronology.* New York: Simon and Schuster, Fireside, 1983. 239 p. Illustrated. Filmography. Discography. Bibliography. Paperbound.

1649. Carr, Roy, and Murray, Charles Shaar. *David Bowie: An Illustrated Record.* New York: Avon; London: Eel Pie Publishing, 1981. 120 p. Illustrated. Discography. Paperbound.

1650. Charlesworth, Chris. *David Bowie, Profile.* New York, London: Proteus Books, 1981. 95p. Illustrated. Discography. Paperbound.

1651. Claire, Vivian. *David Bowie! The King of Glitter Rock.* New York, London: Flash Books, 1977. 75 p. Illustrated. Paperbound.

1652. Edwards, Henry, and Zanetta, Tony. *Stardust: The David Bowie Story.* New York: McGraw-Hill, 1986. 433 p. Illustrated. Bibliography. Discography. Index.

1653. Gett, Steve. *David Bowie.* Port Chester, NY: Cherry Lane Books, 1985. 48 p. Illustrated. Paperbound.

1654. Gillman, Peter, and Gillman, Leni. *Alias David Bowie: A Biography.* New York: H. Holt, 1987. 511 p. Illustrated. Discography. Filmography. Videography. Index.

1655. Goddard, Peter. *David Bowie: Out of the Cool.*
Photographs by Philip Kamin. New York: Beaufort Books,
1983. 125 p. Illustrated. Paperbound.

1656. Hoggard, Stuart. *Bowie, Changes: The Illustrated David
Bowie Story.* 3d ed. Revised and updated by Chris
Charlesworth. London, New York: Omnibus Press,
1983. 83 p. Illustrated. ***

1657. Hopkins, Jerry. *Bowie.* New York: Macmillan, 1985. 286
p. Illustrated. Discography. Filmography. Videography.
Index.

1658. Kamin, Philip, and Goddard, Peter. *David Bowie: The
World Tour.* Toronto: Musson, 1983. ***

1659. Lynch, Kate. *David Bowie: A Rock 'n' Roll Odyssey.*
London, New York: Proteus Books, 1984. 181 p.
Illustrated. Bibliography. Paperbound.

1660. Matthew-Walker, Robert. *David Bowie: Theatre of
Music.* Abbotsbrook, Buckinghamshire, England: Kensal
Press, 1986. 198 p. Illustrated. Discography.
Filmography. Bibliography. Index. Paperbound.

1661. Miles, Barry. *David Bowie Black Book.* London:
Omnibus Press, 1980. 125 p. Illustrated. Paperbound.

1662. O'Regan, Denis. *David Bowie's Serious Moonlight: The
World Tour.* Text by Chet Flippo. Introduction by David
Bowie. Garden City, NY: Doubleday, Dolphin, 1984. 256
p. Illustrated. Paperbound.

1663. Pitt, Kenneth. *Bowie: The Pitt Report.* London, New
York: Omnibus Press, 1985. 223 p. Illustrated. Index.
Paperbound.

1664. Rock, Mick. *Ziggy Stardust: Bowie, 1972/1973.* New York: St. Martin's Press, 1984. 128 p. Illustrated. Paperbound. ***

BOY GEORGE. Mus.

1665. *The Best of Boy George & Culture Club.* Edited by Richard Rosenfeld. New York: Gallery Books, 1984. 48 p. Illustrated. Paperbound.

1666. *The Boy George Fact File.* Photographs by Armando Gallo. London, New York: Omnibus Press, 1984. 34 p. Illustrated. Discography. Paperbound.

1667. Brompton, Sally. *Chameleon: The Boy George Story.* Tunbridge Wells, Kent, England: Spellmount, 1984. 153 p. Illustrated. Paperbound.

1668. Cohen, Scott. *Boy George.* New York: Berkley Books, 1984. 158 p. Illustrated. Paperbound.

1669. David, Maria. *Boy George and Culture Club.* Produced by Ted Smart and Gerald Hughes. Edited by David Gibbon. Designed by Philip Clucas. New York: Greenwich House, 1984. 61 p. Illustrated.

1670. Dietrich, Joe. *Boy George and Culture Club.* Port Chester, NY: Cherry Lane Books, 1984. 32 p. Illustrated. Paperbound.

1671. Gill, Anton. *Mad about the Boy: The Life and Times of Boy George and Culture Club.* New York: Holt, Rinehart and Winston, Owl, 1984. 128 p. Illustrated. Discography. Videography. Paperbound.

1672. Ginsberg, Merle. *Boy George.* New York: Dell, 1984. 191 p. Illustrated. Paperbound.

1673. Rimmer, Dave. *Like Punk Never Happened: Culture Club and the New Pop.* London, Boston: Faber and Faber, 1985. 191 p. Bibliography. Paperbound.

1674. Robins, Wayne. *Boy George and Culture Club.* New York: Ballantine Books, 1984. 146 p. Illustrated. Discography. Videography. Paperbound.

BROWN, JAMES. Mus.

1675. Brown, James, and Tucker, Bruce. *James Brown, the Godfather of Soul.* New York: Macmillan; London: Collier Macmillan, 1986. 336 p. Illustrated. Discography. Index.

1676. *James Brown: The Man [Motion Picture].* Sterling Educational Films, 1974. 15 min., sd., col., 16mm.

Summary: The influence of the singer on his people is described in this work, as is his step-by-step ascent from a Georgia reform school to wealth and fame.

BRUBECK, DAVE. Mus.

1677. *Dave Brubeck [Motion Picture].* New York: Time-Life Multimedia, 1978. 1 reel, 52 min., sd., col., 16 mm.

Summary: This film focuses on the performances of the Dave Brubeck Quartet on a twenty-five city tour commemorating their silver jubilee. Includes interviews with Brubeck and his colleagues in which his life and work are discussed. Also issued as a videorecording.

CARMICHAEL, HOAGY. Mus. 12/27/81

1678. Carmichael, Hoagy. *The Stardust Road.* Bloomington: Indiana University Press, Midland, 1983. 156 p. Illustrated. Paperbound. ***

CARROLL, DIAHANN. Mus.

1679. Carroll, Diahann, and Firestone, Ross. *Diahann: An Autobiography.* Boston: Little, Brown, 1986. 247 p. Illustrated. Index.

CHARLES, RAY. Mus.

1680. Charles, Ray, and Ritz, David. *Brother Ray: Ray Charles' Own Story.* New York: Dial Press, 1978. 316 p. Illustrated. Discography.

CLAPTON, ERIC. Mus.

1681. Coleman, Ray. *Clapton: An Authorized Biography.* New York: Warner Books, 1986. 368 p. Illustrated. Discography. Index. Paperbound.

1682. Pidgeon, John. *Eric Clapton: A Biography.* Rev. ed. London: Vermilion, 1985. 123 p. Illustrated. Discography. Index. Paperbound.

1683. Shapiro, Harry. *Slowhand: The Story of Eric Clapton.* London, New York: Proteus Books, 1984. 160 p. Illustrated. Discography. Paperbound.

CLOONEY, ROSEMARY. Mus.

1684. Clooney, Rosemary, and Strait, Raymond. *This for Remembrance: The Autobiography of Rosemary Clooney, an Irish-American Singer.* New York: Playboy Press, 1977. 250 p. Illustrated.

COLLINS, JUDY. Mus.

1685. Claire, Vivian. *Judy Collins.* New York: Flash Books, 1977. 78 p. Illustrated. Discography.

1686. Collins, Judy. *Trust Your Heart: An Autobiography.* Boston: Houghton Mifflin, 1987. 231 p. Illustrated. ***

COLLINS, PHIL. Mus.

1687. Collins, Phil. *Collins on Collins [Sound Recording].* New York: Atlantic Recording, 1985. 1 sound disc, 55 min., 33 1/3 rpm, stereo, 12 in.

This disc is accompanied by a printed list of questions. Also, disc side A has recorded questions and answers; side B, answers only. Summary: Collins discusses his success and his musical group, Genesis. He talks about his fans, the use of humor in his act, and other aspects of his life and work.

1688. Kamin, Philip, and Goddard, Peter. *Genesis: Peter Gabriel, Phil Collins, and Beyond.* Introduction by Phil Collins. New York, Toronto: Beaufort Books, 1984. 116 p. Illustrated. Paperbound.

1689. Kamin, Philip. *Phil Collins.* Wauwatosa, WI: Robus Books, 1985. 32 p. Illustrated. Discography. Paperbound.

CROSBY, BING. Mus. 10/14/77

1690. Barnes, Ken. *The Crosby Years.* New York: St. Martin's Press, 1980. 216 p. Illustrated. Discography. Filmography. Bibliography.

1691. Bauer, Barbara. *Bing Crosby.* Pyramid Illustrated History of the Movies. New York: Pyramid Publications, 1977. 159 p. Illustrated. Bibliography. Filmography. Index.

1692. *Bing Crosby Album.* Text by Linda Rosenbaum. Edited by Milburn Smith. Art director, Maryann Cook. New York: H. Shorten, 1977. 78 p. Illustrated. Paperbound.

1693. *Bing Crosby: A Pictorial Tribute.* Edited by James W. Bowser. Written by Joseph L. Koenig. New York: Dell, 1977. 85 p. Illustrated. Paperbound.

1694. Church, John Thomas. *Bing: The Melody Lingers On.* New York: Todays Communication, 1977. 64 p. Illustrated.

1695. Crosby, Gary, and Firestone, Ross. *Going My Own Way.* Garden City, NY: Doubleday, 1983. 304 p. Illustrated.

1696. Crosby, Kathryn. *My Life with Bing.* Wheeling, IL: Collage, 1983. 351 p. Illustrated. ***

1697. O'Connell, Sheldon, and Atkinson, Gord. *Bing: A Voice for All Seasons.* Foreword by Rich Little. Introduction by Phil Harris. Kerry, Ireland: Kerryman Tralee, 1984. 251 p. Illustrated. Discography. Filmography. Index. Paperbound.

1698. Shepherd, Donald, and Slatzer, Robert F. *Bing Crosby: The Hollow Man.* New York: St. Martin's Press, 1981. 326 p. Illustrated. Filmography. Discography. Index.

1699. Thomas, Bob. *The One and Only Bing.* Tribute by Bob Hope. New York: Grosset & Dunlap, 1977. 150 p. Illustrated. Filmography. Discography.

1700. Zwisohn, Laurence J. *Bing Crosby: A Lifetime of Music.* Foreword by James Van Heusen. Los Angeles: Palm Tree Library, 1978. 147 p. Illustrated. Discography.

DAVIS, MILES. Mus.

1701. Carr, Ian. *Miles Davis: A Biography.* Foreword by Len Lyons. New York: Morrow, 1982. 310 p. Illustrated. Bibliography. Discography. Index.

1702. Chambers, Jack. *Milestones 1: The Music and Times of Miles Davis to 1960.* New York: Beech Tree Books, 1983. 345 p. Illustrated. Bibliography. Index.

1703. Chambers, Jack. *Milestones 2: The Music and Times of Miles Davis since 1960.* New York: Beech Tree Books, 1985. 416 p. Illustrated. Bibliography. Index.

1704. Nisenson, Eric. *'Round about Midnight: A Portrait of Miles Davis.* New York: Dial Press, 1982. 244 p. Illustrated. Discography. Index. Paperbound.

DIAMOND, NEIL. Mus.

1705. Grossman, Alan; Truman, Bill; and Yamanaka, Roy Oki. *Diamond, a Biography.* Chicago, New York: Contemporary Books, 1987. 235 p. Illustrated. Song listing. Discography.

1706. *Neil Diamond—I'm Glad You're Here with Me Tonight [Video recording].* Stamford, CT: Vestron Musicvideo, 1986? 1 videocassette, 60 min., sd., col.

Summary: Looks at the public and private worlds of Diamond, and offers a collection of his performances from around the world.

1707. Wiseman, Rich. *Neil Diamond, Solitary Star.* New York: Dodd, Mead, 1987. 324 p. Illustrated. Discography. Index.

DURAN DURAN Mus. (Simon Le Bon, Nick Rhodes, Andy Taylor, John Taylor, and Roger Taylor.)

1708. David, Maria. *Duran Duran.* New York: Crescent Books, 1984. 60 p. Illustrated.

1709. *Duran Duran: The Book of Words.* Edited by De Graaf Garrett. Foreword by Simon Le Bon. Milwaukee, WI: Hal Leonard Books, 1984. 96 p. Illustrated. Discography. Videography. Paperbound.

1710. Gaiman, Neil. *Duran Duran: The First Four Years of the Fab Five.* New York: Proteus Books, 1984. 126 p. Illustrated. Discography. Paperbound.

1711. Goldstein, Toby. *Duran Duran.* New York: Ballantine Books, 1984. 149 p. Illustrated. Discography. Videography. Paperbound.

1712. Kent, Cynthia C. *Duran Duran.* New York: Kensington, Zebra, 1984. 174 p. Illustrated. Discography. Videography. Paperbound.

DYLAN, BOB. Mus.

1713. Cott, Jonathan. *Dylan.* Garden City, NY: Doubleday, Rolling Stone Press Book, 1984. 246 p. Illustrated.

1714. Dowley, Tim, and Dunnage, Barry. *Bob Dylan: From a Hard Rain to a Slow Train.* Tunbridge Wells, Kent, England: Midas Books; New York: Hippocrene Books, 1982. 177 p. Illustrated. Discography. Bibliography.

1715. Mellers, Wilfrid. *A Darker Shade of Pale: A Backdrop to Bob Dylan.* New York: Oxford University Press, 1985. 255 p. Illustrated. Discography. Bibliography. Index. Paperbound.

1716. Shelton, Robert. *No Direction Home: The Life and Music of Bob Dylan.* New York: Morrow, Beech Tree Books, 1986. 573 p. Illustrated. Bibliography. Discography. Index.

1717. Williams, Don. *Bob Dylan: The Man, the Music, the Message.* Old Tappan, NJ: F. H. Revell, 1985. 160 p. Illustrated. Bibliography. Paperbound.

ELLINGTON, DUKE. Mus. 5/24/74

1718. Collier, James Lincoln. *Duke Ellington.* New York: Oxford University Press, 1987. 340 p. Illustrated. Discography. Index.

1719. *Duke Ellington, King of Jazz [Filmstrip].* Jazz Masters Cassette/Filmstrip Series. New York: Merit Audio Visual, 1982. 1 filmstrip, 67 fr., col., 35mm; 1 sound cassette, 14 min.
    Summary: Biographical sketch of jazz pianist and composer, Ellington; the development of his music and career is followed, accompanied by musical examples.

1720. Ellington, Mercer, and Dance, Stanley. *Duke Ellington in Person: An Intimate Memoir.* Boston: Houghton Mifflin, 1978. 236 p. Illustrated. Index.

1721. George, Don R. *Sweet Man, the Real Duke Ellington.* New York: Putnam, 1981. 272 p. Illustrated. Index.

1722. Jewell, Derek. *Duke: A Portrait of Duke Ellington.* New York: Norton, 1977. 264 p. Illustrated. Discography. Bibliography. Index.

FELICIANO, JOSE. Mus.

1723. *Jose Feliciano: Against All Odds [Filmstrip].* Spanish-American Leaders of 20th Century America. BFA Educational Media, 1974. 57 fr., col., 35mm, and phonodisc: 33 1/3 rpm.

Summary: Deals with the accomplishments of Feliciano showing how Spanish Americans have overcome handicaps such as poverty, lack of education, discrimination, and physical disabilities to make significant contributions to the American society.

FITZGERALD, ELLA. Mus.

1724. Colin, Sid. *Ella: The Life and Times of Ella Fitzgerald.* London: Elm Tree Books, 1986. 151 p. Illustrated. Discography. Bibliography. Index.

FLACK, ROBERTA. Mus.

1725. *Roberta Flack [Motion Picture].* Washington, DC: WETA-TV, 1971. 20 min., sd., col., 16mm.

Credits: Producer and writer, Cherrill Anson; director and editor, David W. Powell. Released by Indiana University Audio Visual Center.

FRANKLIN, ARETHA. Mus.

1726. *Aretha Franklin: Soul Singer [Motion Picture].* McGraw-
Hill Contemporary Films, 1968. 1 film reel, 25 min., sd.,
col., 16mm.
   Summary: A biographical profile of soul singer Aretha
Franklin; originally part of an ABC News production entitled,
"The Singers: Two Profiles."

GARFUNKEL, ART. Mus., See: SIMON AND GARFUNKEL.
Mus.

GARNER, ERROLL. Mus. 1/2/77

1727. Doran, James M. *Erroll Garner, the Most Happy Piano.*
Foreword by Dan Morgenstern. Studies in Jazz, No. 3.
Metuchen, NJ: Scarecrow Press, 1985. 481 p. Illustrated.
Discography. Filmography. Bibliography. Index.

GILLESPIE, DIZZY. Mus.

1728. *Dizzy [Motion Picture].* El Cerrito, CA: Flower Films,
1965. 1 reel, 20 min., sd., b&w, 16mm. Also issued as a
videorecording, this film focuses on Gillespie talking about
his beginnings and music theories—in addition to playing
his trumpet.

1729. Gillespie, Dizzy, and Fraser, Al. *To Be, or Not . . . to
Bop: Memoirs.* Garden City, NY: Doubleday, 1979. 552
p. Illustrated. Discography. Index.

1730. Horricks, Raymond. *Dizzy Gillespie and the Be-Bop
Revolution.* Selected Discography by Tony Middleton.
Jazz Masters Series. Tunbridge Wells, Kent, England:

Spellmount; New York: Hippocrene Books, 1984. 95 p.
Illustrated. Discography. Bibliography.

GOODMAN, BENNY. Mus.

1731. *Benny Goodman [Filmstrip].* The Great Composers.
New York: Brunswick Productions, 1976. 1 filmstrip, 43
fr., col., 35mm.
Summary: Captioned filmstrip tells the story of Goodman
and describes the major influences affecting his life and work.
Music plates of themes from best-known works are provided.

1732. Goodman, Benny. *Benny, King of Swing: A Pictorial
Biography Based on Benny Goodman's Personal
Archives.* Introduction by Stanley Baron. New York:
Morrow, 1979. 63 p. Illustrated.

HAGGARD, MERLE. Mus.

1733. Haggard, Merle, and Russell, Peggy. *Sing Me Back
Home: My Story.* New York: Times Books, 1981. 287 p.
Illustrated.

HALL AND OATES. Mus. (Daryl Hall and John Oates.)

1734. Gooch, Brad. *Hall and Oates.* New York: Ballantine
Books, 1984. 147 p. Illustrated. Discography.
Videography. Paperbound.

1735. Tosches, Nick; Hall, Daryl; and Oates, John.
Dangerous Dances: The Authorized Biography. New
York: St. Martin's Press, 1984. 144 p. Illustrated.

Music Celebrities Sources

HAMPTON, LIONEL. Mus.

1736. *One Night Stand [Motion Picture].* Toronto: CFTO-TV,
    1972. 60 min., sd., col., 16mm.
    Summary: Explores the career of jazz musician, Lionel
Hampton.

HARRISON, GEORGE. Mus.

1737. Harrison, George. *I, Me, Mine.* Illustrations by Roy
    Williams. New York: Simon and Schuster, 1980. 398 p.
    Illustrated. Song listing. Index.

1738. Michaels, Ross. *George Harrison: Yesterday and
    Today.* New York: Flash Books, 1977. 96 p. Illustrated.
    Discography. Paperbound.

HORNE, LENA. Mus.

1739. Buckley, Gail Lumet. *The Hornes: An American Family.*
    New York: Knopf, 1986. 262 p. Illustrated.

1740. Haskins, James, and Benson, Kathleen. *Lena: A Personal
    and Professional Biography of Lena Horne.* New York:
    Stein & Day, 1984. 226 p. Illustrated. Index.

1741. Haskins, James. *Lena Horne.* New York: Coward-
    McCann, 1983. 160 p. Illustrated. Index.

1742. Howard, Brett. *Lena.* Los Angeles: Holloway House,
    1981. 218 p. Paperbound.

IDOL, BILLY. Mus.

1743. Gooch, Brad. *Billy Idol.* New York: Ballantine Books, 1985. 151 p. Illustrated. Discography. Videography. Paperbound. ***

IGLESIAS, JULIO. Mus.

1744. Daly, Marsha. *Julio Iglesias.* New York: St. Martin's Press, 1986. 131 p. Illustrated. Index.

1745. Garcia, Elizabeth. *Julio.* New York: Ballantine Books, 1985. 127 p. Illustrated. Discography. Paperbound.

1746. Gett, Steve. *Julio Iglesias: The New Valentino.* Port Chester, NY: Cherry Lane Books, 1985. 48 p. Illustrated. Paperbound.

1747. Rovin, Jeff. *Julio!* Toronto, New York: Bantam Books, 1985. 212 p. Illustrated. Paperbound.

JACKSON, MICHAEL. Mus.

1748. Bego, Mark. *Michael!* New York: Pinnacle Books, 1984. 180 p. Illustrated. Discography. Paperbound.

1749. Brown, Geoff. *Michael Jackson, Body and Soul: An Illustrated Biography.* Toronto: Musson, 1984. 128 p. Illustrated. ***

1750. George, Nelson. *The Michael Jackson Story.* New York: Dell, 1984. 191 p. Discography. Illustrated. Paperbound.

1751. Honeyford, Paul. *The Thrill of Michael Jackson.* New York: Quill, 1984. 64 p. Illustrated. Paperbound.

1752. Jackson, Michael. *Moonwalk*. New York: Doubleday, 1988. 283 p. Illustrated. ***

1753. Kamin, Philip, and Goddard, Peter. *Michael Jackson & the Jacksons: Live on Tour in '84*. Toronto: Methuen, 1984. 95 p. Illustrated. Paperbound.

1754. *Latham, Caroline. Michael Jackson Thrill*. New York: Kensington, Zebra, 1984. 191 p. Illustrated. Discography. Paperbound.

1755. McDougal, Weldon A. *The Michael Jackson Scrapbook: The Early Days of the Jackson 5*. New York: Avon, 1985. 128 p. Illustrated. Paperbound.

1756. *The Magic of Michael Jackson*. Cresskill, NJ: Starbook, 1984. 64 p. Illustrated. Discography. Paperbound.

1757. Marsh, Dave. *Trapped: Michael Jackson and the Crossover Dream*. Toronto, New York: Bantam Books, 1985. 259 p. Illustrated. Paperbound.

1758. *Michael Jackson*. Introduction by Robin Katz. New York: Gallery Books, 1984. 62 p. Illustrated. Discography.

1759. Pitts, Leonard, Jr. *Papa Joe's Boys: The Jacksons Story*. Cresskill, NJ: Sharon Starbook, 1983. 96 p. Illustrated. Discography. Paperbound.

1760. Regan, Stewart. *Michael Jackson*. Designed by Philip Clucas. Produced by Ted Smart, and David Gibbon. New York: Greenwich House, 1984. 64 p. Illustrated.

1761. *Those Incredible Jackson Boys*. Cresskill, NJ: Sharon Starbook, 1984. 192 p. Illustrated. Paperbound.

JAGGER, MICK. Mus.

1762. Blake, John. *His Satanic Majesty: Mick Jagger.* New York: Holt, Rinehart and Winston, Owl, 1986. 192 p. Paperbound. ***

1763. Jagger, Mick. *Mick Jagger in His Own Words.* Compiled by [Barry] Miles. New York: Delilah/Putnam, 1982. 127 p. Illustrated. Paperbound.

1764. Schofield, Carey. *Jagger.* New York: Beaufort Books, 1985. 248 p. Illustrated. Bibliography. Index. Paperbound.

JENNINGS, WAYLON. Mus.

1765. Allen, Bob. *Waylon & Willie: The Full Story in Words and Pictures of Waylon Jennings & Willie Nelson.* New York: Quick Fox, 1979. 127 p. Illustrated. Discography. Paperbound.

1766. Cunniff, Albert. *Waylon Jennings.* New York: Kensington, Zebra, 1985. 237 p. Illustrated. Discography. Paperbound.

1767. Denisoff, R. Serge. *Waylon: A Biography.* Knoxville: University of Tennessee Press, 1983. 375 p. Illustrated. Discography. Bibliography. Index.

1768. *Waylon Jennings America [Videorecording].* Produced by John Goodhue and John Ware. Burbank, CA: RCA/Columbia Pictures Home Video, 1986. 1 videocassette, 30 min., sd., col., 1/2 in.
Summary: Dramatized songs plus sequences where Jennings explains his life and the background for a song as if he were talking to psychiatrist.

JOEL, BILLY. Mus.

1769. Gambaccini, Peter. *Billy Joel: A Personal File.* New York: Quick Fox, 1979. 128 p. Illustrated. Discography. Paperbound.

1770. Geller, Debbie, and Hibbert, Tom. *Billy Joel: An Illustrated Biography.* New York: McGraw-Hill, 1985. 127 p. Illustrated. Discography. Paperbound.

1771. McKenzie, Michael. *Billy Joel.* New York: Ballantine Books, 1985. 151 p. Illustrated. Discography. Videography. Paperbound.

1772. Myers, Donald M. *Headliners: Billy Joel.* New York: Tempo Books, 1981. 170 p. Illustrated. Discography. Paperbound.

1773. Tamarkin, Jeff. *Billy Joel: From Hicksville to Hitsville.* Port Chester, NY: Cherry Lane Books, 1984. 48 p. Illustrated. Discography. Paperbound.

JOHN, ELTON. Mus.

1774. John, Elton, and Peebles, Andy. *The Elton John Tapes.* New York: St. Martin's Press, 1981. 55 p. Illustrated. Paperbound.

1775. Nutter, David, and Taupin, Bernie. *Elton: It's a Little Bit Funny.* Dedication by Elton John. Harmondsworth, Middlesex, England; New York: Penguin, 1977. 142 p. Illustrated. Paperbound.

1776. Roland, Paul. *Elton John.* London, New York: Proteus Books, 1984. 125 p. Illustrated. Discography. Paperbound.

JONES, QUINCY. Mus.

1777. Horricks, Raymond. *Quincy Jones.* Popular Musicians, 2. Selected discography by Tony Middleton. Tunbridge Wells, Kent, England: Spellmount; New York: Hippocrene Books, 1985. 127 p. Illustrations. Filmography. Videography. Discography.

KNIGHT, GLADYS & THE PIPS. Mus. (William Guest, Merald Knight, Edward Patten.)

1778. Knight, Gladys. *Gladys Knight and the Pips with Ray Charles [Videorecording].* New York: Time-Life Video, 1980. 1 videocassette, 75 min., sd., col. 1/2 in.

Summary: A concert performance by Gladys Knight and the Pips, with a surprise appearance by Ray Charles. Also includes off-stage interviews and some secret rehearsal scenes.

LAUPER, CYNDI. Mus.

1779. Kamin, Philip, and Goddard, Peter. *Cyndi Lauper.* New York: McGraw-Hill, 1986. 96 p. Illustrated. Paperbound.

1780. Morreale, Marie, and Mittelkauf, Susan. *The Cyndi Lauper Scrapbook.* Toronto, New York: Bantam Books, 1985. 42 p. Illustrated. Discography. Paperbound.

1781. Willis, K. K. *Cyndi Lauper.* New York: Ballantine Books, 1984. Illustrated. Discography. Videography. Paperbound.

LEE, PEGGY. Mus.

1782. Towe, Ronald. *Here's to You: The Complete Bio-Discography of Miss Peggy Lee.* R. Towe Music, 1986. 542 p. Bibliography. Index. ***

LENNON, JOHN. Mus. 12/8/80

1783. Baird, Julia, and Giuliano, Geoffrey. *John Lennon, My Brother.* New York: H. Holt, 1988. ***

1784. Coleman, Ray. *John Winston Lennon; Volume 1, 1940-1966.* London: Sidgwick & Jackson, 1984. 350 p. Illustrated. Discography. Song listing. Index.

1785. Cott, Jonathan, and Doudna, Christine, eds. *The Ballad of John and Yoko.* Foreword by Jann S. Wenner. New York: Doubleday, Rolling Stone, 1982. 340 p. Illustrated. Index.

1786. Goldman, Albert Harry. *The Lives of John Lennon.* New York: Morrow, 1988. Bibliography. Index. ***

1787. Green, John. *Dakota Days.* New York: St. Martin's Press, 1983. 260 p. Illustrated.

1788. *John Lennon [Videorecording].* National Broadcasting Corporation, 1980. 1 videocassette, 52 min., sd., col., 1/2 in., VHS.

Summary: Segment of the "Tomorrow Show" originally broadcast the day after Lennon's death, which contained an interview with the show's host, Tom Snyder, of Lennon from the mid-1970s in which Lennon talked about his music and his life. Also includes an interview by Snyder of Lucia Robinson, a journalist who had written an in-depth item on Lennon during his househusband years, and an interview with Jack Douglas who was the engineer for Lennon's last record.

1789. *The Lennon Companion.* Edited by Elizabeth M. Thomson and David Gutman. New York: Schirmer Books, 1988. ***

1790. Lennon, John, and Ono, Yoko. *Heart Play: Unfinished Dialogue [Sound Recording].* New York: Polydor, 1983. 1 sound disc, 33 1/3 rpm, stereo, 12 in.

Summary: An interview recorded in 1980. It was also issued as a cassette.

1791. Lennon, John. *Reflections and Poetry [Sound Recording].* Brooklyn, NY: Silhouette Music, 1984. 2 sound discs, analog, 33 1/3 rpm, 12 in.

Summary: Presents Lennon's last interview, recorded Dec. 8, 1980, in New York City. He and Yoko Ono discuss their work and personal lives. Lennon also reads three of his poems, two of which were taken from his private tapes.

1792. Pang, May, and Edwards, Henry. *Loving John.* New York: Warner Books, 1983. 336 p. Illustrated. Paperbound.

1793. Ryan, David Stuart. *John Lennon's Secret.* London, Washington, DC: Kozmik Press Centre, 1982. 251 p. Illustrated. Bibliography. Index.

1794. Shotton, Pete, and Schaffner, Nicholas. *The Beatles, Lennon and Me.* New York: Stein and Day, 1983. 399 p. Illustrated. Index. Paperbound.

1795. Wiener, Jon. *Come Together: John Lennon in His Time.* New York: Random House, 1984. 379 p. Illustrated. Bibliography. Index. Paperbound.

LERNER, ALAN JAY. Mus.

1796. Lerner, Alan Jay. *The Street Where I Live.* New York, London: Norton, 1978. 333 p. Illustrated. Index. Paperbound.

LIBERACE. Mus. 2/4/87

1797. Liberace. *The Wonderful Private World of Liberace.* New York: Harper & Row, Hannibal Books, 1986. 222 p. Illustrated.

1798. Thorson, Scott, and Thorleifson, Alex. *Behind the Candelabra: My Life with Liberace.* New York: E. P. Dutton, 1988. 242 p. Illustrated. ***

LITTLE RICHARD. Mus. See: RICHARD, LITTLE. Mus.

LLOYD WEBER, ANDREW. Mus.

1799. McKnight, Gerald. *Andrew Lloyd Webber.* New York: St. Martin's Press, 1984. 278 p. Illustrated. Discography. Index.

LOMBARDO, GUY. Mus. 11/5/77

1800. Cline, Beverly Fink. *The Lombardo Story.* Introduction by Lebert Lombardo. Don Mills, Ontario, Canada: Musson, 1979. 158 p. Illustrated. Song listing. Discography. Index.

1801. Richman, Saul. *Guy*. Foreword by Lawrence Welk. New York: Rich Guy, 1978. 189 p. Illustrated.

LYNN, LORETTA. Mus.

1802. *Coal Miner's Daughter [Videorecording]*. Universal City, CA: MCA Home Video, 1985. 1 videocassette, 124 min., sd., col., 1/2 in., VHS.

Credits: Screenplay by Tom Rickman; directed by Michael Apted. Originally produced as a motion picture in 1980 with Sissy Spacek, Tommy Lee Jones, Beverly D'Angelo and Levon Helm. Summary: The story of Lynn, who as a child bride and the mother of four at eighteen, still found time to sing and write songs. Badgered into making a record and going to Nashville, she got her chance in the Grand Ole Opry, which launched her career.

1803. Lynn, Loretta, and Vecsey, George. *Loretta Lynn: Coal Miner's Daughter*. New York: Warner Books, Bernard Geis, 1977. 269 p. Illustrated. Discography. Index. Paperbound.

McCARTNEY, PAUL. Mus.

1804. Doney, Malcolm. *Lennon and McCartney*. Tunbridge Wells, Kent, England: Midas Books; New York: Hippocrene Books, 1981. 128 p. Illustrated. Discography.

1805. Flippo, Chet. *Yesterday: The Unauthorized Biography of Paul McCartney*. New York: Doubleday, 1988. 400 p. Illustrated. Bibliography. Index. ***

1806. Hamilton, Alan. *Paul McCartney*. Illustrated by Karen Heywood. London: H. Hamilton, 1983. 59 p. Illustrated.

1807. McCartney, Mike. *The Macs: Mike McCartney's Family Album*. New York: Delilah/Putnam, 1981. 192 p. Illustrated. Paperbound.

1808. Mendelssohn, John. *Paul McCartney: A Biography in Words & Pictures*. Edited by Greg Shaw. Sire Books; New York: Chappell Music, 1977. 55 p. Illustrated. Discography. ***

1809. Pascall, Jeremy. *Paul McCartney &Wings*. Edited by Pamela Harvey. Designed by Rob Burt. Secaucus, NJ: Chartwell Books, 1977. 96 p. Illustrated.

1810. Salewicz, Chris. *McCartney*. New York: St. Martin's Press, 1986. 263 p. Bibliography. Index.

MADONNA. Mus.

1811. Bego, Mark. *Madonna!* New York: Pinnacle Books, 1985. 189 p. Illustrated. Discography. Videography. Filmography. Paperbound.

1812. Kelleher, Ed, and Vidal, Harriette. *Madonna*. New York: Leisure Press, 1987. 384 p. ***

1813. McKenzie, Michael. *Madonna, Lucky Star*. Chicago: Contemporary Books, 1985. 94 p. Illustrated. Paperbound.

1814. *Madonna*. New York: New American Library, Signet, 1985. 54 p. Illustrated. Paperbound.

MANDRELL, BARBARA. Mus.

1815. Mandrell, Louise, and Collins, Ace. *The Mandrell Family Album*. Nashville, TN: Thomas Nelson, 1983. 192 p. Illustrated. Discography.

MANILOW, BARRY. Mus.

1816. Bego, Mark. *Barry Manilow: An Unauthorized Biography*. New York: Grosset & Dunlap, Tempo, 1977. 139 p. Illustrated. Discography. Paperbound.

1817. Clark, Alan. *The Magic of Barry Manilow*. New York: Prize Books, 1981. 48 p. Illustrated. Discography. Paperbound.

1818. Lulow, Kalia. *Barry Manilow*. New York: Ballantine Books, 1985. 149 p. Discography. Paperbound.

1819. Manilow, Barry. *Sweet Life: Adventures on the Way to Paradise*. New York: McGraw-Hill, 1987. 274 p. Illustrated. Discography. Index.

1820. Peters, Richard. *Barry Manilow: An Illustrated Biography*. New York: Delilah/Putnam, 1983. 95 p. Illustrated. Discography.

MENUDO. Mus. (Miguel Cancel, Johnny Lozada, Ricardo Omar, Ray Reyes, Carlos Rivera, and Roy Rosello.)

1821. Greenberg, Keith Elliot. *Menudo!* Translated by Noel Hernandez. New York: Pocket Books, 1983. 63 p. Illustrated. Paperbound.

1822. Molina, Maria. *Menudo.* Photographs by Juan Ruiz. Translation from the Spanish by Elizabeth Garcia. New York: Julian Messner, 1984. 96 p. Illustrated.

MERCER, JOHNNY. Mus. 6/25/76

1823. Mercer, Johnny. *Our Huckleberry Friend: The Life, Times, and Lyrics of Johnny Mercer.* Collected and edited by Bob Bach and Ginger Mercer. Designed by Christopher Simon. Secaucus, NJ: Lyle Stuart, 1982. 252 p. Illustrated.

MONK, THELONIOUS. Mus. 2/17/85

1824. *Music in Monk Time [Videorecording].* San Francisco: Video Arts, 1983. 1 videocassette, sd., col., with b&w sequences, 1/2 in., VHS.

Credits: Written and produced by Paul C. Matthews and Stephen Rice. Directed by John Goodhue. Summary: A retrospective tribute to Thelonious Sphere Monk. It blends the history of Monk's early career in Harlem with archival footage of him playing his own compositions.

MURRAY, ANNE. Mus.

1825. *Annie North of 60 [Motion Picture].* MPI Productions, 1974. 2 reels, 52 min., sd., col., 16mm.

Credits: Director, Bill Rhodes. Photographers, Jim Mercer, and Bill Rhodes. Summary: Follows singer Anne Murray as she tours northern Canada.

1826. Livingstone, David. *Anne Murray, the Story So Far.* New York: Collier Books, 1981. 136 p. Illustrated. Discography. Paperbound.

NELSON, WILLIE. Mus.

1827. Bane, Michael. *Willie: An Unauthorized Biography of Willie Nelson.* New York: Dell, Bryans, 1984. 253 p. Illustrated. Index. Paperbound.

1828. Fowler, Lana Nelson, comp. *Willie Nelson Family Album.* Amarillo, TX: H. M. Poirot, 1980. 160 p. Illustrated. Bibliography. Discography. Paperbound.

1829. Nelson, Susie. *Heart Worn Memories: A Daughter's Personal Biography of Willie Nelson.* Austin, TX: Eakin Press, 1987. 228 p. Illustrated. Index.

1830. Nelson, Willie, and Shrake, Bud. *Willie: An Autobiography.* New York: Simon and Schuster, 1988. 334 p. Illustrated. Index. ***

1831. Scobey, Lola. *Willie Nelson, Country Outlaw.* New York: Kensington, Zebra, 1982. 414 p. Paperbound.

OSMOND, MARIE. Mus.

1832. Daly, Marsha. *The Osmonds: A Family Biography.* New York: St. Martin's Press, 1983. 135 p. Illustrated.

1833. *Side by Side [Motion Picture].* Beverly Hills, CA: Interplanetary Pictures, 1978. 1 reel, 16 min., sd., col., 16mm, or 35mm.
   Summary: Documents the seventeen-year show business career of the Osmond family, stressing their close family relationships.

PETERSON, OSCAR. Mus.

1834. Palmer, Richard. *Oscar Peterson.* Jazz Masters Series. Tunbridge Wells, Kent, England: Spellmount; New York: Hippocrene Books, 1984. 93 p. Illustrated. Discography.

PRESLEY, ELVIS. Mus. 8/16/77

1835. Cabaj, Janice M. Schrantz. *The Elvis Image.* Smithtown, NY: Exposition Press, 1982. 184 p. Illustrated.

1836. Carr, Roy, and Farren, Mick. *Elvis Presley: The Illustrated Record.* New York: Harmony Books, 1982. 191 p. Illustrated. Discography. Paperbound.

1837. *The Complete Elvis.* Edited by Martin Torgoff. Art direction by Ed Caraeff. New York: Delilah, 1982. 253 p. Illustrated. Bibliography.

1838. Cotten, Lee. *All Shook Up: Elvis Day-by-Day, 1954-1977.* Rock & Roll Reference Series, 13. Ann Arbor, MI: Pierian Press, 1985. 580 p. Illustrated. Tables. Bibliography. Index.

1839. De Barbin, Lucy, and Matera, Dary. *Are You Lonesome Tonight?: The Untold Story of Elvis Presley's One True Love and the Child He Never Knew.* New York: Villard Books, 1987. 294 p. Illustrated. Bibliography.

1840. Dundy, Elaine. *Elvis and Gladys.* New York: Dell, 1985. 386 p. Illustrated. Bibliography. Index. Paperbound.

1841. *Elvis—in Days Gone By [Sound Recording].* Staten Island, NY: Ron D'Ambra Enterprises, 1979. 2 sound discs, 33 1/3 rpm.

Summary: On these discs, Presley discusses the start of his singing career, his experiences in the U. S. Army, and his career aspirations.

1842. *Elvis on Tour [Videorecording].* New York: MGM/UA Home Video, 1972. 1 videocassette, 93 min., sd., col., VHS.

Summary: Interviews and live performances with Presley have been produced and directed by Pierre Adidge and Robert Abel.

1843. *Elvis, That's the Way It Is [Videorecording].* Culver City, CA: MGM/UA Home Video, 1987. 1 videocassette, 109 min., sd., col., 1/2 in.

Summary: Informal documentary of Elvis's 1970 concert tour, featuring off-stage moments, interviews with fans, and performances of a variety of numbers including Patch It Up, All Shook Up, Blue Suede Shoes, Heartbreak Hotel, Suspicious Minds, Love Me Tender, Bridge over Troubled Waters, You've Lost That Loving Feeling, I Can't Help Falling in Love with You.

1844. *Elvis, the King Speaks [Sound Recording].* Seattle, WA: Great Northwest Music, 1976. 1 sound disc, 33 1/3 rpm, stereo.

Summary: In a 1961 press conference in Memphis, Tennessee, Presley answers questions about his life and work.

1845. Gibson, Robert, and Shaw, Sid. *Elvis, a King Forever.* Poole, Dorset, England: Blandford Press, 1985. 176 p. Illustrated. Paperbound.

1846. Harbinson, W. A. *The Illustrated Elvis.* New York: Putnam, Perigee, 1987. 160 p. Illustrated. Paperbound.
***

1847. Hodge, Charlie, and Goodman, Charles. *Me 'n Elvis.* Memphis, TN: Castle Books, 1984. 194 p. Illustrated. ***

1848. Latham, Caroline. *Priscilla and Elvis: The Priscilla Presley Story.* New York: New American Library, Signet, 1985. 189 p. Illustrated. Bibliography. Paperbound.

1849. Mann, May. *Elvis, Why Won't They Leave You Alone?* New York: New American Library, Signet, 1982. 214 p. Illustrated. Paperbound.

1850. Marsh, Dave. *Elvis.* Art direction by Bea Feitler. New York: Times Books, 1982. 245 p. Illustrated. Discography. Filmography. Bibliography. ***

1851. Moody, Raymond A., Jr. *Elvis after Life: Unusual Psychic Experiences Surrounding the Death of a Superstar.* Atlanta, GA: Peachtree Publishers, 1987. 158 p.

1852. Peters, Richard. *Elvis, the Golden Anniversary Tribute: Fifty Fabulous Years, 1935-1985, in Words and Pictures.* Salem, NH: Salem House, 1984. 128 p. Illustrated. Discography. Paperbound.

1853. Presley, Priscilla Beaulieu, and Harmon, Sandra. *Elvis and Me.* New York: Putnam, 1985. 320 p. Illustrated.

1854. *Rock 'n' Roll Disciples [Videorecording].* Monticello Productions, 1984. 1 videocassette, 28 min., sd., col., VHS.

A documentary, also issued under the title, *Mondo Elvis*, the focus here is the infatuation approaching religious fervor displayed by some of his fans following Presley's death.

1855. Rooks, Nancy, and Gutter, Mae. *The Maid, the Man, and the Fans: Elvis Is the Man.* New York: Vantage, 1984. 51 p. Illustrated. Bibliography.

1856. Roy, Samuel. *Elvis, Prophet of Power.* Brookline, MA: Branden, 1985. 195 p. Illustrated. Bibliography. Index.

1857. Stanley, David, and Wimbish, David. *Life with Elvis.* Foreword by Jimmy Draper. Old Tappan, NJ: F. H. Revell, 1986. 223 p. Illustrated.

1858. Stanley, Rick, and Haynes, Michael K. *The Touch of Two Kings.* T2K [Press], 1986. 186 p. Illustrated. Paperbound.

1859. Stearn, Jess. *Elvis, His Spiritual Journey.* Norfolk, VA: Donning, 1982. 252 p. Illustrated. Paperbound.

1860. Stern, Jane, and Stern, Michael. *Elvis World.* New York: Knopf, 1987. 196 p. Illustrated. Bibliography.

1861. *This is Elvis [Videorecording].* Burbank, CA: Warner Home Video, 1983. 1 videocassette, 144 min., sd., col., VHS.

This biography of Presley draws on interviews with many of the people who knew him best, plus documentary footage. Cast: Presley, David Scott, Paul Boensch III, Johnny Harra, Lawrence Koller, Rhonda Lyn, Debbie Edge, and Larry Raspberry.

1862. Tobler, John, and Wootton, Richard. *Elvis: The Legend and the Music.* New York: Crescent Books, 1983. 192 p. Illustrated. Bibliography. Filmography. Discography. Index.

1863. Vellenga, Dirk, and Farren, Mick. *Elvis and the Colonel.* New York: Delacorte Press, 1988. 278 p. Illustrated. Discography. Index. ***

PREVIN, ANDRE. Mus.

1864. Bookspan, Martin, and Yockey, Ross. *André Previn: A Biography.* Garden City, NY: Doubleday, 1981. 398 p. Illustrated. Index.

1865. Ruttencutter, Helen Drees. *Previn.* New York: St. Martin's/Marek, 1985. 234 p. Illustrated.

PRINCE. Mus.

1866. Bream, Jon. *Prince: Inside the Purple Reign.* New York: Collier Books, 1984. 112 p. Illustrated. Discography. Paperbound.

1867. Feldman, Jim. *Prince.* New York: Ballantine Books, 1985. 146 p. Illustrated. Discography. Videography. Paperbound.

1868. Ivory, Steven. *Prince.* New York: Perigee, 1984. 175 p. Illustrated. Discography. Paperbound.

1869. Olmeca. *Prince.* New York: Proteus Books, 1984. 28 p. Illustrated. Discography. Paperbound.

1870. Prince. *Prince in His Own Words.* Edited by Dave Fudger. Picture research by Valerie Boyd. London: Omnibus Press; Port Chester, NY: Cherry Lane Books, 1984. 33 p. Illustrated. Paperbound.

1871. Rowland, Mark, and Rochlin, Margy. *Prince, His Story in Words and Pictures: An Unauthorized Biography.* New York: Lorevan, Critic's Choice, 1985. 174 p. Illustrated. Discography. Paperbound.

1872. *The Year of the Prince.* Cresskill, NJ: Sharon Starbook, 1984. 48 p. Illustrated.

RICHARD, LITTLE. Mus.

1873. White, Charles. *The Life and Times of Little Richard: The Quasar of Rock.* Foreword by Paul McCartney. New

York: Harmony Books, 1984. 269 p. Illustrated. Discography. Filmography. Index.

RICHIE, LIONEL. Mus.

1874. Nathan, David. *Lionel Richie: An Illustrated Biography.* Introduction by Dionne Warwick. New York: McGraw-Hill, 1985. 127 p. Illustrated. Discography. Paperbound.

1875. Plutzik, Roberta. *Lionel Richie.* New York: Dell, 1985. 185 p. Illustrated. Discography. Paperbound.

ROBESON, PAUL. Mus. 1/23/76

1876. Hamilton, Virginia. *Paul Robeson: The Life and Times of a Free Black Man.* New York: Dell, Laurel-Leaf, 1979. 218 p. ***

1877. Nazel, Joseph. *Paul Robeson: Biography of a Proud Man.* Los Angeles: Holloway House, 1980. 216 p. Bibliography. Paperbound.

1878. Noble, Gil. *Paul Robeson: The Tallest Tree in Our Forest* [Motion Picture]. New York: Phoenix Films, 1977. 3 reels. 90 min., sd., col., 16mm.

Summary: This is a documentary on the life and career of the singer, actor, and political activist. It includes archival footage and still photographs, and presents interviews with Robeson's friends and admirers.

1879. *Paul Robeson, the Great Forerunner.* By the editors of *Freedomways.* New York: Dodd, Mead, 1978. 383 p. Illustrated. Bibliography. Index.

1880. *Paul Robeson, Tribute to an Artist [Motion Picture]*. New York: Janus Films, 1979. 1 film reel, 29 min., sd., col., 16 mm.

Summary: This film focuses on the life and art of singer, Paul Robeson.

1881. *A Profile of Paul Robeson [Videorecording]*. Washington, DC: Greater Washington Educational Telecommunications Association, 1975. 1 videocassette. 58 min., sd., b&w and col., VHS.

Summary: The life and accomplishments of the talented Robeson are covered—from his days as a football star and exemplary student at Rutgers University, and focusing on his singing and acting careers in the United States and abroad, to his political and social activism in support of American Blacks and oppressed people worldwide.

1882. Robeson, Paul. *Paul Robeson Speaks: Writings, Speeches, Interviews, 1918-1974*. Edited, with an introduction and notes, by Philip S. Foner. New York: Brunner/Mazel, 1978. 623 p. Illustrated. Bibliography. Index.

1883. Robeson, Susan. *The Whole World in His Hands: A Pictorial Biography of Paul Robeson*. Secaucus, NJ: Citadel, 1981. 254 p. Illustrated. Paperbound.

RODGERS, RICHARD. Mus. 12/30/79

1884. Nolan, Frederick. *The Sound of Their Music: The Story of Rodgers & Hammerstein*. London: Dent, 1978. 272 p. Illustrated. Bibliography. Index.

1885. *Rodgers and Hammerstein [Filmstrip]*. Brunswick Productions, 1973. 45 fr., col., 35mm.

Summary: This is a strip (with captions) describing the careers of composer Richard Rodgers and lyricist Oscar Hammerstein II.

1886. Rodgers, Dorothy. *A Personal Book.* New York: Harper & Row, 1977. 188 p. Illustrated.

1887. *Words and Music [Videorecording].* New York: MGM/UA Home Video, 1986. 1 videocassette, 122 min., sd., col., VHS.
Summary: This video (originally issued as a motion picture in 1948) presents the story of the partnership of Richard Rodgers and Lorenz Hart. An exceptional cast includes: June Allyson, Perry Como, Judy Garland, Lena Horne, Gene Kelly, Mickey Rooney, and Ann Sothern.

ROGERS, KENNY. Mus.

1888. Hume, Martha. *Kenny Rogers, Gambler, Dreamer, Lover.* Photographs by John Reggero. New York: New American Library, Plume, 1980. 159 p. Illustrated. Discography. Paperbound.

THE ROLLING STONES. Mus. (Mick Jagger, [Brian Jones], Keith Richards, Charlie Watts, Ron Wood, and Bill Wyman.)

1889. Aftel, Mandy. *Death of a Rolling Stone: The Brian Jones Story.* New York: Delilah Books, 1982. 205 p. Illustrated. Paperbound.

1890. Booth, Stanley. *Dance With the Devil: The Rolling Stones and Their Times.* New York: Random House, 1984. 383 p. Illustrated.

1891. Charone, Barbara. *Keith Richards, Life as a Rolling Stone.* Garden City, NY: Doubleday, Dolphin, 1982. 198 p. Illustrated. Discography. Paperbound.

1892. Dalton, David, and Farren, Mick, comps. *Rolling Stones in Their Own Words.* New York: Delilah/Putnam, 1983. 127 p. Illustrated. Paperbound.

1893. Dalton, David. *The Rolling Stones: The First Twenty Years.* New York: Knopf, 1981. 191 p. Illustrated.

1894. Dowley, Tim. *The Rolling Stones.* New York: Hippocrene Books, 1983. 156 p. Illustrated. Discography. Filmography. Bibliography.

1895. Flippo, Chet. *On the Road with the Rolling Stones: 20 Years of Lipstick, Handcuffs, and Chemicals.* Garden City, NY: Doubleday, Dolphin, 1985. 178 p. Paperbound.

1896. *Gimme Shelter [Videorecording].* New York: Columbia Pictures Home Entertainment, 1980. 1 videocassette, 90 min., sd., col., 1/2 in., VHS.
   Originally issued as a motion picture in 1970. Summary: Vignettes from the Rolling Stones' 1970 United States concert tour.

1897. Kamin, Philip, and Goddard, Peter. *The Rolling Stones: Live.* London: Sidgwick & Jackson, 1982. 130 p. Illustrated. Paperbound. ***

1898. Kamin, Philip, and Goddard, Peter. *The Rolling Stones: The Last Tour.* New York: Beaufort Books, 1982. 125 p. Illustrated. Paperbound.

1899. Leibovitz, Annie, et al. *The Rolling Stones on Tour.* Introduction by Mick Jagger. Paris: Dragon's Dream, 1978. 143 p. Illustrated. Paperbound. ***

1900. Martin, Linda. *The Rolling Stones in Concert.* Produced by Ted Smart and David Gibbon. New York: Crescent Books, 1982. 96 p. Illustrated. Discography.

1901. Norman, Philip. *Symphony for the Devil: The Rolling Stones Story.* New York: Linden Press/Simon and Schuster, 1984. 413 p. Illustrated.

1902. Norman, Philip. *The Stones.* London: Elm Tree Books, 1984. 373 p. Illustrated. Index. ***

1903. Palmer, Robert. *The Rolling Stones.* Design by Mary Shanahan. Garden City, NY: Doubleday, Rolling Stone, 1983. 256 p. Illustrated. Discography. Bibliography.

1904. Pascall, Jeremy. *The Rolling Stones.* Designed by Rob Burt. Secaucus, NJ: Chartwell Books, 1977. 96 p. Illustrated. Filmography. Discography.

1905. *The Rolling Stones.* Edited by David Dalton. New York: Delilah/Putnam, 1982. 126 p. Illustrated. Bibliography. Discography. ***

1906. Sanchez, Tony. *Up and Down with the Rolling Stones.* New York: Morrow, 1979. 309 p. Illustrated. Paperbound.

1907. Schofield, Carey. *Jagger.* New York: Beaufort Books, 1985. 248 p. Illustrated. Bibliography. Index. Paperbound. ***

RONSTADT, LINDA. Mus.

1908. Berman, Connie. *Linda Ronstadt: An Illustrated Biography.* London, Carson City, NV: Proteus, 1980. 117 p. Illustrated. Discography. Paperbound.

1909. Claire, Vivian. *Linda Ronstadt.* New York: Flash Books, 1978. Illustrated. Discography. Paperbound.

1910. Kanakaris, Richard. *Linda Ronstadt, a Portrait.* Los Angeles: L. A. Pop, 1977. 79 p. Illustrated. Discography.

1911. Moore, Mary Ellen. *The Linda Ronstadt Scrapbook.* New York: Sunridge Press, 1978. 121 p. Illustrated. Paperbound.

ROSS, DIANA. Mus.

1912. Brown, Geoff. *Diana Ross.* New York: St. Martin's Press, 1981. 144 p. Illustrated. Discography. Index. Paperbound.

1913. Taraborrelli, J. Randy; Wilson, Reginald; and Minger, Darryl. *Diana.* Garden City, NY: Doubleday, Dolphin, 1985. 245 p. Illustrated. Discography. Videography. Paperbound.

SEEGER, PETE. Mus.

1914. Dunaway, David King. *How Can I Keep from Singing: Pete Seeger.* New York: McGraw-Hill, 1981. 386 p. Illustrated. Bibliography. Discography. Index.

1915. *Roger Ebert, Film Critic; Pete Seeger, Folk Singer* [*Sound Recording*]. Washington, DC: National Public Radio, 1981. 1 sound cassette, 60 min., analog.

Summary: Ebert surveys the American movie scene and recalls his own initiation into moviegoing and reviewing. Seeger looks back at his travels with Woody Guthrie, his years with the Almanac Singers and the Weavers, and at his years on the "blacklist," which effectively restricted his appearances during the 1960s revival of folk music he helped inspire.

SIMON AND GARFUNKEL. Mus. (Paul Simon and Art Garfunkel.)

1916. Cohen, Mitchell S. *Simon & Garfunkel: A Biography in Words and Pictures.* Edited by Greg Shaw. Sire Books; New York: Chappell Music, 1977. 55 p. Illustrated. Discography. Bibliography. Paperbound.

1917. Humphries, Patrick. *Bookends: The Simon and Garfunkel Story.* London, New York: Proteus Books, 1982. 128 p. Illustrated. Discography. Paperbound.

1918. Matthew-Walker, Robert. *Simon and Garfunkel.* New York: Hippocrene Books; Tunbridge Wells, Kent, England: Baton Press, 1984. 165 p. Illustrated. Discography. Filmography. Bibliography. Index.

SIMON, PAUL. Mus. See: SIMON AND GARFUNKEL. Mus.

SLICK, GRACE. Mus.

1919. Rowes, Barbara. *Grace Slick: The Biography.* Garden City, NY: Doubleday, 1980. 215 p. Illustrated.

SONDHEIM, STEPHEN. Mus.

1920. Zadan, Craig. *Sondheim & Co.* 2d ed. New York: Harper & Row, 1986. 408 p. Illustrated. Playography. Discography. Index.

SPRINGFIELD, RICK. Mus.

1921. Gillianti, Simone. *Rick Springfield.* New York: Wanderer Books, 1984. 64 p. Illustrated. Discography. Paperbound.

SPRINGSTEEN, BRUCE. Mus.

1922. Gambaccine, Peter. *Bruce Springsteen.* New York: Perigee, Perigee/Delilah Book, 1985. 159 p. Illustrated. Discography. Paperbound.

1923. Halbersberg, Elianne. *The Boss Bruce Springsteen.* Cresskill, NJ: Sharon Starbook, 1984. 95 p. Illustrated. Discography. Paperbound.

1924. Hilburn, Robert. *Springsteen.* Art direction by Howard Klein. New York: Rolling Stone Press, 1985. 256 p. Illustrated.

1925. Humphries, Patrick, and Hunt, Chris. *Bruce Springsteen, Blinded by the Light.* New York: H. Holt, Owl Book, 1985. 176 p. Illustrated. Discography. Paperbound.

1926. Kamin, Philip, and Goddard, Peter. *Springsteen Live.* New York: Beaufort Books, 1984. 126 p. Illustrated. Paperbound.

1927. Lynch, Kate. *Springsteen: No Surrender.* London, New York: Proteus Books, 1984. 126 p. Illustrated. Discography.

1928. Marsh, Dave. *Born to Run: The Bruce Springsteen Story.* Garden City, NY: Doubleday, Delilah, 1979. 176 p. Illustrated. Paperbound.

1929. Marsh, Dave. *Glory Days: Bruce Springsteen in the 1980s.* New York: Pantheon Books, 1987. 478 p. Illustrated. Bibliography. Index.

1930. Meyer, Marianne. *Bruce Springsteen.* New York: Ballantine Books, 1984. 176 p. Illustrated. Discography. Videography. Paperbound.

1931. St. Pierre, Roger. *Bruce Springsteen: An Independent Story in Words and Pictures.* Romford, England: Anabas Publishing, 1985. Illustrated. Paperbound. ***

1932. Slaughter, Mike. *Bruce Springsteen: An American Classic.* Port Chester, NY: Cherry Lane Books, 1984. 30 p. Illustrated. Discography. Paperbound.

STEWART, ROD. Mus.

1933. Burton, Peter. *Rod Stewart: A Life on the Town.* London: New English Library, 1977. 120 p. Illustrated. ***

1934. Jasper, Tony. *Rod Stewart.* Secaucus, NJ: Chartwell Books, 1977. 91 p. Illustrated.

1935. Nelson, Paul, and Bangs, Lester. *Rod Stewart.* New York: Delilah/Putnam, 1981. 159 p. Illustrated. Paperbound.

STING. Mus.

1936. Cohen, Barney. *Sting: Every Breath He Takes.* New York: Berkley Books, 1984. 150 p. Illustrated. Discography. Paperbound.

1937. Gett, Steve. *Sting*. Port Chester, NY: Cherry Lane Books, 1985. 48 p. Illustrated. Paperbound.

1938. Nikart, Ray. *Sting and the Police*. New York: Ballantine Books, 1984. 149 p. Illustrated. Discography. Videography. Paperbound.

STYNE, JULE. Mus.

1939. Taylor, Theodore. *Jule: The Story of Composer Jule Styne*. New York: Random House, 1979. 293 p. Illustrated. Index.

TURNER, TINA. Mus.

1940. Fissinger, Laura. *Tina Turner*. New York: Ballantine Books, 1985. 163 p. Illustrated. Discography. Videography. Paperbound.

1941. Ivory, Steven. *Tina!* New York: Putnam, Perigee, 1985. 189 p. Illustrated. Discography. Paperbound.

1942. Mills, Bart. *Tina*. New York: Warner Books, 1985. 127 p. Illustrated. Discography. Filmography.

1943. Turner, Tina, and Loder, Kurt. *I, Tina*. New York: Morrow, 1986. 236 p. Illustrated. Discography.

1944. Wynn, Ron. *Tina: The Tina Turner Story*. New York: Collier Books, 1985. 158 p. Illustrated. Discography.

TWITTY, CONWAY. Mus.

1945. Cross, Wilbur, and Kosser, Michael. *The Conway Twitty Story: An Authorized Biography.* Garden City, NY: Doubleday, Dolphin, 1986. 213 p. Illustrated. Discography.

WATERS, ETHEL. Mus. 9/1/77

1946. DeKorte, Juliann. *Ethel Waters: Finally Home.* Old Tappan, NJ: F. H. Revell, 1978. 128 p. Illustrated.

1947. Knaack, Twila. *Ethel Waters, I Touched a Sparrow.* Introduction by Ruth Bell Graham. Waco, TX: Word Books, 1978. 128 p. Illustrated.

WELK, LAWRENCE. Mus.

1948. Sanders, Coyne Steven, and Weissman, Ginny. *Champagne Music: The Lawrence Welk Show.* Foreword by Bobby Burgess. New York: St. Martin's Press, 1985. 146 p. Illustrated. Bibliography. Index.

1949. Schwienher, William K. *Lawrence Welk, an American Institution.* Chicago: Nelson-Hall, 1980. 288 p. Illustrated. Bibliography. Index.

1950. Welk, Lawrence, and McGeehan, Bernice. *This I Believe.* Englewood Cliffs, NJ: Prentice-Hall, 1979. 197 p. Illustrated.

1951. Welk, Lawrence, and McGeehan, Bernice. *You're Never Too Young.* Englewood Cliffs, NJ: Prentice-Hall, 1981. 187 p. Illustrated.

WHITING, MARGARET. Mus.

1952. Whiting, Margaret, and Holt, Will. *It Might As Well Be Spring: A Musical Autobiography.* New York: Morrow, 1987. 384 p. Illustrated. Discography. Index.

WONDER, STEVIE. Mus.

1953. Dragonwagon, Crescent. *Stevie Wonder.* New York: Flash Books, 1977. 94 p. Illustrated. Discography.

1954. Elsner, Constanze. *Stevie Wonder.* London: Everest Books, 1977. 360 p. Illustrated. Discography. Index.

1955. Fox-Cumming, Ray. *Stevie Wonder.* London: Mandabrook Books, 1977. 123 p. Discography. Paperbound. ***

1956. Haskins, James, and Benson, Kathleen. *The Stevie Wonder Scrapbook.* New York: Grosset & Dunlap, 1978. 159 p. Illustrated. Bibliography.

1957. Peisch, Jeffrey. *Stevie Wonder.* New York: Ballantine Books, 1985. 146 p. Illustrated. Discography. Videography. Paperbound.

1958. Ruuth, Marianne. *Stevie Wonder.* Los Angeles: Holloway House, 1980. 95 p. Illustrated. Paperbound.

1959. Swenson, John. *Stevie Wonder.* New York: Perennial Library, 1986. 159 p. Illustrated. Discography. Paperbound.

WYNETTE, TAMMY. Mus.

1960. Wynette, Tammy, and Dew, Joan. *Stand By Your Man.* New York: Simon and Schuster, 1979. 349 p. Illustrated. Index.

PART IV
SPORTS CELEBRITIES SOURCES

Chapter 26
Reference Books

Section 1
Bibliographies and Guides

1961. Davis, Lenwood G., and Daniels, Belinda S., comps. *Black Athletes in the United States: A Bibliography of Books, Articles, Autobiographies, and Biographies on Black Professional Athletes in the United States, 1800-1981.* Westport, CT: Greenwood Press, 1981. 265 p. Index.

Focusing on black athletes in the professional sports of baseball, basketball, boxing, football, golf, and tennis, this work lists major reference books, histories and other non-fiction, biographical books and articles. The selection criteria were to identify the first black athlete in a major sport; the best-known; those having a body of significant biographical materials; and those currently newsworthy. There are 3,871 entries, intermittently annotated.

1962. Gratch, Bonnie; Chan, Betty; and Lingenfelter, Judith; comps. *Sports and Physical Education: A Guide to the Reference Resources.* Westport, CT; London: Greenwood Press, 1983. 198 p. Index.

A unique, dependable reference bibliography for English-language sources in sports, physical education, and several allied fields published since 1970. Excluded are sports requiring no physical ability, or which are not competitive. Also excluded are non-equestrian animal sports, and motor sports. Arrangement is classified by sport or related category, then subdivided by type of source: bibliographies, biographies (containing biographical information for twenty or more individuals), equipment catalogs, dictionaries, encyclopedias, directories, statistical sources, and miscellaneous. Personal/corporate author, title and subject indexes.

1963. Smith, Myron J. *The Dodgers Bibliography: From Brooklyn to Los Angeles.* Foreword by Roy Campanella. Sports Teams and Players Bibliography Series, No. 1. Westport, CT: Meckler Books, 1988. 153 p. Illustrated. Index.

Stresses published (non-newspaper) items written in this century. Comprised of three main sections: Reference Works and General Histories, Team Bibliography, and Player Bibliography. The last section of seventy-one pages contains collective and individual biographies. Appendix II: Visual and Computer Database Sources.

1964. Tomlinson, Gerald. *The Baseball Research Handbook.* Preface by John Thorn. Kansas City, MO: Society for American Baseball Research, 1987. 120 p. Bibliography. Index. ***

"How-to" explanation, bibliography (chapter 3), and publishing guide for the beginning researcher. (Information from the publisher's brochure.)

1965. Zucker, Harvey Marc, and Babich, Lawrence J., comps. *Sports Films: A Complete Reference.* Jefferson, NC: McFarland, 1987. 612 p. Illustrated. Index.

Lists 2,000 English language films concerning spectator sports, released through December, 1984. Not included are films made for television or cable, industrial, educational or promotional films, newsreels, or pornographic films. Arrangement is by sport with film citations by title followed by release date, country of origin, distributor, running time, credits, and synopsis. "Athletes in Films," is a chapter containing biographical sketches and credits of sports figures who have pursued dual careers. This is followed by "Actor's Portrayals," a section which lists by athlete's name the actor(s) who portrayed them. There are general and title indexes.

Section 2
Biographical Dictionaries

1966. Alliss, Peter. *The Who's Who of Golf.* Research by Michael Hobbs. Englewood Cliffs, NJ: Prentice-Hall, 1983. 381 p. Illustrated. Index.

An international biographical dictionary attempting ". . . to include all who have achieved considerable success at the game." (Introduction.) The period of coverage is from approximately 1850 through 1982. Arrangement is geographical, then alphabetical. The sketches vary in length, however, each has the minimum information elements: birthplace and date, money winnings, and tournament victories. Photographs accompany most sketches.

1967. *Biographical Dictionary of American Sports, Baseball.* Edited by David L. Porter. New York: Greenwood Press, 1987. 713 p. Index.

Volume I of a planned four-volume set which is intended as "a scholarly, comprehensive biographical dictionary of notable American athletic figures." Each volume covers about 500 athletes. Categories for the volumes yet to be published: football (vol. II, to be published late 1988); auto racing, golf, harness and thoroughbred racing, lacrosse, skiing, soccer, tennis, and track and field (vol. III—outdoor sports); and, basketball, bowling, boxing, gymnastics, ice hockey, figure and speed skating, swimming and diving, weightlifting, and wrestling (vol. IV—indoor sports). "Other" sports figures, e.g., sportscasters, writers, promoters, will also be covered in the final volumes. Criteria for inclusion: born or raised in the U.S.; exceptional accomplishments in a sport; and, significant impact on his or her sport. In the baseball volume, signed essays are contributed by over 100 experts. A balance between personal biography and athletic achievement is the editorial intent. The essays are about a page long and conclude with a bibliography. Included in the appendices are lists of players by position, place of birth, and league (major; negro).

1968. Ferguson, Bob. *Who's Who in Canadian Sport*. Toronto: Summerhill Press, 1985. 354 p. Illustrated. Index

The achievements of 2,800 Canadian athletes, amateur and professional, living and dead, and representing nearly every sport are gathered in this dictionary. Sketches, averaging about a paragraph, concentrate on the individual's sports career with personal information limited to name, birth-date/place, marital status, spouse's name, children's names, and educational background. The book concludes with lists: Canadian National Champions; Canadian Olympic Teams (1904-1984); and, Canadian Halls of Fame members. Sport/personality cross-reference index.

1969. Grimsley, Will, et al. *101 Greatest Athletes of the Century*. Supervising editor, Ben Olan. New York: Bonanza Books, 1987. 320 p. Illustrated.

Grimsley, and the Associated Press Sports Staff, offer their list of sport superstars, some eighty percent of whom are Americans. Each athlete is described in a section of two or three pages, including several illustrations. The choice for outstanding all-around athletes of this century: Jim Thorpe and Babe Didrikson Zaharias.

1970. *International Who's Who in Tennis.* Dallas, TX: World Championship Tennis, vol. 1-, 1983-. Illustrated. Index. (Annual)

"Entries have been accepted from 8,000 individuals [including senior, junior, professional, amateur and veteran players] representing 102 countries plus 4,000 commercial entities from 72 different nations." (Foreword.) There is a biographical list, a commercial list, and a name index subdivided by country. Depth of biographical content varies, with a minimal insertion usually giving name, country of residence, and specialization within the sport, e.g., umpire.

1971. James, Bill. *The Bill James Historical Baseball Abstract.* New York: Villard Books, 1986. 721 p. Illustrated. Table. Bibliography. Index.

James, described as "the guru of baseball statistics," also writes an annual called, *The Baseball Abstract.* Less statistics-laden than the "Abstract," this work devotes a section to a history of the game's eleven decades, and another to a biographical part called "The Players," described in the introduction as the "Who-Was-Better-Than-Whom" section. Here one finds a standardized annotation giving Hall of Fame information, position comparison, offensive won-lost record, career value rating, and one or more paragraphs of career appraisal. The final section is a table of records, by position.

1972. Lesser, Eugene. *Eugene Lesser's Sports Birthdays.* San Francisco, CA: E. Buryn, 1985. Unpaged. Illustrated. Index. Paperbound.

A chronological listing of several hundred sports stars. The vast majority are men and women from professional teams. One or two persons are intermittently featured in a biographical sketch. The sketches are followed by a line or so for those "also born today."

1973. Mallon, Bill; Buchanan, Ian; and Tishman, Jeffrey. *Quest for Gold: The Encyclopedia of American Olympians.* New York: Leisure Press, 1984. 495 p. Illustrated. Table. Index. Paperbound.

"[The U.S.A.] has produced the most Olympic athletes, the most Olympic gold medalists, and the most Olympic medalists—by far" (Preface). Medal winners from the 1896 games to the (boycotted) 1980 Moscow games are described in a line or a paragraph. There is a list of Olympic records, and an index of all competitors.

1974. Smith, Ken. *Baseball's Hall of Fame*. 9th ed. New York: Tempo Books, 1979. 226 p. Paperbound.

Presents the history, rules, and honorees (through 1978 in the edition inspected), of the National Baseball Hall of Fame and Museum in Cooperstown, New York. Written by the Hall's Director, biographies, physical description, and career statistics of some 170 members comprise the principal portion of this work.

1975. *Who's Who in International Tennis*. Edited by David Emery. New York: Facts on File, 1983. 128 p. Illustrated.

This book attempts to cover the world of superstar tennis—the top-seeded young players, the veterans nearing career end, plus an introduction to the would-be champions. Given the publication date, one wonders how Boris Becker missed inclusion in the latter category. Information given: birth place/date, home, height, weight, career highlights, descriptive/evaluative paragraph(s), and a photograph.

Section 3
Encyclopedias

1976. Hollander, Zander, ed. *The Modern Encyclopedia of Basketball*. 2d ed. An Associated Features Book. Garden City, NY: Doubleday, Dolphin, 1979. 624 p. Illustrated. Table. Bibliography. Index. Paperbound.

Included are a history of the sport, yearly roundups, all-time records, most valuable players, and all-time team and player directories. Biographical articles of a page or so, with photograph, are given for the superstar players and coaches, college and professional. Arrangement is by topical chapter.

1977. *The New York Times Encyclopedia of Sports.* Edited by Gene Brown. Introduction by Frank Litsky. New York: Arno Press, 1979-1980. 15 vols. Illustrated. Bibliography. Table. Index.

As does *The New York Times Encyclopedia of Film* for motion pictures, this source presents facsimile reprints of sports stories, many with biographical content, from *The New York Times*, between the years 1906-1979. The material is divided by sport into separate volumes, with each main sport or group introduced by an historical essay and explanation of the rules and game progress. The volumes have indexes and statistical tables.

1978. Riffenburgh, Beau. *The Official NFL Encyclopedia.* New York, Scarborough, ON: New American Library, NAL Books, 544 p. Illustrated.

"This is the NFL's book about itself." (Introduction.) The audience is both football novice and aficionado. The careers of Hall of Fame inductees are presented in a chapter of biographical paragraphs, each with photograph and position statistics. Some other chapters: Roots of Pro Football; Teams of the NFL; All-Time Roster; and, Rules of the NFL.

1979. Rust, Art, and Rust, Edna. *Art Rust's Illustrated History of the Black Athlete.* Garden City, NY: Doubleday, 1985. 435 p. Illustrated. Index.

In this subject encyclopedia there are ten chapters, the first two on baseball, and the remainder on: boxing, football, basketball, track, horse racing, golf, ice hockey and tennis. Biographical sketches follow an introductory essay on each sport. The major athletes are described in several pages, the minor players in a paragraph.

Section 4
Yearbooks

1980. *Hockey's Heritage.* Edited by the Curator of the Hockey
Hall of Fame. Toronto: Hockey Hall of Fame, 1969-.
Illustrated. Table. Index. (Annual)

Supersedes *Hockey Hall of Fame Book.* Supplements are
issued in years when *Hockey's Heritage* is not published. In
the 1982 issue examined, short biographical sketches of
players, executives or referees elected to the Hall are
presented. The concluding section lists trophies and various
records.

1981. Hollander, Zander, ed. *The Complete Handbook of Pro
Basketball, 1982 Season.* New York: New American
Library, Signet, 1981. 319 p. Illustrated. Table.
Paperbound. (Annual)

The issue examined begins with essays on three
professional players (Larry Bird, Isaiah Thomas and, Bernard
King) followed by the main section of team analysis and
paragraph-long sketches of each player with his statistics.
Concluding portions contain tabular data on the college draft,
NBA statistics, radio/TV game broadcast coverage, and the
league schedule.

1982. Hollander, Zander, ed. *The Complete Handbook of Pro
Hockey, 1986 Season.* New York: New American Library,
Signet, 1985. 287 p. Illustrated. Table. Paperbound.
(Annual)

Sketches of all the current National Hockey League
players include their age, height, weight, and position, followed
by a career statistical table. Arrangement is by team.
Biographical features (the 1986 issue has articles on Wayne
Gretzky and Pelle Lindbergh), scouting reports, "featurettes" on
colorful players, trophy winners, and team schedules are some
of the other contents.

1983. *National Baseball Hall of Fame and Museum Yearbook.* Cooperstown, NY: The Hall of Fame, 19(?)-. Illustrated. (Annual) ***

Section 5
Indexes

1984. *Physical Education Index.* Cape Girardeau, MO: BenOak, vol. 1-, 1978-. (Quarterly)

Subject index to about 200 periodicals published in English or having summaries in English. Coverage is given to pertinent articles in dance, health, physical education, physical therapy, recreation, sports and sports medicine. Included are, "biographies, reports and obituaries about outstanding professionals." (Preface.) The fourth issue is an annual cumulation.

1985. *Sport and Fitness Index. Index des Sports et de la Condition Physique.* Ottawa, Ontario, Canada: Sport Information Resource Centre, 1984-. (Monthly)

Monthly issues include some which are combined. Continues *Sport and Recreation Index* (1977-1984); and, *Sport Articles* (1974-1977). The Centre combined its data base of some 90,000 citations to books, articles, theses, and documents into the eight-volume publication, *Sport Bibliography.* This is continued by annual cumulations of *Sport and Fitness Index*, and its precursor, and currently numbers some 140,000 citations. All major sport, physical education, physical fitness and recreation journals published in English or French are indexed. Arrangement is by major sport or fitness subject where biographical material may be found by searching through the citations alphabetized by author. Far easier and vastly more thorough access can be had by computer; in Canada the data base can be searched through CAN/OLE, and in the U.S. through the SDC/Orbit service. The Centre also does on-demand searches.

1986. *The Sports Periodicals Index.* Ann Arbor, MI: National
      Information Systems, vol. 1-, 1985-. (Monthly)

About eighty-five (the count in the issues examined)
popular North American sport periodicals are analyzed by
subject and name-as-subject in this annotated index.
Biographical articles are entered by sport, then by the
subheading, "profiles." (For example: Football; Profiles;
Bartkowski, Steve.) Cross-references are made from surnames
to the relevant sport. A table of contents lists subject headings
generated from the articles indexed for that month.

Section 6
Directories

1987. *The Comprehensive Directory of Sports Addresses.*
      Ludlow, VT: Global Sports Productions, vol. 1-, 1980-.
      (Biennial)

The third edition of this work covering amateur and
professional sport and which is intended for fans, collectors,
administrators, and job seekers, was published in 1987. A
supplement titled, *Quarterly Update Subscription Service* is
obtainable by subscribers. Contents include sections by sport:
baseball, basketball, football, hockey, lacrosse, soccer,
vollyball, tennis, motor sports, and running; and, by
information category: sports museums, media sources,
organizations, publications, international sports, collecting, and
N.C.A.A. colleges and universities.

1988. Soderberg, Paul; Washington, Helen; and Jacques Cattell
      Press; comps. *The Big Book of Halls of Fame in the
      United States and Canada: Sports.* New York, London:
      Bowker, 1977. 1042 p. Index.

As stated in the preface, the dual purposes of this source
are to create an awareness of the hundreds of halls in North
America, and to focus attention on the tens of thousands of

persons honored. Two additional volumes are in preparation which are to cover entertainment, business, culture, science, collegiate, city and state halls. Arrangement is alphabetical within individual sports. Description for each hall includes name, location, contact person, officers, admission data or criteria, and location of nearby halls. This is followed by a list of honorees with a biographical sketch of each. There are indexes by category, name, location and members.

Section 7
Individual Celebrity Sources

DI MAGGIO, JOE. Spo.

1989. Moore, Jack B. *Joe DiMaggio, a Bio-bibliography.* Popular Culture Bio-bibliographies. New York: Greenwood Press, 1986. 252 p. Tables. Index.

In the main part of this work, Moore presents an account of the salient facts of DiMaggio's life, and analyzes the reasons for his enshrinement as a sports and popular culture hero. This section is followed by a comprehensive narrative bibliography entitled, "Literature About Joe DiMaggio."

LOUIS, JOE. Spo. 4/12/81

1990. Davis, Lenwood G., and Moore, Marsha L., comps. *Joe Louis: A Bibliography of Articles, Books, Pamphlets, Records, and Archival Materials.* Foreword by James E. Newton. Westport, CT: Greenwood Press, 1983. 232 p. Table. Index.

A comprehensive, unannotated English-language bibliography of 2,799 items. Arrangement is chronological by publication date within six sections: Works by Joe Louis; Major

Books and Pamphlets about Joe Louis; General Books and Pamphlets about Joe Louis; Articles about Joe Louis; Periodicals about Joe Louis; and, Obituaries. Author index.

Chapter 27
Collective Biographies

1991. Allen, Maury. *Baseball's 100: A Personal Ranking of the Best Players in Baseball History.* New York: A&W Visual Library, 1981. 316 p. Illustrated. Paperbound.

The author considered the changing conditions of the game since 1900, then rated the players during this period from one to one hundred (hitters against pitchers, batters against fielders, pitchers against relievers). Willie Mays is number one; Roger Maris, number one hundred. Each player is featured in an illustrated biographical sketch of two pages.

1992. Alliss, Peter. *Peter Alliss's Supreme Champions of Golf.* New York: Scribner, 1986. 200 p. Illustrated.

Fifteen golfers are in Alliss's pantheon of greats. Each of the roughly twelve-page sketches is illustrated with a portrait and several photographs, concluding with a summary of career highlights. The champions: Walter Hagen, Gene Sarazen, Bobby Jones, Henry Cotton, Byron Nelson, Sam Snead, Ben Hogan, Bobby Locke, Peter Thomson, Arnold Palmer, Gary Player, Jack Nicklaus, Lee Trevino, Tom Watson, Severiano Ballesteros.

1993. Appel, Martin, and Goldblatt, Burt. *Baseball's Best: The Hall of Fame Gallery.* Rev. ed. New York: McGraw-Hill, 1980. 439 p. Illustrated. ***

1994. Bartlett, Roland W. *The Fans Vote!: 100 Baseball Superstars.* Palm Springs, CA: ETC Publications, 1983. 239 p. Illustrated. Bibliography. Index. Paperbound.

Two panels, each consisting of twenty enthusiastic baseball fans, selected those players believed to be the greatest of all time. Subtitle to the contrary, the book presents brief biographies of eighty-three, and extensive biographies of forty-one players. Of the latter group, thirty-two are Hall of Fame members as of 1982.

1995. Benyo, Richard. *The Masters of the Marathon.* Introduction by Erich Segal. New York: Atheneum, 1983. 242 p. Illustrated. Bibliography.

After a two-chapter history of the marathon (including that apocryphal story from the battle and defeat of the Persians by the Greeks in 490 B.C., in which a youth, Pheidippides, ran from the plains of Marathon to Athens, and as he expired, shouted, "Nike!," [Victory!]), Benyo writes of fourteen of the modern masters of the famous 26-mile, 385-yard run: Spiridon Loues, Clarence DeMar, Johnny Kelly (The Elder), Jim Peters, Emil Zatopek, Johnny Kelly (The Younger), Abebe Bikila, Derek Clayton, Frank Shorter, Bill Rodgers, Waldemar Chierpinski, Toshihiko Seko, Grete Waitz, and Alberto Salazar.

1996. *Champions of American Sport [Motion Picture].* New York: Modern Talking Picture Service, 1981. 1 film reel, 25 min., sd., col., 16mm.

Summary: Introduces the viewer to some of America's great athletes through interviews and action footage.

1997. Cohen, Scott. *Jocks.* New York: Simon and Schuster, 1983. 92 p. Illustrated. Paperbound.

This is a chiefly illustrated work containing one-page profiles of famous athletes including: Kent Hrbek, Eric Heiden, John McEnroe, Ricky Davis, Guillermo Vilas, Brian Goodell, Kevin McHale, Phil and Steve Mahre, John Elway, Wayne Gretzky, Steve Garvey, Reggie Jackson, "Sugar Ray" Leonard, and Bjorn Borg.

1998. *The Combat Sport: Boxing Yesterday and Today* *[Motion Picture.]* Community Film Group, 1988? 1 film reel, sd., col.

Summary: Interwoven with scenes of training gymnasiums and actual bouts are interviews with a number of world champions and boxing notables including "Marvelous Marvin" Hagler, "Sugar Ray" Leonard, Jake La Motta, Ray "Boom Boom" Mancini, Ingemar Johansson, Jose Torres, and Angelo Dundee.

1999. *Days of the Champions [Motion Picture].* Geneva, Switzerland: Montres Rolex; Trans World International, 1974. 22 min., sd., col., 16mm.

Summary: The lifestyles of Arnold Palmer, Jean Claude Killy, and Jackie Stewart, three prominent athletes competing on an international level in three markedly dissimilar sports, are examined in this film released by J. Walter Thompson Company.

2000. Dickey, Glenn. *The History of American League Baseball, since 1901.* Introduction by Reggie Jackson. New York: Stein and Day, Scarborough Book, 1982. 325 p. Table. Bibliography. Index. Paperbound.

See annotation below.

2001. Dickey, Glenn. *The History of National League Baseball, since 1876 (Updated).* New York: Stein and Day, 1982. 312 p. Illustrated. Bibliography. Index.

Dickey's two histories of the professional baseball big leagues concentrate on teams, events, and people. Although somewhat uneven in coverage, their particular strength seems to lie in the latter category. Access to the biographical information is through a personal name index.

2002. Dickey, Glenn. *The History of Professional Basketball since 1876.* Introduction by Earvin (Magic) Johnson. New York: Stein and Day, 1982. 319 p. Illustrated. Table. Bibliography. Index.

Covers the players, teams and coaches for the more than eighty years since the formation of the old National Basketball League. Jumping Joe Fulks, George Mikan, Bob Cousy, Bill Russell, Wilt Chamberlain, Jerry West, Bill Walton, Kareem Abdul-Jabbar, Larry Bird, Magic Johnson, John Havlicek, Dick Motta, Red Auerbach, and Lenny Wilkins are some of the men featured in the book.

2003. Frayne, Trent. *Famous Women Tennis Players.* New York: Dodd, Mead, 1979. 223 p. Illustrated. Index.

This book is the "mixed doubles partner" of Frayne's *Famous Tennis Players,* New York: Dodd, Mead, 1977. In it he spotlights the tennis careers of twelve women champions (Martina Navratilova, Chris Evert, Billie Jean King, Evonne Goolagong, Virginia Wade, Althea Gibson, Margaret Smith Court, Maureen Connolly, Alice Marble, Helen Jacobs, Helen Wills, and Suzanne Lenglen). Each biographical sketch of about twenty pages is illustrated by an action photograph.

2004. Gallagher, Mark. *50 Years of Yankee All-Stars.* New York: Leisure Press, 1984. 224 p. Illustrated. Paperbound.

"Yankee All-Star players have included Babe Ruth, Lou Gehrig, Joe Di Maggio and Mickey Mantle, players for whom the term "Superstar" may be more fitting." (Introduction.) Career profiles of eighty top New York Yankee players are presented, including statistics and a portrait.

2005. *Going for the Gold: The Story of Black Women in Sports [Motion Picture].* San Francisco: Modern Talking Picture Service, 1983. 1 film reel, 20 min., sd., col., 16mm.

Summary: Interviewer Jayne Kennedy talks to several of the outstanding Black women athletes in the United States, who tell how they had to strive for the success they have achieved.

2006. *Greatest Sports Legends [Videorecording].* Magnetic Video, 1978. 1 videocassette, 60 min., sd., b&w, with color sequences, 1/2 in.

Summary: Paul Hornung interviews Joe Frazier, Jesse Owens, Eddie Arcaro, and Sam Snead. The four also narrate film clips showing their career highlights.

2007. *Great Legends of Baseball [Videorecording]*. Greatest Sports Legends. Magnetic Video, 1978. 1 videocassette, 60 min., sd., b&w, with color sequences, 1/2 in.

Summary: This is a VHS format video containing career highlights and interviews with Ted Williams, Willie Mays, Bob Feller and Joe Di Maggio.

2008. Gutman, Bill. *Baseball's Belters: Jackson, Schmidt, Parker, Brett.* New York: Grosset & Dunlap, Tempo, 1981. 210 p. Table. Paperbound.

Four of baseball's current heavy hitters are scrutinized in career biographies emphasizing pivotal games played. Statistical tables, arranged by year, conclude the book.

2009. Hill, Jimmy. *Great Soccer Stars.* London, New York: Hamlyn, 1978. 176 p. Illustrated.

The author has selected 100 great soccer players (footballers), from all times and all countries. He did not presume to name the 100 greatest. Each sketch is a page or so, giving name, club, country, photograph, and personal and career data. Among the footballers ". . . who have impressed [him] with some particular talent or some particular personality," are: Alan Ball, George Best, Zlatko Cajkowski, Alfredo di Stefano, Garrincha, Nandor Hidegkuti, Josef Masopust, Pele, Luis Suarez, and Dino Zoff.

2010. Hobbs, Michael. *50 Masters of Golf.* Ashbourne, Derbyshire, England: Moorland, 1983. 192 p. Illustrated.

While this work is a survey of great players since the beginning of the sport, Hobbs disclaims that his is a selection of the top fifty of all time. He does, however, acknowledge the preeminence of Harry Vardon, Bobby Jones, Ben Hogan, and Jack Nicklaus. Almost half the entries are of American golfers, with Britain claiming a fair share. The career sketches range from three to seven pages. Each has a photograph.

2011. Holway, John. *Blackball Stars: Negro League Pioneers.* Westport, CT: Meckler Books, 1988. 400 p. Illustrated. Bibliography. ***

2012. Honig, Donald. *Baseball America: The Heroes of the Game and the Times of Their Glory.* New York: Macmillan, 1985. 342 p. Illustrated. Index.

This is a baseball history so rich in its biographical content, made easily accessible through a six-page name index, that it rightly belongs among sport collective biographies. Coverage is from baseball's beginnings into the 1980s.

2013. Honig, Donald. *Mays, Mantle, Snider: A Celebration.* New York: Macmillan; London: Collier Macmillan, 1987. 151 p. Illustrated. Index. ***

2014. Keylin, Arleen, and Cohen, Jonathan, eds. *The New York Times Sports Hall of Fame.* Introduction by Gerald Eskenazi. New York: Arno Press, 1981. 184 p. Illustrated. Bibliography.

This is another Arno Press collection of *New York Times* obituaries. The quality of reproduction from the microfilm originals is sometimes poor, although the publisher states that ". . . in many cases new type has been set to assure legibility." Almost 100 athletes from a number of sports are included.

2015. Lamb, Kevin. *Football Stars, 1985.* Chicago: Contemporary Books, 1985. 120 p. Illustrated. Paperbound.

Forty National Football League stars "still fighting for their jobs whether they have to or not." (Introduction.) Each of the twenty-eight teams is represented, leaving only twelve at-large openings. A selection of Lamb's choices: Marcus Allen, Kenny Easley, John Elway, Mark Gastineau, Dave Krieg, Steve Largent,

Dan Marino, Walter Payton, Lee Roy Selmon, and Kellen Winslow.

2016. Leifer, Neil. *Neil Leifer's Sports Stars.* Text by Peter Bonventre. Foreword by Roone Arledge. Garden City, NY: Doubleday, Dolphin, 1985. 255 p. Illustrated.

The color photographs which fill most of this book constitute a Leifer pictorial sports Hall of Fame. Bonventre's one-page anecdotal narratives accompany the photographs. There are sixty-two stars profiled, most of them from the United States. They include: Steve Cauthen, Martina Navratilova, Carl Lewis, Debbie Armstrong, Kareem Abdul-Jabbar, Valerie Brisco-Hooks, Muhammad Ali, Dorothy Hamill, Nate Archibald, and Mary Lou Retton.

2017. Linn, Ed. *Steinbrenner's Yankees.* New York: Holt, Rinehart and Winston, Owl, 1982. 322 p.

". . . An intimate, interwoven group portrait of the most colorful, most successful, and most tormented ballclub in history . . .," featuring George Steinbrenner III, with major support from Reggie Jackson and Billy Martin. The action takes place during the first years of baseball free agency.

2018. McIlvanney, Hugh. *McIlvanney on Boxing: An Anthology.* New York: Beaufort Books, 1982. 190 p. Illustrated.

Most of the pieces in this four-part fight anthology originally appeared in *The Observer.* Many are about Muhammad Ali. And while a majority of the essays are about particular fights, all have biographical content. Besides Ali, there is material on Joe Frazier, George Foreman, Ken Norton, Henry Cooper, Carlos Ortiz, "Sugar Ray" Leonard, Thomas Hearns, Larry Holmes, Leon Spinks, and a number of others.

2019. Masterson, Dave, and Boyle, Timm. *Baseball's Best: The MVPs.* Chicago: Contemporary Books, 1985. 359 p. Illustrated. Index. Paperbound.

Ranking next to election to its Hall of Fame, the Most Valuable Player award is baseball's most coveted honor. This work covers fifty-three years of MVP awards in both major leagues—from Lefty Grove and Frankie Frisch in 1931, to Ryne Sandberg and Willie Hernandez in 1984. Three-page profiles include lifetime statistics, career and personal biographical information, and a photograph.

2020. Moore, Kenny. *Best Efforts: World Class Runners and Races.* Garden City, NY: Doubleday, 1982. 286 p.

A first person narrative with significant biographical content, Moore begins with anecdotes and observations about the participating runners, the bloody terrorist attack, and other incidents before and during the 1972 Munich Olympics. Following this beginning, chapters are devoted to individual running greats: Ron Clarke, John Akii-Bua, Roger Bannister, Steve Prefontaine, Filbert Bayi, John Walker, Lasse Viren, Bill Rodgers, Mary Decker, Henry Rono, Grete Waitz, Eamonn Coghlan, and Sebastian Coe.

2021. *The NFL's Inspirational Men and Moments [Videorecording].* Mt. Laurel, NJ: NFL Films Video, 1980. 1 videocassette, 52 min., sd., col., 1/2 in., Beta or VHS.

Summary: A collection of football shorts, ranging from a verse rendition of Super Bowl III to a retrospective on Quarterback Roger Staubach and accounts of the achievements of outstanding football teams and personalities. Contents: Joe and the Magic Bean; Don't Quit; Roger Staubach, All-American Hero; Ballad of a Team; If; Images; They Said It Couldn't Be Done; and, Symbiosis.

2022. Pachter, Marc, et al. *Champions of American Sport.* Foreword by Red Smith. Washington, DC: National Portrait Gallery; New York: Abrams, 1981. 288 p. Illustrated.

This is the catalog of a 1981 exhibition held at the National Portrait Gallery, Smithsonian Institution. It is not intended to be an ultimate list of 100 sports heroes and heroines, but to suggest an overview. The biographical sketches average about a page, however, it is the illustrated matter—black and white and color portraits, and action photographs, archival photographs, and reproductions of artistic renderings—which constitutes the focus of this work.

2023. Riger, Robert. *The Athlete: An Original Collection of 25 Years of Work*. Prologue by Jim McKay. New York: Simon and Schuster, 1980. 239 p. Illustrated.

Through his work with ABC Sports and *Sports Illustrated*, Riger has photographed, made drawings, and interviewed many athletes in every sport. While the illustrative matter forms the core of his work, there is significant career biographical material in the interviews he has conducted with sports greats: Eddie Arcaro, Jim Brown, Jack Nicklaus, Billie Jean King, Jim Clark, Billy Kidd, Peggy Fleming, Branch Rickey, Vince Lombardi, Muhammad Ali, Pele, Gordie Howe, and Nancy Lopez. Other parts of the book address the craft of sports photo-journalism and the technical aspects of television sports coverage.

2024. Ritter, Lawrence, and Honig, Donald. *The 100 Greatest Baseball Players of All Time*. Rev. ed. New York: Crown Publishers, 1986. 273 p. Illustrated. Index.

Players whose careers flourished after 1900 were considered for inclusion. They are listed in "more or less random sequence." The essays focus entirely on baseball achievements, ranging in length from Babe Ruth's or Joe Di Maggio's eight pages (including photographs) to those of two pages for Ed Walsh, Hank Aaron, Steve Carlton, Addie Joss, and others. There are an index and a listing of players by position.

2025. Roebuck, Nigel. *Grand Prix Greats: A Personal Appreciation of 25 Famous Formula 1 Drivers*. Foreword by Murray Walker. Wellingborough, England: P. Stephens, 1986. 216 p. Illustrated.

While there are a number of world champions represented among the drivers profiled in this book, some of lesser renown are included simply because Roebuck found them to be fascinating personalities both in and out of a race car—in keeping with his intention to write personal, anecdotal profiles. Each piece is about seven pages with several more of photographs, plus a full-page color portrait painted by Craig Warwick. Among the best-known drivers are: Mario Andretti, Jimmy Clark, Juan Manuel Fangio, Niki Lauda, Stirling Moss, Jochen Rindt, Pedro Rodriguez, and Jackie Stewart.

2026. Seitz, Nick. *Superstars of Golf.* Swing Studies by Bob Toski. Norwalk, CT: Golf Digest, 1978. 192 p. Illustrated. Table.

Ten golfers, all members of the million-dollar club, and winners of one or more of the four major championships, have been selected for inclusion in this collective biography. Sketches average eighteen pages of personal data, and contain analyses of playing technique, and "off-course" illustrations. The superstars: Lee Trevino, Hale Irwin, Tom Watson, Raymond Floyd, Arnold Palmer, Johnny Miller, Al Geiberger, Jack Nicklaus, Gary Player, and Tom Weiskopf.

2027. Soar, Phil, and Tyler, Martin. *Soccer: The World Game.* New York: St. Martin's Press, 1978. 184 p. Illustrated. Index.

Primarily a history of the game, there are also biographical profiles, each several pages long, on nineteen of the world's elite players: Gordon Banks, Franz Beckenbauer, George Best, Bobby Charlton, Giorgio Chinaglia, Charlie Cooke, Johan Cruyff, Alfredo di Stefano, Eusebio, Geoff Hurst, Kevin Keegan, Stanley Matthews, Rinus Michels, Bobby Moore, Gerd Muller, Pele, Ferenc Puskas, Kyle Rote Jr., and Helmut Schoen.

2028. Westcott, Rich. *Diamond Greats: Profiles and Interviews with 65 of Baseball's History Makers.* Westport, CT: Meckler Books, 1988. 389 p. Illustrated.

This necessarily opinionated work representing Westcott's choices for all-time best baseball players is easily capable of starting as many sports tavern arguments as it settles. Hall of Famers, The Old Guard, Most Valuable Players,

Men of Special Distinction, Home Run Kings, Batting Champs, RBI Leaders, Pitchers of Excellence, and Solid Performers, are the categories by which the book is arranged. Each sketch is about five pages long.

Chapter 28
Periodicals

2029. *Baseball Digest.* Evanston, IL: Century Publishing, vol. 1-, 1942-. (Monthly)

Stories focusing on aspects of players' careers are emphasized. One recent issue examined has an article previewing the best pitchers for 1988: Roger Clemens and Jack Morris for the AL; Rick Reuschel and Rick Sutcliffe for the NL. Indexed by: *Sports Periodicals Index.*

2030. *Baseball Illustrated.* New York: Lexington Library, vol. 1-, 1964?-. (Annual)

Features on professional players and teams.

2031. *Baseball Scene.* Palisades, NY: Tiger Press, vol. 1-, 1987?-. (9 issues yearly)

Yet another illustrated fan magazine covering America's Favorite Pastime, *Baseball Scene* enlivens its pages with superstar features like those in the March, 1988 issue on Andre Dawson and Mark McGwire.

2032. *Baseball Stars.* New York: 36th St. Publishing, vol. 1-, 1986?-. (Annual)

The 1987 issue examined contains thirty illustrated biographical sketches of players from both major leagues.

2033. *Basketball Digest.* Evanston, IL: Century Publishing, vol.
1-, 1973-. (Monthly)

Features teams and players, past and present. Similar in
content to *Baseball Digest* (above), and *Hockey Digest* (below).
Indexed by: *Sports Periodicals Index.*

2034. *Basketball Weekly.* Detroit, MI: Football News Co., vol.
1-, 1967-. (Weekly)

Coverage of all aspects of basketball: current stories on
teams and personalities, regular columns of basketball
comment, statistics, scores, schedules, and analysis.

2035. *Football Digest.* Evanston, IL: Century Publishing, vol.
1-, 1971-. (10 issues yearly)

With similar content and format as *Hockey Digest*
(below), this magazine covers the game, teams, and players—
present and past. Indexed by: *Sports Periodicals Index,
Sportsearch.*

2036. *Football Forecast.* Baltimore, MD: Baltimore Bulletin,
Inc., vol. 1-, 1978-. (21 issues yearly)

Interviews/profiles of players and coaches in "big-time
football," e.g., University of Southern California; Chicago Bears.

2037. *Football News.* Detroit, MI: Football News, vol. 1-,
1939-. (20 issues yearly)

Contains articles on players, officials, and coaches, past
and present.

2038. *Goal: The National Hockey League Magazine.* New
York: National Hockey League Services, 1980?-. (7 issues
yearly)

Goal is the official publication of the major North
American professional hockey association. Occasional
biographical pieces can be found interspersed with league
news.

2039. *Golf Digest.* Norwalk, CT: Golf Digest, vol. 1-, 1950-. (Monthly)

Title varies: *Arrowhead Golf Digest* (Spring, 1950). Similar in content and intended audience to *Golf Magazine* (below). In-depth profiles of golfers. Indexed (some selectively) by: *Physical Education Index, Sports Periodicals Index, Magazine Article Summaries.*

2040. *Golf Magazine.* New York: Times Mirror Magazines, vol. 1-, 1959-. (Monthly)

Running title: *Golf.* Similar in content and intended audience to *Golf Digest* (above). Contains profiles of people in golf. Indexed (some selectively) by: *Access, Magazine Index, Magazine Article Summaries, Physical Education Index, Sports Periodicals Index.*

2041. *Golf World.* Southern Pines, NC: Golf World, Inc., vol. 1-, 1947-. (43 issues yearly)

A publication similar in content and readership (but not circulation) to *Golf Magazine,* and *Golf Digest* (above). Indexed by: *Sports Periodicals Index.*

2042. *Hockey.* Norwalk, CT: Golf Digest, vol. 1-, 1975-. (8 issues yearly)

Almost every issue has articles with career biographical information on the players and others associated with the game.

2043. *Hockey Digest.* Evanston, IL: Century Publishing, vol. 1-, 1972-. (8 issues yearly)

With similar content and format as *Football Digest* (above), this magazine gives in-depth treatment of teams, players, and all aspects of professional hockey. Indexed by *Sports Periodicals Index.*

2044. *The Hockey News.* New York: Whitney Communications, vol. 1-, 1947-. (Weekly)

During the hockey season, frequency is weekly, becoming monthly in June, then bimonthly July and September. Coverage of junior hockey through the professional leagues. Indexed in: *Sport and Fitness Index.*

2045. *Hoop.* New York: Professional Sports Publications, vol. 11-, 1984-. (8 issues yearly)

Continues: *NBA Today: Official League Newspaper* (1981-1984). Cover-to-cover news, features, and statistics of the NBA and CBA.

2046. *Inside Sports.* Evanston, IL: Inside Sports, Inc., vol. 1-, 1979-. (Monthly)

Publication intermittent between Nov. 1979 and Sept. 1983. *Inside Sports* is a *Sports Illustrated* clone which features in-depth profiles and interviews of sports personalities. Indexed by: *Sports Periodicals Index, Access.*

2047. *Pro Football Weekly.* Northbrook, IL: Football World, Inc., vol. 1-, 1968-. (Weekly)

Publishes thirty issues each year (on a weekly basis during football season). Has supplements: *Pro Football Weekly's Football Almanac,* and *Draft Update.* Covers the game with features and statistics on teams and players.

2048. *The Ring.* New York: The Ring, vol. 1-, 1922-. (Monthly)

Ring is the perennial bible of boxing containing news, statistics, and feature articles. Indexed by: *Sports Periodicals Index.*

2049. *Score: Canada's Golf Magazine.* Toronto: Controlled Media Communications, no. 1-, 1981-. (Quarterly)

Found interspersed among other golf articles, are interviews or profiles of prominent PGA or LPGA professionals.

2050. *Sport.* New York: MVP Sports, Inc., vol. 1-, 1946-. (Monthly)

An all-sports fan magazine comparable to *Sports Illustrated*, below. Illustrated feature stories on all aspects of college and professional sports, and interviews with the participants are standard fare. Indexed (some selectively) by: *Magazine Index, Magazine Article Summaries, Sports Periodicals Index, Readers' Guide to Periodical Literature.*

2051. *The Sporting News.* St. Louis, MO: Sporting News, vol. 1-, 1886-. (Weekly)

Subtitle: "The nation's oldest and finest sports publication." Contains timely news and feature coverage, including biographical material on athletes, in a tabloid format. Indexed by: *Magazine Index, Access, Sports Periodicals Index.*

2052. *Sports Illustrated.* Los Angeles: Time Inc., vol. 1-, 1954-. (53 issues yearly)

Articles in this popular magazine deal with the totality of the sports scene—from women's bathing attire to franchise litigation. Biographical pieces have a clear sporting connection, or are about some sports person. Indexed (some selectively) by: *Biography Index, Magazine Index, Abridged Readers' Guide to Periodical Literature, Readers' Guide to Periodical Literature, Magazine Article Summaries, Book Review Index.*

2053. *Stock Car Racing.* Alexandria, VA: Lopez Publications, vol. 1-, 1966?-. (Monthly)

Other title: *Stock Car Racing Magazine.* Required reading for students and practitioners of closed wheel oval track racing in America, this magazine contains all the relevant news, plus features on the drivers.

2054. *Tennis.* Norwalk, CT: Tennis Features, vol. 1-, 1965-. (Monthly)

"Official monthly publication of the United States Professional Tennis Association." Featured are articles and news, international in scope, concerning the game and its players. Indexed by: *Magazine Article Summaries, Sports Periodicals Index.*

2055. *Tennis U. S. A.* Radnor, PA: Chilton Publications, vol. 1-, 1979-. (Monthly)

This is the official publication of the United States Lawn Tennis Association. Supersedes: *Official USLTA News* (1928?-1979). As does its more youthful competitor, *Tennis*, above, this periodical contains interviews, features, and news. Indexed by: *Magazine Article Summaries, Sports Periodicals Index.*

2056. *Track & Field News.* Los Altos, CA: Track & Field News, Inc., vol. 1-, 1948-. (Monthly)

The single, most important periodical in its field, it covers the sport thoroughly, amateur and professional, high school level to the Olympics. Contains interviews and profiles of the athletes. Indexed by: *Sports Periodicals Index.*

2057. *Women's Sports and Fitness.* Palo Alto, CA: Women's Sports Publications, vol. 6-, 1984-. (11 issues yearly)

Continues: *Women's Sports* (1979-1984). This is a publication of the Women's Sports Foundation with profile/interview, how-to, historic, personal experience, travel, new product, and review articles. Indexed by: *Magazine Index, Sports Periodicals Index, Physical Education Index.*

Chapter 29
Computerized Databases

2058. *Dow Jones News/Retrieval Sports Report* Princeton, NJ: Dow Jones.

Subject: sports news. Contents: full-text news stories and statistics on professional and amateur sports. Coverage: the file began in 1981 and is continuously updated. Address: P.O. Box 300, Princeton, NJ 08543-0300. Telephone: (609) 452-2000.

2059. *SIRLS Data Base.* Waterloo, ON, Canada: University of Waterloo, Faculty of Human Kinetics and Leisure Studies.

Subject: sociology of leisure and sport. Contents: international coverage of journals, conference proceedings, unpublished papers, theses, monographs, and government publications. Coverage: 1963-1979. 16,000 references with abstracts. Corresponding print source: *Sociology of Leisure and Sport Abstracts.* Address: University of Waterloo, Waterloo, ON N2L 3G1 Canada. Telephone: (519) 885-1211.

2060. *Sport Database.* Ottawa, ON, Canada: Sport Information Resource Centre.

Subjects: sports; sports medicine; physical education; sports facilities; sport history. Contents: full coverage, with a North American concentration, of all aspects of sports— approximately 200,000 records. Coverage: 1949- (monographic material only). Updated every month. Corresponding print source: *Sport and Fitness Index.* Address:

449

333 River Rd., Ottawa, ON K1L 8H9 Canada. Telephone: (613) 748-5658.

2061. *Telesports.* Dallas, TX: Telesports, Inc. ***

Subject: current, full text information on sports, including league, team, and individual statistics. Address: 8547 Manderville Ln., Dallas, TX 75231. Telephone: (214) 692-8787.

Chapter 30
Organizations

2062. AMERICAN ALLIANCE FOR HEALTH, PHYSICAL EDUCATION, RECREATION AND DANCE—ARCHIVES

1900 Association Dr.
Reston, VA 22091
(703) 476-3423

Holdings: maintains biographical archives. Services: on-site use by prior permission. Publications: *Journal of Physical Education, Recreation and Dance*; *Update*; *Health Education*; *Research Quarterly*; *Leisure Today*.

2063. ASSOCIATION OF SPORTS MUSEUMS AND HALLS OF FAME

101 W. Sutton Pl.
Wilmington, DE 19810
(302) 475-7068

Purpose: to support and improve the quality of halls of fame. Holdings: has biographical archives. Maintains a hall of fame and museum. For library information, see 2067, below. Services: public use by appointment. Publications: bimonthly newsletter.

2064. BRITISH COLUMBIA SPORTS HALL OF FAME AND MUSEUM

The Pacific National Exhibition
Hastings at Renfrew

British Columbia Pavilion
Vancouver, BC V5K 4W3
Canada
(604) 253-2311

Purpose and holdings: Showcases British Columbia's sports heritage and sports champions by means of photographs, trophies and medallions, and memorabilia. Serves as the major research center for BC sport. Services: reference assistance; photocopying.

2065. CANADA'S SPORTS HALL OF FAME AND LIBRARY

Exhibition Place
Toronto, ON M6K 3C3
Canada
(416) 595-1046

Goal: To preserve and promote Canadian achievements in sport; to maintain open display and library facilities throughout the year. Holdings: photographs, memorabilia and printed resources; biographical files and photograph files on over 330 Hall of Fame honorees.

2066. CANADIAN GOLF MUSEUM AND LIBRARY

Alymer East, Quebec
Correspondence: 1962 Lauder Dr.
Ottawa, ON K2A 1B1
Canada

Goal: to assemble and maintain items for the collection. Holdings: the library has books dating from 1875, manuscripts, and audio visual materials. Services: reference service is provided for queries by mail or in person.

2067. CITIZENS SAVINGS ATHLETIC FOUNDATION

9800 S. Sepulveda Blvd.
Los Angeles, CA 90045
(213) 670-7550

Objective: to collect, organize, and make accessible a very extensive collection of amateur and professional sports materials (particularly in the area of history), and to serve as the library for the Association of Sports Museums and Halls of Fame (see 2063, above). Holdings: books, periodicals, newspapers, college and university annuals. Services: reference in-house or by mail; on-site use of the collection.

2068. CLEVELAND PUBLIC LIBRARY
    Fine Arts Dept., Mears Baseball Collection
    325 Superior Ave.
    Cleveland, OH 44114
    (216) 623-2848

Purpose: to collect and make available some 2,000 baseball titles (books, magazines, newspapers) dating from 1880. Services: reference for on-site, telephone, and mail inquiries; photocopying; interlibrary loan.

2069. HOCKEY HALL OF FAME AND MUSEUM
    Exhibition Place
    Toronto, ON M6K 3C3
    Canada
    (416) 595-1345

Purpose: "The Hockey Hall of Fame is a shrine to the history and study of hockey." The honored members are selected from three categories: builder, player and referee. Holdings: photographs, books, clippings, artifacts from the late 1800s to the present. As of March, 1987, there have been sixty *HHFM Library Biographies* produced. Services: public use by appointment.

2070. INDIANAPOLIS MOTOR SPEEDWAY HALL OF FAME MUSEUM
    4790 West 16th St.
    Indianapolis, IN 46222
    (317) 248-6747

The Hall contains twenty-five winning race cars and other artifacts. Library holdings: 500 volumes pertaining to automobile racing, passenger cars, and related references. Photos of starting line-up since 1911. Biographical information pertaining to all starting drivers since 1911.

2071. INTERNATIONAL BOXING HALL OF FAME

P.O. Box 425
Canastota, NY 13032
(315) 697-7095

Purpose: to bring honor to outstanding boxers. Holdings: a library of boxing literature and museum artifacts is being assembled. Publication: quarterly newsletter.

2072. INTERNATIONAL TENNIS HALL OF FAME AND TENNIS MUSEUM

194 Bellevue Ave.
Newport, RI 02840
(401) 849-6378/3990

Holdings: tennis histories, biographies, how-to books, serials. There are biography clippings files, scrapbooks and photographs. Services: the library opens by appointment for use by researchers and scholars.

2073. KEENELAND ASSOCIATION LIBRARY

Keeneland Race Course
Box 1690
Lexington, KY 40592
(606) 254-3412

Purpose: "To collect, maintain and provide service to the public through a comprehensive library of thoroughbred horse racing and breeding and horse sports materials." Holdings: 5,500 books, 1,100 bound periodical volumes, and 200,000 photographic negatives of American racing, clippings, and pamphlets. Services: on-site use of collection by the public; reference in-house, or by telephone or mail; photocopying. Guide to the collection: Amelia K. Buckley, *The Keeneland Association Library: Guide to the Collection.* Lexington: University of Kentucky Press, 1958.

2074. NAISMITH MEMORIAL BASKETBALL HALL OF FAME

1150 W. Columbus Ave.
Springfield, MA 01101
(413) 781-6500

Purpose: to promote basketball, and preserve its artifacts and memorabilia. Holdings: books on coaching, administration, and rules, and an extensive photograph collection. Services: the library may be used after prior appointment. Publication: a quarterly newsletter.

2075. NATIONAL ASSOCIATION FOR GIRLS & WOMEN IN SPORT (See: AMERICAN ALLIANCE FOR HEALTH PHYSICAL EDUCATION RECREATION AND DANCE, above.)

2076. NATIONAL ASSOCIATION FOR STOCK CAR AUTO RACING

1801 Speedway Blvd.
Daytona Beach, FL 32015
(904) 253-6713

Holdings: 100,000 photographs of stock car racing in the United States. Services: mail or telephone requests accepted from researches; photographic reproduction service.

2077. NATIONAL BASEBALL HALL OF FAME, MUSEUM AND LIBRARY

Main St.
Cooperstown, NY 13326
(607) 547-9988

Goal: to support the service objectives of the Hall of Fame and Museum. Holdings: some 5,000 books, periodicals, A-V materials, clippings and photographs files. The official records of the major leagues are here. Services: in-house use of collection; reference; photocopying.

2078. NATIONAL BASKETBALL ASSOCIATION

645 Fifth Ave.
New York, NY 10022
(212) 826-7000

Purpose: to promote professional basketball, and supervise franchises in the NBA. Holdings: Photographic archive of team action. Services: referral to franchise teams for team and personality photographs.

2079. NATIONAL FOOTBALL FOUNDATION
    1865 Palmer Ave.
    Larchmont, NY 10538
    (914) 834-0474

Purpose: to promote secondary school and college football; research the sport's history and biography; honor the outstanding players and coaches of the college game by selection to the Hall of Fame (see: National Football Foundation's College Football Hall of Fame, below). Holdings: 1,200-volume library. Services: on-site use by prior application. Publication: bimonthly newsletter.

2080. NATIONAL FOOTBALL FOUNDATION'S COLLEGE FOOTBALL HALL OF FAME
    Kings Island Dr.
    Kings Island, OH 45034
    (513) 241-5410

Purpose: to honor players and coaches of college football through a hall of fame. Library holdings: biographical information on the honorees; archives; manuscripts; film loan library. Services: on-site use by prior application.

2081. NATIONAL FOOTBALL LEAGUE
    410 Park Ave.
    New York, NY 10022
    (212) 758-1500

Purpose: overall administration of twenty-eight NFL professional football member teams. Publication: *Record Fact Book.*

2082. NATIONAL HOCKEY LEAGUE
    1155 Metcalfe St., No. 960
    Montreal, PQ H3B 2W2
    Canada
    (514) 871-9220

Purpose: to promote professional hockey, and operate franchises in the NHL. Publication: *Goal*.

2083. NATIONAL MUSEUM OF RACING

Union Ave.
Saratoga Springs, NY 12866
(518) 584-0400

Purpose: To promote thoroughbred racing and honor its outstanding people and horses. Collection: art works, trophies, racing silks, information on the sport. Services: inquire regarding research services.

2084. NEDERLANDSE SPORT FEDERATIE

P.O. Box 80555
The Hague
Netherlands
(Tel.) 31-070-632963

Purpose: to collect and supply sports literature and information for serious study. Holdings: 2,000 books, 1,000 periodicals, photograph file, and a special collection of around 3,000 Dutch and international athlete biographies. Services: photograph duplication.

2085. NORTH AMERICAN SOCIETY FOR SPORT HISTORY

101 White Hall
Penn State University
University Park, PA 16802
(814) 865-7591

Purpose: to encourage the study of sport history. Holdings: archives open to users by prior approval. Publications: *Journal of Sport History*; newsletter.

2086. PGA/WORLD GOLF HALL OF FAME

Gerald R. Ford Blvd.
P.O. Box 1908
Pinehurst, NC 28374
(919) 295-6651

Purpose: to promote this worldwide sport by honoring its great participants. Holdings: a modest library of golf books; archives containing biographies of inductees; tournament records. The Hall displays a wide assortment of golfing memorabilia. Services: this facility is new; inquire about services.

2087. PROFESSIONAL GOLFER'S ASSOCIATION OF AMERICA, LIBRARY

100 Ave. of the Champions
Palm Beach Gardens, FL 33410
(303) 626-3600

Goal: to promote an interest in golf literature by providing the most complete research library in the field (use by permission). Holdings: Scottish records from the 1500s, periodicals, clippings file, and 16,000 golf books including many biographical sources. Services: on-site use by permission; reference.

2088. PRO FOOTBALL HALL OF FAME

2121 George Halas Dr. N.W.
Canton, OH 44708
(216) 456-8207

Purpose: accommodate the needs of the Hall staff and other researchers and writers (by appointment, or via correspondence). Holdings: 5,500 game programs, 1,000 team media guides, 575 periodicals, 1575 book volumes, 17,000 photographs, and 80 file drawers of clippings. Specific biographical information includes files on over 5,000 former players with emphasis on the 135 current Hall enshrinees. Services: reference; photocopying.

2089. RACQUET AND TENNIS CLUB LIBRARY

370 Park Ave.
New York, NY 10022
(212) 753-9700

Goal: to assemble and make available to researchers a specialized tennis collection. Holdings: 16,500 books, and 45 periodical titles. Services: on-site use by qualified individuals; mail or telephone inquiries; reference; photocopying. Publications: collection catalog.

2090. SAN DIEGO HALL OF CHAMPIONS
   1649 El Prado
   Balboa Park
   San Diego, CA 92101
   (619) 234-2544

Purpose: to operate a museum and hall of fame displaying items honoring champions in all sports. Library holdings: books, periodicals, films, audio and video tapes. Services: on-site use by prior application. Publication: quarterly newsletter.

2091. SPORT INFORMATION RESOURCE CENTRE (SIRC)
   333 River Rd.
   Ottawa, ON K1L 8B9
   Canada
   (613) 746-5357

Purpose: to collect and make available periodicals and selected monographs in the fields of sport, physical education and recreation. Holdings: over 14,000 books, 1,000 journals, and 60,000 articles in the field. Services: reference (including computerized searching of the SIRC database); on-site use of the materials. Publications: *Sport and Fitness Index*, and *Sport Bibliography*.

2092. STOCK CAR HALL OF FAME
   Highway 34
   Box 500
   Darlington, SC 29532
   (803) 393-2103

Purpose: to operate the Stock Car Hall of Fame, and the Joe Weatherly Museum. Collection: cars, engines, and car parts; photographs; trophies; biography and memorabilia of the drivers honored in the Hall.

2093. TORONTO METROPOLITAN LIBRARY

Science and Technology Dept.
789 Yonge St.
Toronto, ON M4W 2G8
Canada
(416) 928-5296

Purpose: to collect and make available materials on sports (emphasis on Canadian items). Holdings: clippings files, pamphlets, books, periodicals, and over 1,200 biographical files on Canadian sports figures. Services: on-site, telephone and mail reference queries; in-house use of collection; (limited) interlibrary loan; photocopying.

2094. UNITED STATES GOLF ASSOCIATION

Golf House
Far Hills, NJ 07931
(201) 234-2300

Purpose: to serve as a governing body for golf in the United States. Library holdings: over 8,000 volumes and an archive of around 10,000 pictures. The USGA also administers Golf House Museum, housing a large collection of memorabilia. Publication: *Golf Journal*.

2095. UNITED STATES HOCKEY HALL OF FAME

Hat Trick Ave.
Box 657
Eveleth, MN 55734
(218) 744-5167

Purpose: to honor U.S. hockey champions. Library collection: biographies of the Hall honorees, magazines, programs, newspapers. Services: on-site use of materials by prior application. Publication: enshrinee biography booklet.

2096. UNITED STATES TENNIS ASSOCIATION

Education and Research Center
729 Alexander Rd.
Princeton, NJ 08540
(609) 452-2580

Goal: serve the information requirements of players, educators, researchers and enthusiasts; publish the results of Center investigations. Holdings: large collection of films. Services: film rentals; mail and telephone reference. Publications: annual film list; over 60 USTA items are currently in print.

2097. UNIVERSITY OF ILLINOIS

Applied Life Studies Library
146 Main Library
Urbana, IL 61801
(217) 333-3615

Holdings: large collection of books and periodicals on physical education, and general materials on sport, including biographies of athletes. Services: on-site use by public; reference; interlibrary loan; photocopying. Publication: collection catalog.

2098. UNIVERSITY OF MONTREAL

Physical Education Library
C. P. 6128, Succursale A
Montreal, PQ H3C 3J7
Canada
(514) 343-6765

Holdings: strong collection (28,000 items, primarily in English and French) in physical education, sport history and biography, recreation, leisure, and sport sciences. Services: in-house use of collection by the public; reference; interlibrary loan; photocopying.

2099. UNIVERSITY OF NOTRE DAME LIBRARIES

International Sports and Games Research Collection
Notre Dame, IN 46556
(219) 283-6506

Goal: to collect and provide access to printed materials and memorabilia concerning the history and biography of sport and physical education. Holdings: 20,000 books, 1,000 journals, and 250,000 programs and other file items including photographs. Services: on-site use of collection; reference; interlibrary loan; photocopying.

2100. UNIVERSITY OF WATERLOO
    Faculty of Human Kinetics and Leisure Studies
    SIRLS, an Information Retrieval System for the Sociology
    of Leisure and Sport
    Waterloo, ON N2L 3G1
    Canada
    (519) 885-1211 ext. 2560

Goal: to collect and provide bibliographical access (including access via computer) to materials treating the social sciences aspects of sport and leisure. Holdings: books, articles, reports, documents and theses. Services: in-house collection use by the public; reference assistance for on-site, mail and telephone inquiries (including on-demand searches of the SIRLS database); photocopying. Publication: *Sociology of Leisure and Sports Abstracts.* 1979-. (quarterly).

2101. WOMEN'S SPORTS FOUNDATION
    342 Madison Ave., Suite 728
    New York, NY 10173
    (212) 972-9170 (800) 227-3988

Goal: to provide information, opportunities and the means for women of all ages to develop skills in the sport of their choice and so provide them with the benefits of a physically active lifestyle. Library holdings: a small library containing books, periodicals, vertical files, photographs, slides, and other significata about women's sports (including biographical materials on athletes, coaches, officials, etc.). Some memorabilia on well known individuals, and Hall of Fame information on inductees. Services: in-house use of materials; reference assistance.

Chapter 31
Commercial Sources and Services

2102. ABRAMS, HARVEY (Bookstore)

P.O. Box 732
State College, PA 16801

For sale: mail order sports books.

2103. ALL SPORT PHOTOGRAPHIC (Collector Source)

All Sport House
55-57 Martin Way
Morden, Surrey
England
(Tel.) 01 543 0988

For sale: photographs of international sporting personalities.

2104. ARTHUR, S. E. (Service)

4 Ty Brith Gardens, Usk
Gwent NP51BY
England
(Tel.) 029 13 3368

For sale: mail order golf books.

2105. AUSTIN BOOK SHOP (Bookstore, Service)

104-29 Jamaica Ave.
Richmond Hill, NY

Mail: Box 36, Kew Gardens, NY 11415

(718) 441-1199

For sale: baseball books from the earliest days to the present; out-of-print search service.

2106. AUTOBOOKS EAST (Bookstore)

P.O. Box 1

Babylon, NY 11702

For sale: mail order auto racing books.

2107. BADDIEL, SARAH (Service)

43 Kendal Rd., Gladstone Park

London NW10

England

(Tel.) 01 452-7243

For sale: mail order golf books.

2108. BALIOTTI, DANIEL (Collector Source)

45 East 34th St.

New York, NY 10016

(212) 686-4617

For sale: action photographs of professional and amateur sports stars.

2109. BASEBALL BOOKS ONLY (Bookstore, Service)

5672 East Scarlett St.

Tucson, AZ 85711

(602) 747-5394

For sale: baseball; sporting books; out of print book searching.

2110. BIG LEAGUE GAME CO. (Service)

321 E. Superior St.

Duluth, MN 55802

(218) 722-1275

For sale: mail order sports books; out of print book searching.

2111. BOOK MART (Bookstore, Collector Service)
985 Main St.
Brockton, MA 02401
(617) 588-0124
For sale: sports books; memorabilia.

2112. DONOVAN, RICHARD E. (Bookstore)
1904 E. Main St.
Endicott, NY 13760
For sale: golf books.

2113. FINNEY, JACK (Bookstore)
Box 152-F
Indianapolis, IN 46234
(317) 271-9030
For sale: auto racing books.

2114. GOLF BOOKS (Service)
7 Tower Grove
Weybridge, Surrey KT13 9LX
England
(Tel.) 01 686-1080
For sale: mail order golf books.

2115. GRANT BOOKS (Service)
Victoria Square
Droitwich, Worcestershire
England
(Tel.) 029 923 680
For sale: mail order golf books.

2116. HARTLEY, R. A. (Service)
542 Kings Dr.

Wembley, Middlesex HA9 9JD
England
(Tel.) 01 904-6413

For sale: mail order boxing books; boxing biography.

2117. HOFFMAN LANE BOOKS-NICKLAS & PARKER
(Bookstore)

P.O. Box 711
Cooperstown, NY 13326

For sale: mail order golf books.

2118. LE VAN, PHILIP G. (Bookstore)

2443 Liberty St.
Allentown, PA 18104
(215) 432-6147

For sale: golf books.

2119. LITTLE, PAT (Collector Source)

212 South Allen St.
State College, PA 16801
(814) 237-7026

For sale: photographs of big-league college sports,
including superstar coaches.

2120. MARKETING EVALUATIONS, INC. (Service)

P.O. Box 671
Port Washington, NY 11050-9882
(516) 944-8833

For sale: yearly evaluative surveys of the public
popularity of 500-600 active and retired athletes, coaches and
managers.

2121. NFL CREATIVE SERVICES (Collector Source)

10880 Wilshire Blvd.
Los Angeles, CA 90024
(213) 475-0571

For sale: photographs of NFL personalities and games.

2122. PFB PHOTO LIBRARY (Collector Source)
11a Hyde Park Crescent
Leeds LS6 2NW
England
(Tel.) 0532 789869
For sale: photographic archive of international sport.

2123. RAPHAEL, DICK (Collector Source)
189 Friend St.
Boston, MA 02114
(617) 523-4664
For sale: photographs of U.S. sports figures and sports action.

2124. RISING TROUT SPORTING BOOKS (Bookstore)
P.O. Box 1719
Guelph, ON N1H 6Z9
Canada
For sale: mail order sports books.

2125. SPORTS BOOKS ETC. (Bookstore)
7073 Brookfield Plaza
Springfield, VA 22150
(703) 451-1884
For sale: sports books.

2126. SPORTS ILLUSTRATED (Collector Source)
c/o Picture Sales, Room 1919
1271 Avenue of the Americas
New York, NY 10020
(212) 841-3663
For sale: photographs from the archives of *Sports Illustrated*.

2127. SPORTS PRODUCTS, INC., BOOK DEPT. (Service, Collector Source)

412 Main St.
P.O. Box 392
Ridgefield, CT 06877
(203) 438-3055
For sale: mail order sports books; posters.

2128. (E.) TATRO—BOOKS (Bookstore)

60 Goff Rd.
Wethersfield, CT 06109
For sale: baseball books; boxing; golf; Olympic games.

2129. VANASSE, ANNE (Bookstore)

P.O. Box 93
Carversville, PA 18913
For sale: mail order sports books.

Chapter 32
Fan Clubs (FC)

2130. BECKER, BORIS.

Boris Becker FC
c/o Randy Pagel
P.O. Box 1491
Oshkosh, WI 54902-1491

2131. CONNORS, JIMMY.

Jimmy Connors FC
c/o Terry Flasch
8864 62nd Ave. N.
Brooklyn Park, MN 55428

Jimmy Connors FC
c/o Lois Jolson
6864 Selfridge St.
Forest Hills, NY 11375

Chapter 33
Individual Biographies

ABDUL-JABBAR, KAREEM. Spo.

2132. Abdul-Jabbar, Kareem, and Knobler, Peter. *Giant Steps.* Toronto: Bantam, 1983. 324 p. Illustrated.

ALI, MUHAMMAD. Spo.

2133. *The Baddest Daddy in the Whole World [Motion Picture].* New Yorker Films, 1974. 52 min., sd., col., 16mm.

Summary: Explores the life of fighter Muhammad Ali as he prepares for a bout. Examines his rigorous training ritual and provides some insights into his beliefs and ideas about boxing and his personal popularity.

2134. Kaletsky, Richard. *Ali and Me: Through the Ropes.* Introduction by Mel Allen, Nat Loubet, and John F. X. Condon. Bethany, CT: Adrienne Publications, 1982. 88 p. Illustrated. Table. Paperbound.

2135. *Muhammad Ali—Skill, Brains, and Guts! [Motion Picture].* Macmillan Films, 1975. 90 min., col., 16mm.

Summary: This slickly produced biography of Ali reconfirms his power of wit is as strong as his power in the ring. He is the unabashed star of any interview, the fight sequences, and opponent-taunting sequences.

2136. Pacheco, Ferdie. *Fight Doctor.* Introduction by Muhammad Ali. New York: Simon and Schuster, 1977. 237 p. Illustrated.

2137. Walker, Robert. *Muhammad Ali: His Fights in the Ring.* Speldhurst, Kent, Eng.: Midas Books, 1978. 154 p. Illustrated. Table. Index.

ALLEN, MARCUS. Spo.

2138. Cobbs, Chris. *Marcus Allen, Super Raider.* New York: Scholastic, 1984. 122 p. Illustrated. Paperbound.

ANDRETTI, MARIO. Spo.

2139. Engel, Lyle Kenyon. *Mario Andretti, World Driving Champion.* New York: Arco, 1979. 159 p. Illustrated. Index. Paperbound.

ASHE, ARTHUR. Spo.

2140. Ashe, Arthur, and Amdur, Neil. *Off the Court.* New York: New American Library, 1981. 230 p. Illustrated.

2141. *Love, Tennis: Highlighting Players from the United States Indoor Men's Open Tennis Championships [Videorecording].* Maryland Center for Public Broadcasting, 1971? 10 videocassettes. 290 min., sd., col., VHS.
        Summary: Lew Gerrard and Don Candy demonstrate techniques of tennis and comment on slow motion action from

the U.S. Indoor Men's Tennis Championships. Includes interviews with Arthur Ashe, Cliff Richie, and William Riordan.

AUERBACH, ARNOLD (RED). Spo.

2142. Auerbach, Arnold, and Fitzgerald, Joe. *On and Off the Court.* New York: Macmillan; London: Collier Macmillan, 1985. 256 p. Index.

2143. Auerbach, Arnold, and Fitzgerald, Joe. *Red Auerbach: An Autobiography.* Foreword by John Havlicek. New York: Putnam, 1977. 331 p. Illustrated. Index.

BALLESTEROS, SEVERIANO. Spo.

2144. Ballesteros, Severiano, and Doust, Dudley. *Seve: The Young Champion.* Illustrations by Jim McQueen. Foreword by Lee Travino. Norwalk, CT: Golf Digest/Tennis, 1982. 156 p. Illustrated. Table. Index.

BENCH, JOHNNY. Spo.

2145. Bench, Johnny, and Brashler, William. *Catch You Later: The Autobiography of Johnny Bench.* New York: Harper & Row, 1979. 245 p. Illustrated. Index.

2146. *The Tools of Ignorance [Motion Picture].* W & W Films, 1972. 26 min. sd., col., 16 mm.
Summary: Bench discusses his job as catcher for the Cincinnati Reds and explains how catchers have overcome the stigma of the tools of ignorance—an expression referring to the specialized gear worn by catchers.

BIRD, LARRY. Spo.

2147. Smith, L. Virginia. *Larry Bird, from Valley Hick to Boston Celtic.* L.V. Smith, 1982. 179 p. Illustrated. Paperbound.

BORG, BJORN. Spo.

2148. Borg, Bjorn, and Scott, Eugene L. *My Life and Game.* New York: Simon and Schuster, 1980. 184 p. Illustrated.

2149. Borg, Marina. *Love Match: My Life with Bjorn.* New York: Dial Press, 1981. 153 p. Illustrated.

BRADSHAW, TERRY. Spo.

2150. Bradshaw, Terry, and Diles, David. *Terry Bradshaw: Man of Steel.* Preface by Pete Rozelle. Foreword by Roger Staubach. Grand Rapids, MI: Zondervan Publishing House, 1979. 195 p. Illustrated. Tables.

BRETT, GEORGE. Spo.

2151. Garrity, John. *The George Brett Story.* New York: Coward, McCann & Geoghegan, 1981. 248 p. Illustrated.

BRYANT, PAUL (BEAR). Spo. 1/26/83

2152. *'Bama and the Bear.* Salt Lake City, UT: Great American Sports, 1983. 199 p. Illustrated. Paperbound.

2153. Bynum, Mike. *Bryant, the Man, the Myth.* Atlanta, GA: Cross Roads Books, 1979. 191 p. Illustrated. Table.

2154. Bynum, Mike. *High Tide.* Foreword by Steve Sloan. Atlanta, GA: Cross Roads Books, 1978. 193 p. Illustrated.

2155. Bynum, Mike, and Brondfield, Jerry. *We Believe: Bear Bryant's Boys Talk.* College Station, TX: We Believe Trust Fund at the Bank of A&M, 1980. 229 p. Illustrated.

2156. Ford, Tommy. *Bama under Bear: Alabama's Family Tides.* Rev. ed. Foreword by Charley Thornton. Huntsville, AL: Strode Publishers, 1983. 288 p. Illustrated. Table.

2157. Herskowitz, Mickey. *The Legend of Bear Bryant.* New York: McGraw-Hill, 1987. 241 p. Illustrated.

2158. *Remembering Bear.* Written by the Staff of the *Birmingham News.* Indianapolis, IN: News & Features Press, 1983. 110 p. Illustrated. Tables.

CAUTHEN, STEVE. Spo.

2159. Axthelm, Pete. *The Kid.* New York: Viking Press, 1978. 265 p. Illustrated.

CHAMBERLAIN, WILT. Spo.

2160. Libby, Bill. *Goliath: The Wilt Chamberlain Story.* New York: Dodd, Mead, 1977. 248 p. Illustrated.

DAWKINS, DARRYL. Spo.

2161. Dawkins, Darryl, and Wirt, George. *Chocolate Thunder: The in-Your-Face, All-over-the-Place, Death-Defyin',*

Mesmerizin', Slam-Jam Adventures of Double-D. Chicago: Contemporary Books, 1986. 164 p. Illustrated.

DEMPSEY, JACK. Spo. 5/31/83

2162. Dempsey, Jack, and Dempsey, Barbara Piattelli. *Dempsey.* Introduction by Joseph Durso. New York: Harper & Row, 1977. 320 p. Illustrated. Index.

2163. Roberts, Randy. *Jack Dempsey, the Manassa Mauler.* Baton Rouge: Louisiana State University Press, 1979. 310 p. Illustrated. Bibliography. Index.

DICKERSON, ERIC. Spo.

2164. Dickerson, Eric, and Delsohn, Steve. *On the Run.* Chicago: Contemporary Books, 1986. 130 p. Illustrated. Paperbound.

DI MAGGIO, JOE. Spo.

2165. De Gregorio, George. *Joe DiMaggio: An Informal Biography.* New York: Stein and Day, 1981. 269 p. Illustrated. Bibliography. Index.

2166. Kahn, Roger. *Joe & Marilyn: A Memory of Love.* New York: Morrow, 1986. 269 p. Illustrated.

ERVING, JULIUS. Spo.

2167. *Dr. J's Basketball Stuff [Videorecording].* Directed by Ken Ross, Steve Koontz, and Albert Kestnbaum. Livonia,

MI: CBS/Fox Video Sports, 1987. 1 videocassette, 60 min., sd., col., 1/2 in.

Summary: Erving presents ways to improve basic basketball skills. Also shown are film clips from the All Star Weekend held in Seattle in 1987, and the tributes paid to Dr. J on his retirement.

EVERT, CHRIS. Spo.

2168. Lloyd, Chris Evert, and Amdur, Neil. *Chrissie, My Own Story*. New York: Simon and Schuster, 1982. 238 p. Illustrated.

2169. Lloyd, Chris Evert; Lloyd, John; and Thatcher, Carol. *Lloyd on Lloyd*. New York: Beaufort Books, 1986. 206 p. Illustrated.

FLEMING, PEGGY. Spo.

2170. *Peggy Fleming, a Special Performance [Motion Picture]*. New York: ABC Sports, 1981. 1 film reel, 38 min., sd., col., 16mm.

Summary: This segment from ABC's television program, "Wide World of Sports," shows Fleming's ice skating artistry as she performs in a wide variety of moods and settings. Also provides a behind-the-scenes look at the skater.

FLUTE, DOUG. Spo.

2171. Siegel, Barbara, and Siegel, Scott. *Doug Flute*. Avon Superstars. New York: Avon, 1985. 60 p. Illustrated. Table. Paperbound.

FOYT, A. J. Spo.

2172. Engel, Lyle Kenyon. *The Incredible A. J. Foyt.* Rev. ed. New York: Arco, 1977. 187 p. Illustrated. Table.

2173. Foyt, A. J., and Neely, William. *A.J.* New York: Times Books, 1983. 246 p. Illustrated. Table.

GOODEN, DWIGHT. Spo.

2174. Deutsch, Jordan. *Dwight Gooden, Dale Murphy.* Avon Superstars. New York: Avon, 1986. 63 p. Illustrated. Table. Paperbound.

2175. Gooden, Dwight, and Woodley, Richard. *Rookie.* Garden City, NY: Doubleday, 1985. 177 p. Illustrated.

GRAZIANO, ROCKY. Spo.

2176. Graziano, Rocky, and Corsel, Ralph. *Somebody Down Here Likes Me Too.* New York: Stein & Day, 1981. 273 p. Illustrated. Index.

GRETZKY, WAYNE. Spo.

2177. Fischler, Stan. *The Great Gretzky.* New York: Quill, Stuart L. Daniels, 1982. 158 p. Illustrated. Paperbound.

2178. Gretzky, Walter, and Taylor, Jim. *Gretzky: From the Back Yard Rink to the Stanley Cup.* Toronto: McClelland and Stewart, 1984. 281 p. Illustrated. Table.

2179. Jones, Terry. *The Great Gretzky: The Greatest Single Season in Hockey History*. Chicago: Contemporary Books, 1982. 136 p. Illustrated. Table. Paperbound.

2180. *Wayne Gretzky: Hockey My Way [Videorecording]*. Toronto: Ohlmeyer Communications; New York: Coliseum Video, 1986. 1 videocassette, 50 min., sd., col., 1/2 in., VHS.

Credits: Produced by Simon Christopher Drew; directed by Aiken Scherberger; written by Jack Hutchinson; and presented by Wayne Gretzky. Summary: Profile of Gretzky, with tips on playing hockey and clips of several hockey games.

2181. Wilner, Barry. *Wayne Gretzky: Countdown to Immortality*. West Point, NY: Leisure Press, 1982. 232 p. Illustrated. Table. Paperbound.

HAMILL, DOROTHY. Spo.

2182. *Dorothy on Ice [Motion Picture]*. New York: Modern Talking Picture Service, 1976. 1 reel, 5 min., sd., col., 16mm.

Summary: An interview with the Olympic figure skater, intercut with her skating to music.

HAMILTON, SCOTT. Spo.

2183. Steere, Michael. *Scott Hamilton, a Behind-the-Scenes Look at the Life and Competitive Times of America's Favorite Figure Skater: An Unauthorized Biography*. New York: St. Martin's Press, 1985. 347 p. Illustrated. Index.

JABBAR, KAREEM ABDUL. Spo. See: ABDUL-JABBAR, KAREEM. Spo.

JACKSON, REGGIE. Spo.

2184. Allen, Maury. *Mr. October: The Reggie Jackson Story.*
      New York: New American Library, Signet, 1982. 253 p.
      Illustrated. Paperbound.

2185. Allen, Maury. *Reggie Jackson, the Three Million Dollar
      Man.* Photographs by Louis Requena. New York: Harvey
      House, 1978. 62 p. Illustrated.

2186. O'Connor, Dick. *Reggie Jackson: Yankee Superstar.* Rev.
      ed. New York: Scholastic Book Services, 1978. 106 p.
      Illustrated. Table. Paperbound.

2187. Jackson, Reggie. *Reggie Jackson's Scrapbook.* Edited by
      Robert Kraus. New York: Windmill Books, 1978. 120 p.
      Illustrated. Table.

2188. Jackson, Reggie, and Lupica, Mike. *Reggie: The
      Autobiography.* New York: Villard Books, 1984. 332 p.

JENNER, BRUCE. Spo.

2189. Jenner, Bruce, and Finch, Phillip. *Decathlon Challenge:
      Bruce Jenner's Story.* Englewood Cliffs, NJ: Prentice-Hall,
      1977. 213 p. Illustrated.

2190. Jenner, Chrystie, and Wood, Patricia. *I Am Chrystie.*
      Millbrae, CA: Les Femmes, 1977. 187 p. Illustrated.
      Paperbound.

2191. *Ten for Gold [Motion Picture].* Minneapolis, MN:
      Concept Productions, 1978. 1 reel, 29 min., sd., col.,
      16mm.
      Summary: Deals with Olympic decathlon champion
      Jenner's six-year quest for a gold medal. Includes footage of the
      1976 Olympics in Montreal.

JOHNSON, EARVIN (MAGIC). Spo.

2192. Johnson, Earvin, and Levin, Richard. *Magic.* New York: Viking Press, 1983. 231 p. Illustrated.

KING, BILLIE JEAN. Spo.

2193. King, Billie Jean, and Deford, Frank. *Billie Jean.* New York: Viking Press, 1982. 220 p. Illustrated.

KNIGHT, BOBBY. Spo.

2194. Feinstein, John. *A Season on the Brink: A Year with Bob Knight and the Indiana Hoosiers.* Introduction by Al McGuire. New York: Macmillan, 1986. 311 p. Illustrated.

LANDRY, TOM. Spo.

2195. St. John, Bob. *The Man Inside . . . Landry.* Waco, TX: Word Books, 1979. 251 p. Illustrated. Bibliography.

LEONARD, SUGAR RAY. Spo.

2196. Goldstein, Alan. *A Fistful of Sugar.* New York: Coward, McCann & Geoghegan, 1981. Illustrated. Tables.

2197. *Joining Hands Together [Motion Picture].* Washington, DC: United Way, 1983. 1 film reel, 12 min., sd., col., 16mm.

Summary: World welter-weight boxing champion Leonard tells three personal, heartwarming stories.

2198. Toperoff, Sam. *Sugar Ray Leonard & Other Noble Warriors.* New York: McGraw-Hill, 1987. 212 p.

LEWIS, CARL. Spo.

2199. Devaney, John. *Carl!: The Story of an American Hero.* Toronto, New York: Bantam Books, 1984. 127 p. Illustrated. Paperbound.

LLOYD, CHRIS EVERT. Spo. See: EVERT, CHRIS. Spo.

LOPEZ, NANCY. Spo.

2200. Lopez, Nancy, and Schwed, Peter. *The Education of a Woman Golfer.* New York: Simon and Schuster, 1979. 191 p. Illustrated.

2201. *Nancy Lopez, a Winner [Sound Recording].* Waco, TX: SMI International, 1979. 1 sound cassette.

Summary: Lopez delivers an inspirational/biographical message on athletic achievement.

LOUIS, JOE. Spo. 4/12/81

2202. *Joe Louis for All Time [Videorecording].* New York: ABC Video Enterprises, 1984. 2 videocassettes, 89 min., sd., col., 3/4 in., U-matic.

Credits: Directed by Peter Tatum; writer, Budd Schulberg; and, producers, Jack Healy, et al. Summary: A documentary on the life of Louis, heavyweight champion of the world from 1937 to 1949.

2203. *Joe Louis—the Brown Bomber [Motion Picture].* Highlights of History. Anargyros Film Library, 1972. 4 min., si., b&w, super 8mm.

Summary: Shows Louis as he trained, talked to the press, and was drafted into the Army. Includes scenes of Yankee Stadium, people at home listening to the fight on the radio, and Ezzard Charles, the new heavyweight champion.

2204. Louis, Joe; Rust, Edna; and Rust, Art, Jr. *Joe Louis, My Life.* New York: Harcourt Brace Jovanovich, 1978. 277 p. Illustrated. Tables.

2205. Mead, Chris. *Champion: Joe Louis, Black Hero in White America.* New York: Scribner, 1985. 330 p. Illustrated. Index.

McENROE, JOHN. Spo.

2206. Adams, Ian. *John McEnroe: Rebel without Applause.* London: Corgi Books, 1982. 186 p. Illustrated. Paperbound.

2207. Cross, Tania. *McEnroe, the Man with the Rage to Win.* London: Arrow Books, 1982. 155 p. Illustrated. Table. Paperbound.

2208. Evans, Richard, and McEnroe, John. *McEnroe, a Rage for Perfection: A Biography.* New York: Simon and Schuster, 1982. 192 p. Illustrated. Index.

MARINO, DAN. Spo.

2209. Marino, Dan, and Delsohn, Steve. *Marino!* Chicago: Contemporary Books, 1986. 95 p. Illustrated. Paperbound.

MARTIN, BILLY. Spo.

2210. Allen, Maury. *Damn Yankee: The Billy Martin Story.*
New York: Times Books, 1980. 302 p. Illustrated.

2211. Martin, Billy, and Golenbock, Peter. *Number 1.* New
York: Delacorte Press, 1980. 272 p.

2212. Schoor, Gene. *Billy Martin.* Garden City, NY:
Doubleday, 1980. 228 p. Illustrated.

2213. Smith, Norman Lewis. *The Return of Billy the Kid.* New
York: Coward, McCann & Geoghegan, 1977. 213 p.
Illustrated.

MAYS, WILLIE. Spo.

2214. Einstein, Charles. *Willie's Time: A Memoir.* New York:
Lippincott, 1979. 352 p.

2215. Mays, Willie, and Sahadi, Lou. *Say Hey: The
Autobiography of Willie Mays.* New York: Simon and
Schuster, 1988. 286 p. Illustrated. Index. ***

MONTANA, JOE. Spo.

2216. Holmstrom, John. *Dan Marino, Joe Montana.* Avon
Superstars. New York: Avon, 1985. 63 p. Illustrated.
Table. Paperbound.

2217. Montana, Joe, and Raissman, Bob. *Audibles: My Life in
Football.* New York: Morrow, 1986. 205 p. Illustrated.

MUHAMMAD ALI. Spo. See: ALI, MUHAMMAD. Spo.

MURPHY, DALE. Spo.

2218. Murphy, Dale, and Patton, Curtis. *Ask Dale Murphy.* Introduction by Furman Bisher. Chapel Hill, NC; Dallas, TX: Algonquin/Taylor Book, 1987. 102 p. Illustrated. Paperbound.

NAVRATILOVA, MARTINA. Spo.

2219. Navratilova, Martina, and Vecsey, George. *Martina.* New York: Knopf, 1985. 287 p. Illustrated.

NICKLAUS, JACK. Spo.

2220. Argea, Angelo, and Edmondson, Jolee. *The Bear and I: The Story of the World's Most Famous Caddie.* Foreword and commentary by Jack Nicklaus. New York: Atheneum/SMI, 1979. 148 p. Illustrated.

2221. Nicklaus, Jack, and Bowden, Ken. *On and Off the Fairway: A Pictorial Autobiography.* New York: Simon and Schuster, 1978. 255 p. Illustrated.

PALMER, ARNOLD. Spo.

2222. Palmer, Arnold. *Charge! Winning in Life [Sound Recording].* Chicago: Nightingale-Conant, 1984. 6 sound cassettes, analog, accompanying notes.

Contents: The Palmer philosophy; Charging ahead—the competitive drive; Winning in business—Arnie, incorporated; The right stuff—winning ways; Personal lessons from Arnie—a balanced lifestyle; Family and friends—never say die; and, Planning for the future.

PATERNO, JOE. Spo.

2223. Hyman, Mervin D., and White, Gordon S., Jr. *Joe Paterno: Football My Way*. Preface by Joe Paterno. New York: Collier Books; London: Collier Macmillan, 1978. 309 p. Illustrated. Table. Index. Paperbound.

PAYTON, WALTER. Spo.

2224. Payton, Walter, and Jenkins, Jerry B. *Sweetness*. Chicago: Contemporary Books, 1978. 162 p. Illustrated. Table.

2225. *Walter Payton, Winning in Life [Videorecording]*. Chicago: Nightingale-Conant Video, 1986. 1 videocassette, 55 min., sd., col., 1/2 in., VHS.
  Credits: Producer/writer, Bob Smith; director, Bill Heitz. Cast: Payton, Mike Ditka, Jerry Richard, Connie Payton, and Matt Suhey. Summary: Payton shares his insights on winning in life, and his "game plan" for living life fully.

PELE. Spo.

2226. Bodo, Peter; Hirshey, David; and Pele. *Pele's New World*. New York: Norton, 1977. 223 p. Illustrated.

2227. Pele and Fish, Robert L. *My Life and the Beautiful Game: The Autobiography of Pele*. Garden City, NY: Doubleday, 1977. Illustrated. Table.

PETTY, RICHARD. Spo.

2228. Libby, Bill, and Petty, Richard. *"King Richard": The Richard Petty Story.* Garden City, NY: Doubleday, 1977. 322 p. Illustrated.

2229. Petty, Richard, and Neely, William. *King Richard I: The Autobiography of America's Greatest Auto Racer.* New York: Macmillan; London: Collier Macmillan, 1986. 268 p. Illustrated. Index.

PLUNKETT, JIM. Spo.

2230. *Jim Plunkett [Motion Picture].* Sports Action Profiles. Oxford Films, 1972. 22 min., sd., col., 16mm.
Credits: Director, Jeffrey Pill. Summary: Traces the life and career of professional football quarterback, Plunkett.

2231. Plunkett, Jim, and Newhouse, Dave. *The Jim Plunkett Story: The Saga of a Man Who Came Back.* New York: Arbor House, 1981. 256 p. Illustrated.

RETTON, MARY LOU. Spo.

2232. Retton, Mary Lou; Karolyi, Bela; and Powers, John. *Mary Lou: Creating an Olympic Champion.* New York: McGraw-Hill, 1986. 170 p. Illustrated.

RICHARDS, RENEE. Spo.

2233. Richards, Renee, and Ames, John. *Second Serve: The Renee Richards Story.* New York: Stein and Day, 1983. 373 p. Illustrated.

RODGERS, BILL. Spo.

2234. *The Pursuit of Excellence [Motion Picture].* Pittsburgh, PA: WQED, 1978. 2 reels, 50 min., sd., col., 16mm.
Summary: Profiles two of America's top long-distance runners, Rodgers, and Frank Shorter, as they prepare for the 1978 Boston Marathon.

2235. Rodgers, Bill, and Concannon, Joe. *Marathoning.* Rev. ed. Foreword by Amby Burfoot. New York: Simon and Schuster, Fireside, 1982. 344 p. Illustrated. Paperbound.

ROSE, PETE. Spo.

2236. *4192!: A Celebration of Pete Rose, Baseball's Record-Breaking Hitter.* By United Press International. Foreword by Sparky Anderson. Chicago: Contemporary Books, 1985. 85 p. Illustrated. Table. Paperbound.

2237. Rose, Pete, and Bodley, Hal. *Countdown to Cobb: My Diary of the Record-Breaking 1985 Season.* St. Louis, MO: Sporting News, 1985. 224 p. Illustrated. Paperbound.

2238. Rose, Pete, and McCoy, Hal. *The Official Pete Rose Scrapbook.* Rev. ed. New York: New American Library, Signet, 1985. 128 p. Illustrated. Table. Paperbound.

RUSSELL, BILL. Spo.

2239. Russell, Bill, and Branch, Taylor. *Second Wind: The Memoirs of an Opinionated Man.* New York: Random House, 1979. 265 p.

2240. Russell, Bill, and McSweeny, William. *Go Up for Glory.* New York: Coward, McCann & Geoghegan, Berkley, 1980. 171 p.

RYAN, NOLAN. Spo.

2241. Ryan, Nolan, and Libby, Bill. *The Other Game.* Waco, TX: Word Books, 1977. 216 p. Illustrated.

SEAVER, TOM. Spo.

2242. Schoor, Gene. *Seaver: A Biography.* Chicago: Contemporary Books, 1986. 344 p. Illustrated. Table.

SHRIVER, PAM. Spo.

2243. Shriver, Pam; Deford, Frank; and Adams, Susan B. *Passing Shots: Pam Shriver on Tour.* New York: McGraw-Hill, 1987. 211 p. Illustrations.

SIMPSON, O. J. Spo.

2244. Baker, Jim. *O. J. Simpson's Most Memorable Games.* New York: Putnam, 1978. 288 p. Illustrated. Table.

STAUBACH, ROGER. Spo.

2245. Staubach, Roger, and Luksa, Frank. *Time Enough to Win.* Waco, TX: Word Books, 1980. 237 p. Illustrated. Table.

STENGEL, CASEY. Spo. 9/29/75

2246. Allen, Maury. *You Could Look It Up: The Life of Casey Stengel.* New York: Times Books, 1979. 310 p. Illustrated. Index.

2247. Creamer, Robert W. *Stengel: His Life and Times.* New York: Simon and Schuster, 1984. 349 p. Illustrated. Index.

STRAWBERRY, DARRYL. Spo.

2248. Saxon, Walt. *Darryl Strawberry.* New York: Dell, 1985. 187 p. Illustrated. Table. Paperbound.

2249. Strawberry, Darryl, and Castellano, Dan. *Darryl!* Chicago: Contemporary Books, 1986. 79 p. Illustrated. Paperbound.

TAYLOR, LAWRENCE. Spo.

2250. Taylor, Lawrence, and Falkner, David. *LT: Living on the Edge.* New York: Times Books, 1987. 225 p. Illustrated. Table.

TORVILL & DEAN (Jayne Torvill and Christopher Dean). Spo.

2251. *Donald K. Donald Productions . . . Presents . . . Torvill & Dean, the World Tour.* London: Michael Linnit and Michael Edgley Holdings, 1986. 37 p. Illustrated. ***

2252. *Torvill & Dean, Path to Perfection [Videorecording].* Produced and directed by John Davis. New York: Thorn

EMI Video, 1984. 1 videocassette, 52 min., sd., col., 1/2 in.

Summary: A documentary about the 1983 world ice-dancing champions, including eight routines.

2253. Torvill, Jayne; Dean, Christopher; and Hennessy, John. *Torvill & Dean.* New York: St. Martin's Press, 1983. 208 p. Illustrations. Index.

TREVINO, LEE. Spo.

2254. Trevino, Lee, and Blair, Sam. *The Snake in the Sandtrap [and Other Misadventures on the Golf Tour].* New York: Holt, Rinehart, and Winston, 1985. 166 p. Illustrated.

2255. Trevino, Lee, and Blair, Sam. *They Call Me Super Mex.* New York: Random House, 1982. 202 p. Illustrated.

UNSER, BOBBY. Spo.

2256. Scalzo, Joe, and Unser, Bobby. *The Bobby Unser Story.* Garden City, NY: Doubleday, 1979. 203 p. Illustrated.

WALKER, HERSCHEL. Spo.

2257. Cromartie, Bill. *There Goes Herschel.* New York: Leisure Press, 1983. 256 p. Illustrated. Table. Paperbound.

2258. Prugh, Jeff. *The Herschel Walker Story.* New York: Ballantine Books, 1983. 173 p. Illustrated. Paperbound.

WALSH, BILL. Spo.

2259. Dickey, Glenn. *America Has a Better Team: The Story of Bill Walsh and San Francisco's World Champion 49ers.* Introduction by Herb Caen. Tribute by Dianne Feinstein. San Francisco: Harbor Publishing, 1982. 175 p. Illustrated. Table. Paperbound.

WEAVER, EARL. Spo.

2260. Pluto, Terry. *The Earl of Baltimore: The Story of Earl Weaver, Baltimore Orioles Manager.* Piscataway, NJ: New Century, 1982. 207 p. Illustrated. Table. Index.

2261. Weaver, Earl, and Stainback, Berry. *It's What You Learn after You Know It All That Counts: Updated to Include the 1982 Season.* New York: Simon and Schuster, Fireside, 1982. 306 p. Table. Paperbound.

WINFIELD, DAVE. Spo.

2262. Schoor, Gene. *Dave Winfield: The 23 Million Dollar Man.* Briarcliff Manor, NY: Stein and Day, 1982. 184 p. Illustrated. Index.

YARBOROUGH, CALE. Spo.

2263. Yarborough, Cale, and Neely, William. *Cale: The Hazardous Life and Times of America's Greatest Stock Car Driver.* New York: Times Books, 1986. 246 p. Illustrated.

NAME INDEX

493

TITLE INDEX

SUBJECT INDEX

Numbers refer to citation numbers, not page numbers. Major works by and about individual celebrities are italicized. Superseded periodicals and book or film titles are listed if they appear as annotated information in the bibliography.

Aaron, Henry, 2024
Abbott & Costello, 568
Abbott, Bud, See: Abbott & Costello
Abdul-Jabbar, Kareem, 2002, 2016, *2132*
About Music and Writers/BMI, 1437
Academy of Country Music, 1497
Academy of Motion Picture Arts and Sciences, 655
Academy Players Directory, 491
Access, 74
"Acting Shakespeare," 1115
Actors and actresses, See also: Celebrities; Entertainers
　anecdotes, sex secrets, scandals, etc., 524, 570, 585
　audio-visual sources, 480, 552
　Australia, 468

bibliographies and guides, 405
biographical dictionaries, 444-449, 452-455, 463, 467, 490, 1368-1370
characters played, 441, 466, 480
child actors, See: Child actors
collective biography, 520, 522-524, 526, 529-530, 533-536, 538, 541-542, 544-547, 552-554, 556-559, 561-565, 571, 576, 581-586
commercial sources and services, 698-773
cowboy films, 550, 569
criticism of individual artists, 552, 583, 618, 631, 647, 940, 1047, 1109, 1160, 1179, 1182, 1198, 1203-1204, 1220, 1250, 1257, 1260

915, 977, 981, 983, 1007-
1008, 1058, 1075, 1079,
1083, 1100, 1105, 1132,
1200, 1232, 1244, 1290,
1312-1314, 1317, 1319,
1321
directories, 492
film, video or recorded
biography of individuals,
810, 817, 840, 856, 902,
904, 954, 956, 978, 984,
1055, 1136-1138, 1194-
1195, 1230, 1253
Great Britain, 427, 609
interviews, 502, 506, 518,
536, 541, 546, 551, 594-
595, 597, 605, 608, 620,
647
obituaries, 611
United States, 423, 427, 459
Dire Straits, 1409
Disney, Walt, 542
Ditka, Mike, 2225
Diving, See: Swimming and
diving
The Dodgers (baseball team),
1963
Domino, Fats, 1410
Donahue, Phil, *311-313*
Donat, Robert, 558
Don Quixote, 285
Douglas, Jack, 1788
Douglas, Kirk, 93, *935-936*
Douglas family, 538
Downs, Hugh, *314*
Draft Update, 2047
Dreesen, Tom, 521
Dress & Vanity Fair, 149
Dreyer, Carl Theodor, 540
Dreyfuss, Richard, 536
Duel, Peter, 570
Duke, Patty, See: Astin, Patty
Duke

Dunaway, Faye, 91, 937
Dundee, Angelo, 1998
Dunne, Irene, 542, 546
Duran Duran (musical group),
1408, 1560, *1708-1712*
Durante, Jimmy, 97, *315*, 521
Duvall, Robert, 938
Dylan, Bob, 1400, 1417, 1538,
1561, *1713-1717*
Easley, Kenny, 2015
Eastwood, Clint, 780, *939-946*
Ebert, Roger, *1915*
Ebony, 119
Eddy, Nelson, 544
Edge, Debbie, 1861
Edwards, Blake, 536
8mm Collector, 598
Eisenhower, Dwight, 402
Eisenstein, Sergei, 461, 540
Ellington, Duke, 1404, 1414-
1415, *1718-1722*
Elliott, Cass, 101
Elliott, Denholm, 563
Ellis, Anita, 1401
Elway, John, 1997, 2015
Emmy Magazine, 605
Encyclopaedia Britannica, 44
*Encyclopedia of Rock Music on
Film*, 1339
*Encyclopedia of Television Series,
Plots and Specials*, 651
Encyclopedias, See: Films and
television—encyclopedias;
Music—encyclopedias,
etc.
Entertainers, See also: Actors and
actresses; Celebrities;
Comedians; Musicians and
composers
anecdotes, sex secrets,
scandals, etc., 572
biographical dictionaries,
453-455, 1368-1370

Track and field, See also: Sports
  biographical dictionaries,
      1967, 1979
  collective biographies, 2020
  film, video or recorded
      biography of individuals,
      2191, 2234
  history, 1979
  periodicals, 2056
Tracy, Spencer, 557
Trans-Oceanic Trouser Press,
      1488
Travanti, Daniel J., 570
Travis, Merle, 1411
Travolta, John, 567, 570, 572,
      804, *1276-1278*
Trevino, Lee, 1992, 2026, *2254-
      2255*
Truffaut, François, 517, *1279*
Tubb, Ernest, 1411
Turner, Grant, 1411
Turner, Joe, 1401
Turner, Kathleen, *1280*
Turner, Lana, 561, 564, *1281-
      1283*
Turner, Tina, *1940-1944*
Turpin, Ben, 560
TV, See: Films and television
TV Guide, 619
*TV Guide . . ., Cumulative
      Supplement*, 484
TV Guide . . ., Supplement, 484
TV Guide 25 Year Index, 484
TV Mirror, 621, 643
TV Special, 612
Twentieth Century Fox Corporate
      Archive (UCLA), 489
20th Century Fox Film
      Corporation Library, 193
Twisted Sister, 1408
Twitty, Conway, *1945*
Ullman, Liv, 845, *1284-1287*
Ultra Violet, *1292*

United Artists Corporation
      (collection), 697
United States Golf Association,
      2094
United States Hockey Hall of
      Fame, 2095
United States Indoor Men's
      Tennis Championships,
      2141
United States Professional Tennis
      Association, 2054
United States Tennis Association,
      2096
Universal City Studios, 194
University of California, Berkeley,
      692
University of California, Davis,
      693
University of California, Los
      Angeles, 694
University of Illinois, 2097
University of Montreal, 2098
University of Notre Dame
      Libraries, 2099
University of Southern California
      Cinema Library, 489
University of Southern California
      Library, Archives of
      Performing Arts, 695
University of Waterloo, 2100
Unser, Bobby, *2256*
Update, 2062
USA Today, 70
Ustinov, Peter, 563, *1288*
U2, 1409
Vadim, Roger, 581
Valentino, Rudolph, 92, 101, 400,
      584
Vancouver Sun, 58, 158
Van Halen, 1408
van Itallie, Jean-Claude (papers),
      672
Van Ronk, Dave, 1423